THEORIZING
Criminal Justice

Eight Essential Orientations

Peter B. Kraska

Eastern Kentucky University

D0103255

WAVELAND
PRESS, INC.
Long Grove, Illinois

For information about this book, contact:
Waveland Press, Inc.
4180 IL Route 83, Suite 101
Long Grove, IL 60047-9580
(847) 634-0081
info@waveland.com
www.waveland.com

Contents

Preface

You've heard the expression, "This money is burning a hole in my pocket." The idea for this book has been burning a hole in my head for ten years. Its completion has meant a major release of cranial pressure. The relief, I think, comes from asking explicitly what bothers a lot of academics in our field of study: how can we profess to be studying the criminal justice system and trends in crime control without textbooks in CJ theory, without courses in CJ theory, and most importantly, without a well-recognized theoretical infrastructure about criminal justice? Our introductory criminal justice courses focus mostly on theories of crime and give little or no attention to making theoretical sense of the system charged with safeguarding society. Our graduate and undergraduate curriculums in both criminology and criminal justice assume that studying theory involves concentrating on theories of *crime*. And even though our discipline has developed an impressive body of theoretical research and literature about crime, these explanations are inadequate (not irrelevant) for explaining criminal justice and crime control behavior. Although there are important interconnections, the behavior of our legal system, or trends in social control, are substantially different objects of study than crime behavior. It seems that the time is right for our discipline to embrace the development of theories about both crime and criminal justice.

Fortunately the task of exposing a theoretical infrastructure about criminal justice in no way falls on my shoulders. Numerous academics have theorized criminal justice and worked diligently to lay the foundation for a vibrant area of scholarship. Scholars such as David Duffee, Samuel

Walker, Richard Quinney, Allen Liska, Jonathan Simon, David Garland, Bill Chambliss, and Meda Chesney-Lind have examined and attempted to explain the behavior of the criminal justice system and developments in crime control over the last thirty years. My task has been to gather elements from this body of knowledge and to present them in an accessible, intelligible, and interesting framework.

The approach I've taken centers on the notion of metaphor—making sense of criminal justice by relating it to something else. The predominant metaphor used in our field is "system" (e.g., criminal justice as system). While the system metaphor has been fruitful and gained widespread acceptance, organizing our understanding through a single framework limits our theoretical gaze. As is the case with crime behavior, the story of criminal justice behavior is complex and paradoxical, necessitating an assortment of theoretical orientations. This book explores the implications of eight different orientations for *thinking* about the nature of the criminal justice system—each telling the story of criminal justice from a different point of view or reference. Looking at our multi-faceted object of study through numerous theoretical lenses yields a more complete understanding even as it exposes the complexity, confusion, and contradictions of our intellectual terrain.

The eight metaphors selected demonstrate a wide breadth of concepts and ideas. However, they *in no way* should be construed as the *only* ways of thinking about criminal justice. Certainly other possibilities exist, and I have no doubt excluded metaphors that are perceived by some as "essential." Hopefully I'll have the opportunity to include a few more metaphors if I'm fortunate enough to write a second edition.

I've discovered that approaching our field of study from multiple directions (plowing with less conventional equipment, to continue the use of metaphors) can generate criticism from those accustomed to certain traditions. For example, it seems some crime theorists feel strongly that pre-existing theories about crime are sufficient for explaining criminal justice behavior. They could read this book as presenting "models" of criminal justice functioning (which a few criminologists have already done using crime theory). While the theoretical orientations outlined have some similarities to "models," they are primarily interpretive constructs designed to guide the assignment of meaning to criminal justice trends, issues, experiences, and phenomena. Rather than describing specific functions, they identify orientations of understanding.

An additional problem might stem from giving equal weight to all the theoretical orientations. The ground covered by each metaphor constitutes "turf" for many. Those strongly aligned with the system metaphor may not appreciate being discussed as one perspective among many; similarly, those aligned with the oppression metaphor could resent the parity. The intention was to present differing ways of thinking in the hope of cultivating theoretical tolerance.

Another point of confusion might be the book's use of the term "theory." Unlike other more established disciplines, our field tends to restrict theory within rather narrow parameters—namely, quantitatively testable systems. The use of metaphor, or theoretical orientations, avoids this restriction by embracing a broader view of the activity of theorizing. It allows us to examine underlying assumptions, embedded values, and practical implications—as well as the all-important task of laying the groundwork for developing testable theoretical systems.

I hope these potential criticisms are outweighed by the central objective of the book: the presentation of a broad theoretical infrastructure for the study of criminal justice. Academic leaders in both criminology and criminal justice studies have asserted repeatedly that academic legitimacy and respectability will only come with the recognition and development of criminal justice theory. No claim is made here that traditional crime theories are not useful and sometimes interrelated to the study of criminal justice (see, for example, CJ as oppression). Rather, the approach of this book emphasizes the obvious and clear distinction between the two objects of study; further, it affirms that theorizing criminal justice is as challenging, intellectually stimulating, and useful as is theorizing crime.

Otwin Marenin noted in the late 1990s that "criminal justice is an academic discipline in practice but not yet in theory." After teaching in criminology and criminal justice for over 15 years and witnessing to the central place—economically, politically, and culturally—crime control and CJ have taken in our society, I think that Marenin's statement identifies a glaring gap in our responsibility as educators to our undergraduate and graduate students. I realize that numerous academics do indeed teach criminal justice theory in different courses, but there is no collective recognition or effort in our coursework, curriculums, or even in our introductory books to expose students to the varied ways in which our field thinks theoretically about criminal justice phenomena and issues. This is unfortunate. As demonstrated in this book, a deep and engaging body of literature already exists, and a new and exciting genre of criminal justice theory is emerging. In exposing students to the various stories of criminal justice growth and behavior, we can cultivate a more thoughtful approach to this important object of study—going beyond describing how the system functions or assessing what does or doesn't work to control crime.

My students have been my most important inspiration. I've used the materials found in this book at the introductory undergraduate and advanced graduate levels with the same positive results—students appreciate and yes, even enjoy, the critical thinking skills encouraged by filtering the subject through different metaphors. Their feedback has been invaluable.

I would also like to thank those colleagues who reviewed this book and have patiently listened to and responded to my ideas over the years. I am especially grateful to my good friend Vic Kappeler, who has shared with me an enthusiasm for thinking about trends in social control and criminal justice-based controls since we went to graduate school together. Other colleagues who have helped include Jonathan Simon, Carole Garrison, Kevin Haggerty, Otwin Marenin, Ralph Weisheit, David Garland, Jeff Ferrell, and Dennis Longmire.

Working with Waveland has been a wonderful experience. This project took a potentially fatal turn after my lower left leg had a run-in with an 8-ton oak log. The editor, Carol Rowe, remained upbeat and kind, providing me with just the right amounts of encouragement, space, and assistance to finish this project.

I would finally like to thank my lovely partner-in-life, Shannon Leigh. She has contributed substantially to the ideas developed in each of the chapters. Fortunately I don't have to thank her for her patience while I holed myself away working on this book. This project has taken so long that our life has managed to continue unaltered along its beautiful path.

Criminal Justice Theory
Why Ask Why?

> Theory is not some kind of flight from reality. . . . Theoretical work seeks to change the way we think about an issue and ultimately change the practical ways we deal with it.
> —David Garland (1990, p. 277)

> Criminal justice is an academic discipline in practice but not yet in theory.
> —Otwin Marenin and John Worrall (1998, p. 465)

A strong theoretical infrastructure is the heart and soul of any academic discipline. It provides the lenses through which academics, students, and learned practitioners make sense of their object of study. This book confronts a major shortcoming of our discipline: despite over thirty years of research and development, criminal justice studies and criminology do not have a recognizable body of theoretical scholarship *about the criminal justice system and crime control* (Bernard & Engel, 2001; Garland, 2001; Hagan, 1989; Marenin & Worrall, 1998). As the articles in this book demonstrate, some theoretical work exists; the problem is that until very recently it has taken a distant backseat to other concerns.

The knee-jerk reaction to this observation might be: "Wait a minute, our leading journals and books contain an impressive body of theoretical work." Herein lies a key source of confusion. In criminology and criminal justice, the term *theory* by default refers to theories explaining crime. Our

1

field's impressive body of theoretical scholarship is focused almost exclusively on the causes of crime. Our "theory courses" focus primarily on the why of crime.[1] Even our introduction to criminal justice textbooks, which have the criminal justice system as their explicit object of study, dedicate their discussions of theory to crime causation.[2]

If theory work has been reserved for understanding crime, where has that left the theoretical study of the criminal justice system and crime control? Generally speaking, studying criminal justice has meant determining the most efficient and effective crime control practices through an endeavor known as applied or evaluative research.[3] Under this approach, theory-work is relevant to criminal justice only insofar as theories of crime causation point to more effective crime control policies (Einstadter & Henry, 1995; Gibbons, 1994). While criminological theories no doubt bear significantly on our crime control policies, it is an inadequate framework for making theoretical sense of criminal justice and crime control behavior and their place in historical and contemporary society.[4]

Consequently, criminal justice studies, an academic field that assumes disciplinary status, has yet to take seriously the task of developing theories *about* criminal justice. Our object of study when theorizing criminal justice is not crime or crime rates; rather, it is the entire criminal justice apparatus and a host of crime-control practices. Our theoretical questions might

---

[1] "Theory courses" generally fall under the purview of criminology—an area of study which focuses on: 1) how the law is formed; 2) why the law is broken; and, 3) society's reaction to crime. Although theory work takes place in each of these three areas, it is the *why of crime* that receives the bulk of theoretical attention. Indeed, many criminologists view the study of criminal justice as relevant only insofar as it points to better crime control approaches (Gibbons, 1994). The view that criminal justice is the "how to" component of criminology leaves little room for the endeavor pursued in this book—theorizing our formal reaction to crime (the criminal justice apparatus). See Einstadter and Henry (1995) for an excellent, and rare, discussion of the linkages between our theories of crime and their criminal justice implications.

[2] This is not an either/or argument. Most academics agree that understanding the why of crime is a crucial part of criminal justice studies, and vice versa. Thus, avoiding theorizing about criminal justice and crime control phenomena within our introductory courses makes little intellectual or academic sense, as would avoiding theories of crime.

[3] Of course, even in applied and evaluative studies, theory is an integral part of the research, policy recommendation, and policy implementation process. On one of my visits to the National Institute of Justice I talked to a newly graduated Ph.D. from a respected doctoral program about a few criminal justice issues. It took only a few minutes to notice that this person was annoyed. When I asked why, he told me proudly that he concentrated only on studying "criminal justice" and did not bother himself with "theory." It was clear that his doctoral training had socialized him into thinking that criminal justice studies was somehow an atheoretical, strictly practical endeavor—a common yet untenable position. It is well established in the philosophy and social science literature that it is impossible to conduct "theory-less" research—no matter how applied, practical, or policy-oriented it may seem (Bernstein, 1976; Carr & Kemmis, 1986; Denhardt, 1984; Fay, 1977; Habermas, 1972, 1974; Popper, 1963).

[4] It is important to point out that many well-known criminological theories, if put into practice, would not result in criminal justice-based solutions. Rather, sociological theories stressing economic difficulties and family violence problems point to social service-oriented solutions—such as better employment opportunities and early childhood assistance for at-risk youths.

include, for example: How do we make sense of transformations occurring in crime control practices? or, What are the driving forces that shape the function and character of the criminal justice apparatus? or What accounts for the steep growth in power and size of the criminal justice apparatus over the last 30 years? Answering these types of questions will lead to an academic field that is theoretically aware and reflective about crime *and* the entity of criminal justice (Weer, 2001).

The purpose of this book is to help invigorate this ongoing theoretical project by mapping out the complex terrain of various ways of thinking about criminal justice—referred to as *theoretical orientations* (T.O.s and, to avoid monotony, sometimes "theoretical frameworks"). Notice that the goal is not to develop *a theory* of criminal justice. Instead, the objective is to establish that our area of study is and should be *multi-theoretical*: a discipline that has at its disposal numerous theoretical lenses through which it studies and makes sense of an increasingly complex criminal justice and crime control network.

As we will discover, these eight theoretical lenses are essential for a more complete intellectual understanding of our field of study and the criminal justice apparatus. They are the foundation for a well informed engagement in action by all those involved in the community of criminal justice—academic policy advisors, policy makers, the media, criminal justice personnel, and theoreticians.

Varieties of Theory

Watching paint dry, grass grow, or a cat sleep might be more exciting to many people than theorizing. Theory development conjures up images of academic eggheads dreaming up conceptual models that are divorced from reality, hopelessly complex, and irrelevant—expressed with a superior attitude.

I would like to be able to claim that this is an untrue stereotype promoted by the intellectually lazy; unfortunately I can't. I have read books (and had professors) that fit this image. However, as a former Alaskan fishing guide who has been chased by grizzly bears, I can say on good authority that—believe it or not—theorizing can actually be exciting. If you have an interest in making sense of our confusing society or how to navigate your way through our increasingly complex world more effectively, then theorizing can provide stimulating insights and answers.

To theorize is to speculate why. Probably all of us, a thousand times a day, theorize about an infinite number of topics: Why did those people look at me like that?, Why is my significant other angry?, What is making that awful clicking sound under my car's hood?, or What does it mean when my dog spins in circles for no apparent reason? All of these questions require us to assign meaning to our observations, contemplate reasons, assign blame, or speculate about causes. In other words, we engage theory to help us to make sense of the world around us and—just as importantly—to maneuver competently through that world.

Whereas most people take theorizing for granted, academics (people who by definition have an appetite for making sense of phenomena such as historical events, literature, or ancient cultures) consciously and systematically construct and employ theory. In criminal justice/criminology, for example, we study, interpret, and make theoretical sense of the history of crime and drug wars, the writings of Cesare Beccaria and Michel Foucault, or urban gang subculture. In order to understand these phenomena, we impose theoretical frameworks. These frameworks include organizing concepts, causal attributions, and various ideological assumptions (underlying beliefs and values).

On a more mundane level, the interpretation of even the most simple descriptive statistic—3 percent of all reported crimes end in punishment—invokes theory. One academic might interpret this statistic as evidence of a lenient system in need of repair; another might see it as a sign of a healthy system that metes out punishment in judicious fashion.[5] The statistic remains static; what it *means* depends on the theoretical framework employed.

While the omnipresence of theory in everyday life and in academic work demonstrates its fundamental nature, it simultaneously poses a difficulty. The definition and use of theory varies. We often say, "my theory is," when we are merely making a prediction. When we put forward an approach to solve a particular problem we sometimes refer to it as theory (e.g., "my theory is that we should try to rehabilitate sex offenders"). Assessing blame for someone's actions involves determining causation and is also a form of theory. When academics articulate a philosophical statement about a set of values designed to guide our actions, they sometimes call it "theory" (e.g., John Rawl's *Theory of Justice*).[6]

Probably the most well known conception of theory is the scientific (or positivistic) view to which most of us were exposed in grade school. This approach sees theorizing as making a generalized statement of a relationship between two or more observable events. A hypothesis is formulated and tested using quantitative measures and analysis.

The scientific view of theory is an invaluable mainstay of our field. However, if adhered to too rigidly (a perspective sometimes referred to as "logical

---

[5] This statistic is found at the exit point of the criminal justice funnel, where large numbers of arrestees are poured into the top while only a select few are punished at the bottom. The funnel was one of the first metaphorical tools used to shed light on the nature of criminal justice *system* functioning.

[6] Several criminal justice books have been written using this more philosophical approach to theory (see for example, Braithwaite & Pettit, 1990; Ellis & Ellis, 1989). This conception of theory has a long tradition beginning with the work of early Greek philosophers (Carr & Kemmis, 1986). Criminology is not unfamiliar with theory that promotes a reform agenda using a guiding philosophical framework. The best known is labeled classical theory or the classical school.

positivism"), it can inhibit our full appreciation of the power, complexity, and usefulness of theory. This approach, for example, has the disadvantage of judging the worth of a particular theory on the *sole* basis of whether or not it best fits quantitative data collected through traditional scientific means. A theory can and often does help us in better understanding phenomena, even if it is not amenable to quantitative testing or if the results of that testing are ongoing or vary over time. Theory testing in our complicated area of study often raises as many questions as it answers. In addition, logical positivism does not acknowledge the integral role that norms, values, and ideology play in theory development and the process of theorizing. Attempting to exclude or ignore this dimension of theory is especially problematic when your object of study entails such value-laden concepts as "justice," "human rights," "safety," "democracy," and "crime."[7] Is there an approach where we can capture the multi-faceted nature of theory without sacrificing our scientific rigor? Fortunately the objective of this book is not to develop testable theoretical systems. Instead, it pursues the broader goal of developing various ways of thinking about criminal justice—an approach that concentrates on developing "theoretical orientations" that include various organizing concepts.

Theoretical Orientations as Metaphor

After years of trying to figure out the different conceptions of and limitations placed on the term theory, I came across an inspiring presentation in the field of organizational studies. Gareth Morgan (1986), in his work *Images of Organization*, identified an array of theoretical frameworks through which we might better understand organizations. It wasn't the explanatory strength of one or the other that mattered; rather, it was how each directed a person's gaze in a unique way—yielding constructive answers, ideas, perspectives, and insights.

Morgan referred to these theoretical frameworks as "metaphors." Metaphors are tools that help us understand something by associating it with something else whose characteristics are familiar to us. Morgan made sense of organizations using the metaphors of "biological organisms," "machines," "cultures," "political systems," and "psychic prisons." Each metaphor enabled the reader to perceive organizations in differing ways.[8]

---

[7] Where does theory begin and ideology end? Logical positivism demands a clear separation between fact and value. However, there is no question remaining in the academic world that ideology and values are an inseparable dimension of theoretical work. The difficulty for our field has been admitting this reality while retaining the notion that the archetype crime and justice scholar is a value-neutral scientist (Bernard & Engel, 2001; Duffee & O'Leary, 1971; Sullivan, 1994; Williams, 1984). Fortunately, the notion of theoretical *orientations* allows for more flexibility (and for me to sidestep the debate). See Garland (1990) for an excellent discussion of the disadvantages of restricting theorizing to the tenets of logical positivism.

[8] Nicole Rafter (1990) similarly suggests that our discipline needs to examine more carefully its disciplinary underpinnings using a social constructionist approach to knowledge production. Also, see Kraska (1993, 2001) for more detailed discussions of metaphors as they relate to criminal justice study and practice.

I've chosen a similar approach. The theoretical frameworks discussed in this book could also be conceived of as metaphors: for example, criminal justice as a system, criminal justice as politics, criminal justice as industry, criminal justice as oppression, or criminal justice as myth construction. While not specific theories in and of themselves, they are models commonly used throughout the literature and in the practicing world that *orient* our thinking about criminal justice and crime control in particular ways—hence, the term *theoretical orientations*.[9] Each of the eight orientations selected provide us with a unique theoretical gaze, framing our interpretation of criminal justice phenomena, guiding the questions we might ask, influencing the type of research we might conduct, and affecting how we act in the real world.[10]

I did not choose these theoretical orientations because they yield the most accurate or "true" representation of reality. (Indeed, the multitheoretical approach guards against the ethnocentric tendency to proclaim one orientation as truth to the exclusion of all others.) Rather, the selection decision was made through a twelve-year process of reading the literature, talking to academic colleagues, staying involved in the practicing world, and listening closely to students. The eight theoretical orientations selected are the most often used in crime and justice studies and the most likely to shed a unique light on our subject matter. They are not meant to be exhaustive. They capture in broad terms the numerous *ways of thinking* about criminal justice in our field. This book is designed to showcase the fact that our field's theoretical strength emanates from its diversity—a diversity that extends beyond the eight metaphors outlined here.[11]

---

[9] A helpful discussion of the difference between a theory and a theoretical orientation is found in Wagner (1984). Consistent with Wagner's work, the chapters do not posit individual theories ready-made for measuring and testing. Instead they provide frameworks for understanding (Wagner labels them "orienting strategies") that include speculations about causation as well as an underpinning of norms, values, and beliefs. This is similar to Ritzer's (1983) use of the term.

[10] This approach is not unknown to our discipline. Nanette Davis (1975:5) examined sociological theories of crime and deviance using the concept of metaphor. Metaphor, according to Davis (1975:5), "summarizes the symbolic and cognitive style of theoretical work and its research problems. [It operates] as a set of propositions that uses a relatively well-understood set of phenomena as an explanatory analogy for a set of phenomena that is inadequately conceptualized."

[11] I began with too many orientations for one book. It was tempting to include every well-known professor or piece or work in the field that at one time theorized criminal justice. I wanted to avoid, however, making this book a mere who's who exercise. As mentioned above, criminal justice textbooks were of little help. The most common coverage of criminal justice theory includes a brief mention of either conflict vs. consensus or Packer's "crime control vs. due process model." I opted to exclude the conflict vs. consensus model as a separate orientation because it glosses over a rich body of theorizing in our field, telling us too little about too much (it is discussed in the oppression section). See Duffee (1990) for an insightful discussion of the unproductive nature of this dichotomy and how recent scholarship demonstrates its inherent flaws.

What Is Our Object of Study?

What exactly do these orientations explain? So far we have established that they *do not* attempt to explain crime, nor do they attempt to offer differing policy prescriptions for controlling crime (for example, a rehabilitation model, economic reordering, or a deterrence model).[12] The object of study for this book is, at its most basic level, the entity we call criminal justice. Just as some academics study plant life (botanists), the medical industry (medical researchers), or our political system (political scientists), the orientations in this book focus on making theoretical sense of the criminal justice apparatus (CJA).

Apparatus Over System

Why use the label criminal justice *apparatus* (CJA) instead of the criminal justice *system* (CJS)? Pinning down and labeling our precise object of study is challenging. A few key questions illuminate the difficulty.

- Should we use the term criminal justice *system*, when the notion of "system" pre-frames our thinking about criminal justice from a systems theory perspective, precluding other possibilities?

- Does the notion of the "criminal justice system" refer *only* to "the state's [*government's*] distribution of penal sanctions and the administration of agencies involved in law enforcement, prosecution, and punishment" (Duffee, 1980, p. 1)?

- Should we include in our conception of criminal justice other entities outside the formal criminal law system that are arguably an integral part of the character, functioning, and make-up of contemporary crime control and criminal justice? Examples might include the private police industry, for-profit and nonprofit corrections organizations, social service agencies, the military, the media, the public, the legislative body, and even academics.

The first four theoretical orientations covered in this book are primarily concerned with the formal criminal justice system. The next four broaden the object of study to include the practices of numerous state and nonstate responses to the crime problem that fall outside the formal CJS. Therefore, several interrelated objects of study are subsumed under the label *criminal justice* apparatus: 1) crime control practices carried out by state and non-state entities; 2) the formal creation and administration of criminal law carried out by legislators, the police, courts, corrections, and juvenile justice subcomponents; and 3) others involved in the criminal justice enterprise, such as the media, academic researchers, and political

---

[12] Although the focus on this book is not on theories promoting solutions or strategies, some of the theoretical orientations do imply certain prescriptive measures. For example, the systems orientation suggests a vision of controlling crime where all the components of the CJS work in seamless harmony.

interest groups. The following questions are a sample of the type of inquiry we're interested in when theorizing the criminal justice apparatus.

- What elements in the historical development of the CJA continue to exert the most influence today?

- What theoretical basis drove justice reform efforts in the past? Why did they succeed or fail?

- What accounts for the steep growth in power and size of the CJA over the last 30 years?

- How do we interpret current and possible future trends associated with the CJA?

- On what theoretical basis can we best understand current practices in the CJA (e.g., racial profiling, death penalty, erosion of constitutional safeguards, privatization, etc.)?

- How does the CJA affect the larger society in which it operates; conversely, what societal forces shape the CJA?

- How do we best make sense of the behaviors of criminal justice practitioners?

- What best explains the internal functioning and practices of criminal justice agencies?

Micro and Macro Levels of Explanation

As these questions demonstrate, social scientists often examine a phenomenon on differing levels. For example, if I wanted to make theoretical sense of obesity, I could speculate that the cause might be genetic or the result of failing to develop self-control mechanisms. Such theories operate at the smallest level of explanation, referred to as "micro-level theorizing." They look to the individual for causes and focus on matters of process (how a person becomes obese). By contrast, a "macro-theory" of obesity might look to the overall opportunity structure in certain countries that compels overeating (lots of fattening, fast-food items available and advertised incessantly) or the influence of a self-indulgent culture that emphasizes pleasure above sacrifice and restraint. Macro-theories have a broader gaze, explaining phenomena through an examination of how society is constituted, arranged, and organized—what sociologists often refer to as social structure.

The bulk of the questions at the end of the previous section lead to macro-level theorizing. The last two questions address issues of process and individual behavior, micro-level theorizing. All eight theoretical orientations found in this book can operate at the micro, macro, or in-between levels, although some are more suited to one level or another.

The Practicality of Theory

Now that we have identified our object of study, I would like to return to the utility of theory. We discussed earlier that theory is an integral part of academic and everyday life, and whether we recognize it or not it is enmeshed in how we interpret the world around us and in our actions. Theoretical orientations are the filters we use to interpret and assign meaning to empirical observations. The actions that follow the assignment of meaning are affected by the filters selected. A large part of becoming educated is developing an awareness of our personal theoretical frameworks so that our actions emanate from conscious reflection—something referred to as *praxis*, or "informed action" (Denhardt, 1984). Theory and practice are one in the realm of informed action. Theory is a prerequisite for responsible practice.

The first tangible use of criminal justice theory then is profound: it informs and guides practice, just as practice informs theory. The bias against theory by some in the practicing community is misguided, as is the prejudice some theoreticians have about learning from real-world practices and practitioners.[13]

The second beneficial outcome of theorizing is enhanced understanding. The criminal justice apparatus is transforming at bewildering speed. Increasingly punitive laws and policies, a media industry that thrives on crime and crime-control themes, unrestrained criminal justice system growth, and a confusion about the overall moral purpose of the criminal justice system all signal an entanglement of perplexity that is dizzying for even the most seasoned criminal justice analyst.[14] De-tangling this perplexity using numerous theoretical orientations is like deciphering one of those children's color-coded pictures that require different colored lenses to detect the images. It is only through gazing at the entanglement of criminal justice through differing colors (orientations)—and then comparing the images yielded—that we can more clearly understand our object of study.

Finally, rigorous theorizing is essential for conducting quality research. Crime and justice scholars carry out numerous types of research developing theory, testing theory, evaluating policy, or describing phenomena using qualitative and/or quantitative data. No matter the type, it is impossible to conduct theory-less research (see note 2). Theory influences the questions asked, the selection of the phenomenon under study, the way in which data are collected, the interpretation of those data, and

---

[13] Kurt Lewin's (1952) articulation of the symbiotic relationship between theory and practice has had a profound impact on academe in recent years. Nearly every area of study associated with a profession has experimented with what the literature labels "action research" or "critical action research." The objective of action research is to contribute simultaneously to social theory while bringing about constructive social change.

[14] See Garland (2001, pp. 6–20) for a revealing overview of the major changes that have faced the criminal justice apparatus over the last thirty years.

the type of policies recommended. As noted above, even the practices generated from a researcher's policy recommendation are imbued with theory, no matter how practical they may appear. To avoid theory is to remain ignorant of its influence.

Theoretical Awakening

We have established in this chapter that theorizing is misunderstood, ubiquitous, unavoidable, essential for a discipline's healthy heart and soul, critical to our thorough understanding of the criminal justice apparatus, a prerequisite for competent practice, and almost as exciting as being chased by a grizzly bear.

Criminal justice and criminology have not placed a high priority on developing a theoretical infrastructure about the criminal justice apparatus. However, the eight theoretical orientations in this book, and their associated readings, should demonstrate that criminal justice theory has nevertheless been an influential presence all along. In the last several years a growing number of criminology and criminal justice scholars are taking theorizing the criminal justice system and crime control seriously. Many of the selections in this work, and the information included in the overviews to each orientation, demonstrate this trend.[15] Moreover, even within the discipline of criminology—where the tradition has been to study criminal justice only as a means to controlling crime—the new journal *Theoretical Criminology* has devoted the bulk of its attention to theoretical examinations of the criminal justice system, crime control, and social control in contemporary society.

This book's overall goal is to acknowledge, learn, and use criminal justice theory; a challenging endeavor but one not meant to be mind-numbingly complex. In fact, theorizing has some similarities to the gentle art of storytelling. Contrast the story told, for example, by a person who sees criminal justice as a growth industry with the story told by someone who believes criminal justice is a forced reaction to the crime problem. The first storyteller would spin a tale of self-promotion and hardhearted bureaucracy building, while the second would weave a plot where the government reacts rationally to whatever threatens our security and safety. Each of the orientations in this book filter the criminal justice apparatus through different theoretical lenses and tells a unique story about its history, growth, behaviors, motivations, functioning, and its possible future.

---

[15] Three books stand out as excellent early examples of crime and justice scholars theorizing criminal justice: Duffee's (1980) *Explaining Criminal Justice: Community Theory and Criminal Justice Reform,* Quinney's (1974) *Critique of Legal Order: Crime Control in Capitalist Society,* and King's (1981) *The Framework of Criminal Justice.* Although written from differing ideological orientations, each book's explicit object of theorizing is the criminal justice apparatus. David Duffee's (1980) work provides the most comprehensive and rigorous theorizing about the criminal justice system to date.

In addition, some of these lenses can be combined to construct a prism through which to begin new filtering processes.

Eight Theoretical Orientations

Each chapter is dedicated to a single theoretical orientation, and the overview presents the major elements, followed by articles selected to illustrate each framework's understanding of criminal justice. Some overviews are more comprehensive than others; this should not be interpreted as an indication of preference or superiority. A more in-depth overview merely means that the T.O. being discussed is either more complicated to summarize and/or its literature is more extensive. Packer's theoretical orientation, for example, has generated roughly fifty journal articles and books, whereas the criminal justice as oppression scholarship numbers in the thousands.

Figure 1 summarizes the eight orientations in grid form, highlighting a few key features and characteristics of each. While perhaps ominous at first glance, the grid is a visual representation of the "big picture." It maps the territory covered in the book. Most readers with some background in criminal justice and/or the social sciences will recognize most of these ways of thinking. My hope is that this organizational scheme will play a role in recognizing criminal justice theory as a worthwhile area of research and scholarship—and as an essential component of teaching criminology and criminal justice.

As the reader works through these eight orientations, it should become apparent that they overlap and oftentimes complement one another. Separating the various ways of thinking about criminal justice into categories helps organize our thinking. However, it also creates artificial boundaries, diminishing the explanatory strength of the frameworks. The last four orientations, for example, are often used simultaneously within a single study. The categorization for purposes of instruction should not curtail the natural inclination to find similarities and links among the orientations and possibilities of combining their insights to fashion more powerful tools for analysis.

Figure 1   Theoretical Orientations

Features	Rational/Legal	System	Packer's C.C. vs. D.P.	Politics
Intellectual tradition	neoclassical; legal formalism; classical	structural-functionalism; biological sciences; organizational studies	liberal legal jurisprudence; legal realism; socio-legal studies	political science; public administration
Key concepts employed	rational-legalistic; rule-bound; taken for granted	functional; equilibrium; efficiency; technology; external forces; open system; closed system	value-cluster; efficiency; crime control values; due process values; needs-based values	ideology; conflict; symbolic politics; policy making/implementing; state; community
Central objects of study	cj system; rational decisions; law enforcement	cj system; what works; technology; subsystem focus	cj system; criminal law process; police and courts	cj system; legislators; policy making and implementing
Purpose of the cj system and apparatus	control crime; punish offenders; maintain peace and security	control crime primary focus; various sub-purposes; efficient processing of accused; maintain safety in society	control crime overall; purpose is ambiguous and tension-filled between crime control, due process, and need-based values	purpose contingent on political climate; cj is tool for political capital; rational administration of policy
Why the rapid cj expansion in the last 30 years?	legal reaction to increased law-breaking (forced reaction theory)	cj system reacting to increases in crime (forced reaction theory)	pendulum swing toward crime control values; choosing punitiveness	politicians exploiting problem; politicized drug war; shift in ideology
Underlying conception of crime	definition of crime is not questioned; crime is a rational choice	definition of crime is not questioned; crime is a rational choice	definition of most crimes not questioned; status offenses are over-reach of criminal law; crime is a rational choice	image/definition of crime community-driven; partisan ideology also drives image of crime; crime is a political construct

Assumptions about agency and practitioner motives	well-intended; protecting; serving; rule following; law abiding; professionalism	rational decision makers; efficient; adapting to external forces	role/goal conflict; mixed messages; mimic the value-messages provided from public	responsive to politics; interest-based; ideological pulls; power-players
Level of emphasis on reform	strong emphasis on rules; policies	strong on efficiency; technology; rational decision making; control discretion	minimal as applied in the discipline; but could be a strong emphasis based on the tone of Packer's book	varies; strong emphasis on policy reform for most; some use mostly as a way to understand
Solutions to problems facing cja	more resources; greater efficiency; reduce discretion; professionalism	seamless harmony; what works; research; reduce discretion; new technology; efficiency	healthy balance of values; ensure system of checks and balances; decriminalization	de-politicize; research; local democratic control; control interest groups
Issues and controversies of concern	deterrence; defending the virtues and honor of the cjs	abuse of discretion; cutting-edge technology; streamline/centralize operations	erosion of constitutional rights; governmental intrusiveness	federalization; symbolic politics; ideological intensification
Methodological tendency	Legal research; advocacy research	quantitative policy and evaluative research; macro-quantitative studies	legal research; socio-legal studies	historical research; quantitative; interpretive
What the future might hold	crime-control efforts intensify; increased professionalism; forced reaction to terrorism threat	greater system integration; enhanced technology; greater efficiency; well-coordinated response to terrorism threat	pendulum swings between crime control and due process; crime control's continued emphasis likely with war on terrorism	interest group influence intensifies; irrational policies due to partisan ideology; further federalization of cjs due to war on terrorism

(continued)

Figure I Theoretical Orientations (continued)

Features	Social Constructionist	Growth Complex	Oppression	Late-Modern
Intellectual tradition	interpretive school; symbolic interactionism; social constructionism; cultural studies	Weber; Frankfurt School; critical public administration	Marx; feminism; critical sociology; race studies	Foucault; governmentality literature; postmodernism
Key concepts employed	myth; reality; culture; symbols; legitimacy; moral panic; impression-management institutional theory	bureaucracy building; privatization profit; complex; technical rationality; merging complexes	dangerous classes; gender; patriarchy; racism; class bias; conflict model; structural thinking; dialectics; praxis	actuarial justice; neo-liberal politics; exclusive society; safety norm; incoherence in cj policy
Central objects of study	entire cj apparatus; myth; media; organization culture; legitimacy; use of language	entire cj apparatus; dynasty building; privatization	entire cj apparatus; inequality; patriarchy; racism	entire cj apparatus and beyond; impact of late modern changes
Purpose of the cj system and apparatus	purpose is relative, socially constructed; management of appearances; maintain legitimacy	growth in size and power; financial gain; political gain; build bureaucracy	oppress marginalized in society; controlling those perceived as threatening status quo	purpose is confused; technical management of excluded; fetish for safety; complex of controls
Why the rapid cj expansion in the last 30 years?	moral panics; media exploitation; runaway cultural process; crime as scapegoat	dynasty building; growth complex; merging private with public; cj with military	control of threatening groups; marginalized used as scapegoats; crisis in state legitimacy	crisis in state sovereignty; risk aversive society; growth complex; moral indifference
Underlying conception of crime	definition of crime relative; myths about crime rampant; moral overcriminalization; moral entrepreneurs guiding definition	definition of crime driven by desire to expand; image manipulated for purposes of cj growth; crime is raw material for industry	definition of crime driven by those with economic, cultural, and political power; definition of crime is a product of race/gender/class inequality	negligence and safety threats defined as criminal; late modern controls do not require acts to be defined as criminal

Assumptions about agency and practitioner motives	constructing problems for existing solutions; reacting to moral panics; culturally-bound; managing appearances	self-serving; power-building; quest for immortality; means over ends; bureaucratic survival; technical over moral thinking	institutional racism; sexism; classism; often unaware of oppressive end-result of their own activities	navigating through massive transformations; late modern forces; good intentions; disturbing results
Level of emphasis on reform	low to moderate; most use only as a way to understand; some emphasis on reforming culture and myth-busting	low to moderate; primarily used to understand; some emphasis on methods of limiting growth	strong on promoting economic/social justice; eliminating racial and gender oppression	low to moderate; primarily a needed intellectual exercise; better theory leads to understanding, leading to better practice
Solutions to problems facing cja	myth-busting; deconstruct moral panics; media accountability	beware of growing complex; limit growth; resist privatization; watchdogs needed	reduce size and power of cja; emphasis on social/economic measures; social justice	few recommendations; latent concern for freedom; mostly analytical orientation
Issues and controversies of concern	media/bureaucrat/political exploitation; mythology; symbolic war rhetoric; images of race/gender	exponential growth; private/public; military/police blur	violence against women; drug war's impact on marginalized; racial profiling	growth of system; changes in social control; rise of surveillance society
Methodological tendency	interpretive methodologies; cultural studies	descriptive; quantitative; investigative; historical	qualitative and quantitative; historical; critical ethnography	recent historical analysis; some quantitative being done on new penology
What the future might hold	moral panics intensify; irrational policies; media and governmental influence grows in construction of myths, especially in light of war on terrorism	merging growth industries; runaway growth in power and size due to war on terrorism	cj apparatus becomes more oppressive to poor, women, and minorities; war on terrorism used to further control and oppress	uncertainties and fears of risk intensify; enhanced soft control measures; blurring of traditional distinctions; terrorism threat intensifies; security-conscious society

References

Bernard, T., & Engel, R. (2001). Conceptualizing criminal justice theory. *Justice Quarterly, 18*(1), 1–30.

Bernstein, R. J. (1976). *The restructuring of social and political theory*. London: Methuen University Press.

Braithwait, J., & Pettit, P. (1990). *Not just deserts: A republican theory of criminal justice*. Oxford: Clarendon Press.

Carr, W., & Kemmis, S. (1986). *Becoming critical: Education, knowledge and action research*. London: The Falmer Press.

Davis, N. J. (1975). *Sociological constructions of deviance: Perspectives and issues in the field*. Dubuque, IA: Wm. C. Brown.

Denhardt, R. B. (1984). *Theories of public organization*. Pacific Grove, CA: Brooks/Cole.

Duffee, D. E. (1980, 1990). *Explaining criminal justice: Community theory and criminal justice reform*. Prospect Heights, IL: Waveland Press.

Duffee, D. E., & O'Leary, V. (1971). Models of correction: An entry in the Packer-Griffiths debate. *Criminal Law Bulletin, 7*(4), 329–352.

Einstadter, W., & Henry, S. (1995). *Criminological theory: An analysis of its underlying assumptions*. New York: Harcourt Brace.

Ellis, R. D., & Ellis, C. S. (1989). *Theories of criminal justice: A critical reappraisal*. Wolfeborro, NH: Longwood Academic.

Fay, B. (1977). *Social theory and political practice*. London: George Allen and Unwin.

Garland, D. (1990). *Punishment and modern society: A study in social theory*. Chicago: The University of Chicago Press.

Garland, D. (2001). *The culture of control: Crime and social order in contemporary society*. Chicago: The University of Chicago Press.

Gibbons, D. C. (1994). *Talking about crime and criminals: Problem and issues in theory development in criminology*. Englewood Cliffs, NJ: Prentice-Hall.

Hagan, J. (1989). Why is there so little criminal justice theory? Neglected macro- and micro-level links between organizations and power. *Journal of Research in Crime and Delinquency, 26*(2), 116–135.

Habermas, J. (1972). *Knowledge and human interests* (J. J. Shapiro, Trans.). London: Heinemann.

Habermas, J. (1974). *Theory and practice* (T. McCarthy, Trans.). London: Heinemann.

King, M. (1981). *The framework of criminal justice*. London: Croom Helm.

Kraska, P. B. (1993). Militarizing the drug war: A sign of the times. In P. B. Kraska (Ed.), *Altered states of mind: Critical observations of the drug war* (pp. 159–206). New York: Garland Press.

Kraska, P. B. (2001). *Militarizing the American criminal justice system: The changing roles of the armed forces and police*. Boston: Northeastern University Press.

Lewin, K. (1952). Group decision and social change. In G. E. Swanson, T. M. Newcomb, & F. E. Hartley (Eds.), *Readings in social psychology*. New York: Holt.

Marenin, O., & Worrall, J. (1998). Criminal justice: Portrait of a discipline in progress. *Journal of Criminal Justice, 26*(6), 465–480.

Morgan, G. M. (1986). *Images of organization*. Newbury Park, CA: Sage.

Popper, K. R. (1963). *Conjectures and refutations*. London: Routledge and Kegan Paul.

Quinney, R. (1974). *Critique of legal order: Crime control in capitalist society*. Boston: Little, Brown.

Rafter, N. H. (1990). The social construction of crime and crime control. *Journal of Research in Crime and Delinquency, 27*(4), 376–389.

Ritzer, G. (1983). *Contemporary sociological theory.* New York: Alfred A. Knopf.

Sullivan, R. R. (1994). The tragedy of academic criminal justice. *Journal of Criminal Justice, 22*(4), 549–558.

Wagner, D. G. (1984). *The growth of sociological theory.* Beverly Hills: Sage.

Weer, S. L. (2001). Personal conversation, October 13.

Williams, T. (1984). The demise of the criminological imagination: A critique of recent criminology. *Justice Quarterly, 1*(1), 91–106.

Criminal Justice as Rational/Legalism

Theorizing unveils what we take for granted. The common reference to *taking something for granted* often overlooks the fact that we supply whatever we take for granted with tremendous power. It remains unquestioned and possesses unnoticed influence and authority. A girl, for example, being raised in a society oppressive to women, may never seriously question her oppressed status and the system of male privilege that restricts her freedom. What oppresses her remains invisible.

The first way of thinking about criminal justice, the rational/legal theoretical orientation, is taken for granted by many people.[1] It contains a host of assumptions, ideas, and values about the law, punishment, and crime control that seem obvious and to many irrefutable. Consequently, it is a highly influential theoretical orientation about criminal justice apparatus, especially with the public and with those who work in the system. Compared to several of the other theoretical orientations covered in this book, this one does not constitute a well-defined area of scholarship. It exists, instead, as a way of thinking dispersed throughout various literatures in criminology/criminal justice.

---

[1] It is important to recognize that what I call the rational/legal orientation was a radical and controversial proposal for reform in the early to mid-1700s.

Rational/Legal Thinking and Assumptions

Criminal justice and crime control activity originates from the need of people to be secure from the harmful acts of others.[2] As the first two articles note, each citizen gives a measure of his or her freedom and power to the government so that it can enforce a set of universally agreed upon laws for the purpose of keeping the public safe and secure (also known as the *social contract*). The system used to enforce these laws, and prescribe fair and effective punishments for those who break them, is guided solely by the rule of law. Legislators and criminal justice practitioners are motivated, thus, by the desire to keep society safe through a fair and impartial legal process and to protect the rights of all individuals irrespective of their social rank or class. Rational, impartial decision-making, based on the rule of law, best typifies criminal justice operations. Extra-legal factors such as ethnicity, gender, income, or politics play no important role.

An academic friend used to be a judge in Sierra Leone and has his Ph.D. in law from Cambridge. Years ago we used to discuss our differing views on the nature of criminal justice behavior. He would chastise me for my cynicism; I would rib him for his idealism. I could not understand how someone who worked with and studied the law so closely could be so trusting about its functioning. One day he talked about his legal training at Cambridge and the importance, given the harsh circumstances he worked under in Sierra Leone, to believe in the highest ideals of the law. He understands from experience the challenges in implementing the rational/legal model and is engaged in a struggle similar to that of the early legal reformist, Cesare Beccaria (see the first article). He believes deeply in the ideals embodied in our legal system and, as a result, processes his analysis of the U.S. criminal justice system through rational/legal lenses. Consequently, he focuses on the way the system is supposed to work in its ideal form—finding plenty of evidence that, at least in the United States, its ideals are being realized.

A key strength of the rational/legal orientation lies in its theoretical simplicity. Consider the answer to one of the questions asked in the first chapter: "What accounts for the steep growth in power and size of the CJA over the last 30 years?" Answer: *Criminal justice growth is a forced reaction to increased law-breaking*. The forced reaction theory[3] of criminal justice development and growth is straightforward and very appealing to the general public: increased power and growth is an inescapable reaction to a worsening crime and security problem, an unavoidable outgrowth of a society in greater need of criminal justice-based controls. Each of the articles provided for this section demonstrates a strong adherence to forced

---

[2] A key assumption made here is that, due to people's inherent desire to pursue their own ends regardless of consequences to others, a well-functioning society must keep in place a superordinate force that prohibits and punishes what Hobbes called "brutish" behavior.
[3] Shannon Weer deserves the credit for the terminology "forced reaction theory."

reaction theorizing. They emphasize not only the symbolic value of punishment in modern society but also the importance of enlarging the role of legal controls as a responsible means of addressing crime.

Defenders of Our Response to Crime

Cesare Beccaria wrote *Of Crimes and Punishments* in 1764. He was influenced by his friends, Pietro and Alessandro Verri, who had formed "the academy of fists," an intellectual circle intent on reforming how criminals were treated. Pietro was writing a book on torture, and Alessandro was an official at a Milan prison, thoroughly familiar with the conditions in that institution. Beccaria's work was an attempt to halt torture, secret accusations, the arbitrary power of judges, inequality in sentencing, and the use of capital punishment. Beccaria was influenced by the Enlightenment philosophers. Two key philosophies grounded his work: social contract and utility. Beccaria believed that punishment was justified only to ensure that all citizens abide by the social contract of not causing harm to others. He emphasized that punishment should fit the crime and should be prescribed by carefully conceived legislation; it should also be swift and certain. He recommended that imprisonment should replace torture and capital punishment. The utilitarian aspect of his recommendations was that the punishment selected should satisfy the greatest public good.

In article 2, Ernest van den Haag continues the application of utilitarian principles. Justice requires punishing as many of the guilty as possible and sparing as many of the innocent as possible. The criminal act is a choice; punishment increases the cost of crime and thus serves as a deterrent. Van den Haag points out that the emphasis on incarceration as the primary tool for criminal justice is approximately 200 years old and primarily a U.S. invention.

The concluding article by Logan and DiIulio is a reaction to those who do *not* ascribe to the rational/legal theoretical orientation. Their essay critiques points of view that are critical of the government and the criminal justice system. In the process they vindicate the reformist principles laid out by Beccaria in the mid-1700s, defending what has come to be known today as the neoclassical model. They argue that it is a myth that punishment is inherently bad and that the system or society is in need of an overhaul. Reform measures should be limited to increasing the efficiency of what exists, minor changes in rules and operating policies, and only slight modifications in law as determined by a consensus view among society's members.

Unlike other orientations in this book, there is not a specific group of academics in our field that adheres solely to this way of thinking.[4] Its

---

[4] Some academics, however, emphasize that the system works as it was intended. Examples include James Q. Wilson, John DiIulio, and P. J. Waddington.

influence, as a guide for understanding criminal justice and crime control, is less conspicuous when compared to the other orientations that follow; but its omnipresence throughout the literature is undeniable. Beyond academe, the public, lawmakers, and the criminal justice practicing community rely heavily on the rational/legal theoretical orientation—even if its presence sometimes goes unnoticed.

Of Crimes and Punishments

Cesare Beccaria

> *Beccaria's short treatise was published in 1764 and consisted of an introduction, conclusion, and 46 topics (excerpts from 13 of the topics are included here).*

Introduction

. . . If we look into history we shall find that laws, which are, or ought to be, conventions between men in a state of freedom have been, for the most part the work of the passions of a few, or the consequences of a fortuitous or temporary necessity; not dictated by a cool examiner of human nature, who knew how to collect in one point the actions of a multitude, and had this only end in view, *the greatest happiness of the greatest number.* . . .

Of the Origin of Punishments

Laws are the conditions under which men, naturally independent, united themselves in society. Weary of living in a continual state of war, and of enjoying a liberty which became of little value, from the uncertainty of its duration, they sacrificed one part of it, to enjoy the rest in peace and security. The sum of all these portions of the liberty of each individual constituted the sovereignty of a nation and was deposited in the hands of the sovereign, as the lawful administrator. But it was not sufficient only to

These excerpts are from a version of Beccaria's work translated from the French by E. D. Ingraham (second American edition, 1819, Philadelphia: Philip H. Nicklin) available at http://www.constitution.org/cb/crim_pun.txt

establish this deposit; it was also necessary to defend it from the usurpation of each individual, who will always endeavour to take away from the mass, not only his own portion, but to encroach on that of others. Some motives therefore, that strike the senses were necessary to prevent the despotism of each individual from plunging society into its former chaos. Such motives are the punishments established, against the infractors of the laws. I say that motives of this kind are necessary; because experience shows, that the multitude adopt no established principle of conduct; and because society is prevented from approaching to that dissolution, (to which, as well as all other parts of the physical and moral world, it naturally tends,) only by motives that are the immediate objects of sense, and which being continually presented to the mind, are sufficient to counterbalance the effects of the passions of the individual which oppose the general good. Neither the power of eloquence nor the sublimest truths are sufficient to restrain, for any length of time, those passions which are excited by the lively impressions of present objects.

Of the Right to Punish

. . . No man ever gave up his liberty merely for the good of the public. Such a chimera exists only in romances. Every individual wishes, if possible, to be exempt from the compacts that bind the rest of mankind. . . .

It was necessity that forced men to give up apart of their liberty. It is certain, then, that every individual would choose to put into the public stock the smallest portion possible, as much only as was sufficient to engage others to defend it. The aggregate of these, the smallest portions possible, forms the right of punishing; all that extends beyond this, is abuse, not justice.

Observe that by *justice* I understand nothing more than that bond which is necessary to keep the interest of individuals united, without which men would return to their original state of barbarity. All punishments which exceed the necessity of preserving this bond are in their nature unjust. . . .

Consequences of the Foregoing Principles

The laws only can determine the punishment of crimes; and the authority of making penal laws can only reside with the legislator, who represents the whole society united by the social compact. No magistrate then, (as he is one of the society,) can, with justice, inflict on any other member of the same society punishment that is not ordained by the laws. . . .

If it can only be proved that the severity of punishments, though not immediately contrary to the public good or to the end for which they were intended which is to prevent crimes, be useless, then such severity would be contrary to those beneficent virtues. . . . It would also be contrary to justice and the social compact.

Of the Interpretation of Laws

Judges, in criminal cases, have no right to interpret the penal laws, because they are not legislators. . . . [The role of the judge] is only to examine if a man have or have not committed an action contrary to the laws.

In every criminal cause the judge should reason syllogistically. The *major* should be the general law; the *minor*, the conformity of the action, or its opposition to the laws; the *conclusion*, liberty, or punishment. . .

Of the Proportion between Crimes and Punishment

It is not only the common interest of mankind that crimes should not be committed, but that crimes of every kind should be less frequent, in proportion to the evil they produce to society. Therefore the means made use of by the legislature to prevent crimes should be more powerful in proportion as they are destructive of the public safety and happiness, and as the inducements to commit them are stronger. Therefore there ought to be a fixed proportion between crimes and punishments.

It is impossible to prevent entirely all the disorders which the passions of mankind cause in society. These disorders increase in proportion to the number of people and the opposition of private interests. . . . In political arithmetic, it is necessary to substitute a calculation of probabilities to mathematical exactness. That force which continually impels us to our own private interest, like gravity, acts incessantly, unless it meets with an obstacle to oppose it. . . . Punishments, which I would call political obstacles, prevent the fatal effects of private interest. . . . The legislator acts, in this case, like a skilful architect, who endeavours to counteract the force of gravity by combining the circumstances which may contribute to the strength of his edifice. . . .

Of Estimating the Degree of Crimes

. . . Crimes are only to be measured by the injury done to society.

Of the Intent of Punishments

From the foregoing considerations it is evident that the intent of punishments is not to torment a sensible being, nor to undo a crime already committed. . . . The end of punishment, therefore, is no other than to prevent the criminal from doing further injury to society, and to prevent others from committing the like offence. Such punishments, therefore, and such a mode of inflicting them, ought to be chosen, as will make the strongest and most lasting impressions on the minds of others, with the least torment to the body of the criminal.

Of Torture

The torture of a criminal during the course of his trial is a cruelty consecrated by custom in most nations. It is used with an intent either to make him confess his crime, or to explain some contradictions into which he had been led during his examination, or discover his accomplices, or for some kind of metaphysical and incomprehensible purgation of infamy, or, finally, in order to discover other crimes of which he is not accused, but of which he may be guilty.

No man can be judged a criminal until he be found guilty; nor can society take from him the public protection until it have been proved that he has violated the conditions on which it was granted. . . . . Either he is guilty, or not guilty. If guilty, he should only suffer the punishment ordained by the laws, and torture becomes useless, as his confession is unnecessary, if he be not guilty, you torture the innocent; for, in the eye of the law, every man is innocent whose crime has not been proved. . . .

Of the Advantage of Immediate Punishment

The more immediately after the commission of a crime a punishment is inflicted, the more just and useful it will be. . . . *The degree of the punishment, and the consequences of a crime, ought to be so contrived as to have the greatest possible effect on others, with the least possible pain to the delinquent.* . . .

An immediate punishment is more useful; because the smaller the interval of time between the punishment and the crime, the stronger and more lasting will be the association of the two ideas of *crime* and *punishment*; so that they may be considered, one as the cause, and the other as the unavoidable and necessary effect. . . .

It is, then, of the greatest importance that the punishment should succeed the crime as immediately as possible if we intend that . . . the seducing picture of the advantage arising from the crime should instantly awake the attendant idea of punishment. Delaying the punishment serves only to separate these two ideas, and thus affects the minds of the spectators rather as being a terrible sight than the necessary consequence of a crime, the horror of which should contribute to heighten the idea of the punishment.

There is another excellent method of strengthening this important connection between the ideas of crime and punishment; that is, to make the punishment as analogous as possible to the nature of the crime, in order that the punishment may lead the mind to consider the crime in a different point of view from that in which it was placed by the flattering idea of promised advantages. . . .

Men do not, in general, commit great crimes deliberately, but rather in a sudden gust of passion; and they commonly look on the punishment due to a great crime as remote and improbable. The public punishment, therefore, of small crimes will make a greater impression, and, by deterring men from the smaller, will effectually prevent the greater.

Of the Mildness of Punishments

. . . Crimes are more effectually prevented by the *certainty* than the *severity* of punishment. . . . The certainty of a small punishment will make a stronger impression than the fear of one more severe, if attended with the hopes of escaping. . . .

In proportion as punishments become more cruel, the minds of men, as a fluid rises to the same height with that which surrounds it, grow hardened and insensible. . . . That a punishment may produce the effect required, it is sufficient that the *evil* it occasions should exceed the *good* expected from the crime, including in the calculation the certainty of the punishment, and the privation of the expected advantage. All severity beyond this is superfluous, and therefore tyrannical.

The punishment of death is pernicious to society, from the example of barbarity it affords. If the passions, or the necessity of war, have taught men to shed the blood of their fellow creatures, the laws, which are intended to moderate the ferocity of mankind, should not increase it by examples of barbarity, the more horrible as this punishment is usually attended with formal pageantry. Is it not absurd, that the laws, which detest and punish homicide, should, in order to prevent murder, publicly commit murder themselves? . . .

Of the Punishment of Death

. . . The death of a criminal is a terrible but momentary spectacle, and therefore a less efficacious method of deterring others than the continued example of a man deprived of his liberty, condemned, as a beast of burden, to repair, by his labour, the injury he has done to society. *If I commit such a crime*, says the spectator to himself, *I shall be reduced to that miserable condition for the rest of my life*. . . .

Of Imprisonment

That a magistrate, the executor of the laws, should have a power to imprison a citizen, to deprive the man he hates of his liberty, upon frivolous pretences, and to leave his friend unpunished, notwithstanding the strongest proofs of his guilt, is an error as common as it is contrary to the end of society, which is personal security. . . .

Imprisonment is a punishment which differs from all others in this particular, that it necessarily precedes conviction; but this difference does not destroy a circumstance which is essential and common to it with all other punishments, that it should never be inflicted but when ordained by the law. The law should therefore determine the crime, the presumption, and the evidence sufficient to subject the accused to imprisonment and examination. . . .

Of the Means of Preventing Crimes

It is better to prevent crimes than to punish them. This is the fundamental principle of good legislation, which is the art of conducting men to
the maximum of happiness, and to the minimum of misery. . . . It is impossible to reduce the tumultuous activity of mankind to absolute regularity;
for, amidst the various and opposite attractions of pleasure and pain,
human laws are not sufficient entirely to prevent disorders in society. . . .
To prohibit a number of indifferent actions is not to prevent the crimes
which they may produce, but to create new ones. . . . To what a situation
should we be reduced if every thing were to be forbidden that might possibly lead to, a crime? We must be deprived of the use of our senses: for one
motive that induces a man to commit a real crime, there are a thousand
which excite him to those indifferent actions which are called crimes by
bad laws. If then the probability that a crime will be committed be in proportion to the number of motives, to extend the sphere of crimes will be to
increase that probability. . . . Would you prevent crimes? Let the laws be
clear and simple, let the entire force of the nation be united in their
defence, let them be intended rather to favour every individual than any
particular classes of men, let the laws be feared, and the laws only. The
fear of the laws is salutary, but the fear of men is a fruitful and fatal source
of crimes. . . .

Conclusion

I conclude with this reflection, that the severity of punishments ought
to be in proportion to the state of the nation. Among a people hardly yet
emerged from barbarity, they should be most severe, as strong impressions
are required; but, in proportion as the minds of men become softened by
their intercourse in society, the severity of punishments should be diminished, if it be intended that the necessary relation between the object and
the sensation should be maintained. . . . *That a punishment may not be an
act of violence, of one, or of many, against a private member of society, it
should be public, immediate, and necessary, the least possible in the case
given, proportioned to the crime, and determined by the laws.*

To Secure These Rights

Ernest van den Haag

Although they do many other things, the paramount duty, the *raison d'être*, of governments is to provide a legal order in which citizens can be secure in their lives, their liberties, and their pursuit of happiness. Whether originally granted by God, nature, society, or by the government itself (through a charter or constitution), these rights can be secured only by the government. For the rights of each citizen necessarily are the duties of all other citizens. Unless they give him what his rights entitle him to, and refrain from interfering with his rightful actions, no citizen can exercise his rights. Since not everybody can be counted on to volunteer his duties, our "unalienable" rights could easily be alienated; hence, according to our Declaration of Independence, "To secure these rights governments are instituted among men."

Governments secure rights and duties by specifying them through laws and by enforcing the laws. Laws regulate many activities; criminal (penal) laws, which concern us here, prohibit some activities (crimes) on pain of punishment (penalties). Punishment is administered by many agencies, which, by aggregation more than by systematic organization, form the "criminal justice system." By distributing punishments to those found guilty of violating penal laws, the criminal justice system directly and visibly dispenses "justice." Now, the total of what we call "social justice" depends on many other institutions that more or less equitably distribute income, or opportunities for advancement, or the good things of life generally. These distributions, not decided on directly by the criminal

Ernest Van den Haag, *Punishing Criminals: Concerning a Very Old and Painful Question* (New York: Basic Books, 1975, pp. 3–7). Reprinted by permission of the author.

justice system, are referred to as "distributive justice"; only the distribution of punishments is referred to as "penal," or "criminal" justice. But in both cases the word "justice" connotes an ideal, not an evaluation of reality.

Basically, the criminal justice system deals with three questions.

1. What conduct is prohibited?
2. How is it decided that a person is guilty of prohibited conduct?
3. What is to be done with those found guilty?

I shall focus mostly on the third question, although the other two will be engaged when they are likely to shed light on punishment. Where relevant, I shall also try to indicate the relation of criminal to distributive justice.

Punishment has been the main device for enforcing laws ever since the mists of prehistory lifted. And questions about punishment have been with us since then. What exactly is punishment? What motivates us to punish? What do we intend to accomplish? Is punishment effective? Can punishment deter? What role does it play in determining crime rates? Why do people violate laws? Are they responsible? What kind and what degree of punishment, if any, is just and effective for what kind of crime and for what kind of criminal? Are there means other than punishment to enforce laws? Are these more promising than the present kinds of punishment? How is punishment related to the social order, to justice, and to charity? Could punishment—as is frequently argued—be replaced by other measures such as education, treatment, or redistribution of income and property? Finally, what can be said for and against the three major kinds of punishment now used: death, imprisonment, and fines (including conditional suspensions such as probation and parole), and for and against the alternatives that might be available? . . . .

Many people . . . believe punishment morally unjustifiable and ineffective in enforcing laws, little more than a barbarous relic that merely satisfies an ignoble thirst for revenge. On the other hand, if the laws are not enforced, the citizens, in Lincoln's words "seeing their property destroyed, their families insulted and their lives endangered . . . become tired and disgusted with a government that offers them no protection."[1] Hence, there is insistence as well on the paramount duty of the government to enforce the laws. The issue hinges on the moral legitimacy and effectiveness of punishment as against alternative means of enforcing the laws—and, not least, on the justice of the laws themselves and of their enforcement.

Although the institution of punishment is as old as society, actual punishments, as well as the methods of dispensing them, have changed a great deal. Our present emphasis on incarceration as the main punitive or corrective device is less than two hundred years old and largely an American invention. In the past offenders were imprisoned mainly to hold them for trial. They were then sentenced to be fined, pilloried, flogged, mutilated, or put to death.

Notes

[1] Abraham Lincoln, *On the Perpetuation of our Political Institutions*, 1838.

Deadly Myths about Crime and Punishment in the United States

Charles Logan
John J. DiIulio, Jr.

Myth: In the 1980s, the United States Enacted All Sorts of "Get Tough on Crime" Legislation and Went on an Incarceration Binge

Prison populations have risen sharply over the last decade; that much is true. The myth is that this is due to an unprecedented and purely political wave of punitivity sweeping the nation, as epitomized by the War on Drugs and by legislative demands for longer and mandatory sentences. Several elements of this myth are shattered by a meticulous and authoritative article published recently in *Science* by Patrick A. Langan, a statistician at the Bureau of Justice Statistics.[1]

Langan examined the tremendous increase in state prison populations from 1973 to 1986. He determined that the growth was due to increases in prison admissions, rather than to (alleged but nonexistent) increases in sentence length or time served. He estimated that about 20 percent of the growth in admissions could be accounted for by demographic shifts in age and race. Increases in crime were offset by decreases in the probability of

Excerpted from "Ten Deadly Myths about Crime and Punishment in the U.S.," *Wisconsin Interest* 1 (Winter/Spring 1992), pp. 21–35. Reprinted with permission.

arrest, with the result that combined changes in crime and arrest rates accounted for only 9 percent of admissions growth. Increased drug arrests and imprisonments contributed only 8 percent.[2] By far the strongest determinant, explaining 51 percent of growth in prison admissions, was an increase in the postarrest probabilities of conviction and incarceration.[3] Prosecutors convicted more felons, judges imposed more prison sentences, and more violators of probation or parole were sent or returned to prison. The data suggest that the system may have gotten more efficient but not harsher.

A column in the *Washington Post* captures well the form and spirit of the "imprisonment binge" myth.[4] In "The Great American Lockup," Franklin E. Zimring, a professor of law at Berkeley, claims that we are more punitive now than ever before in history, that the rising tide of imprisonment is a matter of overzealous policy rather than a response to need, and that we must come to our senses and reverse an essentially irrational imprisonment policy.

When Professor Zimring says that we are experiencing a "100-year peak in rates of imprisonment," he does not inform the reader that this is true only when you measure imprisonment on a crude per capita basis. If, however, you wish to describe the *punitivity* of our imprisonment rate, you need to measure the amount of imprisonment relative to the number of crimes for which people may be sent to prison. To get an even more complete measure of punitivity, you should multiply this probability of imprisonment by the length of time served. When just such an index is examined for all the years in which it is available, 1960 through 1986, it becomes clear that we have not been marching steadily forward to an all-time high in punitivity. Instead, this index of "expected days of imprisonment" fell steadily from its high in 1959 (ninety-three days) to about one-seventh of that figure in 1975 (fourteen days). From 1975 through 1986 it returned to about one-fifth (nineteen days) of its 1960 level.[5] Even if we ignore the factor of time served and look only at prison commitments divided by crimes, we see much the same pattern. In 1960 there were sixty-two prison commitments per 1,000 Uniform Crime Index offenses; that number fell to twenty-three in 1970, remained relatively stable during the 1970s, then climbed from twenty-five back to sixty-two between 1980 and 1989.[6]

Thus, when we look at imprisonment per crime rather than per capita, and over thirty rather than ten years, we see that our punishment level is not rocketing to a new high but recovering from a plunge. The myth of the imprisonment binge requires that we focus only on punishment and not on crime, and that we ignore all data prior to about 1980. . . .

Myth: Prisons are Filthy, Violence-Ridden, and Overcrowded Human Warehouses That Function as Schools of Crime

There are two popular and competing images of American prisons. In one image, all or most prisons are hellholes. In the other image, all or most prisons are country clubs. Each image fits some prisons. But the vast majority of prisons in the United States today are neither hellholes nor country clubs. Instead, most American prisons do a pretty decent job of protecting inmates from each other, providing them with basic amenities (decent food, clean quarters, recreational equipment), offering them basic services (educational programs, work opportunities), and doing so in a way that ensures prisoners their basic constitutional and legal rights.

It is certainly true that most prison systems now hold more prisoners than they did a decade ago. The Federal Bureau of Prisons, for example, is operating at over 160 percent of its "design capacity"; that is, federal prisons house 60 percent more prisoners than they were designed to hold. When the federal prison agency's current multibillion-dollar expansion program is completed, it will still house about 40 percent more inmates than its buildings were designed to hold. That is by no means an ideal picture, and much the same picture can indeed be painted for dozens of jurisdictions around the country.

Contrary to the popular lore and propaganda, however, the consequences of prison crowding vary widely both within and between prison systems, and in every careful empirical study of the subject, the widely believed negative effects of crowding—violence, program disruption, health problems, and so on—are nowhere to be found. More broadly, several recent analyses have exploded the facile belief that contemporary prison conditions are unhealthy and harmful to inmates.

For example, in a study of over 180,000 housing units at 694 state prisons, the Bureau of Justice Statistics reported that the most overcrowded maximum security prisons had a rate of homicide lower than that of moderately crowded prisons and about the same as that of prisons that were not crowded.[7] By the same token, a recent review of the prison-crowding literature rightly concluded that "despite familiar claims that crowded prisons have produced dramatic increases in prison violence, illness, and hostility, modern research has failed to establish any conclusive link between current prison spatial and social densities and these problems."[8] Even more compelling was the conclusion reached in a recent and exhaustive survey of the empirical literatures bearing on the "pains of imprisonment." This conclusion is worth quoting at some length:

> To date, the incarceration literature has been very much influenced by a pains of imprisonment model. This model views imprisonment as psychologically harmful. However, the empirical data we reviewed question the validity of the view that imprisonment is universally painful. Solitary confinement, under limiting and humane conditions, long-term imprisonment, and short-term detention fail to show detrimental effects. From a physical health standpoint, inmates appear more healthy than their community counterparts.[9]

Normally, those who for ideological or other reasons are inclined to paint a bleaker portrait of U.S. prison conditions than is justified by the facts respond to such evidence with countervailing anecdotes about a given prison or prison system. Perhaps because good news is no news, most media pundits lap up these unrepresentative prison horror stories and report on "powder keg conditions" behind bars. And when a prison riot occurs, it is now de rigueur for "experts" to ascribe the incident to "overcrowding" and other "underlying factors." For selfish and short-sighted reasons, some prison officials are all too willing to go along with the farce. It is easier for them to join in a Greek chorus about the evils of prison crowding than it is for them to admit that their own poor leadership and management were wholly or partially responsible for the trouble (as it so often is).

Indeed, recent comparative analyses of how different prison administrators have handled crowding and other problems under like conditions suggest that the quality of life behind bars is mainly a function of how prisons are organized, led, and managed.[10]

Overwhelmingly, the evidence shows that crowded prisons can be safe and humane, while prisons with serious problems often suffered the same or worse problems before they were crowded. In short, the quality of prison life varies mainly according to the quality of prison management, and the quality of prison life in the United States today is generally quite good.

More specifically, contrary to the widely influential "nothing works" school of prison-based criminal rehabilitation programs, correctional administrators in a number of jurisdictions have instituted a variety of programs that serve as effective management tools and appear to increase the probability that prisoners who participate in them will go straight upon their release. Recent empirical studies indicate that prisoners who participate in certain types of drug abuse, counseling, and work-based programs may be less likely than otherwise comparable prisoners to return to prison once they return to the streets, as over 95 percent of all prisoners eventually do.[11]

Unfortunately, the recent spate of analyses that support this encouraging conclusion remain empirically thin, technically complex, and highly speculative. Moreover, each of the successful programs embodies a type of highly compassionate yet no-nonsense management approach that may be easier to describe in print than to emulate in practice or export widely. But, taken together with the more general facts and findings mentioned above, these studies—and the simple reality that most of those released from prison never return there—rebut the notion that most or all prisons in the United States are little better than crowded human warehouses that breed crime and other ills.

Myth: The U.S. Criminal Justice System Is Shot Through with Racial Discrimination

Most law-abiding Americans think that criminal sanctions are normally imposed on people who have been duly convicted of criminally violating the life, liberty, and property of their fellow citizens. Many critics, however, harbor a different, ostensibly more sophisticated view. They see prisons as instruments of "social control." To them, America is an oppressive, racist society, and prisons are a none-too-subtle way of subjugating the nation's poor and minority populations. Thus are roughly one of every nine adult African-American males in this country now under some form of correctional supervision—in prison, in jail, on probation, or on parole. And thus in the "conservative" 1980s was this "net of social control" cast over nearly a quarter of young African-American males in many jurisdictions.

There are at least three reasons why such race-based understandings of the U.S. criminal justice system are highly suspect at best. First, once one controls for socioeconomic and related factors, there is simply no empirical evidence to support the view that African-Americans, or the members of other racial and ethnic minorities in the United States, are far more likely than whites to be arrested, booked, indicted, fully prosecuted, convicted, be denied probation, incarcerated, disciplined while in custody (administrative segregation), or be denied furloughs or parole.

In one recent study, for example, the RAND Corporation found that "a defendant's racial or ethnic group bore little or no relationship to conviction rates, disposition times" and other adjudication outcomes in fourteen large urban jurisdictions across the country.[12] Instead, the study found that such mundane factors as the amount of evidence against a defendant, and whether or not a credible eyewitness testified, were strongly related to outcomes. This study echoed the findings of several previous empirical analyses.[13]

Second, the 1980s were many things, but they were not a time when the fraction of African-Americans behind prison bars skyrocketed. In a recent report, the Bureau of Justice Statistics revealed that the number of African-Americans as a percentage of the state prison population "has changed little since 1974; 47 percent in 1974, 48 percent in 1979, and 47 percent in 1986."[14] it is certainly true that the imprisonment rate for African-Americans has been, and continues to be, far higher than for whites. For example, in 1986 the rate of admission to prison per 100,000 residential population was 342 for African-Americans and 63 for whites.[15] But it is also true that crime rates are much higher for the former group than for the latter.

Finally, it is well known that most crime committed by poor minority citizens is committed against poor minority citizens. The typical victims of predatory ghetto criminals are innocent ghetto dwellers and their children, not middle- or upper-class whites.[16] For example, the best available data indicate that over 85 percent of single-offender crimes of violence committed by blacks are committed against blacks, while over 75 percent of such crimes committed by whites are committed against whites.[17] And if every credible opinion poll and victimization survey is to be believed, no group suffers more from violent street crime, "petty" thefts, and drug dealing, and no group is more eager to have courts, cops, and corrections officials crack down on inner-city criminals, than the predominantly minority citizens of these communities themselves.

The U.S. criminal justice system, therefore, may be biased, but not in the ways that elite, anti-incarceration penal reformers generally suppose. Relative to whites and more affluent citizens generally, the system now permits poor and minority citizens to be victimized readily and repeatedly: the rich get richer, the poor get poorly protected against the criminals in their midst. The system is thus rigged in favor of those who advocate community-based alternatives to incarceration and other measures that return violent, repeat, and violent repeat offenders to poor, drug-ravaged, minority communities far from the elites' own well-protected homes, offices, and suites.

Myth: The United States Has the Most Punitive Criminal Justice System in the World

Over a decade ago, the National Council on Crime and Delinquency foisted on the media a statistic it produced in a 1979 report: in terms of severity of punishment, as measured by the number of prisoners per capita, only two countries in the world—the Soviet Union and South Africa—were more ruthlessly repressive than the United States. The media have been parroting this claim ever since, never asking the NCCD why they were so willing to accept Soviet figures at face value, nor why they did not include the 4 or 5 million prisoners held captive in the forced labor camps that have been indispensable to the Soviet economy.[18]

Well, maybe a sloppy attitude toward data didn't matter before; we merely would have been a more distant third. But now . . . according to The Sentencing Project, a Washington-based research group, the United States has moved into first place, with 426 prison and jail inmates per 100,000 population, compared to 333 in South Africa and 268 in the [former] Soviet Union.[19] The media, including commentators as diverse as Tom Wicker and William Raspberry, have reacted just as uncritically to the new figures as they did to the old ones.

While gullibility toward Soviet statistics is the most glaring, it is not the most fatal flaw in this comparison, which also shows American incarceration rates to be much higher than, say, those of European countries, for which we have more reliable figures. The fatal flaw is very simple and very obvious: to interpret incarceration as a measure of the punitivity of a society, you have to divide, not by the population size, but by the number of crimes.

More competent comparative studies have discovered that when you control for rates of serious crime, the difference between the United States and other countries largely, and for some crimes completely, disappears.[20] For example, after controlling for crime rate and adjusting for difference in charge reduction between arrest and imprisonment, the United States in the early 1980s had an imprisonment rate virtually identical to Canada and

England for theft, fell between those two countries in the case of burglary, and lagged well behind each of the others in imprisonments for robbery.[21]

In addition to the myth of the United States as the world's most punitive nation, The Sentencing Project perpetuates in its report several of the other myths we discuss in this essay. It notes that African-American males are locked up at a rate four times greater than their counterparts in South Africa. A fleeting reference to the very high crime rate among black males is immediately buried in an avalanche of references to root causes, poverty, diminished opportunities, the gap between rich and poor, and the failure of schools, health care, and other social institutions—all wrapped up as "the cumulative effect of American policies regarding black males." The report calls for increased spending on supposed "prevention policies and services" such as education, housing, health care, and programs to generate employment. In a truly wacky expression of faith in social engineering, the report urges the General Accounting Office "to determine the relative influence of a range of social and economic factors on crime."

Most of all, The Sentencing Project advocates the expanded use of alternatives to incarceration, but with a unique twist: they recommend racial quotas in the distribution of criminal justice. Independent of any preceding reduction in criminal behavior, the "Justice Department should encourage the development of programs and sanctions designed specifically to reduce the disproportionate incarceration rate of African-American males."[22] The Sentencing Project endorses the language of one such program designed to reduce the incarceration "of ethnic and minority groups where such proportion exceeds the proportions such groups represent in the general population." Methods recommended for such reduction include diversion from prosecution, intensive probation, alternative sentencing, and parole release planning, among others.

That crime rates are very high in this country, particularly among black males, is an unhappy fact. When that fact is taken into account, it exposes as a myth the argument that we are excessively punitive, relative to other countries, in our imposition of imprisonment. . . .

Myth: Punishment is Bad

Underlying all the myths we have discussed so far, and motivating people to believe them, is the biggest myth of all: that punishment itself is inherently wrong. It is largely because they are opposed to punishment generally and to imprisonment in particular that many people argue so strongly that we must address the root causes of crime, that our criminal justice system discriminates, that we are overly punitive and haven't considered alternatives, that prisons are too costly and overcrowded, and that we must look to the courts for reform.

The "Big Myth" is that punishment has no value in itself; that it is intrinsically evil, and can be justified as a necessary evil only if it can be shown to be instrumental in achieving some overriding value, such as social order. Even retributivists, who argue that the primary purpose of the criminal sanction is to do justice by imposing deserved punishment (rather than to control crime through such strategies as rehabilitation, deterrence, or incapacitation), can find themselves caught up in utilitarian terminology when they speak of the "purpose"—rather than the "value"—of punishment.

Andrew von Hirsch provides the major contemporary statement of the justice model in his book *Doing Justice*.[23] Following Immanuel Kant, von Hirsch calls for penal sanctions on moral grounds, as the "just deserts" for criminally blameworthy conduct. Unlike Kant, however, von Hirsch sees deservedness only as necessary, but not sufficient, to justify punishment. There is supposedly a "countervailing moral consideration"—specifically, "the principle of not deliberately causing human suffering where it can possibly be avoided."[24] Accepting this principle, von Hirsch argues that for punishment to be justified, it must also be shown to have a deterrent effect. A utilitarian element has been added.

Von Hirsch's compromise is internally inconsistent, and this is weaker than a purely retributivist justification. The principle that punishment for wrongdoing is deserved, and the principle against all avoidable suffering, are logically incompatible. To say that *some* suffering (that is, punishment) is deserved is to say that we do not believe that all avoidable infliction of pain *should* be avoided. The justice model is stronger when the utilitarian requirement of deterrence is dropped.[25]

The best defense of punishment is not that it upholds the social order, but that it affirms important moral and cultural values.[26] Legal punishment is a legitimate and, if properly defined and administered, even a noble aspect of our culture. Imprisonment, in order to be respectable, does not need to be defined as "corrections," or as "treatment," or as "education," or as "protection of society," or as any other instrumental activity that an army of critics will forever claim to be a failure.

We must reject the false dichotomy between punishment and "humanitarianism." It is precisely within the context of punishment that humanistic concepts are most relevant. Principled and fair punishment for wrongdoing treats individuals as persons and as human beings, rather than objects. Punishment is an affirmation of the autonomy, responsibility, and dignity of the individual.

Punishment in the abstract is morally neutral. When applied in specific instances and in particular forms—including imprisonment—its morality win depend on whether or not it is deserved, justly composed, and proportionate to the wrongfulness of the crime. Where these conditions are met, punishment will not be a necessary evil, tolerable on utilitarian grounds only when hold to the minimum "effective" level. Rather, under those conditions, it will have positive moral value.

Notes

[1] Patrick A. Langan, "America's Soaring Prison Population," *Science* 251 (March 29, 1991): 1568–1573.

[2] The war on drugs probably had a greater effect on state prisons after 1984 and undoubtedly has had a great effect on federal prisons, where over half of last year's admissions were for drug offenses.

[3] Ibid., p. 1572.

[4] Franklin E. Zimring, "The Great American Lockup," *The Washington Post*, February 28, 1991.

[5] Mark Kleiman et al., *Imprisonment-to-Offense Ratios* (Washington, DC: Bureau of Justice Statistics Report, November, 1988), p. 21; we are using his figures without adjustment for underreporting by the UCR, since that adjustment is only possible from 1973 on.

[6] Robyn L. Cohen, *Prisoners in 1990* (Washington, DC: Bureau of Justice Statistics, 1991), p. 7.

[7] Christopher A. Innes, *Population Density in State Prisons* (Washington, DC: Bureau of Justice Statistics, December 1986).

[8] Jeff Bleich, "The Politics of Prison Crowding," *California Law Review* 77 (1989): 1137.

[9] James Bonta and Paul Gendreau, "Reexamining the Cruel and Unusual Punishment of Prison Life," *Law and Human Behavior* 14 (1990): 365.

[10] For example, see Bert Useem and Peter Kimball, *States of Siege: U.S. Poison Riots, 1971–1986* (New York: Oxford University Press, 1989); and John J. DiIulio, Jr., *Governing Prisons: A Comparative Study of Correctional Management* (New York: Free Press, 1987).

[11] For an overview, see DiIulio, *No Escape*, ibid., Chapter 3.

[12] Stephen P. Klein et al., *Predicting Criminal Justice Outcomes: What Matters?* (Santa Monica, CA: RAND Corp., 1991), p. ix.

[13] For example, see Stephen Klein et al., "Race and Imprisonment Decisions in California," *Science* 247 (February 1990): 769–792.

[14] Patrick A. Langan, *Race of Prisoners Admitted to State and Federal Institutions, 1926–86* (Washington, DC: Bureau of Justice Statistics, May 1991), p. 8.

[15] Ibid., p. 7.

[16] See Stewart, op. cit.; and DiIulio, "Underclass," op. cit.

[17] Joan Johnson et al., *Criminal Victimization in the United States, 1988* (Washington, DC: Bureau of Justice Statistics, December 1990), p. 48.

[18] See Ludmilla Alexeyeva, *Cruel and Usual Punishment: Forced Labor in Today's U.S.S.R.* (Washington, DC: AFL-CIO Department of International Affairs, 1987); see also various editions throughout the 1980s of the State Department's annual Country Reports on human rights practices of governments around the world.

[19] Marc Mauer, *Americans Behind Bars: A Comparison of International Rates of Incarceration* (Washington, DC: The Sentencing Project, January 1991). [At mid-year 2001, there were 690 prison and jail inmates per 100,000 population.]

[20] James Lynch, *Imprisonment in Four Countries* (Washington, DC: Bureau of Justice Statistics Special Report, February 1987); see also Alfred Blumstein, "Prison Populations: A System Out of Control?" in Michael Tonry and Norval Morris, *Crime and Justice: A Review of Research*, vol. 10 (Chicago: University of Chicago Press, 1988).

[21] Lynch, op cit., p. 2.

[22] Mauer, op cit., p. 12.

[23] Andrew von Hirsch, *Doing Justice: The Choice of Punishments* (New York: Hill & Wang, 1976).

[24] Ibid., p. 553.

[25] Charles H. Logan, *Private Prisons: Cons and Pros* (New York: Oxford University Press, 1990), pp. 243, 298.

[26] This discussion draws on Charles H. Logan and Gerald G. Gaes, "The Rehabilitation of Punishment" (unpublished, 1991).

Criminal Justice as a System

Most academics in criminology and criminal justice would agree that the systems theoretical orientation has dominated our field's thinking and research about criminal justice. Tracing its history back over 30 years, Samuel Walker deems it our "dominant paradigm." Indeed, the complex of governmental agencies responding to our crime problem is universally known as a "system." As with the rational/legal orientation, however, the system's framework is so entrenched that it is sometimes taken for granted and not approached as one of many different ways to understand our object of study.

The Garden Pond: Systems Theory and Concepts

Every aspect of our physical and mental world, no matter how small or large, can be interpreted through thinking about systems. Last summer we built a garden pond; we constructed it on a hillside, creating a "natural" waterfall comprised of twelve truckloads of rocks collected in our rural neighborhood. Below the waterfall is a three-foot deep pool. A pump at the bottom of the pool directs water up a hidden tube behind the waterfall, onto a large flat rock, then down six feet of rock wall, and back into the pool. It has taken only a year for this structure to be colonized by nature. Beneficial bacteria in the substrata of gravel at the bottom of the pond keep the water clean and clear. A dozen frogs consider it home; birds bathe in the falls and drink the water; the moss has germinated and sent new spores to surrounding rocks; and native Kentucky fish have appeared.

Biologist Ludvig von Bertalanffy's general systems theory and findings about interdependent units that work together to adapt to a changing environment explain many of the properties of the pond. It maintains itself through *homeostasis,* self-regulation by which a system adapts to a change in the environment to restore balance, or *equilibrium.* As an *open system,* the garden pond functions by drawing *inputs* from the external environment, transforming them (*throughputs*), and sending *outputs* back to the environment. It is engaged in an *exchange relationship* with elements outside and within its environment. Closed systems do not interact with environments, leading toward *entropy* or total disorganization (chaos). This mini-ecosystem's *subsystems* operate interdependently, resulting in *non-summativity,* in which the whole is larger than the sum of its parts. The concept that there are many different ways for a system to reach the same end state is known as *equifinality*; the term used for open systems that try to reach specific end states or goals is *teleological.* Open systems interact with other systems, forming *suprasystems.*

The Criminal Justice Organism and System Thinking

Criminal justice is also larger than the sum of its parts. Just as with a biological organism, the criminal justice system contains interacting subsystems (police, courts, and corrections), it has internal and external exchange relationships, it processes inputs (resources, laws, arrestees), and it produces outputs (punishment, reformed offenders, community service). Its structure and operations seek homeostasis, sustaining each other and striving for balance. If this balance is disrupted due to an external change, such as with an increase in crime, the criminal justice system reacts in kind so that it can fulfill its stated objective. As with the rational/ legal orientation, system size and power are determined by the volume of the crime problem (*forced reaction theory*).

System thinking was all the rage in the mid-1900s. It originated out of mathematics and biology and epitomized U.S. society's reliance on the life-improving benefits of science and technology. Talcott Parsons's (1951) theoretical framework, known as "structural-functionalism," dominated sociological thinking in the 1950s. And by the early 1970s, systems theory had established itself in nearly all the social and applied sciences. It was implemented in many spheres of the public and private sector, including the U.S. Department of Defense.

It is critical to recognize that this early effort to employ a system framework was not merely an academic search for the truth. The overarching motivation was similar to that of Beccaria and Bentham's Classical School of thought—reform, carried out by key stakeholders within the criminal justice system itself.[1] Researching and studying criminal justice was primarily a means to make it operate more efficiently and effectively. This was the intellectual and political environment in which social science researchers for the American Bar Foundation (see article 4 by Samuel Walker) and the President's Crime Commission (article 5) made recommendations for reforming the criminal law apparatus.

Contributions to Our Understanding

Thinking about the criminal law apparatus as a system was a huge intellectual leap. Following are three of the more important ways it has affected how we think about and approach the study of criminal justice.

- Sociological thinking is probably best characterized by an ability to make sense of complex phenomena through stepping back and seeing the big picture. Similarly, the system orientation directs our field to think about the hundreds of thousands of police, courts, and corrections agencies as an interacting and interdependent entity. In fact, studying the behavior of criminal justice, as we are doing in this book, would not be possible if it were not assumed by most in our field that this complex of agencies can be viewed in macro-terms.

- The objective in adopting a systems orientation was to improve the operations of the police, courts, and corrections. Our discipline thus has strong reformist roots, meaning that the study of criminal justice (what is) is intermingled with a hoped-for vision of the criminal justice system (what should be). Other orientations discussed in this book do not share this explicit reformist assumption (see chapters 6, 7, and 9).

- With an agenda of reform and improvement, the bulk of criminal justice research has focused on goal attainment: what works to control crime, discretion and rationality in decision making, managerial efficiency, and resource management. The systems orientation established a strong tradition in our field of concentrating on *organizational* and *managerial* concerns within criminal justice agencies (see, for example, Cole, 1970; Eisenstein & Jacob, 1977; Feeley, 1973; Wilson, 1968). Rational policies, reducing discretion, evaluation research, streamlining operations, enhanced information for efficient decision making, and an emphasis on new technology are all accepted elements of the reform agenda.

---

[1] As the Task Force Report (article 5) stated: "systems analysis studies should include development of mathematical models of the criminal justice system and appropriate parts and collection of data needed to apply these models to *improving operations*."

One Orientation, Two Strains

The previous discussion might give the impression that a systems the-oretical orientation is a single, mutually agreed upon approach to under-standing our object of study. Articles 4 and 5, however, will demonstrate to the careful reader that the real-world application of system thinking varies significantly within the discipline. You will notice that applying the systems framework to criminal justice was as much a political process as an academic one. Accordingly, systems theory was not adopted in its entirety—bits and pieces were included or excluded where convenient. For example, much of the literature, including article 5, only concentrates on the internal functioning of the system. The social, political, and eco-nomic context is downplayed or ignored. In addition, some of the prag-matic concerns of the early systems theorists are not unique to this orientation. For example, organizational/managerial research and study-ing and controlling discretion in practitioner decision making are not intrinsic to a systems framework. Several other orientations discussed in this book include organizational studies and a concern about discretion in decision making.

Perhaps the best way to avoid confusion is to divide the application of systems thinking into two strains, both at work today. The first we could call an open system strain. This is what the early sociological researchers involved in the ABF Survey project had in mind when recommending the use of systems theory. It is a more unadulterated use of the systems theo-retical framework than that found in sociology and the hard sciences. It strives to make sense of criminal justice by examining it within its larger social context. It is as concerned with the creation of knowledge as it is the improvement of the justice system. It has a greater willingness to recog-nize and acknowledge the system's complexities and problems; it sees the purpose of the criminal justice system as multi-faceted (control crime, rehabilitate, public service); and its reform agenda is more comprehensive and progressive.

The other strain sees the criminal law apparatus as a closed system and thus applies systems theory in a limited way. Heavy emphasis is placed on improving the technical efficiency of the *crime control* function of agencies through the introduction of new technology and minor adjust-ments in rules and policies. As a result, it is more concerned with how the system is supposed to work from a systems perspective (what ought to be), as opposed to how it works in reality (what is). It takes a more defensive posture toward criticism of the system, unless that questioning is limited to maladies in the system's internal functioning. Researching the system is only worthwhile to the degree that it will improve its internal crime con-trol function.

Which strain holds the most weight in our field? The answer would likely depend on whom you ask. Many in the field, particularly those sociologists who cut their academic teeth on systems theory, would maintain that the open system predominates.[2] However, the more critical orientations found later in the book would argue that despite the rhetoric espousing support for this strain, the closed-system perspective is the actual orientation most widely in use.

References

Cole, G. F. (1970). The decision to prosecute. *Law and Society Review, 4*, 313–343.

Eisenstein, J., & Jacob, H. (1977). *Felony justice: An organizational analysis of criminal courts*. Boston: Little, Brown.

Feeley, M. M. (1973). Two models of the criminal justice system: An organizational perspective. *Law and Society Review, 7*, 407–425.

Habermas, J. (1996). *Between facts and norms: Contributions to a discourse theory of law and democracy*. Cambridge: Polity.

Munro, J. (1971). Towards a theory of criminal justice administration: A general system's perspective. *Public Administration Review* (Nov/Dec), 621–631.

May, T. (1996). *Situating social theory*. Philadelphia: Open University Press.

Parsons, T. (1951). *The social system*. Glencoe, IL: Free Press.

Wilson. J. Q. (1968). *Varieties of police behavior: The management of law and order in eight communities*. Cambridge: Harvard University Press.

---

[2] Systems theory has fallen out of favor in the larger social science world. Since the early- to mid-1970s it came under increasing criticism for accepting things as they are (maintaining the "status quo") and failing to account for the power of conscious individual action within deterministic systems (agency). Interestingly, however, there has been a recent resurgence of interest due primarily to: 1) more elaborate system models that account for conflict, change, uncertainty, and chaos; and 2) the work of Jürgen Habermas (1996) who has successfully incorporated structural-functionalism within a critical school of thought (May 1996).

Origins of the Contemporary Criminal Justice Paradigm
The American Bar Foundation Survey, 1953–1969

Samuel Walker

The Forgotten Survey

"To a large extent, the administration of criminal justice can be characterized as a series of important decisions from the time a crime is committed until the offender is finally released from supervision."[1] Frank Remington's 1956 observation states an apparent truism. The dominant paradigm in American criminal justice today involves a "systems" perspective, in which the administration of justice consists of a series of discretionary decisions about individual criminal cases by officials working in a set of interrelated agencies. The systems approach dominates teaching and research (Cole 1989; Newman and Anderson 1989; Reid 1991) and has shaped most of the reform efforts over the past 25 years. These efforts include attempts to increase the system's overall effectiveness in crime control (President's Commission on Law Enforcement and Administration of Justice 1967a, 1967c), to improve coordination among the various components (Skoler 1977), and to control the exercise of discretion (Gottfredson and Gottfredson 1988; Walker 1988).

Source: *Justice Quarterly*, Vol. 9 No. 1, March 1992. © 1992 Academy of Criminal Justice Sciences. Reprinted with permission of the Academy of Criminal Justice Sciences.

Yet when Remington made this comment on September 24, 1956, it was a new and exciting insight, emerging from the first months of field research by the American Bar Foundation (ABF) Survey of the Administration of Criminal Justice (Remington 1956). Virtually forgotten today, the ABF Survey was largely responsible for creating the current criminal justice paradigm. It undertook the first systematic field observation of criminal justice agencies in operation and marked the emergence of a sociology of the administration of justice (Newman 1966b).

This article explores the history of the ABF Survey. It seeks not only to recover an important lost chapter in the history of American criminal justice, but also to describe the creation of the paradigm that dominates the field. The history of the survey illuminates the process of paradigm creation. The surviving records of the ABF Survey,[2] supplemented by interviews with the key personnel, allow us to reconstruct how a new paradigm or model emerged. This process involved the complex interplay of external political forces, certain key individuals, a major funding agency, the impact of data on scientific thinking, and the dissemination of new ideas.

Of Paradigms and Criminal Justice

Scientific research in every field, Kuhn argues, is dominated by a paradigm, which he characterizes as "some implicit body of intertwined theoretical and methodological belief that permits selection, evaluation, and criticism" (1970: 16–17). He emphasizes the point that a paradigm does not answer all questions. Rather, it defines those unanswered questions which are worthy of scientific inquiry (18). Nor does a paradigm have to be "true"; it simply must appear to be "better," or more persuasive, than its competitors. The history of the ABF Survey illuminates the process by which an earlier paradigm was replaced by the current one. The emergence of a new paradigm, Kuhn points out, represents a scientific revolution (1970: 111–35). This phenomenon involves the development of a new worldview and a new agenda for scientific research.

The history of the ABF Survey provides fresh perspective on the field of criminal justice by illuminating not only the questions that currently dominate research, but also those which once ruled the field and since have been rejected. To summarize briefly the argument of this article, the ABF Survey swept aside a paradigm that we label the Progressive Era Paradigm. It focused attention on questions of political influence over criminal justice agencies and, to a lesser extent, over material resources (e.g., number of employees). Questions of decision making and the interrelationship among criminal justice agencies simply did not enter this paradigm as subjects worthy of research and reform. By the same token, the paradigm established by the ABF Survey renders certain questions irrelevant. . . .

The Fate of the ABF Survey

A certain amount of drama surrounded the survey. Herman Goldstein, one of the principal figures, called it "the project that succeeded in spite of

itself" (H. Goldstein 1988). At a few critical points the project nearly col-
lapsed, beset by external criticism, internal doubt, and a seemingly indi-
gestible volume of field reports. Even then, it suffered the fate of being lost
to the memory of criminal justice studies.

The lack of awareness of the ABF Survey among people currently
engaged in teaching and research raises a question that needs to be
addressed at the outset. If, as this article argues, the ABF Survey played
such a pivotal role in creating the prevailing paradigm, why is it so little
known? Certain publications based on the survey's field research are
extremely well known. LaFave's (1965) *Arrest* is universally regarded as a
classic. Joseph Goldstein's (1960) article on police discretion is generally
recognized as having launched serious discussion of a subject that now
includes a vast, steadily growing literature. Donald Newman's (1966a)
book on plea bargaining is recognized as the pioneering work on that subject. Herman Goldstein (1977, 1979, 1990) has been one of the most fer-
tile thinkers in the field of American policing. Yet most of the academics
who regularly cite these classic works are not aware of their origins.[3]

Several factors account for the paradoxical near-disappearance of the
name of the ABF Survey despite the impact of many of its products. First,
none of the participants wrote his own account of the project as a whole,
to make a case for the significance of its contribution.[4] Second, publication
of the books (Dawson 1969; LaFave 1965; McIntyre 1967; Miller 1969;
Newman 1966a; Remington et al. 1969) that constituted the survey's principal findings was delayed for many years for a variety of organizational
and personal reasons. Third, by the time these books appeared, the field of
criminal justice had been completely transformed. A national crisis over
crime and justice had produced a series of national study commissions,
and a new academic field, "criminal justice," had emerged (Walker 1980:
221–53). The survey's principal findings were incorporated by the reports
of the President's Commission on Law Enforcement and Administration of
Justice (1967a), largely because members of the survey played key roles in
the Commission. Thus the Crime Commission has long been identified as
the principal source of wisdom about the criminal justice system. Virtually
every textbook in the field published after 1967 used the Crime Commission's schematic diagram of the system (President's Commission on Law
Enforcement and Administration of Justice 1967c: 58–59). Yet the two
essential ingredients of the flowchart—that there is a criminal justice "system" and that the system consists of a series of critical decision points—
derive from the ABF Survey.

Origins of the Survey

The ABF Survey originated in 1953 at the suggestion of Supreme
Court Justice Robert H. Jackson. In a speech to the American Bar Association he expressed alarm about the "breakdown, delay and ineffectiveness

of American law enforcement" and urged the bar to take the lead in addressing this crisis. It was difficult to propose meaningful reforms, he continued, because so little was known about the day-to-day administration of justice. To remedy this problem he urged the ABA to begin a program of empirical research. As chair of the new ABA Committee on the Administration of Justice, he offered an 18-item research agenda. The topics included "the significance and reason for failures to report crimes," the "discretion of police not to arrest," and the "discretion of prosecutors not to prosecute." Jackson reminded his audience that effective law enforcement was only one of the two goals of the criminal justice system; protection of individual rights was equally important. Accordingly he recommended research on those "points at which the existing process can be used, purposely or unconsciously, to harass or jeopardize innocent persons" (1953).

Jackson's proposal was part of a growing interest in research within the ABA that had already resulted in the creation of the American Bar Foundation in 1953. The survey became the ABF's first major project and for several years was its largest, accounting for 57 percent of the foundation's budget at one point (American Bar Foundation 1955–1956). Subsequent ABF leaders believed that the survey was instrumental in establishing the foundation as a center for high-quality legal research (Heinz 1988). . . .

The ABA established an advisory committee for the project,[5] retained a panel of expert consultants,[6] and hired University of Wisconsin Law Professor Frank Remington as director of research. Remington assembled a staff, and field research began on February 6, 1956 (Remington 1988). Remington fleshed out the details of the research plan with Lloyd Ohlin, the consultant on field research, who also played a critical advisory role. Remington was the key figure in shaping the survey, and deserves much of the credit for creating the new criminal justice paradigm.

The Research Design: Rejecting the Progressive Era Paradigm

The ABF Survey's findings were a product of its methodology, namely the systematic direct observation of criminal justice agencies in operation. Survey leaders began with a strong sense that the most important aspects of the administration of criminal justice were not known (Ohlin 1988; Remington 1988).[7] This assumption reflected discontent with the prevailing paradigm of criminal justice, known here as "the Progressive Era Paradigm."

The Progressive Era Paradigm

The Progressive Era Paradigm was based on the numerous crime commission studies of the previous 30 years. The Cleveland Survey of Criminal Justice (1922) established the model for the 44 state and local studies published by 1940 (American Bar Foundation 1955: 5–7; Walker 1980: 169–80). This extraordinary burst of interest in criminal justice reached its peak in 1931 with the publication of the federal Wickersham Commission reports (National Commission 1931a).

The Progressive Era paradigm of the administration of criminal justice was shaped by two characteristics: methodology and reformist ideology. Crime commission investigators relied entirely on available official data and undertook no direct observations of criminal justice agencies in operation. Thus, for example, they examined arrest data but never observed police officers at work (Cleveland 1922: 3–82).[8] They discussed the problem of police personnel standards, using official data on background characteristics and disciplinary actions, but conducted no independent research on police officers' backgrounds or attitudes.[9]

The treatment of prosecution demonstrates most clearly how methodology and conclusions about the administration of justice were shaped by an a priori set of ideological assumptions. All of the crime commissions expressed alarm over the "mortality" of cases, noting that few arrests resulted in prosecution, trial, conviction, or imprisonment (Cleveland Survey of Criminal Justice 1922: 89–96; Illinois Association for Criminal Justice 1929; Missouri Crime Survey 1926; Moley 1930). They discovered the phenomenon now known as plea bargaining, although they did not understand it in the same terms as it is understood today.[10] The crime commissions assumed that the "mortality" of cases was evidence of a "failure" to punish wrongdoers. The unexamined assumption appears to have been that persons arrested and charged with crimes were presumptively guilty and that any refusal to prosecute, convict, and punish was a "failure." The Cleveland Survey stated that matter succinctly: "a high percentage of cases which fail at various stages is an indication of something wrong in earlier stages" (1922: 89).

The explanation of "failure" was guided by the ideological assumptions of Progressive Era reform. The major problems in the administration of justice (as in other parts of government) were political interference, unqualified justice system personnel, inadequate resources, and a lack of data. The reform agenda called for public-spirited members of the community to mobilize, to break the power of the corrupt political machines, to appoint good police chiefs and other top officials, to establish high personnel standards, to provide agencies with adequate resources, and to arm them with "facts" (Cleveland Survey 1922: 649–52; Illinois Association 1929; Walker 1980: 125–60).

To the modern criminal justice expert, this reform strategy seems hopelessly naive. It shows no awareness of the phenomenon of discretion, or of its underlying dynamics. It includes no appreciation of the possibility that a "good" person—a police officer whose qualifications met the standards, or a prosecutor with the proper credentials—might do the "wrong" thing. That is, there is no sense that such officials might be affected by excessive workloads, conflicting public expectations, or self-serving bureaucratic interests—in short, all of the factors that have been identified by the sociology of criminal justice.

The Progressive Era paradigm of the justice system posited a series of semiautonomous agencies where officials administered the law in an impersonal, "ministerial" fashion: that is, they did what the law required. Any exercise of discretion was an unwarranted and probably illegal departure from an official's legal mandate.[11] This was the model for the administration of justice which the survey's planners believed was inadequate and which the survey eventually swept away.

The Original Research Plan

[Arthur Sherry of the University of California Law School submitted a 190-page plan for a survey that would test research methods in preparation for an 18-state national study.] Sherry's original *Plan* called for a study of the "organization, administration and operation" of (1) police, (2) prosecution and defense, (3) courts, and (4) probation, sentence, and parole. Curiously, it deferred research on the "extremely specialized" subject of correctional institutions until some "unspecified later date" (American Bar Foundation 1955: 18–19, 22).

The essence of the research plan was its flexibility and openendedness. The *Plan* conceded the lack of "the very knowledge which it is hoped the survey will produce." Sherry argued that the survey's planners could not bind themselves to "fixed and predetermined procedures and methods" (American Bar Foundation 1955: 19, 22, 24). In short, the survey was designed as an exploratory ethnographic study. Insofar as a literature existed—the crime commission studies—the planners rejected it as inadequate.[12]

The field research would not be completely unstructured, however. To guide the field observers, the *Plan* included a "Topical Outline" of questions for each justice agency (American Bar Foundation 1955: 107–93). These questions posed an inherent dilemma and a latent threat to the survey because the questions were developed with the help of the survey's consultants, and their views inevitably reflected the prevailing paradigm. Although the survey's planners sensed that this paradigm was inadequate, they were forced to use recognized experts for inescapable practical and political reasons. These experts would make the project credible in the eyes of the principal sponsors, the ABA and the Ford Foundation. In addition, their extensive contacts in the professional community would help to overcome the difficult problem of obtaining access to the agencies to be studied. This point proved to be especially important in regard to the police, where consultant O. W. Wilson's stature in the field helped to overcome the deeply ingrained hostility to observation by outsiders.

The tension between the traditional assumptions of the consultants and the potentially new insights was most evident in policing. At that time, O. W. Wilson was the leading authority on police professionalization (Bopp

1977). He was a protege of August Vollmer, the "father" of professionalization, and his textbook, *Police Administration* (Wilson 1950), was rapidly
establishing itself as the "bible" on the subject (Sherman 1974; Walker
1980). The *Plan*'s "Topical Outline" for research on the police was essentially a slightly revised version of the table of contents of Wilson's book
(American Bar Foundation 1955: 107–27; Wilson 1950). This outline represented a formalistic approach to police administration, emphasizing
organizational structure, agency jurisdiction, the number and distribution
of employees, the adequacy of equipment, formal record-keeping systems,
and so on. No attention was given to actual police work, particularly the
exercise of discretion.[13] Years later, Remington (1988) and Herman Goldstein (1988) still joked about Wilson's obsession with such trivia as the
number of batons on hand at a police department headquarters.

The topical outline deviated from Wilson's perspective in only one significant respect: the final section outlined research on "Areas of Activity
Where Civil Liberties May Be Jeopardized" (American Bar Foundation
1955: 124). This section probably was added by Sherry to reflect Justice
Jackson's concerns. It used rather strong language regarding the potential
"tyranny" from "unrestrained government" and noted the tension between
the "ideal of individual freedom and the necessity of group security"
(American Bar Foundation 1955: 125). Written in the mid-1950s, when
the Supreme Court's due process revolution was still in its most tentative
stage, these comments reflected a prescient insight into the problems of
law enforcement.

Creating a New Paradigm

The critical turning point in the survey—that is, the moment when a
new paradigm took shape—occurred when Remington and Ohlin began to
dispense with the original topical outline and to point the research in a
new direction. The process of redirecting the survey did not occur over-
night, of course. The surviving documents from the survey suggest that it
took place over a period of many months, as Remington, Ohlin, and others
tried to make sense of the observations that were flowing in from the field.
This outcome was by no means inevitable; in other circumstances, the survey might well have produced a report or reports consistent with the Progressive Era paradigm. Indeed, at some points it appeared that the entire
project might collapse under its own weight and produce nothing of value
(H. Goldstein 1988).

Several factors account for the eventual success of the survey and its
role in creating a new paradigm. The first was the sheer weight of the evidence in the form of field reports. Second, by training and experience,
Remington and Ohlin were especially well prepared to grasp the significance of these data. Third, most of the consultants remained relatively
uninvolved, giving Remington and Ohlin a free hand. Finally, the broader

objectives of the Ford Foundation included a patient, laissez-faire attitude that allowed the project to overcome a period of disarray and to formulate a coherent, albeit delayed, product.

The Impact of the Data

The field research had an immediate and profound effect on the researchers: they were overwhelmed by the pervasiveness of discretionary decision making. It was not only that the innumerable routine decisions had profound implications for individuals, but also that these decisions were guided by no formal standards and were largely ad hoc accommodations designed to "get the job done." In the process, the members of the team also observed a great deal of lawlessness, racism, and casual unprofessional conduct.[14] Yet, as Herman Goldstein (1988) recalled later, their attention was caught by the phenomenon of decision making, not by the lawlessness.

On his first night with Milwaukee detectives, John Warner spent the entire evening drinking in bars (Field Report 10027). Police operations in Detroit's vice-ridden Thirteenth Ward were beyond belief—and the source of innumerable "war stories" 30 years later. Goldstein (1988) observed the police routinely breaking into buildings to obtain evidence or make arrests, harassing homosexuals, and arresting prostitutes in massive "sweep" arrests by the "whore squad." A "clean-up squad" staged massive raids on gambling activities.[15] One suspect was interrogated with a fake polygraph machine made from a kitchen colander (Field Reports 11084). Officers patrolled the Thirteenth Ward in what they called the "heavy cruiser": an unmarked Buick with four officers (the "big four") and an arsenal of weapons in the trunk (shotguns, rifles, sledge hammers, axes) (Field Reports 11037–11042). The heavy cruiser's reputation was so notorious that in the Michigan state penitentiary, persons arrested by the "big four" in the "heavy cruiser" had special status (H. Goldstein 1988).

The police were not the only source of war stories. Defense attorneys often misrepresented their activities to their clients. They regularly promised arrested prostitutes that they would secure their release through a writ of habeas corpus. Because prosecutors usually dismissed charges in any event, the "habeas corpus" action was a sham (Field Report 11042). Prosecutors often detained suspects on the false pretext that there was a delay in checking their fingerprint records (Field Report 11051).

Officials not only flouted the law; often they were completely ignorant of it. Herman Goldstein recalled that a member of the team once asked a Wisconsin police chief about the exclusionary rule then in effect in the state. "Oh, we never exclude anyone from the courtroom," the chief assured him (H. Goldstein 1988). Further research confirmed that the exclusionary rule had no evident effect on police behavior in Wisconsin; Goldstein never recalled hearing anyone mention "probable cause." On April 2, after only eight weeks of field research, O. W. Wilson conceded, "It seems to me that areas of activity where civil liberties may be jeopardized

have not yet been adequately explored or reported" (memo to Frank Remington, April 2, 1956). This was a remarkable admission from the nation's
leading expert on police administration, whose authoritative textbook did
not mention the problem (Wilson 1950).

The willful mistreatment of black citizens was pervasive. Bruce Olson
observed that the Pontiac, Michigan police beat and severely injured a
black individual for photographing police officers while they were bowling
(the photographs were part of an Urban League campaign to identify officers accused of brutality) (Field Report 11242). Roy McLaren contrasted
police actions in the predominantly Italian Third Ward in Milwaukee with
those in the predominantly black Sixth Ward. The "Italian hoodlums
[were] very cagey and hard to deal with" because they were fairly knowledgeable about the law of search and seizure; they knew that a search
could not precede arrest. The unrestrained frisking of black suspects in the
Sixth Ward was due to the fact that "the people who are searched don't
know any better" (Field Reports 10288).

Building a New Paradigm

The observations in the field reports could have been accommodated
easily into the Progressive Era paradigm. For example, the Wickersham
Commission's report *Lawlessness in Law Enforcement* (National Commission 1931b) documented widespread police misconduct. The survey staff
could have embraced the long-standing recommendations for better leadership, higher personnel standards, the application of modern management techniques, and so on.

Instead Remington and Ohlin placed a new interpretation on the data.
The surviving records document the process by which they began to fashion a new paradigm. On March 15, after only five weeks of research, Ohlin
advised the field research team that "the outlines prepared by the consultants are not to be taken as a day-to-day guide for research." Instead, he
said, the researchers should give more attention "to an investigation of
processes than is indicated by the outlines" (memo to O. W. Wilson, March
15, 1956). On May 11 Remington advised the team that they would need
to return to Milwaukee for a "clean-up" trip; they had not given "sufficient
attention to . . . the 'main stream'" of policing, the "actual practices of
arrest, search and seizure, handling of persons in custody . . . and other
such matters" (memo to Herman Goldstein and Lloyd Ohlin, May 11,
1956). On June 7 Remington commented, "The criminal law seemed to be
used increasingly for purposes which are not at all punitive or even necessarily rehabilitative in the usual sense of that term." On the next day he
advised the field team that they had not adequately covered "either the
exercise of discretion by the police; the relation with the county attorney
or the relationship between a proceeding under city ordinance and a proceeding under state statute" (memo to all field research personnel, June 7,
1956; memo to Lloyd Ohlin, June 8, 1956).

These memos embodied the elements of what would become the modern criminal justice paradigm: the problems in administration arising from the substantive criminal law; the pervasiveness of discretion; the extent to which illegal behavior was not simply a matter of "bad people"; the fact that the various criminal justice agencies were interrelated in such a way that they constituted a criminal justice system. The overall design of this paradigm would not be clear for a few years, but the essentials were identified during the late winter and spring of 1956.

The "pilot project" phase, in short, served its intended purpose: the testing of field research methods allowed the staff to identify the key issues and to reshape the research to focus on them, and the project proceeded. Thus, when the field research began in Michigan in November 1956, the staff had a clearer sense of purpose. As a result, the Michigan research was regarded as far superior to the earlier research in Kansas and Wisconsin (Goldstein 1988; Remington 1988). The Michigan data constituted three of the seven volumes of the 1958 *Pilot Project Report* (American Bar Foundation 1958) and was the basis for the 1967 *Law Enforcement in the Metropolis*, a description of the criminal justice system in Detroit (McIntyre 1967).

The Roles of Remington and Ohlin

Frank Remington and Lloyd Ohlin played the critical roles in reshaping the survey's research objectives. Remington's role was most important in day-to-day operations. Members of the field research team recorded their observations each day into a dictograph and sent them to ABF offices for transcription. Remington studied these reports and sent back his comments, noting issues that should be investigated further, ambiguities that needed to be clarified, and areas that had been neglected. Remington also sent copies of the field reports and his memos to the consultants. His comments on the field reports, often based on conservations with Ohlin, represented the "moment of creation" of the new paradigm.

Several aspects of Remington's background prepared him for his role in the ABF Survey. First, he was heir to the tradition of legal realism, which emerged in the 1930s. Realism stressed the need for empirical research on the gap between the "law-on-the-books" and the "law-in-action" (K. Hall 1989: 269–71; Kalman 1986). Although realism never became the dominant mode of legal scholarship, it remained an important minority perspective. It had a foothold in the University of Wisconsin Law School (Friedman 1985: 594), where Remington received his degree and subsequently taught.

In addition, Remington's appreciation for the problematic nature of criminal justice administration was heightened by two early research projects. First, he observed a restitution program in the Detroit prosecutor's office. This exposed him to the processes of informal negotiation and the various considerations that enter case disposition (Remington 1988).

Second and even more important was his subsequent role as director of the Wisconsin criminal code revision between 1950 and 1956 (Remington 1954). This responsibility forced him to confront the extent to which certain aspects of the substantive criminal law created enormous administrative problems, particularly in gambling, alcohol, and sex offenses. The interaction between law and administration was complex: unrealistic laws created administrative problems, and administration easily undermined the intent of the laws themselves. This experience heightened Remington's awareness of the extent to which the "law-on-the-books" often reflected grand moralistic statements and of how often the day-to-day administration created innumerable problems that were solved through various "accommodations," "bargains," and "distortions" (Ohlin and Remington 1958).[16] None of the earlier crime commission reports exhibited any awareness of this phenomenon; they all assumed that the substantive criminal law was a given and that any failure to enforce it fully was a sign of some political or moral failing. Sensitivity to the problematic nature of the criminal laws laid the foundation for the new paradigm.

Lloyd Ohlin, the special consultant on research, also had experiences that sensitized him to the complexities of the administration of justice. From 1947 to 1950 he was the staff criminologist-actuary at the Illinois State Penitentiary at Joliet, one of a long series of distinguished criminologists to hold that position (Jacobs 1977: 35). Although the job itself involved statistical analysis, working at the penitentiary acquainted him with the realities of day-to-day prison life, particularly the gap between official policy and actual practice (Ohlin 1988). This insight was reinforced by his subsequent participation in the "Wisconsin Project." In 1953 the state of Wisconsin began a complete overhaul of its correctional system, and Ohlin researched the process of institutional change.[17] This project increased his appreciation of the difficulties of translating official policy into administrative practice (Ohlin 1960, 1988). . . .[The field research was completed in mid-1957. A seven-volume *Pilot Project Report* was published in 1958. Volume 1 covered the administration of the survey itself; volumes 2, 3, and 4 described the criminal justice system in Detroit; volume 5 covered Milwaukee County, Wisconsin; volume 6 covered Sedgwick County, Kansas; volume 7 contained a set of essays by the consultants on selected problems. The survey staff decided to abandon the national study and to analyze the existing field reports to identify the key issues. The "pilot project" became the "final" phase of the survey. Publication of the final volumes in 1969 brought the ABF Survey to a close, 13 years after the field research had begun (Hazard 1969).]

The New Paradigm: Dissemination and Impact

The delay in publishing the five books that represented the survey's major product masked the full impact of the project. Although that impact was profound, it was indirect in important respects. Much of it occurred through the participation of survey veterans in national-level projects that began in the mid-1960s. Two factors characterize the dissemination process. First, that process was influenced heavily by the rapidly changing political environment of criminal justice. Second, the survey had a far greater and more evident effect on some aspects of criminal justice than on others.

The Politics of Criminal Justice, 1956–1969

In the 1960s, a national crisis arose over issues of crime, law, and justice. The most obvious indicator of this crisis was the fact that in 1964 criminal justice (under the rubric of "law and order") became an issue in a presidential election campaign. It became even more important in 1968. . . . This crisis was the result of several factors: the civil rights movement, controversial Supreme Court rulings on the police, a series of urban riots (1964–1968), and a dramatic rise in the crime rate (Walker 1980: 221–24).

One result of the crisis was the creation of several national commissions. In 1963 the ABA launched its *Standards for Criminal Justice* project (American Bar Association 1980), and the American Law Institute (1974) began work on a *Model Code of Pre-Arraignment Procedure*. Even more important, in 1965 President Lyndon Johnson created a President's Commission on Law Enforcement and Administration of Justice, along with a new Office of Law Enforcement Assistance (OLEA), which provided the first significant federal financial assistance to criminal justice. The field of criminal justice was transformed by the reports of the President's Crime Commission in 1967, together with the creation of the Law Enforcement Assistance Administration (LEAA) and the advent of the first substantial federal financial assistance to criminal justice in 1968.

In two respects, the explosion of activity related to criminal justice had major consequences for the dissemination of the survey's findings. First, it created a vast constituency for detailed knowledge about the operations of the criminal justice system. The veterans of the survey who continued their interest in the subject (along with several who were brought in to write the books) were perfectly situated to advance the ideas that emerged from the survey. (The exact channels of participation and influence are described below.)

Second, certain aspects of the crisis created great interest in the specific findings of the survey. The civil rights movement raised issues of race discrimination throughout the criminal justice system, especially by the police. This situation focused attention on discretionary decision making and on whether those decisions represented patterns of discrimination. The survey's material could not be used to answer that question precisely because it involved qualitative rather than quantitative research.[18] Nonetheless, it provided persuasive evidence that controls over routine decision making were lacking and that there was a great deal of misconduct.

At the same time, the most controversial decisions of the Supreme Court involving the police focused attention on the appropriate method of controlling police behavior. The controversy over the exclusionary rule was (and remains) fundamentally a question of who should control the police, and by what method. Indeed, the survey was immersed in that controversy several years before the Supreme Court's 1961 decision in *Mapp*. The issue was raised by the California Supreme Court's decision in *People v. Cahan*, which imposed the rule in that state. By chance, the survey was dominated by people with great interest in the subject. The entire project was top-heavy with Californians, who were informed of developments in their state. Two of the consultants, O. W. Wilson and Fred E. Inbau, were among the leading opponents of judicial supervision of police activity.

The survey's material did not resolve that issue either, but it influenced the ensuing debate. On the one hand, the field reports suggested that the rule had no effect in Wisconsin; on the other, it provided overwhelming evidence of the pervasiveness of discretion, the lawlessness of that decision making, and the need for controls of some sort.

The national crisis over the police—a combined product of the civil rights movement, the Supreme Court, and rising crime rates—helps to explain the disparate impact of the survey's findings. As we shall discuss in detail below, the survey's impact on the police was far more direct and more sustained than on any other aspect of criminal justice.

Patterns of Impact

The principal findings that constituted the new paradigm included the following interrelated propositions: (1) the criminal process is extremely complex as a result of the nature of the substantial criminal law; (2) as a consequence, the police role is extremely complex; (3) the administration of justice is pervaded by discretion; (4) decision making is (or was at the time) unstructured by legal norms or formal controls; and (5) the various justice agencies make up a criminal justice "system" in which the actions of one agency affect and are affected by other agencies.

The complexity of the criminal process.   In many respects, recognition of the complexity of the criminal process was the cornerstone of the survey's findings because so many of the other propositions flow from it. The Progressive Era paradigm had assumed that the criminal process was devoted to law enforcement in the narrowest sense, concentrating on the arrest, prosecution, and punishment of criminal offenders. The various crime commission reports assumed that any deviation from full enforcement was evidence of some political, institutional, or moral failure. The survey's field research, however, revealed a very different picture, in which the criminal process was used routinely to handle a broad range of social problems including alcohol abuse, mental illness, family difficulties, petty financial disputes, and other miscellaneous matters. Moreover, the substantive criminal law was complex because it often reflected conflicting expectations about morality and standards of public order.

Recognition of the complexity of the criminal process spurred new thinking and research on a number of related points. One such point involved recognition of the need to reduce the scope of the criminal law. Kadish (1967), who studied the *Pilot Project Report* in 1958, wrote an influential article on "the crisis of overcriminalization." Packer's (1968) extremely important book, *The Limits of the Criminal Sanction*, reflected the influence of both the survey and the Model Penal Code (American Law Institute 1962). The flurry of interest on diversion of chronic alcoholics (Aaronson et al. 1984; Nimmer 1971, 1974) was stimulated largely by the survey's findings. The first scholarly article on police handling of domestic disturbances (Parnas 1967) was suggested by Remington and based in part on survey field reports.

The complexity of the police role.   Recognition of the complexity of the criminal process generally had important ramifications for the police role. LaFave's (1965) classic study, based on the survey's field reports, documented the effect on arrest decisions. Perhaps even more important for a basic understanding of the police, the survey's findings set in motion a broad rethinking of the police role. Ultimately, the idea that the police are primarily crime fighters was replaced by the new conventional wisdom that they are primarily peacekeepers.

Much of the credit for the triumph of this idea belongs to Herman Goldstein, a member of the original survey field research team. He promulgated this idea through two particularly influential channels. First, he coauthored with Remington the discussion of the police role in the President's Crime Commission's (1967b) *Task Force Report: The Police*. He then served as reporter for the ABA's (1980) *Standards Relating to the Urban Police Function* and played a major role in the ABA's detailed and authoritative analysis of the police role. Goldstein pursued the implications of the survey's findings on this subject for three decades. His intellectual quest ultimately led him to propose the concept of "problem-oriented policing" (H. Goldstein 1979, 1990). Together with the closely related concept "community policing" (Greene and Mastrofski 1988), problem-oriented policing emerged as the most important new idea in policing in the 1980s (U.S. Department of Justice 1988–1989).

The pervasiveness of discretion and the absence of legal or formal controls.   Recognition of the pervasive exercise of discretion is perhaps the single most important contribution of the survey. Certainly it is the crucial element that was missing from the earlier crime commission reports. From the first weeks of the field research, the entire team noticed the pervasiveness of discretion. At that time, they were struck less by the illegality of so much police behavior than by the sheer fact that so much decision making had so little relationship to the law on the books. Although the decisions by prosecutors and correctional officials were less horrific than many police actions, they were equally unguided by legal norms or formal controls.

The impact of the survey on the question of police discretion is the easiest to trace. The first serious discussion of the subject, Joseph Goldstein's (1960) article in the *Yale Law Journal*, was a direct product of the 1958 summer seminar. Remington (1960) examined the law of "on-the-street" police activity from a fresh perspective. LaFave (1965) produced the classic discussion of arrest discretion. Meanwhile Herman Goldstein (1963, 1967) made several important contributions to the rapidly developing literature on the subject. He played a major role in helping to forge the consensus that "abolishing" police discretion was both unwise and unworkable, and that the best approach was to control it through administrative rule making (Davis 1975; Walker 1993).

With respect to plea bargaining, Donald Newman's (1956, 1966a) work launched serious discussion of the subject.[19] In corrections, Sanford Kadish (1960–1961) was one of the first to challenge the claim of correctional officials that their actions were rehabilitative rather than judicial or penal and therefore should be immune from formal legal controls.

In an indirect fashion, the survey helped to undermine the philosophy of rehabilitation. The first significant challenge to the rehabilitative ideal, on the grounds that it involved an enormous expansion of discretion and created numerous due process problems, was made by Francis Allen in 1959 (Allen 1964). Although Allen was not formally a member of the ABF Survey, he took a great interest in it and was informed by its findings (Allen 1988).

The survey's findings on discretion provided a new perspective on official lawlessness, especially on the part of the police. The Wickersham Commission report *Lawlessness in Law Enforcement* (National Commission 1931b) had documented police misconduct, but the problem was defined in the terms of the Progressive Era paradigm. In brief, it called for better people: both more highly qualified police executives and higher standards for rank-and-file officers. The survey recast the problem in terms of two issues. First, misconduct was only one form of the pervasive exercise of discretion. Second, much misconduct was a result of police response to public demands for the control of crime and disorder. The traditionally offered solution, hiring better cops, would address neither issue.

Criminal justice as a "system."   It may be too much to claim that Frank Remington was the very first person to articulate the "systematic" nature of the administration of justice, but his 1956 memos certainly make him a strong candidate.[20] More important is the fact that the idea of a system was embodied in the 1958 *Pilot Project Report* and eventually in the books that emerged from the survey.

The idea of a criminal justice system was popularized by the President's Crime Commission. The schematic diagram of the system which has been so influential in criminal justice teaching was developed in fact by the Commission's Task Force on Science and Technology, directed by Alfred Blumstein. The crucial point is not the narrow question of who drew the original flowchart, but who suggested the systems approach in the first place. Blumstein, who was trained in operations research, had a "systems" orientation before he ever thought about criminal justice. In 1965 he was employed by the Institute for Defense Analysis (IDA), which did work for the Defense Department. In fact, because it was politically sensitive to hire defense contractors to work on domestic criminal justice issues, the decision to allow the IDA to work for the President's Crime Commission was made by the attorney general and the secretary of defense (Blumstein 1988).

Blumstein and the IDA were hired because a "systems" perspective already had been adopted by the Crime Commission. It is impossible to determine with any precision how and when this decision was made. Nonetheless, Ohlin was one of the Commission's four associate directors and undoubtedly brought the survey's perspective to bear on this new project. At the same time, Remington, Herman Goldstein, and others who were well acquainted with the survey's findings were active in the Commission's work.

Summary.   The survey's findings, in short, had an enormous impact on thinking about discretion in general, police discretion in particular, and plea bargaining. Probably they were also responsible for the idea of a criminal justice system. The survey had some effect on thinking about correctional decision making and about sentencing discretion, although it is difficult to trace the patterns of influence directly.

The Dominance of the New Paradigm

Paradigms, Kuhn (1970) argues, organize scientific inquiry by defining the problems worth investigating. Viewing the field of criminal justice in these terms offers a new perspective on the debates and controversies that have dominated research and public policy making over the past 25 years. This perspective dramatizes the extent to which the antagonists share common ground. The principal division has been defined according to Packer's (1968) classic distinction between "crime control" and "due process." In a somewhat cruder formulation, this division appears as a conflict between "conservative" and "liberal" policy positions, or, cruder still, between the advocates of "punishment" and "rehabilitation" (Walker 1989).

When viewed from the perspective of a paradigm, however, it becomes apparent that scholars and policy advocates on both sides are working within the framework of the prevailing criminal justice paradigm. The advocates of both crime control and due process focus primarily on decision making (Walker 1993). The former approach decision making out of concern for excessive leniency; the latter approach it out of concern for fairness and equality. The policy debates between the advocates of crime control and of due process turn on the question of how best to control decision making in order to achieve their respective goals. Much research is directed toward answering the questions raised by these debates. A few selected examples illustrate the point.

With respect to the police, the advocates of "crime control" charge that the exclusionary rule inhibits effective crime fighting by the police. The advocates of "due process," meanwhile, allege systematic race discrimination in arrest, stop and frisk, and other on-the-street decisions. Both issues focus on police decision making and on the related question of the proper controls over police discretion. The prevailing paradigm, with its emphasis on decision making, defines the terms of these debates.

By the same token, research and policy making over the past 30 years with respect to bail have focused almost exclusively on decision making. Two bail reform movements have taken place in this period. The first, which peaked in the 1960s, emphasized the damaging effect of the money bail system on the poor. Bail reform, of which the 1966 federal Bail Reform Act was the highwater point, sought to restructure bail decision making in order to achieve justice for the poor. By 1970, however, the political mood of the country had changed dramatically, and a new emphasis on crime control through preventive detention dominated. The preventive detention movement also sought to control bail decision making, but for very different purposes. The focus on decision making as the heart of the problem in the administration of justice remained, even as the political mood changed and the objectives of reform shifted (Goldkamp 1979; Goldkamp and Gottfredson 1985; Thomas 1976).

Sentencing reform also has been dominated by a focus on decision making. As with police discretion, "due process" advocates have focused largely on race discrimination. (On this issue, the death penalty has been the most heavily contested ground in both litigation and research.) Meanwhile "crime control" advocates have sought to fight crime through various mandatory imprisonment laws or sentencing guideline procedures. Every sentencing reform proposal offered or implemented over the past 30 years has attempted to solve "the problem" by controlling judicial decision making. In a broader sense, the enormous interest in prediction and classification, which has consumed so much energy among scholars over the past 15 years, reflects the effort to provide better tools for decision making (Gottfredson and Tonry 1987).

The Survey and Criminal Justice Education

The survey also had an important effect on criminal justice education. Between the late 1960s and the early 1970s, criminal justice as a distinct field of study appeared. The number of college- and university-based academic programs increased enormously, and in many instances the term "criminal justice" replaced "law enforcement" or "police studies." The dominant model of criminal justice education became the "systems" approach, with emphasis on the *administration* of justice (as opposed to theoretical criminology), and with equal attention to the various components of police, courts, and corrections. This approach is reflected in the organization of the leading textbooks in the field today (Cole 1989; Newman and Anderson 1989; Reid 1991).

More than any other program, the School of Criminal Justice at the State University of New York at Albany (SUNY-Albany, as it is generally called) established the dominant model. Frank Remington and Lloyd Ohlin were deeply involved in the development of the SUNY-Albany program. Both were retained as consultants, and advised establishing a curriculum organized around a "systems" approach (Remington 1988). The first dean of the School of Criminal Justice, Richard A. Myren, who worked with Remington, was influenced by his views and by the ABF Survey, and was recommended for the deanship by Remington (Remington 1988).

Remington influenced the teaching of criminal justice in yet another way. He was the moving force behind, and first author of, an innovative casebook on the administration of criminal justice based on the ABF Survey (Remington et al. 1969). *Criminal Justice Administration: Cases and Materials* never dominated teaching about criminal justice in law schools (although it remained an important minority perspective), but it provided the model for the social science-oriented textbooks that currently dominate the field. In this respect alone, the ABF Survey exerts a continuing influence over criminal justice studies. . . .

. . . A paradigm, Kuhn (1970) points out, reflects a general worldview. [For example,] the Marxist worldview is different from that held by non-Marxists. Thus the debates between Marxist and non-Marxist criminologists have been relatively unfruitful simply because they are dialogues representing two different worldviews. They do not have a common understanding of what issues are important and deserving of scientific inquiry. The problems associated with decision making are relatively unimportant to someone who regards the entire criminal justice machinery as unjust and invalid. In Kuhnian terms, Marxist criminology is not "wrong"; at this particular moment it is simply not persuasive to the majority of the scientists in the field.

Finally, Kuhn's perspective cautions adherents of the prevailing paradigm to recognize that there is nothing permanent or timeless about their viewpoint. This paradigm, which organizes their thinking, research, and policy proposals, was the product of a scientific revolution that replaced an earlier paradigm. Science, however, like time, marches on. We cannot predict what kind of scientific revolution lies in the future and will overthrow the assumptions shared by virtually everyone reading this article.

Notes

[1] Frank Remington, memo to field staff, September 24, 1956. Unless noted otherwise, all documents cited herein are located in the ABF Survey files at the Criminal Justice Library at the University of Wisconsin Law School.

[2] The original field reports, along with many internal memoranda and documents, are housed in the Criminal Justice Library at the University of Wisconsin Law School. Additional documents are housed in the library of the American Bar Foundation, Chicago, and in the archives of the Ford Foundation, New York.

[3] This observation is based in part on the author's informal survey of professors of criminal law regarding LaFave's (1965) *Arrest*. Virtually everyone recognized the book immediately as a classic in the field; yet no one was aware of the ABF Survey, which provided the raw material.

[4] Newman (1966b) published an excellent short overview of the survey's contributions to the sociology of criminal justice, but he did not develop his argument at length, and the article itself remained somewhat obscure.

[5] Justice Robert H. Jackson died in 1954. He was replaced by William J. Donovan (1954–1957) and subsequently by many other distinguished persons.

[6] The consultants were Sanford Bates, consultant on sentencing, probation, and parole; Edmond F. DeVine, special consultant; Fred E. Inbau, consultant on prosecution and defense; Benjamin A. Matthews, consultant on courts; Lloyd E. Ohlin, consultant on field research; and O. W. Wilson, consultant on police.

[7] Remington later commented that it was possible to review the entire literature on on-the-street police behavior in a day.

[8] The first direct observation of police officers on patrol appears to have been made by Warner (1940), who used these observations to propose the Uniform Arrest Act (Warner 1942).

[9] The first research on police officers from the perspective of occupational sociology was Westley's (1970) 1950 dissertation on the Gary, Indiana police—a study that was not published in full until 1970.

[10] McDonald (1985: 2–3) argues that the early crime commission studies discovered plea bargaining. These studies, however, only noted the phenomenon of case attrition (which they called "mortality") and did not understand the sociological dynamics of plea "bargaining" or plea "negotiations," as it is currently understood. Credit for that discovery belongs to Newman (1956).

[11] This view is clearest in the discussions of police discretion through the early 1950s. See in particular Jerome Hall's (1953) influential article on the subject.

[12] The research contemplated by the survey was not completely without precedent. Samuel Warner (1940) had observed police at work in 1940. Donald Newman's (1956) initial research on plea bargaining preceded the survey. As the survey was being planned, Professor Caleb Foote (1954, 1957) at the University of Pennsylvania Law School was engaged in a series of path-breaking observations of both bail setting and the police in Philadelphia. The important point about these studies, however, is that they were so few and so isolated. The significance of the survey was its comprehensive approach to the entire criminal justice system, which produced conclusions about general phenomena.

[13] Wilson was committed so deeply to his original approach that even the fourth edition of Police Administration (Wilson and McLaren 1977) did not discuss discretion or any of the other issues that derived from the survey.

[14] The observation of misconduct raised serious ethical questions, the full dimensions of which were not apparent until much later. Access to the agencies was obtained only by promising confidentiality and giving repeated assurances that the survey was a "fact-finding" and not a "fault-finding" project. Nonetheless, one wonders why the members of the field team did not feel any pangs of conscience about not reporting some of the grosser abuses of particular citizens. For his part, Herman Goldstein (1988) now feels that he was

"pretty naive" at the time and believes that he may not have seen the worst police behavior at all. Also, the social and political climate was very different in the mid-1950s: the impulse to expose official misconduct in the pursuit of social justice was not as strong as it became in the 1960s.

[15] ABF Survey Field Reports 11037–11042 describe the "whore squad" and the "heavy cruise," 11051 the harassment of "fags" and the collusion with federal officials on illegal searches, 11056 various illegal practices, 11066 and 11115 an illegal entry, and so on. A general summary is given in 11105.

[16] An important aspect of the history of the ABF Survey, which cannot be treated fully here because of space limitations, is the interaction between the staff members, particularly Remington and Ohlin, and the development of the Model Penal Code. There is evidence that Remington and Ohlin brought to the deliberations on the Model Penal Code a fresh awareness of the relationship between the substantive criminal code and its administration (American Law Institute 1956: 208–58; Ohlin and Remington 1958).

[17] An incredible tragedy sabotaged publication of Ohlin's Wisconsin Project Research: a cleaning person accidentally burned virtually his entire manuscript. Ohlin, who already was committed to another job in New York City, never found the time to rewrite the manuscript (Ohlin 1988). A portion survives in Ohlin (1960).

[18] One of the clearest indicators of the survey's impact on criminal justice research is found in criminologist Daniel Glaser's reaction to the *Pilot Project Report*. He found the *Report* "fascinating" and stressed the "need for more effort to obtain quantitative data" on the problems of (for example) police misconduct. In short, the survey had identified the overriding issue; the task now was to specify the frequency of various outcomes (Glaser, letter to John C. Leary, ABF, May 13, 1959).

[19] Newman's doctoral dissertation on plea bargaining preceded the ABF Survey. He did not participate in the survey's field research, but was brought in to write the volume titled *Conviction*. It is an interesting commentary on the status of criminal justice studies in the field of criminology that Newman completed his dissertation at the University of Wisconsin in the face of repeated questions about whether his subject was "really sociology" (Newman 1988).

[20] Credit for the first recognition of the "systemic" nature of the administration of justice probably belongs to Alfred Bettman, author of the Wickersham Commission *Report on Prosecution*. Bettman noted the "organic unity of administration" and cited 10 critical decision points (National Commission 1931c: 164, 172–73). The development of criminal justice studies would have been very different if Bettman's insights had not been disregarded.

References

Aaronson, David E., C. Thomas Dienes, and Michael C. Musheno (1984) *Public Policy and Police Discretion: Processes of Decriminalization.* New York: Clark Boardman.

Allen, Francis (1964). "Legal Values and the Rehabilitative Ideal." In Francis Allen (ed.), *The Borderland of Criminal Justice*, pp. 25–41. Chicago: University of Chicago Press.

——— (1988) Interview with author.

American Bar Association (1980) *Standards Relating to the Urban Police Function.* Vol. 1: *Standards for Criminal Justice.* 2nd ed. Boston: Little, Brown.

American Bar Foundation (1955) *A Plan for a Survey.* Chicago: American Bar Foundation.

——— (1955–1956) *Annual Report.* Chicago: American Bar Foundation.

——— (1958) *Pilot Project Report.* Chicago: American Bar Foundation.

——— (1959) *History and Status Report* (July). Chicago: American Bar Foundation.

—— (1961–1962) *Annual Report*. Chicago: American Bar Foundation.

American Law Institute (1956) *Proceedings*. Philadelphia: American Law Institute.

—— (1962) *Model Penal Code*. Philadelphia: American Law Institute.

—— (1974) *Model Code of Pre-Arraignment Procedure*. Philadelphia: American Law Institute.

Blumstein, Alfred (1988) Interview with author.

Bopp, William J. (1977) *O. W.: O. W. Wilson and the Search for a Police Profession*. Port Washington, NY: Kennikat.

Cleveland Survey of Criminal Justice (1922) *Criminal Justice in Cleveland*. Cleveland: The Cleveland Foundation.

Cole, George (1989) *The American System of Criminal Justice*. 5th ed. Pacific Grove, CA: Brooks/Cole.

Davis, Kenneth C. (1975) *Police Discretion*. St. Paul: West.

Dawson, Robert O. (1969) *Sentencing: The Decision as to Type, Length and Conditions of Sentence*. Boston: Little, Brown.

Foote, Caleb (1954) "Compelling Appearance in Court: Administration of Bail in Philadelphia." *University of Pennsylvania Law Review* 102 (No. 3): 1031–1079.

—— (1957) "Safeguards in the Law of Arrest." *Northwestern University Law Review* 52 (March–April): 16–45.

Friedman, Lawrence M. (1985) *A History of American Law*. 2nd ed. New York: Simon and Schuster.

Goldkamp, John S. (1979) *Two Classes of Accused*. Cambridge, MA: Ballinger.

Goldkamp, John S. and Michael R. Gottfredson (1985) *Policy Guidelines for Bail: An Experiment in Court Reform*. Philadelphia: Temple University Press.

Goldstein, Herman (1963) "Police Discretion: The Ideal versus the Real." *Public Administration Review* 23 (September): 148–56.

—— (1967) "Administrative Problems in Controlling the Exercise of Police Authority." *Journal of Criminal Law, Criminology, and Police Science* 58 (2): 160–72.

—— (1977) *Policing a Free Society*. Cambridge, MA: Ballinger.

—— (1979) "Improving Policing: A Problem-Oriented Approach." *Crime and Delinquency* 25 (April): 236–58.

—— (1988) Interview with author.

—— (1990) *Problem-Oriented Policing*. New York: McGraw-Hill.

Goldstein, Joseph (1960) "Police Discretion Not to Invoke the Criminal Process: Low-Visibility Decisions in the Administration of Justice." *Yale Law Journal* 69 (No. 4): 543–588.

Gottfredson, Don M. and Michael Tonry (1987) *Prediction and Classification: Criminal Justice Decision Making*. Chicago: University of Chicago Press.

Gottfredson, Michael R. and Don M. Gottfredson (1988) *Decision-Making in Criminal Justice: Toward the Rational Exercise of Discretion*. 2nd ed. New York: Plenum.

Greene, Jack R. and Stephen Mastrofski (1988) *Community Policing. Rhetoric or Reality?* New York: Praeger.

Hall, Jerome (1953) "Police and Law in a Democratic Society." *Indiana Law Journal* 28 (Winter): 133–77.

Hall, Kermit L. (1989) *The Magic Mirror: Law in American Society*. New York: Oxford University Press.

Hazard, Geoffrey C. (1969) "Epilogue to the Criminal Justice Survey." *ABA Journal* 55 (November): 1048–49.

Heinz, John R. (1988) Interview with author.

Illinois Association for Criminal Justice (1929) *Illinois Crime Survey.* Reprint ed. Montclair, NJ: Patterson Smith.

Jackson, Robert F. (1953) "Criminal Justice: The Vital Problem of the Future." *ABA Journal* 39 (August): 743–46.

Jacobs, James B. (1977) *Stateville: The Penitentiary in Mass Society.* Chicago: University of Chicago Press.

Kadish, Sanford H. (1960–1961) "The Advocate and the Expert-Counsel in the Peno-Correctional Process." *Minnesota Law Review* 45: 803–41.

——— (1967) "The Crisis of Overcriminalization." *Annals of the American Academy of Political and Social Science* 374 (November): 157–70.

——— (1988) Interview with author.

Kalman, Laura (1986) *Legal Realism at Yale.* New Haven: Yale University Press.

Kuhn, Thomas S. (1970) *The Structure of Scientific Revolutions.* 2nd ed. Chicago: University of Chicago Press.

LaFave, Wayne R. (1965) *Arrest: The Decision to Take the Suspect into Custody.* Boston: Little, Brown.

McDonald, William F. (1985) *Plea Bargaining: Critical Issues and Common Practices.* Washington, DC: U.S. Government Printing Office.

McIntyre, Donald M., Jr. (1967) *Law Enforcement in the Metropolis.* Chicago: American Bar Foundation.

Miller, Frank (1969) *Prosecution: The Decision to Charge a Suspect With a Crime.* Boston: Little, Brown.

Missouri Crime Survey (1926) *The Missouri Crime Survey.* New York: Macmillan.

Moley, Raymond (1930) *Our Criminal Courts.* New York: Minton, Balch.

National Commission on Law Observance and Enforcement (1931a) *Reports.* Washington, DC: U.S. Government Printing Office.

——— (1931b) *Report on Lawlessness in Law Enforcement.* Washington, DC: U.S. Government Printing Office.

Newman, Donald J. (1956) "Pleading Guilty for Considerations: A Study of Bargain Justice." *Journal of Criminal Law, Criminology, and Police Science* 46 (March-April): 780–90.

——— (1966a) *Conviction: The Determination of Guilt or Innocence without Dial.* Boston: Little, Brown.

——— (1966b) "Sociologists and the Administration of Criminal Justice." In Arthur B. Shostak (ed.), *Sociologists at Work*, pp. 177–87. Homewood, IL: Dorsey.

——— (1988) Interview with author.

Newman, Donald J. and Patrick R. Anderson (1989) *Introduction to Criminal Justice.* 4th ed. New York: Random House

Nimmer, Raymond T. (1971) *Two Million Unnecessary Arrests.* Chicago: American Bar Foundation.

——— (1974) *Diversion.* Chicago: American Bar Foundation.

Ohlin, Lloyd (1960) "Conflicting Interests in Correctional Objectives." In Richard E. Cloward, (eds.), *Theoretical Studies in Social Organization of the Prison*, pp. 111–129. New York: Social Science Research Council.

——— (1988) Interview with author.

Ohlin, Lloyd and Frank Remington (1958) "Sentencing Structure: Its Effect upon Systems for the Administration of Criminal Justice." *Law and Contemporary Problems* 23 (Summer): 495–597.

Packer, Herbert (1968) *The Limits of the Criminal Sanction.* Stanford: Stanford University Press.

Parnas, Raymond I. (1967) "The Police Response to Domestic Disturbances." *Wisconsin Law Review* 42 (Fall): 914–69.

President's Commission on Law Enforcement and Administration of Justice (1967a) *The Challenge of Crime in a Free Society.* Washington, DC: U.S. Government Printing Office.

——— (1967b) *Task Force Report: The Police Crime.* Washington, DC: U.S. Government Printing Office.

——— (1976c) *Task Force Report. Science and Technology.* Washington, DC: U.S. Government Printing Office.

Reid, Sue Titus (1991) *Crime and Criminology.* 6th ed. New York: Holt, Rinehart and Winston.

Remington, Frank (1954) "Criminal Law Revision-Codification vs. Piecemeal Amendment." *Nebraska Law Review* 33 (March): 396–407.

——— (1956) "Survey of the Administration of Justice." *National Probation and Parole Association Journal* 2 (July): 260–65.

——— (1960) "The Law Relating to 'On the Street' Detention, Questioning and Frisking of Suspected Persons and Police Arrest Privileges in General." *Journal of Criminal Law, Criminology, and Police Science* 51 (November-December): 386–94.

——— (1988) Interview with author.

Remington, Frank, Donald J. Newman, Edward L. Kimball, Marygold Merci, Herman Goldstein (1969) *Criminal Justice Administration: Materials and Cases.* Indianapolis: Bobbs-Merrill.

Sherman, Lawrence W. (1974) "The Sociology and the Social Reform of the Police, 1950–1973." *Journal of Police Science and Administration* 11: 255–62.

Skoler, Daniel (1977) *Organizing the Non-System.* Lexington, MA: Lexington Books.

Thomas, Wayne (1976) *Bail Reform in America.* Berkeley: University of California Press.

U.S. Department of Justice (1988–1989) *Perspectives on Policing.* Washington, DC: U.S. Government Printing Office.

Walker, Samuel (1980) *Popular Justice: A History of American Criminal Justice.* New York: Oxford University Press.

——— (1988) *The Rule Revolution.* Madison, WI: Institute For Legal Studies.

——— (1989) *Sense and Nonsense about Crime.* 2nd ed. Pacific Grove, CA: Brooks/Cole.

——— (1993). *Taming the System: The Control of Discretion in Criminal Justice 1950–1990.* New York: Oxford University Press.

Warner, Sam Bass (1940) "Investigating the Law of Arrest." *ABA Journal* 26: 151–55.

——— (1942). "The Uniform Arrest Act." *University of Virginia Law Review* 28 (No. 3): 315–347.

Westley, William A. (1970) *Violence and the Police.* Cambridge: MIT.

Wilson, O. W. (1950) *Police Administration.* New York: McGraw-Hill.

Wilson O. W. and Roy C. McLaren (1977) *Police Administration.*

Cases Cited

Mapp v. Ohio 367 U.S. 643 (1961).
People v. Cahan 282 P.2d 905 (1955).

Science and Technology and the Criminal Justice System

The Institute for Defense Analysis

Role of Science and Technology in Criminal Justice

The natural sciences and technology have long helped the police to solve specific crimes. Scientists and engineers have had very little impact, however, on the overall operations of the criminal justice system and its principal components: police, courts, and corrections. More than 200,000 scientists and engineers have applied themselves to solving military problems and hundreds of thousands more to innovation in other areas of modern life, but only a handful are working to control the crimes that injure or frighten millions of Americans each year. Yet, the two communities have much to offer each other: science and technology is a valuable source of knowledge and techniques for combating crime; the criminal justice system represents a vast area of challenging problems.

Equipment

In the traditional view, science and technology primarily means new equipment. And modern technology can, indeed, provide a vast array of devices beyond those now in general use to improve the operations of criminal justice agencies, particularly in helping the police deter crime and apprehend criminals. Some of the more important possibilities are:

This was the first chapter (pp. 1–6) in a task force report to The President's Commission on Law Enforcement and Administration of Justice, 1967. Washington, D.C.

- Electronic computers for processing the enormous quantities of needed data.
- Police radio networks connecting officers and neighboring departments.
- Inexpensive, light two-way portable radios for every patrolman.
- Computers for processing fingerprints.
- Instruments for identifying criminals by their voice, photographs, hair, blood, body chemistry, etc.
- Devices for automatic and continual reporting of all police car locations.
- Helicopters for airborne police patrol.
- Inexpensive, reliable burglar and robbery alarms.
- Nonlethal weapons to subdue dangerous criminals without inflicting permanent harm.
- Perimeter surveillance devices for prisons.
- Automatic transcription devices for courtroom testimony.

Many of these devices are now in existence, some as prototypes and some available commercially. Others still require basic development but are at least technically feasible and worthy of further exploration.

But for many reasons, even available devices have only slowly been incorporated into criminal justice operations. Procurement funds have been scarce, industry has only limited incentive to conduct basic development for an uncertain and fragmented market, and criminal justice agencies have very few technically trained people on their staffs. Much closer communication is needed between criminal justice officials and engineers to identify the problems for the engineers and to enumerate the possibilities for the officials' consideration.

Also, conventional methods of governmental budgeting often tend to restrict the application of new technology. Budgets are traditionally prepared with item categories such as "personnel" and "equipment," rather than with functional or program categories, such as "maintaining general police patrol." Under such circumstances, a reasonable equipment expenditure may loom as a large increase in the equipment budget. For instance, if each car in a 50-vehicle fleet is provided with a $200 piece of equipment, the additional $10,000 might dominate the increase in an item budget. When it is considered, however, that it costs about $100,000 per year to operate a two-man patrol car continuously, an investment of even a few thousand dollars per car, amortized over at least 3 years, is a small cost if it significantly improves patrol operations. Compared to a $5 million budget for "patrol," a $10,000 increment is very small.

The Federal Government, as well as some state and local governments, is moving from item budgeting to program budgeting to obtain a clearer picture of how its resources are being allocated. Such an approach seems particularly appropriate for criminal justice agencies, especially as their operations become more interrelated in a criminal justice system.

In the realm of technology it is far easier to imagine interesting possibilities than to choose the ones in which to invest necessarily limited equipment funds. Technology can fill most reasonable requests and can thereby provide considerable help to law enforcement. But society must decide what devices it wants relative to the price it is willing to pay in dollars, invasion of privacy, and other intangible social costs. It is technically feasible, for example, to cut auto theft drastically by putting a radio transmitter in every car in America and tracking them all continuously. But this might cost a billion dollars and could create an intolerable climate of surveillance. Science can provide the capability, but the public as a whole must participate in the value discussion of whether or not the capability is worth the costs.

This is often a difficult decision to make, since for most inventions, no one can now say what they will do about crime—very little being known of what *anything* will do about crime. Inventions can cut costs or they can increase [the] ability to sense and to act. They provide more options. They make possible actions heretofore impractical. But their value in reducing crime is not known and will remain so until careful field evaluations are conducted. There should be a coordinated national program to identify the equipment requirements, to undertake the most promising developments, and then to conduct field trials that measure intended as well as side effects of new equipment and procedures. The results of these research, development, test, and evaluation efforts must then be disseminated widely so that the entire system can share in the benefits.

Information and Research

One essential for such a research program, as well as for immediate operational improvements, is better information about crime and the criminal justice system. Criminologists, criminal justice officials, and others familiar with the problems of crime control have long emphasized that the lack of adequate, complete, and timely information lies at the root of many of their problems. Information is needed about:

- The extent and nature of crime and its causes, to help in formulating effective crime control programs.
- Current crimes, to aid in immediate apprehension of offenders.
- Past crimes, to help solve them.
- Individual offenders, to help prescribe treatment for them.
- Criminal justice operations, to help officials better allocate their money and manpower.
- Effects on crime of actions taken by the criminal justice system, to help promote the evolution of a more humane and effective system.

Each year, judges in this country pass approximately 2 million sentences; unfortunately, no one knows the likely effect of the sentences on future criminal behavior. The nation's police [officers] spend half of their time on "preventive" patrol, yet no police chief knows how much crime is thereby prevented. Corrections officials, responsible for over 2 million offenders each year, are considering many new treatment programs; to choose among these, they must be able to estimate the amount by which each program can reduce recidivism.

Information about the consequences of actions by the criminal justice system is essential for improving those actions. In this sense the criminal justice system may be compared to a blind man far down the side of a mountain. If he wants to reach the top, he first must move. And it matters little whether his first move is up or down because any movement with subsequent evaluation will tell him which way is up. A step by step process of experimenting, evaluating, and modifying must be undertaken. Both innovation and the subsequent evaluation of its consequences are essential to climbing up. This process is inherently slow and expensive, and it must be conducted with care to avoid misleading results.

Scientists can help by participating in the efficient design of experiments and the evaluation of their results. The fact-finding, analytical, and experimental methods of science can help develop the required information. Once the information is developed, then the modern technology of data collection, retrieval, analysis, and transmission can help process and deliver it where and when it is needed.

Such carefully controlled testing offers some valuable opportunities for making the criminal justice system more efficient and effective. Correctional agencies have experimented with assigning at random a test group of offenders to each of several different treatment programs and evaluating their relative effectiveness in terms of recidivism and social adjustment. The same experimental techniques are being used in the evaluation of drugs and other treatment by the medical sciences. Similarly, police departments can control the distribution of marked and unmarked cars patrolling various precincts to evaluate the effects upon crime rates in these and adjoining precincts. The design of such experiments must be carefully undertaken to avoid spurious experimental effects and to avoid taking otherwise undesirable or unethical actions merely for the sake of the experiment.

Crime control, being largely a social problem, may appear to be outside the realm of the scientists' skills. Indeed, many aspects of the problem do fall outside their scope. The experience of science in the military, however, suggests that a fruitful collaboration can be established between criminal justice officials on one hand and engineers, physicists, economists, and social and behavioral scientists on the other. In military research organizations these different professions, working with military officers in interdisciplinary teams, have attacked defense problems in new ways and have provided insights that were new even to those with long military experience. Similar developments appear possible in criminal justice.

Research, emphasizing the social and behavioral sciences but including all the sciences, must be undertaken on an expanded and continuing basis. Manufacturing industry devotes at least 3 percent of its budget to research, development, test, and evaluation. The Defense Department spends about $7 billion a year on research and development [$53.9 billion in 2003], about 13 percent of its regular budget. In contrast, as recently as 1965, the Justice Department was the only Cabinet department with no share of the roughly $15 billion federal research and development budget. The research and development budget in other criminal justice organizations is negligible. Even if only 1 percent of the criminal justice budget were earmarked for research and development, this would provide about $50 million, and several times that amount needs to be invested each year.

Systems Analysis

Because of the enormous range of research and development possibilities, it is essential to begin not with the technology but with the problem. Technological efforts can then be concentrated in the areas most likely to be productive. Systems analysis is a valuable method for matching the technology to the need. It uses mathematical models of real-life systems to compare various ways of designing and using these systems to achieve specified objectives at minimum cost. This approach is particularly relevant in today's prolific technology, where the problem is less one of producing new devices than of choosing among the many potential opportunities.

These same techniques of systems analysis can often be helpful when applied to the design of some of the operations in police, courts, and corrections agencies, and to relating these parts to the overall criminal justice system. Such analyses provide a framework for study and for experimenting, as in a laboratory, with many possible alternatives prior to actual field implementation. Depending as they do on the development of appropriate data, these analyses stimulate careful collection and evaluation of information, and can thereby help locate critical areas for research.

The use of systems analysis was a major theme of the work of the Task Force. The approach begins with a broad look at the system's objectives and the possible methods for achieving them. The next step is to estimate the costs and benefits of each method for reaching the goal. The overall goals, however, are often difficult to relate in quantifiable terms to the alternatives under consideration. Thus, it is necessary to narrow the focus to those parts and aspects of the criminal justice system that are amenable to systems analysis, and then to present conclusions in appropriately qualified terms.

Despite these limitations, the systems analysis approach has the larger advantage of clarifying goals and making them explicit, drawing attention to ways of achieving them. Decision makers are thereby forced to make conscious choices among the values to be served. This process makes apparent what information is relevant to these choices and stimulates the collection of the appropriate data.

Figure 1 shows an example of the work of the Task Force along these lines—the use of systems analysis in finding how the police patrol force can better deter crime by shortening the time it takes to respond to a call for help. In the step diagram, the objectives are shown on the risers and the means for achieving them on the treads. The support for each of the steps is shown beneath it. By a sequence of analytical and empirical investigations, necessarily interlaced with assumptions and judgment, it was possible to proceed from a basic objective of the criminal justice system—reducing crime—to specific recommendations concerning new technology and operating procedures. There are, of course, other interests involved in the operations of the criminal justice system—protecting the innocent and safeguarding individual privacy, for example. But by narrowing the focus to the crime-reduction objective, it may be possible to suggest new strategies that can then be evaluated in the light of other and broader objectives.

Figure 1 starts with the principal objective of the criminal justice system, reducing crime. One means of doing this is by deterring people who might otherwise commit criminal acts. The police deter primarily by using the patrol force to pose a threat of apprehension, thereby raising the chances of penalties. Field data were collected and analyzed to determine the important factors that lead to apprehension. Among these, response time appeared to be important. This led to a cost-effectiveness analysis which compared means for cutting response time. The results of the analysis suggested that the best allocation of resources would be in automating the communications center operations by such means as using computers to perform some of the dispatching functions, automatic car locators to find the closest car, and other related technological possibilities. These components then can be brought together into a system design. Thus, it was possible to proceed systematically from the broad objectives down to the relevant technological details.

Of course, figure 1 is a highly simplified routing through the process. At each stage, the objectives are much more complex and the means far more numerous than the ones shown. In addition, the support for each step in this example is based on very preliminary work and requires much further development before firm conclusions can be drawn. Furthermore, this work was based on both specific and hypothetical situations, and the conditions examined may not necessarily apply in any given local situation. They are intended more as an illustration of an approach than for the generality of their conclusions.

Figure 1   A Simplified Illustration of a Systems Approach Relating Technology to Crime Control

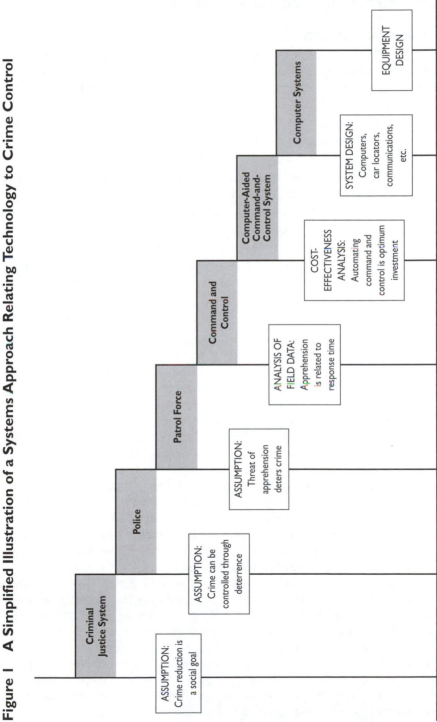

The Science and Technology Task Force

Work of the Task Force

The Science and Technology Task Force was established to investigate in greater detail some of the applications of science and technology to the problems of crime, and especially to improving the criminal justice system. The Task Force sought:

- To identify the problems, immediate and long-term, that science and technology is most likely to help solve, and to suggest the kinds of research and development needed.

- To identify and describe crime control problems in a form more susceptible to quantitative analysis.

- To point out the kinds of important data on crime control and the criminal justice system that are lacking, unreliable, or otherwise unusable, and to propose means of correcting such deficiencies.

- To analyze problems in crime assessment, police, courts, and corrections as an aid to the Commission and its other task forces.

- To suggest organizational formats within which technical devices and systems can be developed, field tested, and rendered useful.

With a scope so broad and time and manpower severely limited, it was necessary to make an early selection of areas to be emphasized. The social and behavioral sciences were deemphasized, largely because these were subjects already receiving treatment elsewhere in the Commission's work. The system sciences—information systems and computer applications, communications systems, and systems analysis—were given primary emphasis. In examining the applicability of technology, the emphasis was placed on identifying requirements rather than on detailed design or selection among equipment alternatives.

Among crimes, the primary focus was on the "Index" crimes—willful homicide, forcible rape, aggravated assault, robbery, burglary, larceny of $50 and over, and auto theft—the predatory crimes which are a principal source of public concern today. Only limited attention was paid to public disorder and vice crimes, and to "white collar crimes," such as illegal price fixing, tax evasion, and antitrust violations.

The organization and emphases in the Task Force's work are illustrated in figure 2. The heavier outlines indicate the subjects of major attention. Of the methods for controlling or reducing crime, the primary focus was on the criminal justice system—the police, courts, and corrections agencies. Within the criminal justice system the greatest potential for immediate improvement by analysis and technological innovation appears to be in police operations. Hence, police problems were emphasized heavily; less attention was given the problems of courts; and still less to the inherently behavioral problems of corrections. . . .

Figure 2   Structure of the Work of the Science and Technology Task Force

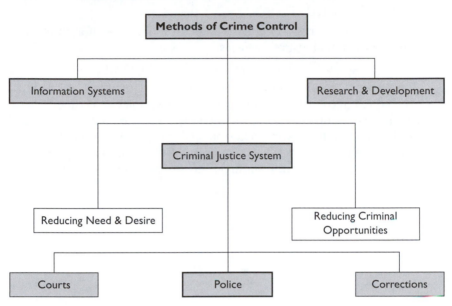

Results of Task Force Work

From its investigations, the Task Force produced a number of preliminary results and recommendations, including:

- A compilation of field data examining certain relationships between police field operations and the apprehension of criminals.
- Procedures for improving police responsiveness to calls at minimum cost.
- An approach which could significantly reduce police radio frequency congestion.
- An outline of a research and development program for the development of a semiautomatic fingerprint recognition system to replace the present manual system under which a criminal cannot ordinarily be traced unless a full set of 10 prints is available.
- Studies examining possible technological innovations for police operations in such areas as alarm systems and nonlethal weapons.
- Statistical approaches concerned with the improvement of allocation of patrol officers in the field.
- A procedure for testing means of reducing unnecessary delays in moving cases through the courts.
- An examination of programmed learning techniques as one means of contributing to the rehabilitation of young offenders.

- Methods for making auto theft more difficult.
- An exploratory attempt to apply system analysis to the overall criminal justice system.
- An outline, but not a detailed design, of a national information system for criminal justice agencies.
- A proposal for a national research and development program.

These specific results and recommendations are intended only to illustrate the potential contributions of science and technology to crime control. They must be developed in detail for each local situation and the extent of their utility must still be ascertained from better data. As illustrations, however, they appear to offer sufficient promise of the potential benefits from science and technology to warrant major efforts in these directions.

Criminal Justice as Crime Control vs. Due Process

Unlike the rational/legal and systems theoretical orientations, the "crime control vs. due process" framework can be attributed to one person—the late legal scholar, Herbert L. Packer. Packer was a law professor and vice-provost at Stanford University.[1] His framework first appeared in a legal journal (Packer, 1964), and it was later incorporated as the middle-third of his critically-acclaimed book, *The Limits of the Criminal Sanction* (1968).

Packer's work has had an enduring impact on our discipline. Nearly every student of crime and justice studies learns this theoretical orientation; it still generates a good deal of debate, research, and theorizing 40 years after its introduction. I suspect that its durability has something to do with its straightforward objective of explaining how criminal law works. "Theoretically grounded *heuristic* models, such as Packer's, are specifically designed to be the exploratory tools of social science explanation" (Henham, 1998, p. 592).

---

[1] George Packer, Herbert Packer's son, recently published *Blood of The Liberals* (2000). He describes his father's event-filled career at Stanford (beginning in the mid-1950s through the next decade) in less than flattering terms.

A heuristic model is a tool that helps us discover and learn. Packer's heuristic tool is comprised of two normative patterns—the crime control model and the due process model. Each model represents a distinct set of values, which operate simultaneously within the criminal justice system. David Duffee (1980) captured the essence of the differences between these two models (see table 1). In brief, the crime control model emphasizes the repression of crime as the most important function of the criminal justice system. It values the most efficient means of producing high

---

Table 1
Duffee's Summary of Packer's Two Models*

Crime Control	Due Process
1. Criminal justice process is positive guarantee of social freedom.	1. Criminal process is most severe social sanction used on free citizens.
2. Criminal acts are major threats to social order.	2. Criminal process can lead to severe limitations on social freedom.
3. To ensure social order we need high rates of apprehension and conviction.	3. Criminal procedures must be of highest quality to ensure freedom.
4. High rates require routine processing of cases with speed and finality.	4. To control abuses of power we have transparency in decisions and credible appeals processes.
5. Uniformity of procedures and plea-bargaining are essential for efficiency.	5. Emphasis on individual attention to cases and a high level of formality in process.
6. Administrative assembly line structure is essential for efficiency.	6. Adversarial process with checks and balances necessary to safeguard from abuse.
7. Successful conclusion is achieved by early culling of people who are not likely to be convicted and gaining quick convictions of the rest with little opportunity for appeal.	7. Successful conclusion is full application of rights in adversary process concerned with determining legal responsibility
8. Conclusion rests on a presumption of guilt, which is a prediction of likely outcome of the case.	8. Presumption of innocence which is directive about how to proceed regardless of the probable outcome.
9. Correction of errors through administrative controls; criminals not released due to mistaken procedures.	9. Correction of errors through appeal; applied on a case-by-case basis; release of offenders, as correction, deters system misbehavior in the future.
10. Confidence in agency and judicial action.	10. Skeptical about the efficacy of punishment applied through governmental mechanisms.

*Modified somewhat due to space limitations.

conviction rates in order to ensure a safe and free society. The due process model values the freedom of individual citizens from unjust acts committed by the state. Procedural safeguards such as the presumption of innocence, transparency of police and judicial proceedings, and credible appeals processes are essential to regulate the government's behaviors.

Packer's Ambivalence about the Criminal Justice System

Over the last 40 years our discipline has lost sight that Packer's two models were only one element of a larger project. As a traditional legal scholar, Packer's overall agenda was explicit:

> The criminal sanction, inflicting as it does a unique combination of stigma and loss of liberty, should be resorted to only sparingly in a society that regards itself as free and open (Packer, 1968, p. 250).

Unlike the rational/legal and systems theoretical orientations, Packer's work reveals a strong ambivalence about the law and its enforcement. On the one hand he placed great faith in the law's potential to prevent crime and to contribute to an orderly society. On the other hand, he stressed how governments often overuse and abuse the law making it necessary to be ever vigilant about controlling its power.

His central objective in the *Limits of the Criminal Sanction* was reformist in nature. He argued for the decriminalization and legalization of most status crimes, such as drug, prostitution, and gambling offenses. The criminal law and its enforcement were powerful and valuable entities in society. Packer believed they should be reserved only for the most serious of situations—and applied only with the utmost caution.

Packer's ambivalence about the criminal justice system was consistent with the historical period in which he compiled his book. Along with the civil rights movement and the dominance of political liberalism, the Warren Court had enacted unprecedented legal safeguards for the processing of the accused. Packer did not assert, as is often assumed in the literature, that there is or should be a competitive *balance* between due process and crime control values. Rather, in the real-world operation of the criminal justice system, he viewed the swing of the pendulum toward due process or toward crime control as a direct result of the socio-political climate of the times. For Packer, crime control values had dominated criminal law processing for most of American history; Packer saw the judicially active rulings of the Warren Court as a long-awaited and appropriate activation of the Bill of Rights. He even foresaw the future instability of the due process revolution and predicted that the pendulum would likely swing back.[2]

---

[2] See Packer (1968), pages 239–246.

Value Clash: A Catalyst for Critique and Thought

As I put this book together, I talked with numerous academic friends about what constitutes our discipline's major theoretical orientations. I was surprised to find that several colleagues did not care at all for Packer's theoretical framework. A few suggested I exclude it despite the evidence, found in textbooks and journal articles, that Packer's model was still an influential force. Aside from the criticism of it being too narrowly focused on legal process, they generally disapproved of how it limits, not enhances, our thinking. Although I do not intend to critique each theoretical orientation in this book, the literature's scrutiny of Packer's work is worth reviewing for two reasons. First, it illustrates how this theoretical orientation is still generating quality scholarship. Second, these debates and the reflection they stimulate add to our understanding of the criminal justice system.

The most common and enduring criticism of Packer's work is that the two models leave much of the story untold. You will notice in article 6 that Packer discusses only two components of the criminal justice system—the police and courts. He excludes from his analysis prisons, jails, probation, and the entire juvenile justice apparatus. By examining only the *legal dimension* of processing the accused through sentencing, Packer failed to notice and incorporate other normative influences.

John Griffith (1970) was the first to point to one alternative he termed the *family model*. Duffee and O'Leary (1974) put together a more coherent argument than Griffith, proposing four different value-clusters specifically associated with the field of corrections. I refer to these in my classes as the "four Rs"—rehabilitation, reintegration, restraint, and reform. Reed and Gaines (1982) also focused on the work of correctional and juvenile justice agencies, adding a new value influence, which they labeled the *social service model*. All three of these early works were attempts at labeling a third normative presence in operation throughout the entire criminal justice system: service to the needs of offenders, victims, and the community—aside from the legal processing of arrestees. We can label this aspect *needs-based justice* (Longmire, 1981). Needs-based values are not limited to corrections and juvenile justice. The police, for example, spend a large percentage of their day on basic order maintenance needs of the communities in which they patrol. These types of service activities do not generally activate the formal legal process.

More recent scholarship has also attempted to expand Packer's framework of competing value systems (Henham, 1998; Huff, Rattner, & Sagarin, 1996; Luna, 1999; McConville, Sanders, & Leng, 1991, 1997; Mears, 1998; Smith, 1997, 1998; Weisberg, 1999). Mike McConville and his colleagues wrote a book in 1991, *The Case for Prosecution,* which relies heavily on Packer's theoretical orientation to make sense of criminal case processing. In 1997, they published an article in the *British Journal of Criminology* restating their orientation. In a scathing rejoinder to their work, David Smith (1997) argued that they had misunderstood and misapplied Packer's crime control and due process models.[3] In article 7, Peter Duff mediates the debate by clarifying and modifying Packer's choice of terms.

From Forced Reaction to Choosing to Act

In discussing the previous orientations we examined how each might explain the recent growth in size and power of the criminal justice system. Both the rational/legal and systems orientations relied on what we called forced reaction theory. The crime control vs. due process orientation requires a different explanation. The pendulum swing toward the crime control model has resulted in tougher punishments, greater efficiency in processing offenders, and fewer constitutional constraints on police power. The causal equation is simple: a high emphasis on crime control values translates into a more powerful and larger crime control apparatus. As opposed to being a forced reaction to a worsening crime problem, CJ growth stems from our society's and the government's value-choices.[4] Note the difference between being *forced* to act, versus *choosing* to act, in a particular fashion.

While this explanation may coincide with Packer's model, it does not necessarily correspond with the central theme of his entire book. Remember Packer was calling for limiting the scope of criminal laws. He viewed the criminalization of behaviors such as drug use as a dangerous overreach of the law's abilities and authority. The following quote makes clear how this worldview furnishes us with another theory of CJS growth.

> Crime is a sociopolitical artifact, not a natural phenomenon. We can have as much or as little crime as we please, depending on what we choose to count as criminal. Only when this basic fact is understood can we begin to deal rationally with the problem of choice by applying relevant criteria for proper uses of the sanction. (Packer, 1968, pp. 365–366)

The size of the crime problem the system deals with, therefore, depends on what the government defines as crime. Without a "war on drugs," for example, the system's growth in power and size over the last 30 years would likely be less significant. Several subsequent theoretical orientations share this line of theorizing with Packer (see especially chapters 6, 7, and 8).

---

[3] This contentious debate is a good example of the clash between the rational/legal orientation (Smith) and the constructionist orientation (McConville et al.). In rigidly filtering reality through their own theoretical orientations, little understanding of the other's perspective takes place. However, the debate allows the reader to view criminal justice processing from two unique perspectives.

[4] Of course, one could argue that those value choices are determined by the extent of the crime problem.

84   Chapter Four

References

Duffee, D. E. (1990). *Explaining criminal justice: Community theory and criminal justice reform*. Prospect Heights, IL: Waveland Press.

Duffee, D. E., & O'Leary, V. O. (1974). Models of correction: An entry in the Packer-Griffith debate. *Criminal Law Bulletin, 7*(4), 329–352.

Griffith, J. (1970). Ideology in criminal procedure or a third "model" of the criminal process. *The Yale Law Journal, 79*(3), 359–417.

Henham, R. (1998). Human rights, due process and sentencing. *British Journal of Criminology, 38*(4), 592–610.

Huff, R., Rattner, A., & Sagarin, E. (1996). *Convicted but innocent: Wrongful conviction and public policy*. Newbury Park, CA: Sage.

Longmire, D. (1981). A popular justice system. *Contemporary Crises, 5*(1), 15–30.

Luna, E. G. (1999). The models of criminal procedure. *Buffalo Criminal Law Review, 2,* 389.

McConville, M., Sanders, A., & Leng, R. (1991). *The case for prosecution*. London: Routledge.

McConville, M., Sanders, A., & Leng, R. (1997). Descriptive or critical sociology: The choice is yours. *British Journal of Criminology, 37*(3), 347–358.

Mears, T. L. (1998). Place and crime. *Chicago-Kent Law Review, 73,* 669.

Packer, G. (2000). *Blood of the liberals*. New York: Farrar, Straus, and Giroux.

Packer, H. L. (1964). Two models of the criminal process. *University of Pennsylvania Law Review, 113,* 1–23.

Packer, H. L. (1968). *The limits of the criminal sanction*. Stanford, CA: Stanford University Press.

Reed, T. E., & Gaines, L. K. (1982). Criminal justice models as a function of ideological images: A social learning alternative to Packer. *International Journal of Comparative and Applied Criminal Justice, 6*(2), 213–222.

Smith, D. J. (1997). Case construction and the goals of criminal process. *The British Journal of Criminology, 37*(3), 319–346.

Weisberg, R. (1999). Foreword: A new agenda for criminal procedure. *Buffalo Criminal Law Review, 2,* 367.

Two Models of the Criminal Process

Herbert L. Packer

The kind of criminal process we have depends importantly on certain value choices that are reflected, explicitly or implicitly, in its habitual functioning. The kind of model we need is one that permits us to recognize explicitly the value choices that underlie the details of the criminal process. In a word, what we need is a normative model or models. It will take more than one model, but it will not take more than two.

Two models of the criminal process will let us perceive the normative antinomy at the heart of the criminal law. These models are not labeled *is* and *ought*, nor are they to be taken in that sense. Rather, they represent an attempt to abstract two separate value systems that compete for priority in the operation of the criminal process. Neither is presented as either corresponding to reality or representing the ideal to the exclusion of the other. The two models merely afford a convenient way to talk about the operation of a process whose day-to-day functioning involves a constant series of minute adjustments between the competing demands of two value systems and whose normative future likewise involves a series of resolutions of the tensions between competing claims.

I call these two models the due process model and the crime control model. In the rest of this chapter I shall sketch their animating presuppositions, and in succeeding chapters I shall show how the two models apply to a selection of representative problems that arise at successive stages of the criminal process. As we examine the way the models operate in each successive stage, we will raise two further inquiries: first, where on a spectrum between the extremes represented by the two models do our present practices seem approximately to fall; second, what appears to be the direction and thrust of current and foreseeable trends along each such spectrum?

There is a risk in an enterprise of this sort that is latent in any attempt to polarize. It is, simply, that values are too various to be pinned down to yes-or-no answers. The models are distortions of reality. And, since they are normative in character, there is a danger of seeing one or the other as good or bad. The reader will have his preferences, as I do, but we should not be so rigid as to demand consistently polarized answers to the range of questions posed in the criminal process. The weighty questions of public policy that inhere in any attempt to discern where on the spectrum of normative choice the "right" answer lies are beyond the scope of the present inquiry. The attempt here is primarily to clarify the terms of discussion by isolating the assumptions that underlie competing policy claims and examining the conclusions that those claims, if fully accepted, would lead to.

Values Underlying the Models

Each of the two models we are about to examine is an attempt to give operational content to a complex of values underlying the criminal law. As I have suggested earlier, it is possible to identify two competing systems of values, the tension between which accounts for the intense activity now observable in the development of the criminal process. The actors in this development—lawmakers, judges, police, prosecutors, defense lawyers— do not often pause to articulate the values that underlie the positions that they take on any given issue. Indeed, it would be a gross oversimplification to ascribe a coherent and consistent set of values to any of these actors. Each of the two competing schemes of values we will be developing in this section contains components that are demonstrably present some of the time in some of the actors' preferences regarding the criminal process. No one person has ever identified himself as holding all of the values that underlie these two models. The models are polarities, and so are the schemes of value that underlie them. A person who subscribed to all of the values underlying one model to the exclusion of all of the values underlying the other would be rightly viewed as a fanatic. The values are presented here as an aid to analysis, not as a program for action.

Some Common Ground

However, the polarity of the two models is not absolute. Although it would be possible to construct models that exist in an institutional vacuum, it would not serve our purposes to do so. We are postulating, not a criminal process that operates in any kind of society at all, but rather one that operates within the framework of contemporary American society.

This leaves plenty of room for polarization, but it does require the observance of some limits. A model of the criminal process that left out of account relatively stable and enduring features of the American legal system would not have much relevance to our central inquiry. For convenience, these elements of stability and continuity can be roughly equated with minimal agreed limits expressed in the Constitution of the United States and, more importantly, with unarticulated assumptions that can be perceived to underlie those limits. Of course, it is true that the Constitution is constantly appealed to by proponents and opponents of many measures that affect the criminal process. And only the naive would deny that there are few conclusive positions that can be reached by appeal to the Constitution. Yet there are assumptions about the criminal process that are widely shared and that may be viewed as common ground for the operation of any model of the criminal process. Our first task is to clarify these assumptions.

First, there is the assumption, implicit in the ex post facto clause of the Constitution, that the function of defining conduct that may be treated as criminal is separate from and prior to the process of identifying and dealing with persons as criminals. How wide or narrow the definition of criminal conduct must be is an important question of policy that yields highly variable results depending on the values held by those making the relevant decisions. But that there must be a means of definition that is in some sense separate from and prior to the operation of the process is clear. . . .

A related assumption that limits the area of controversy is that the criminal process ordinarily ought to be invoked by those charged with the responsibility for doing so when it appears that a crime has been committed and that there is a reasonable prospect of apprehending and convicting its perpetrator. Although police and prosecutors are allowed broad discretion for deciding not to invoke the criminal process, it is commonly agreed that these officials have no general dispensing power. If the legislature has decided that certain conduct is to be treated as criminal, the decision-makers at every level of the criminal process are expected to accept that basic decision as a premise for action. The controversial nature of the occasional case in which the relevant decision-makers appear not to have played their appointed role only serves to highlight the strength with which the premise holds. This assumption may be viewed as the other side of the ex post facto coin. Just as conduct that is not proscribed as criminal may not be dealt with in the criminal process, so conduct that has been denominated as criminal must be treated as such by the participants in the criminal process acting within their respective competences.

Next, there is the assumption that there are limits to the powers of government to investigate and apprehend persons suspected of committing crimes. I do not refer to the controversy (settled recently, at least in broad outline) as to whether the Fourth Amendment's prohibition against unreasonable searches and seizures applies to the states with the same force with which it applies to the federal government.[1] Rather, I am talking about the general assumption that a degree of scrutiny and control must be exercised with respect to the activities of law enforcement officers, that the security and privacy of the individual may not be invaded at will. It is possible to imagine a society in which even lip service is not paid to this assumption. Nazi Germany approached but never quite reached this position. But no one in our society would maintain that any individual may be taken into custody at any time and held without any limitation of time during the process of investigating his possible commission of crimes, or would argue that there should be no form of redress for violation of at least some standards for official investigative conduct. Although this assumption may not appear to have much in the way of positive content, its absence would render moot some of our most hotly controverted problems. If there were not general agreement that there must be some limits on police power to detain and investigate, the highly controversial provisions of the Uniform Arrest Act, permitting the police to detain a person for questioning for a short period even though they do not have grounds for making an arrest, would be a magnanimous concession by the all-powerful state rather than, as it is now perceived, a substantial expansion of police power.

Finally, there is a complex of assumptions embraced by terms such as "the adversary system," "procedural due process," "notice and an opportunity to be heard," and "day in court." Common to them all is the notion that the alleged criminal is not merely an object to be acted upon but an independent entity in the process who may, if he so desires, force the operators of the process to demonstrate to an independent authority (judge and jury) that he is guilty of the charges against him. It is a minimal assumption. It speaks in terms of "may" rather than "must." It permits but does not require the accused, acting by himself or through his own agent, to play an active role in the process. By virtue of that fact the process becomes or has the capacity to become a contest between, if not equals, at least independent actors. As we shall see, much of the space between the two models is occupied by stronger or weaker notions of how this contest is to be arranged, in what cases it is to be played, and by what rules. The crime control model tends to de-emphasize this adversary aspect of the process; the due process model tends to make it central. The common ground, and it is important, is the agreement that the process has, for everyone subjected to it, at least the potentiality of becoming to some extent an adversary struggle.

So much for common ground. There is a good deal of it, even in the narrowest view. Its existence should not be overlooked, because it is, by definition, what permits partial resolutions of the tension between the two models to take place. The rhetoric of the criminal process consists largely of claims that disputed territory is "really" common ground: that, for example, the premise of an adversary system "necessarily" embraces the appointment of counsel for everyone accused of crime, or conversely, that the obligation to pursue persons suspected of committing crimes "necessarily" embraces interrogation of suspects without the intervention of counsel. We may smile indulgently at such claims; they are rhetoric, and no more. But the form in which they are made suggests an important truth: that there *is* a common ground of value assumption about the criminal process that makes continued discourse about its problems possible.

Crime Control Values

The value system that underlies the crime control model is based on the proposition that the repression of criminal conduct is by far the most important function to be performed by the criminal process. The failure of law enforcement to bring criminal conduct under tight control is viewed as leading to the breakdown of public order and thence to the disappearance of an important condition of human freedom. If the laws go unenforced— which is to say, if it is perceived that there is a high percentage of failure to apprehend and convict in the criminal process—a general disregard for legal controls tends to develop. The law-abiding citizen then becomes the victim of all sorts of unjustifiable invasions of his interests. His security of person and property is sharply diminished, and, therefore, so is his liberty to function as a member of society. The claim ultimately is that the criminal process is a positive guarantor of social freedom. In order to achieve this high purpose, the crime control model requires that primary attention be paid to the efficiency with which the criminal process operates to screen suspects, determine guilt, and secure appropriate dispositions of persons convicted of crime.

Efficiency of operation is not, of course, a criterion that can be applied in a vacuum. By "efficiency" we mean the system's capacity to apprehend, try, convict, and dispose of a high proportion of criminal offenders whose offenses become known. In a society in which only the grossest forms of antisocial behavior were made criminal and in which the crime rate was exceedingly low, the criminal process might require the devotion of many more man-hours of police, prosecutorial, and judicial time per case than ours does, and still operate with tolerable efficiency. A society that was prepared to increase even further the resources devoted to the suppression of crime might cope with a rising crime rate without sacrifice of efficiency while continuing to maintain an elaborate and time-consuming set of criminal processes. However, neither of these possible characteristics corresponds with social reality in this country. We use the criminal sanction to cover an increasingly wide spectrum of behavior thought to be antisocial, and the amount of crime is very high indeed, although both level and trend are hard to assess.[2] At the same time, although precise measures are not available, it does not appear that we are disposed in the public sector of the economy to increase very drastically the quantity, much less the quality, of the resources devoted to the suppression of criminal activity through the operation of the criminal process. These factors have an important bearing on the criteria of efficiency, and therefore on the nature of the crime control model.

The model, in order to operate successfully, must produce a high rate of apprehension and conviction, and must do so in a context where the magnitudes being dealt with are very large and the resources for dealing with them are very limited. There must then be a premium on speed and finality. Speed, in turn, depends on informality and on uniformity; finality depends on minimizing the occasions for challenge. The process must not be cluttered up with ceremonious rituals that do not advance the progress of a case. Facts can be established more quickly through interrogation in a police station than through the formal process of examination and cross-examination in a court. It follows that extrajudicial processes should be preferred to judicial processes, informal operations to formal ones. But informality is not enough; there must also be uniformity. Routine, stereotyped procedures are essential if large numbers are being handled. The model that will operate successfully on these presuppositions must be an administrative, almost a managerial, model. The image that comes to mind is an assembly-line conveyor belt down which moves an endless stream of cases, never stopping, carrying the cases to workers who stand at fixed stations and who perform on each case as it comes by the same small but essential operation that brings it one step closer to being a finished product, or, to exchange the metaphor for the reality, a closed file. The criminal process, in this model, is seen as a screening process in which each successive stage—pre-arrest investigation, arrest, post-arrest investigation, preparation for trial, trial or entry of plea, conviction, disposition—involves a series of routinized operations whose success is gauged primarily by their tendency to pass the case along to a successful conclusion.

What is a successful conclusion? One that throws off at an early stage those cases in which it appears unlikely that the person apprehended is an offender and then secures, as expeditiously as possible, the conviction of the rest, with a minimum of occasions for challenge, let alone post-audit. By the application of administrative expertness, primarily that of the police and prosecutors, an early determination of probable innocence or guilt emerges. Those who are probably innocent are screened out. Those who are probably guilty are passed quickly through the remaining stages of the process. The key to the operation of the model regarding those who are not screened out is what I shall call a presumption of guilt. The concept requires some explanation, since it may appear startling to assert that what appears to be the precise converse of our generally accepted ideology of a presumption of innocence can be an essential element of a model that does correspond in some respects to the actual operation of the criminal process.

The presumption of guilt is what makes it possible for the system to deal efficiently with large numbers, as the crime control model demands. The supposition is that the screening processes operated by police and prosecutors are reliable indicators of probable guilt. Once a man has been arrested and investigated without being found to be probably innocent, or, to put it differently, once a determination has been made that there is enough evidence of guilt to permit holding him for further action, then all subsequent activity directed toward him is based on the view that he is probably guilty. The precise point at which this occurs will vary from case to case; in many cases it will occur as soon as the suspect is arrested, or even before, if the evidence of probable guilt that has come to the attention of the authorities is sufficiently strong. But in any case the presumption of guilt will begin to operate well before the "suspect" becomes a "defendant."

The presumption of guilt is not, of course, a thing. Nor is it even a rule of law in the usual sense. It simply is the consequence of a complex of attitudes, a mood. If there is confidence in the reliability of informal administrative fact-finding activities that take place in the early stages of the criminal process, the remaining stages of the process can be relatively perfunctory without any loss in operating efficiency. The presumption of guilt, as it operates in the crime control model, is the operational expression of that confidence.

It would be a mistake to think of the presumption of guilt as the opposite of the presumption of innocence that we are so used to thinking of as the polestar of the criminal process and that, as we shall see, occupies an important position in the due process model. The presumption of innocence is not its opposite; it is irrelevant to the presumption of guilt; the two concepts are different rather than opposite ideas. The difference can perhaps be epitomized by an example. A murderer, for reasons best known to himself, chooses to shoot his victim in plain view of a large number of people. When the police arrive, he hands them his gun and says, "I did it and I'm glad." His account of what happened is corroborated by several eyewitnesses. He is placed under arrest and led off to jail. Under these circumstances, which may seem extreme but which in fact characterize with rough accuracy the evidentiary situation in a large proportion of criminal cases, it would be plainly absurd to maintain that more probably than not the suspect did not commit the killing. But that is not what the presumption of innocence means. It means that until there has been an adjudication of guilt by an authority legally competent to make such an adjudication, the suspect is to be treated, for reasons that have nothing whatever to do with the probable outcome of the case, as if his guilt is an open question.

The presumption of innocence is a direction to officials about how they are to proceed, not a prediction of outcome. The presumption of guilt, however, is purely and simply a prediction of outcome. The presumption of innocence is, then, a direction to the authorities to ignore the presumption of guilt in their treatment of the suspect. It tells them, in effect, to close their eyes to what will frequently seem to be factual probabilities. The reasons why it tells them this are among the animating presuppositions of the due process model, and we will come to them shortly.

It is enough to note at this point that the presumption of guilt is descriptive and factual; the presumption of innocence is normative and legal. The pure crime control model has no truck with the presumption of innocence, although its real-life emanations are, as we shall see, brought into uneasy compromise with the dictates of this dominant ideological position. In the presumption of guilt this model finds a factual predicate for the position that the dominant goal of repressing crime can be achieved through highly summary processes without any great loss of efficiency (as previously defined), because of the probability that, in the run of cases, the preliminary screening processes operated by the police and the prosecuting officials contain adequate guarantees of reliable fact-finding. Indeed, the model takes an even stronger position. It is that subsequent processes, particularly those of a formal adjudicatory nature, are unlikely to produce as reliable fact-finding as the expert administrative process that precedes them is capable of. The criminal process thus must put special weight on the quality of administrative fact-finding. It becomes important, then, to place as few restrictions as possible on the character of the administrative fact-finding processes and to limit restrictions to such as enhance reliability, excluding those designed for other purposes. As we shall see, this view of restrictions on administrative fact-finding is a consistent theme in the development of the crime control model.

In this model, as I have suggested, the center of gravity for the process lies in the early, administrative fact-finding stages. The complementary proposition is that the subsequent stages are relatively unimportant and should be truncated as much as possible. This, too, produces tensions with presently dominant ideology. The pure crime control model has very little use for many conspicuous features of the adjudicative process, and in real life works out a number of ingenious compromises with them. Even in the pure model, however, there have to be devices for dealing with the suspect after the preliminary screening process has resulted in a determination of probable guilt. The focal device, as we shall see, is the plea of guilty; through its use, adjudicative fact-finding is reduced to a minimum. It might be said of the crime control model that, when reduced to its barest essentials and operating at its most successful pitch, it offers two possibilities: an administrative fact-finding process leading (1) to exoneration of the suspect or (2) to the entry of a plea of guilty.

Due Process Values

If the crime control model resembles an assembly line, the due process model looks very much like an obstacle course. Each of its successive stages is designed to present formidable impediments to carrying the accused any further along in the process. Its ideology is not the converse of that underlying the crime control model. It does not rest on the idea that it is not socially desirable to repress crime, although critics of its application have been known to claim so. Its ideology is composed of a complex of ideas, some of them based on judgments about the efficacy of crime control devices, others having to do with quite different considerations. The ideology of due process is far more deeply impressed on the formal structure of the law than is the ideology of crime control; yet an accurate tracing of the strands that make it up is strangely difficult. What follows is only an attempt at an approximation.

The due process model encounters its rival on the crime control model's own ground in respect to the reliability of fact-finding processes. The crime control model, as we have suggested, places heavy reliance on the ability of investigative and prosecutorial officers, acting in an informal setting in which their distinctive skills are given full sway, to elicit and reconstruct a tolerably accurate account of what actually took place in an alleged criminal event. The due process model rejects this premise and substitutes for it a view of informal, nonadjudicative fact-finding that stresses the possibility of error. People are notoriously poor observers of disturbing events—the more emotion-arousing the context, the greater the possibility that recollection will be incorrect; confessions and admissions by persons in police custody may be induced by physical or psychological coercion so that the police end up hearing what the suspect thinks they want to hear rather than the truth; witnesses may be animated by a bias or interest that no one would trouble to discover except one specially charged with protecting the interests of the accused (as the police are not). Considerations of this kind all lead to a rejection of informal fact-finding processes as definitive of factual guilt and to an insistence on formal, adjudicative, adversary fact-finding processes in which the factual case against the accused is publicly heard by an impartial tribunal and is evaluated only after the accused has had a full opportunity to discredit the case against him. Even then, the distrust of fact-finding processes that animates the due process model is not dissipated. The possibilities of human error being what they are, further scrutiny is necessary, or at least must be available, in case facts have been overlooked or suppressed in the heat of battle. How far this subsequent scrutiny must be available is a hotly controverted issue today. In the pure due process model the answer would be: at least as long as there is an allegation of factual error that has not received an adjudicative hearing in a fact-finding context. The demand for finality is thus very low in the due process model.

This strand of due process ideology is not enough to sustain the model. If all that were at issue between the two models was a series of questions about the reliability of fact-finding processes, we would have but one model of the criminal process, the nature of whose constituent elements would pose questions of fact not of value. Even if the discussion is confined, for the moment, to the question of reliability, it is apparent that more is at stake than simply an evaluation of what kinds of fact-finding processes, alone or in combination, are likely to produce the most nearly reliable results. The stumbling block is this: how much reliability is compatible with efficiency? Granted that informal fact-finding will make some mistakes that can be remedied if backed up by adjudicative fact-finding, the desirability of providing this backup is not affirmed or negated by factual demonstrations or predictions that the increase in reliability will be x percent or x plus n percent. It still remains to ask how much weight is to be given to the competing demands of reliability (a high degree of probability in each case that factual guilt has been accurately determined) and efficiency (expeditious handling of the large numbers of cases that the process ingests). The crime control model is more optimistic about the improbability of error in a significant number of cases; but it is also, though only in part therefore, more tolerant about the amount of error that it will put up with. The due process model insists on the prevention and elimination of mistakes to the extent possible; the crime control model accepts the probability of mistakes up to the level at which they interfere with the goal of repressing crime, either because too many guilty people are escaping or, more subtly, because general awareness of the unreliability of the process leads to a decrease in the deterrent efficacy of the criminal law. In this view, reliability and efficiency are not polar opposites but rather complementary characteristics. The system is reliable *because* efficient; reliability becomes a matter of independent concern only when it becomes so attenuated as to impair efficiency. All of this the due process model rejects. If efficiency demands shortcuts around reliability, then absolute efficiency must be rejected. The aim of the process is at least as much to protect the factually innocent as it is to convict the factually guilty. It is a little like quality control in industrial technology: tolerable deviation from standard varies with the importance of conformity to standard in the destined uses of the product. The due process model resembles a factory that has to devote a substantial part of its input to quality control. This necessarily cuts down on quantitative output.

All of this is only the beginning of the ideological difference between the two models. The due process model could disclaim any attempt to provide enhanced reliability for the fact-finding process and still produce a set of institutions and processes that would differ sharply from those demanded by the crime control model. Indeed, it may not be too great an oversimplification to assert that in point of historical development the doctrinal pressures emanating from the demands of the due process model have tended to evolve from an original matrix of concern for the maximization of reliability into values quite different and more far-reaching. These values can be expressed in, although not adequately described by, the concept of the primacy of the individual and the complementary concept of limitation on official power.

The combination of stigma and loss of liberty that is embodied in the end result of the criminal process is viewed as being the heaviest deprivation that government can inflict on the individual. Furthermore, the processes that culminate in these highly afflictive sanctions are seen as in themselves coercive, restricting, and demeaning. Power is always subject to abuse—sometimes subtle, other times, as in the criminal process, open and ugly. Precisely because of its potency in subjecting the individual to the coercive power of the state, the criminal process must, in this model, be subjected to controls that prevent it from operating with maximal efficiency. According to this ideology, maximal efficiency means maximal tyranny. And, although no one would assert that minimal efficiency means minimal tyranny, the proponents of the due process model would accept with considerable equanimity a substantial diminution in the efficiency with which the criminal process operates in the interest of preventing official oppression of the individual.

The most modest-seeming but potentially far-reaching mechanism by which the due process model implements these antiauthoritarian values is the doctrine of legal guilt. According to this doctrine, a person is not to be held guilty of crime merely on a showing that in all probability, based upon reliable evidence, he did factually what he is said to have done. Instead, he is to be held guilty if and only if these factual determinations are made in procedurally regular fashion and by authorities acting within competences duly allocated to them. Furthermore, he is not to be held guilty, even though the factual determination is or might be adverse to him, if various rules designed to protect him and to safeguard the integrity of the process are not given effect: the tribunal that convicts him must have the power to deal with his kind of case ("jurisdiction") and must be geographically appropriate ("venue"); too long a time must not have elapsed since the offense was committed ("statute of limitations"); he must not have been previously convicted or acquitted of the same or a substantially similar offense ("double jeopardy"); he must not fall within a category of persons, such as children or the insane, who are legally immune to conviction ("criminal responsibility"); and so on. None of these requirements has anything to do with the factual question of whether the person did or did not engage in the conduct that is charged as the offense against him; yet favorable answers to any of them will mean that he is legally innocent. Wherever the competence to make adequate factual determinations lies, it is apparent that only a tribunal that is aware of these guilt-defeating doctrines and is willing to apply them can be viewed as competent to make determinations of legal guilt. The police and the prosecutors are ruled out by lack of competence, in the first instance, and by lack of assurance of willingness, in the second. Only an impartial tribunal can be trusted to make determinations of legal as opposed to factual guilt.

In this concept of legal guilt lies the explanation for the apparently quixotic presumption of innocence of which we spoke earlier. A man who, after police investigation, is charged with having committed a crime can hardly be said to be presumptively innocent, if what we mean is factual innocence. But if what we mean is that it has yet to be determined if any of the myriad legal doctrines that serve in one way or another the end of lim-

iting official power through the observance of certain substantive and procedural regularities may be appropriately invoked to exculpate the
accused man, it is apparent that as a matter of prediction it cannot be said
with confidence that more probably than not he will be found guilty.

Beyond the question of predictability this model posits a functional
reason for observing the presumption of innocence: by forcing the state to
prove its case against the accused in an adjudicative context, the presumption of innocence serves to force into play all the qualifying and disabling
doctrines that limit the use of the criminal sanction against the individual,
thereby enhancing his opportunity to secure a favorable outcome. In this
sense, the presumption of innocence may be seen to operate as a kind of
self-fulfilling prophecy. By opening up a procedural situation that permits
the successful assertion of defenses having nothing to do with factual
guilt, it vindicates the proposition that the factually guilty may nonetheless be legally innocent and should therefore be given a chance to qualify
for that kind of treatment.

The possibility of legal innocence is expanded enormously when the
criminal process is viewed as the appropriate forum for correcting its own
abuses. This notion may well account for a greater amount of the distance
between the two models than any other. In theory the crime control model
can tolerate rules that forbid illegal arrests, unreasonable searches, coercive interrogations, and the like. What it cannot tolerate is the vindication
of those rules in the criminal process itself through the exclusion of evidence illegally obtained or through the reversal of convictions in cases
where the criminal process has breached the rules laid down for its observance. And the due process model, although it may in the first instance be
addressed to the maintenance of reliable fact-finding techniques, comes
eventually to incorporate prophylactic and deterrent rules that result in
the release of the factually guilty even in cases in which blotting out the
illegality would still leave an adjudicative fact-finder convinced of the
accused person's guilt. Only by penalizing errant police and prosecutors
within the criminal process itself can adequate pressure be maintained, so
the argument runs, to induce conformity with the due process model.

Another strand in the complex of attitudes underlying the due process
model is the idea—itself a shorthand statement for a complex of attitudes—
of equality. This notion has only recently emerged as an explicit basis for
pressing the demands of the due process model, but it appears to represent,
at least in its potential, a most powerful norm for influencing official conduct. Stated most starkly, the ideal of equality holds that "there can be no
equal justice where the kind of trial a man gets depends on the amount of
money he has."[3] The factual predicate underlying this assertion is that there
are gross inequalities in the financial means of criminal defendants as a
class, that in an adversary system of criminal justice an effective defense is
largely a function of the resources that can be mustered on behalf of the
accused, and that the very large proportion of criminal defendants who are,

operationally speaking, "indigent" will thus be denied an effective defense. This factual premise has been strongly reinforced by recent studies that in turn have been both a cause and an effect of an increasing emphasis upon norms for the criminal process based on the premise.

The norms derived from the premise do not take the form of an insistence upon governmental responsibility to provide literally equal opportunities for all criminal defendants to challenge the process. Rather, they take as their point of departure the notion that the criminal process, initiated as it is by government and containing as it does the likelihood of severe deprivations at the hands of government, imposes some kind of public obligation to ensure that financial inability does not destroy the capacity of an accused to assert what may be meritorious challenges to the processes being invoked against him. At its most gross, the norm of equality would act to prevent situations in which financial inability forms an absolute barrier to the assertion of a right that is in theory generally available, as where there is a right to appeal that is, however, effectively conditional upon the filing of a trial transcript obtained at the defendant's expense. Beyond this, it may provide the basis for a claim whenever the system theoretically makes some kind of challenge available to an accused who has the means to press it. If, for example, a defendant who is adequately represented has the opportunity to prevent the case against him from coming to the trial stage by forcing the state to its proof in a preliminary hearing, the norm of equality may be invoked to assert that the same kind of opportunity must be available to others as well. In a sense the system as it functions for the small minority whose resources permit them to exploit all its defensive possibilities provides a benchmark by which its functioning in all other cases is to be tested: not, perhaps, to guarantee literal identity but rather to provide a measure of whether the process as a whole is recognizably of the same general order. The demands made by a norm of this kind are likely by their very nature to be quite sweeping. Although the norm's imperatives may be initially limited to determining whether in a particular case the accused was injured or prejudiced by his relative inability to make an appropriate challenge, the norm of equality very quickly moves to another level on which the demand is that the process in general be adapted to minimize discriminations rather than that a mere series of post hoc determinations of discrimination be made or makeable.

It should be observed that the impact of the equality norm will vary greatly depending upon the point in time at which it is introduced into a model of the criminal process. If one were starting from scratch to decide how the process ought to work, the norm of equality would have nothing very important to say on such questions as, for example, whether an accused should have the effective assistance of counsel in deciding whether to enter a plea of guilty. One could decide, on quite independent considerations, that it is or is not a good thing to afford that facility to the generality of persons accused of crime. But the impact of the equality norm becomes far greater when it is brought to bear on a process whose contours have already been shaped. If our model of the criminal process affords defendants who are in a financial position to do so the right to consult a lawyer before entering a plea, then the equality norm exerts powerful pressure to provide such an opportunity to all defendants and to regard the failure to do so as a malfunctioning of the process of whose consequences the accused is entitled to be relieved. In a sense, this has been the role of the equality norm in affecting the real-world criminal process. It has made its appearance on the scene comparatively late, and has therefore encountered a system in which the relative financial inability of most persons accused of crime results in treatment very different from that accorded the small minority of the financially capable. For this reason, its impact has already been substantial and may be expected to be even more so in the future.

There is a final strand of thought in the due process model that is often ignored but that needs to be candidly faced if thought on the subject is not to be obscured. This is a mood of skepticism about the morality and utility of the criminal sanction, taken either as a whole or in some of its applications. The subject is a large and complicated one, comprehending as it does much of the intellectual history of our times. It is properly the subject of another essay altogether. To put the matter briefly, one cannot improve upon the statement by Professor Paul Bator:

> In summary we are told that the criminal law's notion of just condemnation and punishment is a cruel hypocrisy visited by a smug society on the psychologically and economically crippled; that its premise of a morally autonomous will with at least some measure of choice whether to comply with the values expressed in a penal code is unscientific and outmoded; that its reliance on punishment as an educational and deterrent agent is misplaced, particularly in the case of the very members of society most likely to engage in criminal conduct; and that its failure to provide for individualized and humane rehabilitation of offenders is inhuman and wasteful.[4]

This skepticism, which may be fairly said to be widespread among the most influential and articulate contemporary leaders of informed opinion, leads to an attitude toward the processes of the criminal law that, to quote Mr. Bator again, engenders "a peculiar receptivity toward claims of injustice which arise within the traditional structure of the system itself; fundamental disagreement and unease about the very bases of the criminal law has, inevitably, created acute pressure at least to expand and liberalize those of its processes and doctrines which serve to make more tentative its judgments or limit its power." In short, doubts about the ends for which power is being exercised create pressure to limit the discretion with which that power is exercised.

The point need not be pressed to the extreme of doubts about or rejection of the premises upon which the criminal sanction in general rests.

Unease may be stirred simply by reflection on the variety of uses to which the criminal sanction is put and by a judgment that an increasingly large proportion of those uses may represent an unwise invocation of so extreme a sanction. It would be an interesting irony if doubts about the propriety of certain uses of the criminal sanction prove to contribute to a restrictive trend in the criminal process that in the end requires a choice among uses and finally an abandonment of some of the very uses that stirred the original doubts, but for a reason quite unrelated to those doubts.

There are two kinds of problems that need to be dealt with in any model of the criminal process. One is what the rules shall be. The other is how the rules shall be implemented. The second is at least as important as the first. As we shall see time and again in our detailed development of the models, the distinctive difference between the two models is not only in the rules of conduct that they lay down but also in the sanctions that are to be invoked when a claim is presented that the rules have been breached and, no less importantly, in the timing that is permitted or required for the invocation of those sanctions.

As I have already suggested, the due process model locates at least some of the sanctions for breach of the operative rules in the criminal process itself. The relation between these two aspects of the process—the rules and the sanctions for their breach—is a purely formal one unless there is some mechanism for bringing them into play with each other. The hinge between them in the due process model is the availability of legal counsel. This has a double aspect. Many of the rules that the model requires are couched in terms of the availability of counsel to do various things at various stages of the process—this is the conventionally recognized aspect; beyond it, there is a pervasive assumption that counsel is necessary in order to invoke sanctions for breach of any of the rules. The more freely available these sanctions are, the more important is the role of counsel in seeing to it that the sanctions are appropriately invoked. If the process is seen as a series of occasions for checking its own operation, the role of counsel is a much more nearly central one than is the case in a process that is seen as primarily concerned with expeditious determination of factual guilt. And if equality of operation is a governing norm, the availability of counsel to some is seen as requiring it for all. Of all the controverted aspects of the criminal process, the right to counsel, including the role of government in its provision, is the most dependent on what one's model of the process looks like, and the least susceptible of resolution unless one has confronted the antinomies of the two models.

I do not mean to suggest that questions about the right to counsel disappear if one adopts a model of the process that conforms more or less closely to the crime control model, but only that such questions become absolutely central if one's model moves very far down the spectrum of possibilities toward the pure due process model. The reason for this centrality is to be found in the assumption underlying both models that the process is an adversary one in which the initiative in invoking relevant rules rests primarily on the parties concerned, the state, and the accused. One could construct models that placed central responsibility on adjudicative agents such as committing magistrates and trial judges. And there are, as we shall see, marginal but nonetheless important adjustments in the role of the adjudicative agents that enter into the models with which we are concerned. For present purposes it is enough to say that these adjustments are marginal, that the animating presuppositions that underlie both models in the context of the American criminal system relegate the adjudicative agents to a relatively passive role, and therefore place central importance on the role of counsel.

One last introductory note. . . . What assumptions do we make about the sources of authority to shape the real-world operations of the criminal process? Recognizing that our models are only models, what agencies of government have the power to pick and choose between their competing demands? Once again, the limiting features of the American context come into play. Ours is not a system of legislative supremacy. The distinctively American institution of judicial review exercises a limiting and ultimately a shaping influence on the criminal process. Because the crime control model is basically an affirmative model, emphasizing at every turn the existence and exercise of official power, its validating authority is ultimately legislative (although proximately administrative). Because the due process model is basically a negative model, asserting limits on the nature of official power and on the modes of its exercise, its validating authority is judicial and requires an appeal to supra-legislative law, to the law of the Constitution. To the extent that tensions between the two models are resolved by deference to the due process model, the authoritative force at work is the judicial power, working in the distinctively judicial mode of invoking the sanction of nullity. That is at once the strength and the weakness of the due process model: its strength because in our system the appeal to the Constitution provides the last and the overriding word; its weakness because saying no in specific cases is an exercise in futility unless there is a general willingness on the part of the officials who operate the process to apply negative prescriptions across the board. It is no accident that statements reinforcing the due process model come from the courts, while at the same time facts denying it are established by the police and prosecutors.

Notes

[1] Mapp v. Ohio, 367 U.S. 643 (1961); Ker v. California, 374 U.S. 23 (1963).

[2] See President's Commission on Law Enforcement and Administration of Justice, *The Challenge of Crime in a Free Society* (Washington, D.C., 1967), chap. 2.

[3] Griffin v. Illinois, 351 U.S. 12, 19 (1956).

[4] *Finality in Criminal Law and Federal Habeas Corpus for State Prisoners*, 76 Harv. L. Rev. 441, 442 (1963).

Crime Control, Due Process and "The Case for the Prosecution"
A Problem of Terminology?

Peter Duff

This short article was prompted by the recent exchange in this journal between Smith (1997) and McConville, Sanders and Long (1997) (henceforth MSL), authors of "The Case for the Prosecution." It is intended simply as an observation about the terms in which the debate is being conducted rather than an independent attempt at theorization. My concern is that confusion over the terminology, stemming directly from the writings of Packer (1969), has obscured the precise nature of the debate. Further argument, I leave to the protagonists.

Essentially, the problem is that the term *crime control* is used in two very different senses. First, it is used to describe the overall purpose of the criminal justice system—i.e., the repression of criminal conduct. Secondly, it is also used as a label—a kind of shorthand—to encapsulate a particular set of values which influences the system. As is well known, Packer's analytical framework contrasted two different "complexes of values": the "crime control model" and the "due process model." His argument was that these sets of values "compete for priority" in the operation of the criminal justice

Duff, Peter. (1998). *British Journal of Criminology 38*(4), pp. 611–615, by permission of the author and Oxford University Press.

process and he sought to show the way in which they were influential in shaping the system and the actions of its functionaries (pp. 153–4). It is fair to say that Smith and MSL do refer to this terminological problem at the outset of their articles but, unfortunately, this insight seems to get lost in the heat of the following argument. Consequently, there is a tendency to use the term *crime control* in two distinct senses—sometimes to describe the goal of the criminal justice system and sometimes to summarize a complex of values which influences its operation—and confusion inevitably follows.

Perhaps I can clarify the problem with a simple change of terminology. The above commentators all clearly agree that the overall purpose of the criminal justice system is the repression of criminal conduct (Packer 1969:158; Smith 1997:320; MSL 1997:355).[1] As Ashworth puts it, in a useful earlier contribution to this debate, the "general justifying aim" of the process is *crime control*. Thus, let us continue to describe the goal of the criminal justice process as *crime control* but let us change the terminology when we are talking about the complex of values which Packer also labels in this way. Let us call it the *efficiency model*. I should stress that this change of nomenclature does not imply that the complex of values it represents is any different from that identified by Packer, nor does it distort his analytical framework in any way. In summarizing the crime control value position, Packer describes it as requiring that "primary attention be paid to the efficiency with which the criminal process operates," as demanding "efficiency of operation" and as an "administrative, almost a managerial, model" (pp. 158–9). In one sense of course, it does not matter what we rename this complex of values, as long as we distinguish it from the goal of crime control, but the term *efficiency model* does seem to capture its essence.

Returning to the present debate, Smith's central accusation is that MSL ignore the fact that the goal of the criminal justice system is crime control and elect due process in its place. The latter rightly refute this allegation because it is perfectly clear that they have always accepted that crime control is the overall aim of the system.[2] But the response of MSL illustrates the terminological problem: ". . . the fundamental *goal* of criminal justice is crime control. . . . To put it another way, in pursuit of crime control, a criminal justice system may select crime control *values*, due process values, or a mixture of both" (p. 356) (emphasis added). What their work actually does is to examine the extent to which the actions of those running the system, particularly the police, draw upon the values of the efficiency model at the expense of the due process model. As they claim, this is a perfectly legitimate enterprise with a long tradition in criminological research (as exemplified in Skolnick's 1966 classic work). In return, MSL accuse Smith of engaging in "descriptive" rather than "critical" sociology or, more bluntly, of being an apologist for police (mal) practice and simply accepting "canteen culture" and its consequences. But this also is perhaps not entirely fair. Smith is "critical" in that he attacks the blind adherence, as he would see it, to the due process model that informs many liberal critiques of the criminal justice process. Given that Smith is clearly starting from a value position closer to that of the efficiency model than most academic researchers, it is inevitable that he is less critical of the police than MSL who are explicitly starting from a due process value position. As I understand it, the purpose of Smith's article is to challenge the common academic conclusion that the criminal justice system currently gives too much weight to the values of efficiency at the expense of due process.

In other words, although I am simplifying somewhat, we might identify the dispute between Smith and MSL as being primarily about the correct balance to be struck in the pursuit of crime control between the values of due process and the values of efficiency. The main thrust of MSL's argument is that insufficient weight is attached in practice to the values of due process while Smith's principal contention is that MSL seriously underestimate the weight which ought to be attached to the values of efficiency.[3] Thus, what is portrayed as each other's misunderstanding of the concepts and fundamentally confused analysis disguises nothing more than what is in essence a difference of opinion about the appropriate compromise to be reached between considerations of efficiency and the need to respect civil liberties in modern liberal society's efforts to repress criminal conduct. . . .

In summary, before this type of debate, which is based on Packer's models of the criminal justice system, proceeds further, it might be as well if the protagonists were to clarify the terminology. I have suggested that it is helpful at the outset to distinguish between the goal, or the "general justifying aim," of the criminal justice system and the types of values which have to be considered and weighed in determining the appropriate mechanisms which society may adopt in its attempt to achieve this goal. In particular, it is profoundly confusing to use the term *crime control* interchangeably to refer both to the goal of the system and to a complex of values that influences what one regards as desirable in the pursuit of that goal. It may help to clarify the issues if the complex of values hitherto labeled as the *crime control model* is renamed as the *efficiency model*. The discerning reader will note that I have made no attempt to explore the theoretical relationships between the goal of crime control and the value complexes of due process and efficiency. As Ashworth notes, these relationships are not fully worked out in Packer's framework (p. 413, n. 4) and it is beyond the scope of this article, and probably my capabilities to address this problem.[4] My principal aim has simply been to clarify what is at issue between Smith and MSL. In essence, the dispute is quite straightforward but this is obscured by the attacks of each protagonist on the other's methodology and grasp of Packer's analytical framework. What the parties are arguing about is the appropriate balance which ought to be struck between considerations of due process and efficiency in the operation of the criminal justice system. That is an important argument but ultimately one's stance probably depends as much upon one's individual judgement than upon methodological purity and dispassionate academic analysis.

Notes

[1] Other theorists might disagree with this view but that need not concern us here.

[2] As Damaska (1973: 575) points out in a useful discussion of Packer's models, it is "conceptually impossible to imagine a criminal process whose dominant concern is a desire to protect the individual from public officials." Smith (pp. 335–6) makes a similar point: "It would make no sense to say that the criminal justice system has the function of delivering due process." His criticism of MSL is that this is precisely what they are saying, an accusation they reject.

[3] Although it need not concern us here, a subsidiary point to dispute is that MSL appear to argue that the lack of influence of due process values is structurally inevitable given a capitalist political system while Smith thinks that the balance struck between the competing value systems is not as determined by structural factors as MSL would have us believe.

[4] It is clear at least that the two value systems are not opposing equivalents nor do they bear the same relationship to the goal of crime control. The values of the efficiency model derive primarily from administrative and economic considerations whereas the values of due process are largely rooted in liberal democratic ideology, "the concept of the primacy of the individual and the complementary concept of limitation on official power" (Packer, p. 165). Efficiency values are largely generated from within the system (although external factors do play a role, for instance, governmental pressure to control public expenditure), whereas the values of the due process model are primarily derived from outside the system. Further, and most important, the due process model severely restricts the way in which the goal of crime control may be pursued whereas the efficiency model does not impinge upon the goal of crime control to nearly the same extent. Packer (pp. 163-5) claims that the due process model, as well as preventing the unbridled pursuit of crime control, also advances that goal to some extent, in that due process values are concerned with increasing the precision of fact-finding and this brings additional public confidence to the process which thereby helps the state's efforts to control crime. Smith echoes this view (pp. 333–4). Damaska (1973:575–6) is rightly skeptical of this admittedly "ancillary" justification of due process and argues it would be more realistic and useful to envisage a "purified" due process model which is concerned solely with protecting individual rights and restricting the powers of public officials.

References

Ashworth, A. (1979), "Concepts of Criminal Justice," *Criminal Law Review*, 412.

Damaska, M. (1973), "Evidentiary Barriers to Conviction and Two Models of Criminal Procedure: A Comparative Study," *University of Pennsylvania Law Review*, 121: 506.

McBarnet, D. (1978), "False Dichotomies in Criminal Justice Research," in J. Baldwin and A. K. Bottomley, eds., *Criminal Justice*, 23–34. London: Martin Robertson.

―――― (1979), "Arrest: the Legal Context of Policing," in S. Holdaway, ed., *The British Police*, 24–40. London: Arnold.

McConville, M., Sanders, A. and Long, R. (1997), "Descriptive or Critical Sociology: The Choice is Yours," *British Journal of Criminology*, 37/3: 347.

Packer, H. (1969), *The Limits of the Criminal Sanction*. Stanford: Stanford University Press.

Skolnick, J. (1966), *Justice Without Trial*. New York: Wiley.

―――― (1989), *Review of Conviction* by D. McBarnet, *Journal of Criminal Law and Criminology*, 73:1329.

Smith, D. J. (1997), "Case Construction and the Goals of Criminal Process," *British Journal of Criminology*, 37/3: 319.

Criminal Justice
as Politics

It would be difficult to exclude the political dimension of criminal justice and crime control when using any of the eight theoretical orientations outlined in this book. After all, we are studying, among other things, the behavior of law and the government. However, viewing the criminal justice apparatus through political lenses means that we wrap our minds around criminal justice using the language and thinking of political scientists.[1] Our interdisciplinary field of study includes, as two of its more important influences, the disciplines of political science and public administration.[2]

---

[1] Acclaimed journalist and member of the Jerry Lee Center of Criminology Ted Gest wrote *Crime and Politics: Big Government's Erratic Campaign for Law and Order* in 2001. He traces the political response to crime in the United States from the mid-1960s to the present. Gest theorizes that partisan politics has largely *determined* criminal justice policies. His work assesses the significance of crime and crime control being defined by politicians and bureaucrats as national-level issues requiring national-level responses. Gest sees national leaders exploiting crime and justice issues, resulting in unethical and ineffective public policies. The theorists included in this section use the political orientation to reach different conclusions.

[2] A large number of academic programs offering degrees in criminal justice are housed within political science programs. Probably the most well-known is the program at Washington State University. Academics with political science and/or public administration educations have made a substantial contribution to the study of criminal justice.

Thinking Politically: The Pursuit of Interests

As Packer's due process/crime control orientation illustrated, there is a constant pull between crime control interests, due process interests, and needs-based justice interests. There are a number of diverse interests throughout the criminal justice system. Obtaining a large enough piece of the resource pie stimulates competing interests: think of the juvenile probation officer trying to make a livable wage, or the large-scale police agency competing to secure a multi-million-dollar grant.

From the standpoint of the political framework, all criminal justice activity and thinking is interest-based. The pursuit of these divergent interests activates *conflict, power struggles, influence building*, and hardened *ideological positions*. Importantly, most political scientists do not interpret the clash of divergent interests as inevitably leading toward chaos, uncertainty, and dysfunction; rather, they interpret these conditions through Aristotelian lenses: diverse interests in democratic societies are essential building blocks for negotiation, resolution, rational policy, and order.[3] Kevin Wright, while emphasizing the existence of divergent interests and power struggles, argues in article 9 that conflict ultimately has a balancing and stabilizing effect on the criminal justice system resulting in functional outcomes.[4]

The political metaphor assumes that politics is at play at all levels of the criminal justice apparatus—from the everyday actions of the corrections or police practitioner, to the political influence of local communities, to agencies involved in criminal justice policy formation and implementation, and to law-making at the national and state levels. Unfortunately this is a large theoretical bite to include in one section of an eight-section book. To complicate matters, the next four orientations covered in this book also employ political concepts and theories. The late-modern orientation (chapter 9), for example, theorizes the influence of macro-political tensions, what they label "neo-liberal" and "neo-conservative" politics (O'Malley, 2000). The oppression orientation (chapter 8) views criminal justice activities as the political repression of groups that threaten state power and legitimacy. To simplify matters, the articles selected for the political orientation concentrate on only a few areas of emphasis.

---

[3] See Duffee (1990) for an excellent discussion of the fallacies and counterproductive consequences of the consensus vs. conflict debate.

[4] Please note that Wright relies on a particular strain of thinking about conflict, developed in Coser's (1954) *The Functions of Social Conflict*. In attempting to integrate structural functionalism with conflict theory, Coser emphasized the functional nature of conflict. Some theorists have focused on the differences in power within conflicts based on economic or political inequalities (Dahrendorf, 1959; Giddens, 1973).

Leftist and Rightist Ideology
in Criminal Justice

Article 8 by Walter Miller, despite being published almost three decades ago, is still the best descriptive discussion of leftist and rightist thinking in our field. His theoretical aims are clear:

> The major contention of this presentation is that ideology and its consequences exert a powerful influence on the policies and procedures of those who conduct the enterprise of criminal justice, and that the degree and kinds of influence go largely unrecognized. Ideology is the permanent hidden agenda of criminal justice. (Miller, 1973, p. 142)

When I teach advanced criminal justice studies at the graduate level, one of the best methods I've found to help students make theoretical sense of criminal justice and crime control is to dissect the inner workings of political ideology. Sam Walker (2001) similarly organizes *Sense and Nonsense about Crime and Drugs: A Policy Guide* around liberal and conservative thinking about crime and criminal justice. He theorizes that rigid ideological positions grounded in questionable assumptions are responsible for irrational and ineffective crime control policies. James Q. Wilson (1980) is generally perceived as representing a rightist perspective; Elliott Currie (1984) is generally perceived as representing a leftist perspective. The writings of each are often juxtaposed in the classroom as an effective heuristic tool to better understand our complex and ambiguous reactions to confronting crime.[5]

Is Wright Right?

Article 9 by Wright represents a mainstream political science orientation. It operates as an effective contrast to the closed-system orientation and is a nice compliment to Packer's competing value-clusters. It illuminates the political nature of the system—concentrating on its policy-making and policy-implementing functions.[6] It addresses how the decisions made by practitioners and agencies occur within the context of *local communities* and how the values and preferences of those communities influence criminal justice behavior. Along with the growth of community policing and community corrections, there has been a surge of interest in the criminal justice literature about the influence of local community poli-

---

[5] Stenson and Cowell (1991) include in their edited book, *The Politics of Crime Control*, an informative debate between Elliot Currie and James Q. Wilson.

[6] For an excellent overview and history of the public policy orientation, see Denhardt's (1984) *Theories of Public Organization*, especially chapter 6, "The Policy Emphasis in Public Administration."

tics on the operations of police, courts, and corrections (see, for example, Cole, Gertz, & Bunger, 2002; Duffee, 1990; Eisenstein, Flemming, & Nardulli, 1988; Miller, 2001).[7]

The Symbolism of Getting Tough

Article 10 by Stuart Scheingold is a classic in the field; it reaffirms what we discover in the other two articles in this section and adds a few important concepts. Scheingold is interested in the national-level political scene—examining the rise and effect of what he calls *the politics of law and order*. Although Scheingold is critical of politicians exploiting crime and criminal justice issues for personal gain, he asserts that campaigns for law and order are symbolic gestures that will not result in meaningful reform (rational/legal orientation) or widespread repression (oppression orientation). *Symbolic politics*, therefore, for all its robust rhetoric, will only affect the actual operating policies of the criminal justice system to the extent allowed by the subcultural norms contained within local criminal justice agencies and local communities. In keeping with Jeffersonian notions of local democratic control, Scheingold prioritizes micro-political influences over macro-political influences when explaining criminal justice thinking and activities.

Two Directions

We could go in two different directions in accounting for the recent growth of the criminal justice apparatus using the political theoretical orientation. From Wright's conflict-as-functional angle, forced reaction theory would suffice. However, the majority of the literature using political filters is skeptical of political claims that a worsening crime problem necessitates an intensified criminal justice response. Since the 1960s, pleas for criminal justice growth have been successful political capital. Conservative law-and-order ideology has become a dominant force in U.S. culture, granting widespread support for *wars* on crime and drugs, whether symbolic or

[7] One could legitimately contend that this book should have included a separate *community* theoretical orientation (Duffee, 1990). I decided to omit it for several reasons: 1) the bulk of literature in this field, while impressive theoretically, examines community-level variables in explaining crime, not formal systems of social control; 2) community-oriented scholars, when they do address the criminal justice system, are merely recommending CJ-based solutions derived from their theory about crime; 3) while community policing reforms are touted as good indications of community theorizing in action, it is questionable whether this reform movement's rhetoric coincides with its community-based action; and 4) the political orientation includes community influence (DeMichelle & Kraska, 2001; Harcourt, 2001). See William Lyons (1999) for a solid use of the political theoretical orientation to make sense of community policing efforts. Lyons's analysis exposes the sobering realities of local communities attempting to form *partnerships* with the police.

real. Even with recent drops in the crime rate, the political push for expansion will likely remain a powerful factor in criminal justice growth.

References

Cole, G., Gertz, M. G., & Bunger, A. (2002). *The criminal justice system: Politics and policies* (8th ed.). Belmont, CA: Wadsworth.

Coser, L. (1956). *The functions of social conflict*. New York: Free Press.

Dahrendorf, R. (1959). *Class and class conflict in industrial society.* Stanford: Stanford University Press.

Denhardt, R. B. (1984). *Theories of public organization*. Pacific Grove, CA: Brooks/Cole.

DeMichelle, M., & Kraska, P. B. (2001). Community policing in battle-garb: Paradox or coherent strategy? In P. B. Kraska (Ed.), *Militarizing the American criminal justice system: Changing roles of the armed forces and police* (pp. 87–104). Boston: Northeastern University Press.

Duffee, D. E. (1990). *Explaining criminal justice: Community theory and criminal justice reform*. Prospect Heights, IL: Waveland Press.

Eisenstein, J., Flemming, R. B., & Nardulli, P. F. (1988). *The contours of justice: Communities and their courts*. New York: HarperCollins.

Gest, T. (2001). *Crime and politics: Big government's erratic campaign for law and order*. New York: Oxford University Press.

Giddens, A. (1973). *The class structure of advanced societies*. London: Hutchinson.

Harcourt, B. E. (2001). *Illusion of order: The false promise of broken windows policing*. Cambridge and London: Harvard University Press.

Lyons, W. (1999). *The politics of community policing: Rearranging the power to punish*. Ann Arbor: University of Michigan Press.

Miller, L. L. (2001). Looking for postmodernism in all the wrong places: Implementing a new penology. *British Journal of Criminology, 41*(2), 168–184.

O'Malley, P. (2000). Criminologies of catastrophe? Understanding criminal justice on the edge of the new millennium. *The Australian and New Zealand Journal of Criminology, 33*(2), 153–167.

Stenson, K., & Cowell, D. (1991). *The politics of crime control*. London: Sage.

Walker, S. (2001). *Sense and nonsense about crime and drugs: A policy guide*. Belmont, CA: Wadsworth.

Ideology and Criminal Justice Policy
Some Current Issues

Walter B. Miller

. . . The term "ideology" may be used in many ways.[1] It will be used here only to refer to a set of general and abstract beliefs or assumptions about the correct or proper state of things, particularly with respect to the moral order and political arrangements, which serve to shape one's positions on specific issues. Several aspects of ideology as used in this sense should be noted. First, ideological assumptions are generally preconscious rather than explicit, and serve, under most circumstances, as unexamined presumptions underlying positions taken openly. Second, ideological assumptions bear a strong emotional charge. This charge is not always evident, but it can readily be activated by appropriate stimuli, in particular by direct challenge. During the process of formation, ideological premises for particular individuals are influenced by a variety of informational inputs, but once established they become relatively impervious to change, since they serve to receive or reject new evidence in terms of a self-contained and self-reinforcing system.

The major contention of this presentation is that ideology and its consequences exert a powerful influence on the policies and procedures of

Originally published by the Northwestern University School of Law, *Journal of Criminal Law and Criminology 64*(2), 141–154. Copyright © 1973 Walter B. Miller. Reprinted with permission of the author.

those who conduct the enterprise of criminal justice, and that the degree and kinds of influence go largely unrecognized. Ideology is the permanent hidden agenda of criminal justice.

The discussion has two major aims. First, assuming that the generally implicit ideological basis of criminal justice commands strong, emotional, partisan allegiance, I shall attempt to state explicitly the major assumptions of relevant divergent ideological positions in as neutral or as nonpartisan a fashion as possible. Second, some of the consequences of such ideologies for the processes of planning, program, and policy in criminal justice will be examined. . . .

Ideological Positions

Right: Crusading Issues

Crusading issues of the right differ somewhat from those of the left; they generally do not carry as explicit a message of movement toward new forms, but imply instead that things should be reconstituted or restored. However, the component of the message that says, "Things should be different from the way they are now," comes through just as clearly as in the crusading issues of the left. Current crusading issues of the right with respect to crime and how to deal with it include the following:

1. *Excessive leniency toward lawbreakers.* This is a traditional complaint of the right, accentuated at present by the publicity given to reform programs in corrections and policing, as well as to judicial activity at various levels.

2. *Favoring the welfare and rights of lawbreakers over the welfare and rights of their victims, of law enforcement officials, and the law-abiding citizen.* This persisting concern is currently activated by attention to prisoners' rights, rehabilitation programs, attacks on police officers by militants, and in particular by a series of well-publicized Supreme Court decisions aimed to enhance the application of due process.

3. *Erosion of discipline and of respect for constituted authority.* This ancient concern is currently manifested in connection with the general behavior of youth, educational policies, treatment of student dissidents by college officials, attitudes and behavior toward law-enforcement, particularly the police.

4. *The cost of crime.* Less likely to arouse the degree of passion evoked by other crusading issues, resentment over what is seen as the enormous and increasing cost of crime and dealing with criminals—a cost borne directly by the hard working and law-abiding citizen— nevertheless remains active and persistent.

5. *Excessive permissiveness.* Related to excessive leniency, erosion of discipline, and the abdication of responsibility by authorities, this

trend is seen as a fundamental defect in the contemporary social order, affecting many diverse areas such as sexual morality, discipline in the schools, educational philosophies, child-rearing, judicial handling of offenders, and media presentation of sexual materials.

Right: General Assumptions

These crusading issues, along with others of similar import, are not merely ritualized slogans, but reflect instead a more abstract set of assumptions about the nature of criminal behavior, the causes of criminality, responsibility for crime, appropriate ameliorative measures, and, on a broader level, the nature of man and of a proper kind of society. These general assumptions provide the basic charter for the ideological stance of the right as a whole, and a basis for distinguishing among the several subtypes along the points of the ideological scale. Major general assumptions of the right might be phrased as follows:

1. The individual is directly responsible for his own behavior. He is not a passive pawn of external forces, but possesses the capacity to make choices between right and wrong—choices which he makes with an awareness of their consequences.

2. A central requirement of a healthy and well functioning society is a strong moral order which is explicit, well-defined, and widely adhered to. Preferably the tenets of this system of morality should be derived from and grounded in the basic precepts of a major religious tradition. Threats to this moral order are threats to the very existence of the society. Within the moral order, two clusters are of particular importance:

   a. Tenets which sustain the family unit involve morally-derived restrictions on sexual behavior, and obligations of parents to maintain consistent responsibility to their children and to one another.

   b. Tenets which pertain to valued personal qualities include: taking personal responsibility for one's behavior and its consequences; conducting one's affairs with the maximum degree of self-reliance and independence, and the minimum of dependency and reliance on others, particularly public agencies; loyalty, particularly to one's country; achieving one's ends through hard work, responsibility to others, and self-discipline.

3. Of paramount importance is the security of the major arenas of one's customary activity—particularly those locations where the conduct of family life occurs. A fundamental personal and family right is safety from crime, violence, and attack, including the right of citizens to take necessary measures to secure their own safety, and the right to bear arms, particularly in cases where official agencies may appear ineffective in doing so.

4. Adherence to the legitimate directives of constituted authority is a primary means for achieving the goals of morality, correct individual behavior, security, and other valued life conditions. Authority in the service of social and institutional rules should be exercised fairly but firmly, and failure or refusal to accept or respect legitimate authority should be dealt with decisively and unequivocally.

5. A major device for ordering human relations in a large and heterogeneous society is that of maintaining distinctions among major categories of persons on the basis of differences in age, sex, and so on, with differences in religion, national background, race, and social position of particular importance. While individuals in each of the general categories should be granted the rights and privileges appropriate thereto, social order in many circumstances is greatly facilitated by maintaining both conceptual and spatial separation among the categories.

Left: Crusading Issues

Crusading issues of the left generally reflect marked dissatisfaction with characteristics of the current social order, and carry an insistent message about the desired nature and direction of social reform. Current issues of relevance to criminal justice include:

1. *Overcriminalization.* This reflects a conviction that a substantial number of offenders delineated under current law are wrongly or inappropriately included, and applies particularly to offenses such as gambling, prostitution, drug abuse, abortion, pornography, and homosexuality.

2. *Labeling and Stigmatization.* This issue is based on a conception that problems of crime are aggravated or even created by the ways in which actual or potential offenders are regarded and treated by persons in authority. To the degree a person is labeled as "criminal," "delinquent," or "deviant," will he be likely to so act.

3. *Overinstitutionalization.* This reflects a dissatisfaction over prevalent methods of dealing with suspected or convicted offenders whereby they are physically confined in large institutional facilities. Castigated as "warehousing," this practice is seen as having a wide range of detrimental consequences, many of which are implied by the ancient phrase "schools for crime." Signaled by a renewed interest in "incarceration," prison reform has become a major social cause of the left.

4. *Overcentralization.* This issue reflects dissatisfaction with the degree of centralized authority existing in organizations which deal with crime—including police departments, correctional systems, and crime-related services at all government levels. Terms which

carry the thrust of the proposed remedy are local control, decentralization, community control, a new populism, and citizen power.

5. *Discriminatory Bias.* A particularly blameworthy feature of the present system lies in the widespread practice of conceiving and reacting to large categories of persons under class labels based on characteristics such as racial background, age, sex, income level, sexual practices, and involvement in criminality. Key terms here are racism, sexism, minority oppression and brutality.

Left: General Assumptions

As in the case of the rightist positions, these crusading issues are surface manifestations of a set of more basic and general assumptions, which might be stated as follows:

1. Primary responsibility for criminal behavior lies in conditions of the social order rather than in the character of the individual. Crime is to a greater extent a product of external social pressures than of internally generated individual motives, and is more appropriately regarded as a symptom of social dysfunction than as a phenomenon in its own right. The correct objective of ameliorative efforts, therefore, lies in the attempt to alter the social conditions that engender crime rather than to rehabilitate the individual.

2. The system of behavioral regulation maintained in America is based on a type of social and political order that is deficient in meeting the fundamental needs of the majority of its citizens. This social order, and the official system of behavioral regulation that it includes, incorporates an obsolete morality not applicable to the conditions of a rapidly changing technological society, and disproportionately geared to sustain the special interests of restricted groups, but which still commands strong support among working class and lower middle-class sectors of the population.

3. A fundamental defect in the political and social organization of the United States and in those components of the criminal justice enterprise that are part of this system is an inequitable and unjust distribution of power, privilege, and resources—particularly of power. This inequity pervades the entire system, but appears in its more pronounced forms in the excessive centralization of governmental functions and consequent powerlessness of the governed, the military-like, hierarchical authority systems found in police and correctional organization, and policies of systematic exclusion from positions of power and privilege for those who lack certain preferred social characteristics. The prime objective of reform must be to redistribute the decision-making power of the criminal justice enterprise rather than to alter the behavior of actual or potential offenders.

4. A further defect of the official system is its propensity to make distinctions among individuals based on major categories or classes within society such as age, sex, race, social class, criminal or non-criminal. Healthy societal adaptation for both the offender and the ordinary citizen depends on maintaining the minimum separation—conceptually and physically—between the community at large and those designated as "different" or "deviant." Reform efforts must be directed to bring this about.

5. Consistent with the capacity of external societal forces to engender crime, personnel of official agencies play a predominantly active role, and offenders a predominantly reactive role, in situations where the two come in contact. Official agents of behavioral regulation possess the capability to induce or enhance criminal behavior by the manner in which they deal with those who have or may have engaged in crime. These agents may define offenders as basically criminal, expose them to stigmatization, degrade them on the basis of social characteristics, and subject them to rigid and arbitrary control.

6. The sector of the total range of human behavior currently included under the system of criminal sanctions is excessively broad, including many forms of behavior (for example, marijuana use, gambling, homosexuality) which do not violate the new morality and forms which would be more effectively and humanely dealt with outside the official system of criminal processing. Legal codes should be redrafted to remove many of the behavioral forms now proscribed, and to limit the discretionary prerogatives of local authorities over apprehension and disposition of violators. . . .

Consequences of Ideology

. . . There is an additional important parameter which must also be considered: that of intensity—the degree of emotional charge which attaches to the assumptions. It is the capacity of these positions to evoke the most passionate kinds of reactions and to become infused with deeply felt, quasi-religious significance that constitutes the crucial element in the difference between testable assumptions and ideological tenets. This dimension has the power to transform plausibility into ironclad certainty, conditional belief into ardent conviction, the reasoned advocate into the implacable zealot. Rather than being looked upon as useful and conditional hypotheses, these assumptions, for many, take the form of the sacred and inviolable dogma of the one true faith, the questioning of which is heresy, and the opposing of which is profoundly evil.

This phenomenon—ideological intensification—appears increasingly to exert a powerful impact on the entire field. Leslie Wilkins has recorded his opinion that the criminal justice enterprise is becoming progressively more scientific and secularized;[2] an opposite, or at least concurrent, trend is here suggested—that it is becoming progressively more ideologized. The consequences are many. Seven will be discussed briefly: Polarization, Reverse Projection, Ideologized Selectivity, Informational Constriction, Catastrophism, Magnification of Prevalence, and Distortion of Opposing Positions.

Polarization. Polarization is perhaps the most obvious consequence of ideological intensification. The more heavily a belief takes on the character of sacred dogma, the more necessary it becomes to view the proponents of opposing positions as devils and scoundrels, and their views as dangerous and immoral. Cast in this framework of the sacred and the profane, of virtuous heroes and despicable villains, the degree of accommodation and compromise that seems essential to the complex enterprise of criminal justice planning becomes, at best, enormously complicated, and at worst, quite impossible.

Reverse Projection. This is a process whereby a person who occupies a position at a given point along the ideological scale perceives those who occupy any point closer to the center than his own as being on the opposite side of the scale. Three aspects of this phenomenon, which appears in its most pronounced form at the extremes of the scale, should be noted. First, if one grants the logical possibility that there can exist a "centrist" position—not a position which maintains no assumptions, but one whose assumptions are "mixed," "balanced," or not readily characterizable—then this position is perceived as "rightist" by those on the left, and "leftist" by those on the right. . . .

Ideologized Selectivity. The range of issues, problems, areas of endeavor, and arenas of activity relevant to the criminal justice enterprise is enormous. Given the vastness of the field relative to the availability of resources, decisions must be made as to task priorities and resource allocation. Ideology plays a paramount but largely unrecognized role in this process, to the detriment of other ways of determining priorities. Ideologized selectivity exerts a constant influence in determining which problem areas are granted greatest significance, which projects are supported, what kinds of information are gathered and how research results are analyzed and interpreted. Divergent resource allocation policies of major federal agencies can be viewed as directly related to the dominant ideological orientation of the agency.

Only one example of ideologized selectivity will be cited here. The increasing use of drugs, soft and hard, and an attendant range of drug-related crime problems is certainly a major contemporary development. The importance of this problem is reflected in the attention devoted to it by academic criminologists. One major reason for this intensive attention is that explanations for the spread of drug use fit the ideological assumptions shared by most academicians (drug use is an understandable product of alienation resulting from the failure of the system to provide adequate meaning and quality to life). Also one major ameliorative proposal, the liberalization of drug laws, accords directly with a crusading issue of the left—decriminalization.

Another contemporary phenomenon, quite possibly of similar magnitude, centers on the apparent disproportionate numbers of low-status urban blacks arrested for violent and predatory crimes, brought to court and sent to prison. While not entirely ignored by academic criminologists, the relatively low amount of attention devoted to this phenomenon stands in sharp contrast to the intensive efforts evident in the field of drugs. Important aspects of the problem of black crime do not fit the ideological assumptions of the majority of academic criminologists. Insofar as the issue is studied, the problem is generally stated in terms of oppressive, unjust and discriminatory behavior by society and its law-enforcement agents—a formulation that accords with that tenet of the left which assumes the capacity of officials to engender crime by their actions, and the parallel assumption that major responsibility for crime lies in conditions of the social order. Approaches to the problem that involve the careful collection of information relative to such characteristics of the population itself as racial and social status run counter to ideological tenets that call for the minimization of such distinctions both conceptually and in practice, and thus are left largely unattended.

Informational Constriction. An attitude which is quite prevalent in many quarters of the criminal justice enterprise today involves a depreciation of the value of research in general, and research on causes of crime in particular. Several reasons are commonly given, including the notion that money spent on research has a low payoff relative to that spent for action, that past research has yielded little of real value for present problems, and that research on causes of crime in particular is of little value since the low degree of consensus among various competing schools and theorists provides little in the way of unified conclusions or concrete guidance. Quite independent of the validity of such reasons, the anti-research stance can be seen as a logical consequence of ideological intensification.

For the ideologically committed at both ends of the scale, new information appears both useless and dangerous. It is useless because the basic answers, particularly with respect to causes, are already given, in their true and final form, by the ideology; it is dangerous because evidence provided by new research has the potential of calling into question ideologically established truths.

In line with this orientation, the present enterprise, that of examining the influence of ideology on criminal justice policy and programs, must be regarded with distaste by the ideologically intense—not only because it represents information of relevance to ideological doctrine, but also because the very nature of the analysis implies that ideological truth is relative.

Catastrophism.   Ideological partisans at both extremes of the scale are intensely committed to particular programs or policies they wish to see effected, and recurrently issue dire warnings of terrible catastrophes that will certainly ensue unless their proposals are adopted (Right: Unless the police are promptly given full power to curb criminality and unless rampant permissiveness toward criminals is halted, the country will surely be faced with an unprecedented wave of crime and violence; Left: Unless society promptly decides to provide the resources necessary to eliminate poverty, discrimination, injustice and exploitation, the country will surely be faced with a holocaust of violence worse than ever before). Such predictions are used as tactics in a general strategy for enlisting support for partisan causes: "Unless you turn to us and our program. . . ." That the great bulk of catastrophes so ominously predicted do not materialize does not deter catastrophism, since partisans can generally claim that it was the response to their warnings that forestalled the catastrophe. Catastrophism can thus serve to inhibit adaptation to real crises by casting into question the credibility of accurate prophets along with the inaccurate.

Magnification of Prevalence.   Ideological intensification produces a characteristic effect on perceptions of the empirical prevalence of phenomena related to areas of ideological concern. In general, targets of ideological condemnation are represented as far more prevalent than carefully collected evidence would indicate. Examples are estimates by rightists of the numbers of black militants, radical conspirators, and welfare cheaters, and by leftists of the numbers of brutal policemen, sadistic prison personnel, and totally legitimate welfare recipients.

Distortion of the Opposition.   To facilitate a demonstration of the invalidity of tenets on the opposite side of the ideological scale it is necessary for partisans to formulate the actual positions of the opposition in such a way as to make them most susceptible to refutation. Opposition positions are phrased to appear maximally illogical, irrational, unsupportable, simplistic, internally contradictory, and, if possible, contemptible or ludicrous. Such distortion impedes the capacity to adequately comprehend and represent positions or points of view which may be complex and extensively developed—a capacity that can be of great value when confronting policy differences based on ideological divergencies.

Implications

What are the implications of this analysis for those who face the demanding tasks of criminal justice action and planning? It might first appear that the prescription would follow simply and directly from the diagnosis. If the processes of formulating and implementing policy with respect to crime problems are heavily infused with ideological doctrine, and if this produces a variety of disadvantageous consequences, the moral would appear to be clear: work to reverse the trend of increased ideological intensification, bring out into the open the hidden ideological agenda of the criminal justice enterprise, and make it possible to release the energy now consumed in partisan conflict for a more direct and effective engagement with the problem field itself.

But such a prescription is both overly optimistic and overly simple. It cannot be doubted that the United States in the latter 20th century is faced with the necessity of confronting and adapting to a set of substantially modified circumstances, rooted primarily in technological developments with complex and ramified sociological consequences. It does not appear too far-fetched to propose that major kinds of necessary social adaptation in the United States can occur only through the medium of ardently ideological social movements—and that the costs of such a process must be borne in order to achieve the benefits it ultimately will confer. If this conception is correct, then ideological intensification, with all its dangers and drawbacks, must be seen as a necessary component of effective social adaptation, and the ideologists must be seen as playing a necessary role in the process of social change.

Even if one grants, however, that ideology will remain an inherent element of the policy-making process, and that while enhancing drive, dedication and commitment it also engenders rigidity, intolerance and distortion—one might still ask whether it is possible to limit the detrimental consequences of ideology without impairing its strengths, Such an objective is not easy, but steps can be taken in this direction. One such step entails an effort to increase one's capacity to discriminate between those types of information which are more heavily invested with ideological content and those which are less so. This involves the traditional distinction between "fact" and "value" statements.[3] The present delineation of selected ideological stances of the left and right provides one basis for estimating the degree to which statements forwarded as established conclusions are based on ideological doctrine rather than empirically supportable evidence. When assertions are made about what measures best serve the purposes of securing order, justice, and the public welfare, one should ask "How do we know this?" If statements appear to reflect in greater or lesser degree the interrelated patterns of premises, assumptions and prescriptions here characterized as "ideological," one should accommodate one's reactions accordingly.

Another step is to attempt to grant the appropriate degree of validity to positions on the other side of the scale from one's own. If ideological commitment plays an important part in the process of developing effective policy, one must bear in mind that both left and right have important parts to play. The left provides the cutting edge of innovation, the capacity to isolate and identify those aspects of existing systems which are least adaptive, and the imagination and vision to devise new modes and new instrumentalities for accommodating emergent conditions. The right has the capacity to sense those elements of the established order that have strength, value, or continuing usefulness, to serve as a brake on over-rapid alteration of existing modes of adaptation, and to use what is valid in the past as a guide to the future. Through the dynamic clash between the two forces, new and valid adaptations may emerge.

None of us can free himself from the influence of ideological predilections, nor are we certain that it would be desirable to do so. But the purposes of effective policy and practice are not served when we are unable to recognize in opposing positions the degree of legitimacy, validity, and humane intent they may possess. It does not seem unreasonable to ask of those engaged in the demanding task of formulating and implementing criminal justice policy that they accord to differing positions that measure of respect and consideration that the true ideologue can never grant.

Notes

[1] A classic treatment of ideology is K. Mannheim, *Ideology and Utopia* (1936). See ch. II.1 "Definition of Concepts." See also G. Myrdal, supra note 3, at 1035–64. There is an extensive literature, much of it sociological, dealing with ideology as it relates to a wide range of political and social phenomena, but the specific relation between ideology and criminal justice has received relatively little direct attention. Among more recent general discussions are E. Shils, *The Intellectuals and the Powers* (1972); Orlans, *The Political Uses of Social Research*, 393 Annals Am. Acad. Polit. & Soc. Sci. 28 (1971); Kelman, *I.Q., Race, and Public Debate*, 2 Hastings Center Rep. 8 (1972). Treatments more specific to crime and criminal justice appear in L. Radzinowicz, *Ideology and Crime* (1966); Andanaes, *Punishment and the Problem of General Prevention*, 8 Int'l Annals Criminology 285 (1969); Blumberg, *The Adversary System*, in C. Bersani, *Crime & Delinq.* 435 (1970); Glaser, *Criminology and Public Policy*, 6 Am. Sociologist 30 (1971).

[2] Wilkins, *Crime in the World of 1990*, 4 Futures 203 (1970).

[3] The classic formulations of the distinction between "factual" and "evaluative" content of statements about human behavior are those of Max Weber.

The Desirability of Goal Conflict within the Criminal Justice System

Kevin N. Wright

The Sociopolitical Environment

The theoretical and philosophical treatises and the structural analyses which advocate a monolithic criminal justice system seem to have conveniently ignored the sociopolitical environment in which the system exists. Such an oversight may be helpful in gaining public attention to one's ideas but is most unfortunate from a practical and pragmatic standpoint. The essence of a system as complex as criminal justice simply cannot be understood from the perspective which considers it as an isolated system. Nor can any proposal for significant planned change of the system claim any validity without considering the effects and constraints of the environment on that system.

In order to understand fully the implications of this idea, it is necessary to assess what type of a system criminal justice is. Numerous authors (Cyert and March, 1963; Emery and Trist, 1965; March and Simon, 1958; Terryberry, 1968) have argued that there are at least two types of social systems: simple and complex. In a simple system, goals can be specified, tasks to accomplish those goals can be undertaken, and progress can be monitored so that the system is self-regulating. These activities are possible

Journal of Criminal Justice, Vol. 9, pp. 211–213, 215, 217. Copyright © 1981. Elsevier Science.

because the internal and external environments of the system are relatively stable. . . . A complex system, on the other hand, does not exist in stable environments but rather finds itself in a complex and rapidly changing, or turbulent, environment which produces unpredictable changes within the system itself. This situation precludes rational, long-range, and macro-planned change. Because the environment is turbulent, and thus drastically and dynamically affecting the system, it is simply impossible to identify and specify a set of goals and to bring about some change to remodel the system (Emery and Trist, 1965, Terryberry, 1968). Duffee (1980:101) has made a very strong case that criminal justice is in fact a complex system:

> There is a wide variety of information available pertaining to the fact that criminal justice is not a monolithic, commonly conceived routine exercise. Criminal justice may well have different meanings in different places, or behave differently under contrasting conditions. Before we attempt to change actual operating agencies so that they might conform to a unitary motive of criminal justice operation, we may wish first to ask why such variations occur, whether these variations are functional equivalents, or whether the contrasting practices provided to the locality in which they are observed contributes to social order that might be lost if all criminal justice agencies behaved appropriately to the expectations of the analyst.

Duffee goes on to argue that criminal justice is, in fact, an institution much like the family or religion, and that its existence and what happens to it are unrelated to goal accomplishment.

Just as Duffee noted that there is a wide variety of information which indicates that criminal justice is not a monolithic system, there is, in particular, considerable information which indicates the political nature of criminal justice. Both conservatives and radicals concur that the basis of criminal justice, criminal law, is generated within an interest structure. (See Pound, 1943; Quinney, 1969:20–30.) Society is characterized by an interest structure in which various kinds of interests are distributed throughout that structure. Laws are the product of different interest groups vying for power to see their interests represented or realized. Theorists differ, however, in their perceptions concerning the output of the process as to whether the result is a product of compromise or domination.

Beyond the law, the actual administration and allocation of justice can also be viewed within the political context. Cole (1973:15–16) has provided one of the most concise reviews of this idea:

> Rather, like all legal institutions, the criminal justice system is "political" since it is engaged in the formulation and administration of public policies where choice must be made among such competing values as the rights of defendants, protection of persons and property, justice and freedom. That various groups in society interpret these values differently is obvious. Decisions result from the influence of the political power of decision makers and the relative strength of competing elites.

Cole (1973:16) continues by noting that there is a wide range of discretion within the administration of justice. Laws are often ambiguous and full enforcement of them is neither possible nor desirable. Decisions must, therefore, be made within the context of the community and its interest structure. Legal personnel, judges and prosecutors, must operate within a political environment. Their decisions must rest on the selection among competing dispositions which reflect dominant political interests. The actions of police executives are similarly influenced by the political nature of the position. To summarize, "in many ways the administration of criminal justice is a community affair; political influentials and interest groups work to insure that the law will be applied in ways consistent with their perception of local values" (Cole, 1973:17). . . .

Suggestions to create a monolithic, unified system deny the very existence of an interest structure characterized by a specific distribution of power. Therefore, to analyze the criminal justice system as if it did not exist within a political environment seems to be particularly naive. There are actors within the system who have a vested interest in its organization and operation, as well as influential persons within the community who want to see their particular interests represented. We know that interests vary from area to area. What is "justice" in an urban area may not be similarly perceived in a rural area. We know that what is "justice" to a police officer may not be "justice" to a young offender and his or her liberal public defender.

Radicals, to a degree, seem to understand the political context of the administration of justice in that their proposals for change are couched in terms of broader social changes. They realize that massive change in the system rests on massive social change. For example, the proponents of prison abolition fairly consistently advocate such change within a proposal for the creation of a society characterized by pervasive equality. (See Hawkins, 1976: 5–12 for a review of the abolitionist movement.) Radicals, however, often fail to consider the likelihood of drastic social change.

Liberals, conservatives, and structural analysts virtually ignore the political environment. They propose massive change in the system without considering the possibility that actors within the system as well as politically influential persons would resist that change. They fail to see that criminal justice is as it is for a reason, that there is a certain rationality in the seemingly structural irrationality of the system. (See Diesing's *Reason in Society* [1962] for a discussion of this conceptualization of rationality.) To create a monolithic, unified system would require a compatible set of values to serve as its basis; our complex society is not constituted in such a manner. Individuals working in the various components of the system, personnel in various jurisdictions, and influence bearers who have an interest in the administration of justice are extremely unlikely to agree on a single set of values. . . .

> In short, the public interest is constantly being defined and redefined. The balance among its various facets is always shifting. As is true in any area of public policy, the choice of ideals in criminal justice is the result

of an unpredictable, ever-changing and very intricate political process. . . . This often means that only incremental rather than sweeping
changes can be made. [Levine, Musheno, & Palumbo, 1980:38, 150]

Furthermore, there are at least three reasons why goal conflict and
fragmentation are advantageous to the processes and functioning of the
system. Conflict makes it possible to represent and protect different societal interests, establishes a system of checks and balances, and promotes a
smoothly operating offender-processing system. . . .

Mediations of Interests and System Adaptation

. . . As Coser (1956:137) has stated, "struggle may be an important
way to avoid conditions of disequilibrium by modifying the basis for power
relations. . . . Conflict, rather than being disruptive and dissociating, may
indeed be a means of balancing and hence maintaining a society as a
going concern." In an environment which is characterized by a high degree
of diversity of interest, conflict may well serve to produce an equilibrium,
a balance, rather than a state of disequilibrium. Interest groups are forced
continually to negotiate and compromise. Differences are thus mitigated,
and the system changes and adapts over time. Given the high diversity of
attitudes about justice and its administration, the conflicts and fragmentation within the criminal justice system probably provide the only means of
maintaining equilibrium among the various interest groups. Thus, a strong
law enforcement orientation can exist in a system which is also committed
to a program of diversion. Lack of specificity is thus an effective device
that allows various and diverse interests to be presented. . . .

Blumstein and Cohen (1973) have suggested that levels of punishment are consistent over time within cultures. They contend that as crime
increases the boundaries of criminality and the severity of punishment will
be modified in order to maintain a consistent level of punishment. Lack of
unification within the criminal justice system seems to sever a similar
function. Discretion, such as corrections mediating a prosecutor's long sentence, allows for an equalization process to occur. In this manner, the motivation of police is modified by the decision of the courts as to what crimes
will be prosecuted. Corrections monitors and modifies court decisions by
implementing forms of early release, thus mitigating the overemphasis of
incapacitation and retribution. The police and the courts monitor correctional decisions by being particularly attuned to previous offenders. This
interactive process within the system makes it possible, at least to some
degree, to maintain levels of punishment at consistent levels. . . .

Conclusions

. . . Any system which exhibits high diversity, even in the form of fragmentation, allows conflicts to be played out and resolved on a continual

basis. Any degree of centralization and unification, on the other hand, promotes rigidification and creates bureaucracy which is known to be an inefficient structure for change. A more unified criminal justice system would be more static, less able to respond to various interests. Greater investments of time and energy would be required to change the system.

As Coser has shown, conflict provides system stability rather than reduces it. The dynamic quality of a fragmented criminal justice system promotes a balance of power between antagonistic interests as it encourages adaptation and change. As societal attitudes and values fluctuate, the system can make corresponding changes. Unification would limit the ability of components to adjust their outputs to specific individual cases, to changes that occur over time, and to overreactions and mistakes by the other components. Furthermore, the balance which results from the exertion of influence on components by other components would be limited.

References

Blumstein, A., and Cohen, J. (1973). A theory of the stability of punishment. *Journal of Criminal Law and Criminology* 64:198–207.

Cole, G. F. (1973). *Politics and the administration of justice.* Beverly Hills: Sage.

Coser, L. A. (1956). *The functions of social conflict.* Glencoe: Free Press.

Cyert, R. M., and March, J. G. (1963). *A behavioral theory of the firm.* Englewood Cliffs: Prentice-Hall.

Diesing, P. (1962). *Reason in society.* Westport, CT: Greenwood Press.

Duffee, D. (1980). *Explaining criminal justice: Community theory and criminal justice reform.* Cambridge, MA: Oelgeschlager, Gunn and Hain.

Emery, F. E., and Trist, E. L. (1965). The causal texture of organizational environments. *Human Relations* 18:21–31.

Hawkins, G. (1976). *The prison: Policy and practice.* Chicago: The University of Chicago Press.

March, J. G., and Simon, H. A. (1958). *Organizations.* New York: John Wiley.

Pound, R. (1943). A survey of social interests. *Harvard Law Review* 57:1–39.

Quinney, R. (1969). *Crime and justice in society.* Boston: Little, Brown.

Terryberry, S. (1968). The evolution of organizational environments. *Administrative Science Quarterly* 12:490–613.

Crime, Culture, and Political Conflict

Stuart A. Scheingold

The Politics of Law and Order

The temptations to politicize crime are very strong. Insofar as politicians share the fears of their fellow citizens, it is only natural that they think about dealing with crime as an important political responsibility. But crime is a political opportunity as well as a responsibility. For the politician casting about for a campaign issue, crime has some compelling attractions. Most fundamentally, the public cares deeply about the issue, and the politician can expect considerable support from the media in capturing the public's attention. Crime is also an issue for which the myth of crime and punishment provides a simple and credible answer that the public is only too happy to embrace. Indeed, once public anxieties are aroused, it would be difficult . . . to sell any answer other than punishment. Finally, punitive solutions tend to bring politicians to office in distinctly favorable circumstances. Given a threat to its security, the public is likely to be permissive with its grants of money and authority.

It could be argued that in the long run, the crime issue is bound to backfire. Crime is, after all, an intractable problem, and there is good reason to doubt whether cracking down will be particularly effective. Will the voters not turn on the erstwhile law-and-order candidates once it becomes clear that they, as elected officials, are unable to deliver on their campaign

Scheingold, Stuart A. *The Politics of Law and Order: Street Crime and Public Policy*, pp. 75–88. New York: Longman, Inc. Permission granted by the author.

promises? Although this could happen, it is really not all that likely because of the sharp discontinuity between politics and policy.

This discontinuity stems from the distance that separates policy makers from the public. To borrow a distinction originally drawn by Murray Edelman, political campaigns are conducted at the "symbolic" level; actual policy making involves a much more "concrete" form of politics.

> For most men most of the time politics is a series of pictures in the mind, placed there by television news, newspapers, magazines, and discussions. The pictures create a moving panorama taking place in a world the mass public never quite touches, yet one its members come to fear or cheer, often with passion and sometimes with action.[1]

The public ordinarily responds to symbols rather than direct experience and is not really aware of the "concrete" effects of public policy. In contrast, political elites who participate regularly in the decisions that actually allocate resources are in a position to appreciate and calculate the costs and benefits of policy choices.

The policy promises made in political campaigns are part of a cycle of symbolic politics and have no necessary connection to concrete problem solving. This cycle is comprised of reassurance from the politicians in return for support from the public. In evoking such widely shared truths as the myth of crime and punishment, politicians tell the public what it wishes to hear, namely, that a complex and troubling problem can be solved in a simple and time-honored fashion. The public thus contributes to its own seduction. Indeed, as Lance Bennett argues, the politician who offers proposals that "fall outside the range of acceptable alternatives dictated by social myth" is asking for trouble.[2]

> Policies become means of affirming the larger images of the world on which they are based. In most policy areas it is more acceptable to suffer failure based on correct theories than it would be to achieve success at the price of sacrificing social values.[3]

Campaign promises, shaped by political myths, provide political leaders with the authority to govern and become "a set of lessons about how people should act and how they should apply values to social dilemmas.[4]

Once in office, there is no reason to assume that political leaders will actually pursue the punitive paths inherent in the myth of crime and punishment. In all likelihood, punitive programs will be developed and presented with the great fanfare appropriate to the symbolic level of politics. Nor should we necessarily think of these policy initiatives as disingenuous. They may or they may not be honest efforts to fulfill campaign promises. Either way, it is at this point that politicians are drawn into interactions with one another and with public officials, and for all these elites the stakes of the policy game are concrete and well understood. It is clear, in the first place, that crime, like other policy problems, is not amenable to simple solutions. In addition, since all reforms tend to alter the status quo and jeopardize vested interests, resistance to punitive policy programs can be taken for granted. Under these circumstances, it is reasonable to expect that even sincere politicians will look for ways to rationalize symbolically what they are unwilling or unable to accomplish concretely.

With these introductory principles in mind, it is time to look more carefully and explicitly at the politics of law and order. . . .

Crime and Politics

. . . There are good reasons for rejecting both the mainstream view of politicization as democracy at work and the Marxist notion of overt manipulation. The crime issue is neither imposed on us by a coalition of media executives and political elites nor does it emerge democratically from an increasingly victimized grass-roots constituency. Instead, what is operative is a complex and unpredictable process in which politicians seeking to obtain or retain office capitalize on public anxieties, which are only tenuously linked to the actual incidence of crime. In sum, the politics of law and order is best understood in terms of political conflict, which is shaped, to a significant degree, by the powerful symbols of American culture that determine how we understand the world around us.

The first problem with the mainstream explanation is that most of us experience crime abstractly and indirectly. We are therefore subjected to confusing and misleading messages by the agents of our vicarious victimization. Do we really know whether the crime rate is increasing or decreasing—much less anything about the rate of change? Consider the following leads to stories about crime appearing in the *New York Times*, clearly one of the more sober and responsible newspapers.

> February 9, 1982: "Homicides Involving Robbery in New York Rising, Study Shows."

> February 27, 1982: "New York City Felonies Rose Far Slower Last Year Than in '80."

> March 25, 1982: "30 of 73 New York Precincts Show Decreases in Felonies."

The issue is not whether these headlines or the stories can be reconciled with one another but whether the casual reader will add up all this information and come to a conclusion or will simply shape that ambiguous information to fit preconceived ideas. Even when the picture is clearer, our response may well be clouded by "extraneous" considerations. It is no doubt true, for example, that the sharp increases in street crime beginning in the middle 1960s contributed to our anxieties and, consequently, to the emergence of crime as a political issue. It is just as certain to me that fear of street crime was inextricably linked to anxieties about the expropriation of the streets by a variety of dissident and disaffected Americans, thus lending impetus to the process of politicization.

The agents of vicarious victimization also give us an exaggerated sense of jeopardy. This is true of neighbors and the news media as well as politicians.[5] It is hardly surprising, then, that the average American is more frightened by crime in general than by the impact of crime on his or her own life.[6] Respondents in several studies—even respondents from high-crime areas—perceived other neighborhoods as more dangerous than their own.[7] There is a parallel inclination to think of the increase in crime nationally as more severe than local increases and to believe that the national increase involves more serious kinds of crime.

> There was a strong tendency to believe that major personal crimes (murder, rape, robbery, assault) were the main factors in the perceived increase in national crime. On the neighborhood level, however, respondents thought that major property crimes (burglary, larceny, and other forms of theft) were equally responsible for an increase in crime.[8]

These same respondents "overwhelmingly agreed that crime affects the behavior of people in general, but were less likely to see crime as an influence on the behavior of people in their own neighborhoods."[9] . . .

At first glance, all of this might seem to lead inevitably to the conclusion that the Marxists have the right idea. Surely the media and the politicians seem to be working hand in glove to build our fears and trigger our punitive impulses. The result is, moreover, clearly manipulative. Crime ends up being portrayed as a cause rather than an effect of social disorganizations; our deep-seated social, economic, and political problems are reduced to the dimensions of cops and robbers.

Manipulative opportunities are, however, much more contingent than the Marxist analysis presented by Quinney would have us believe. The forces generating the politics of law and order are so unstable and uncoordinated that it seems misguided to think of them as a political coalition, much less a conspiracy among ruling elites. Instead, the politics of law and order rests on the attraction of a common target of opportunity—the punitive predispositions of the American public—to a variety of largely independent actors: news and entertainment media, politicians, and the crime-control establishment. Each seeks to market a similar but not identical message to an inconstant public. The generative forces behind the politics of law and order are thus unstable because the purposes of the elites converge and diverge for reasons only tangentially related to crime as such. This underlying instability is increased because law-and-order symbols seem to resonate with varying degrees of intensity, depending on time and circumstance.

Fishman's analysis of the development of a "crime wave" in New York clearly indicates that the connections between the media and public officials are more serendipitous than conspiratorial. News people searching for stories on a slow shift ran across some reports of crime with elderly victims. Crime against the elderly became a theme for linking these discrete events. This theme was picked up by others in the media, thus amplifying the coverage and laying the foundation for a crime wave: "[E]very crime incident that can be seen as an instance of the theme, will be seen and reported as such."[10] The journalists could not provide the "continuous supply of crime incidents" necessary to transform the theme into a wave, but law-enforcement agencies are willing and able to play that role.[11]

> [W]hen the police perceive that the media are interested in a certain type of crime (for example, crimes against the elderly), they include instances of it in the police wire whenever they can. Thus, the police bolster emerging crime waves as long as those waves pertain to crimes the police routinely detect (that is, street crime).
>
> The police-supplied incidents that make up the media's crime wave pool all support prevailing notions of "serious crime." The crime wave pool leads the media to reproduce a common image that "real crime" is crime on the streets, crime occurring between strangers, crime which brutalizes the weak and defenseless, and crime perpetrated by vicious youths.[12] . . .

Perhaps the most uncertain participants in the process of politicization are the media. Media executives are concerned with market shares and ratings, and therefore with entertainment value. Not surprisingly, then, television drama seems to have a cyclical quality to it—corresponding, presumably, to changing public tastes. Medical dramas, crime shows, sporting events, and situation comedies follow one another in a desperate effort to set, or keep up with, fashions. News is also show business. Of course, a good crime story will draw "front page" treatment, but as Fishman's study indicates, the incorporation of that story into a theme that is suitable for subsequent development into a wave is largely fortuitous—an editor in need, stumbling across some reports that seem to hang together. They are, moreover, hung together for purposes of "presentational order"—in other words, according to professional criteria.[13] Thus the media do not sell crime and punishment for its political message but for its payoff in advertising revenue.

It is difficult to estimate how much instability this lends to the generative forces of law and order. No doubt, there is some constancy. The message of crime and punishment is regularly invoked in a variety of adventure programs, not just in crime series. Yet, in times of relative tranquility, those messages may not be particularly seductive. And insofar as the focus is shifted from crime shows per se, the media contribution to fomenting a war against crime is likely to be reduced.

Political leaders operate in a comparably cyclical setting. The law-and-order issue is likely to vary in its appeal, and most political leaders will continue to pursue the issue only, as long as it is electorally salable. The initial precondition for the politics of law and order is a public perception that crime threatens the social order, although other threats to society and other personal insecurities are also germane. In any case, our receptivity to the symbols of law and order are only partially under the control of political leaders. . . .

The only really constant force in the battle on behalf of law and order is the crime-control establishment. Law-enforcement officials have a long-term interest in the myth of crime and punishment. The symbols of law and order reinforce the importance of their skills and enhance their status and rewards. Unlike political leaders and media executives, they have nowhere else to turn, and so they can be expected to continue to plug away at a variety of threats to law and order in a continuing effort to convince the public that with the necessary resources they can successfully thwart these threats. They do have some capability for influencing our sense of threat because they compile the statistics and are the principal source of information for the media. When one combines the incentive of law-enforcement officials to promote the politics of law and order with their opportunities to do so and adds the public's latent receptivity, it is clear that we should not underestimate the law-and-order capabilities of the crime-control establishment. But, ultimately, the politics of law and order depends on a broader configuration of generative forces.

Politics and Policy

The connection between politics and policy is much less direct than either the mainstream or the Marxist view suggests. Quinney claims that political leaders are willing and able to seize upon the pretext provided by the politicization of crime to initiate repressive policies. He draws this conclusion from an analysis of the Law Enforcement Assistance Administration, which, according to his way of thinking, served as the hub of a wheel of repression—providing a clearinghouse for ideas, a conduit for money, and a coordinating agency for programs.

> The major part of LEAA's budget goes to states and localities to improve criminal justice activities and develop new techniques of control. Funds are also provided for training law-enforcement agents and for research to improve criminal justice. The result is a coordinated system of legal control for the advanced capitalist society. All levels of the state and the agencies of the law are linked in a nationwide system of criminal justice.[14]

Wilson is less forthcoming on policy, but he seems to believe that responsible political leaders do, in the long run, take advantage of politicization to implement sensible programs for controlling crime. His own preferences run to proactive policing, deterrent-oriented sentencing, and methadone programs for dealing with heroin-related crimes.[15]

Neither of these two positions takes sufficient account of the discontinuity between political campaigning and policy making. Campaigning is largely a symbolic exercise in which the politicians do their best to conceal what is really at stake. Policy making, in contrast, pitches politicians

headlong into the arena of concrete politics where they must interact with
public officials who are keenly aware of the stakes of the game. These
officials understand, as do most politicians, that crime is not amenable to
simple solutions. Moreover, since all reforms alter the status quo and
threaten vested interests, resistance to law-and-order policies can be
taken for granted. It therefore seems equally naive to assume that policy
consequences of the politics of law and order will be either as repressive
as Quinney argues or as purposefully directed toward crime control as
Wilson implies.

The rise and demise of the LEAA is instructive. The best available
study leads to conclusions altogether different from those developed by
Quinney and at the same time casts substantial doubt on Wilson's view.[16]
The LEAA was established under the Crime Control and Safe Streets Act of
1968, which remains to this day the principal piece of federal legislation
traceable to the politics of law and order. A superficial case can be made
for either Wilson's or Quinney's position, but neither case stands up to
careful scrutiny.

The repressive bias of congressional legislation generally, and the
expenditure of funds by LEAA in particular, is abundantly clear. The Antiriot Act of 1968 was obviously aimed at political dissidents rather than
street criminals and figured in some of the celebrated "political trials" of
the early 1970s.[17] The Crime Control and Safe Streets Act extended the
use of wiretapping and sought to invalidate the Supreme Court's *Miranda*
decision, which broadened the rights of defendants in state criminal proceedings.[18] As to the LEAA itself, a major portion of the funds it expended,
particularly in the early days, went to the police and was used, among
other things, for a variety of threatening hardware that increased police
firepower and surveillance capabilities.

Wilson's position is born out principally by LEAA support of research
and experimentation in law enforcement. LEAA took the lead in funding
extensive studies of victimization that provided a much more reliable picture of patterns of crime and the public's reaction to them. There were also
demonstration grants to fund a variety of experiments involving the diversion of juveniles from the criminal justice system, neighborhood justice to
resolve minor criminal disputes by informal mediation, and reforms aimed
at more effective policing.[19] While it is true that only a small portion of
LEAA funds were so expended, LEAA was continually associated with this
kind of work.

Nonetheless, the essential reality of LEAA before its rather protracted
demise was neither repression nor experimentation, according to Malcolm
Feeley and Austin Sarat, because the agency was never sufficiently purposeful to carry out either mission.

> [C]ritics argued that the bulk of the money made available to the
> states through the Law Enforcement Assistance Administration was
> spent for police equipment, much of which was outlandishly expensive

to say nothing of lethal. With benefit of hindsight, however, these "hardware" purchases appear more ridiculous than repressive (e.g., antiriot tanks for small towns), and, at any rate, such extravagant equipment purchasing did not last long.[20]

The shortcomings of LEAA support to develop effective programs of crime control were rooted not so much in the paucity of funds as in the erratic course of policy.

> With each new administrator came new priorities for discretionary funds, priorities which did not cumulate. Although discretionary funds have been used to support some valuable programs, no truly national approach to crime has been developed.[21]

The politics of law and order was sufficiently powerful to generate campaign promises and follow-up legislation, but relatively little in the way of consistent public policy.

Feeley and Sarat explain the shortcomings of the LEAA in terms consistent with the distinction between concrete and symbolic politics. There were, in particular, two points along the way when concrete interests triumphed over symbolic promises. Those who wrote the act were influenced by a variety of interest groups that blocked a clear legislative mandate. "The result was a failure to specify substantive objectives, specific goals, and a strategy for achieving them. The goals of the Safe Streets Act are almost purely procedural."[22] Implementation was equally problematic as state planning agencies without well-defined legislative objectives attempted to influence well-entrenched law-enforcement officials at the local level.

> As organs of state government, [state planning agencies] must function within an established criminal justice system that is overwhelmingly local in structure, funding, and orientation. As dispensers of funds, they control less than 5 percent of the total criminal justice budget in any state and thus have no real clout especially with respect to larger agencies or in large cities, where the problems of crime are most apparent.[23]

The policy consequences of the political forces that led to the creation of the LEAA were therefore a good deal less imposing than Wilson hoped or Quinney feared. . . .

The politics of law and order grew, in part, out of the increase in street crime that developed in the mid-1960s, but that is only part of the story. The increase in crime must be seen against the many crises of American society during that period. The latter half of the 1960s and the early 1970s were years of rapid and unsettling social change. Traditional norms and values were under pressure in a great many areas of American life, and "law and order" became a symbol of resistance to unwelcome changes of all sorts—in race relations, education, and family life as well as in crime.

Crime tended to become the focal point of much of this discontent because it is such a simple and straightforward issue. There is, in the first place, very little ambiguity about the good guys and the bad guys. Virtually everyone can readily agree that an increase in the crime rate is deplorable. Judgments about changes in race relations, education, and the family are much more elusive and contentious. It is also relatively easy to agree on the right way to solve the crime problem. The myth of crime and punishment informs us that we can control crime by cracking down on criminals firmly and expeditiously. The culture provides no comparable magic wand to wave over the other unsettling features of American life.

But the attractions of punitive solutions go beyond the consensus they engender and their traditional place in American culture. Punishment, as Durkheim has pointed out, provides unequivocal reassurance that the society's norms and values are still intact—fully supported by the powers that be. Punishment also, Lasswell has suggested, has a cathartic effect—assuring us that complicated problems are amenable to simple solutions. At times of stress, we are therefore tempted to seek refuge in the simple world of crime and punishment. Small wonder, then, that crime has become something of a national pastime. It reaffirms our sense of community, and its simple truths are a refreshing change from the frustrating uncertainties of contemporary society.

The upshot is that the generative forces of the politics of law and order are complex and contingent. While the punitive predispositions that fuel the politics of law and order are cultural constants, they surface politically in unpredictable combination with unsettling kinds of social change. Crime per se—or at least a public perception of increasing criminal jeopardy—may be a necessary, but it is hardly a sufficient, condition of the politics of law and order. The politics of law and order thrive only together with a more extended sense of social malaise, which drives the public toward the consolations provided by the myth of crime and punishment. At such times, our problem is not too much crime but, culturally speaking, too little—a need the media are only too happy to meet. Given this climate of opinion, crime becomes a very attractive campaign issue.

An awareness of the complexity and the contingent character of the politics of law and order is the first step toward appreciating the distance that separates campaign promises from changes in operative policy. . . .

The net effect of the politics of law and order will be neither the repression that Marxists fear nor the pragmatic reforms that the mainstream counts on. Instead, we shall see little overall change. Moreover, while such change as does take place will tend to have a punitive bias, this cracking down seems unlikely to make either the police or the criminal courts more effective agents of crime control. There is, in particular, no reason to believe that the punitive drift in criminal process occasioned by the politics of law and order will be effective against the predatory strangers who are the public's primary concern.

The policy limitations of the politics of law and order are, in part, a product of the symbolic character of politicization. Politicians ordinarily gain electoral success by telling the public what it wants to hear. When fear of street crime runs high, politicians have every reason to believe that the public is looking for promises to crack down on criminals firmly and expeditiously. Certainly the politician who, in a climate of fear, champions due process, redemption, or rehabilitation faces an uphill struggle. Thus politicians are more or less forced to promise simple punitive solutions to complicated and intractable problems. Whether they realize it or not during the campaign, political candidates end up making promises that they cannot possibly keep.

The other obstacle to effective reform is the powerfully entrenched values and interests of lawyers and police officers who control the agencies of criminal process. These officials have a stake in the status quo and are resistant to change. This is not to suggest a cynical disregard for public safety and an exclusively self-interested approach to policy choices. There are legitimate differences of opinion about how best to control crime, and, generally speaking, the officials of criminal process are inclined to believe that they are doing the best they can under the circumstances. Certainly they believe that they have a better understanding of how to cope with crime than the politicians, who are poorly informed and who, they feel, yield too readily to political pressures. Moreover, there is probably some recognition by all concerned that whatever is done will have only a marginal impact on crime. With the crime-control stakes relatively low and with no way to demonstrate conclusively that one approach is better than the other, it is understandable that even conscientious public officials tend to be influenced by their own responsibilities. . . .

Notes

[1] Murray Edelman, *The Symbolic Uses of Politics* (Champaign-Urbana: University of Illinois Press, 1967), 5.

[2] W. Lance Bennett, *Public Opinion in American Politics* (New York: Harcourt Brace Jovanovich, 1980), 397.

[3] Ibid.

[4] Ibid.

[5] Wesley G. Skogan and Michael G. Maxfield, *Coping with Crime: Individuals and Neighborhood Reactions* (Beverly Hills, CA: Sage, 1981), 127–62.

[6] I exclude from this generalization the small fraction of the public personally victimized by violent crime who may be expected to have a heightened level of fear.

[7] Fred DuBow, Edward McCabe, and Gail Kaplan, *Reactions to Crime: A Review of the Literature* (Washington, DC: National Institute of Law Enforcement and Criminal Justice, 1979), 4.

[8] James Garofalo, *Public Opinion About Crime: The Attitudes of Victims and Non-Victims in Selected Cities* (Washington, DC: National Criminal Justice Information and Statistics Service, 1977), 15.

[9] Ibid., 32.

[10] Mark Fishman, "Crime Waves as Ideology," *Social Problems* 29 (June 1978): 537.

[11] Ibid., 538.

[12] Ibid., 540.

[13] Ibid., 534–35.

[14] Richard Quinney, *Class, State, and Crime*, 2nd. ed. (New York: Longman, 1980), 129.

[15] James Q. Wilson, *Thinking About Crime* (New York: Vintage, 1977), Chaps. 5, 7, and 8.

[16] Malcolm M. Feeley and Austin D. Sarat, *The Policy Dilemma: Federal Crime Policy and the Law Enforcement Assistance Administration, 1968–1978* (Minneapolis: University of Minnesota Press, 1980).

[17] John T. Eliff, *Crime, Dissent, and the Attorney General: The Justice Department in the 1960's* (Beverly Hills, CA: Sage, 1971), 108–11 and 201–11.

[18] Richard Harris, *The Fear of Crime* (New York: Praeger, 1968), 58–63.

[19] See, for example, *Exemplary Projects* (Washington, DC: National Institute of Law Enforcement and Criminal Justice, 1978). 31 pp.

[20] Feeley and Sarat, *The Policy Dilemma*, 137.

[21] Ibid., 53.

[22] Ibid., 135.

[23] Ibid., 146.

Criminal Justice as Socially Constructed Reality

How do we know what we know? For most of us, our reality and truths are taken for granted. We resist the notion that reality is relative, constructed from our history of experiences and interactions with others. It is more comforting to assume that there is a pre-existing, objective reality. Those who have a different view of reality are wrong-thinking and are misinterpreting the objective truths of the real world.

The next theoretical orientation we will examine—criminal justice as socially constructed reality—does not assume reality is predetermined. It sees reality as being *socially constructed*. Our reality is the result of an intricate process of learning and constructing meanings and definitions of situations through language, symbols, and interactions with other people. Anthropologists call a set of shared beliefs, myths, values, practices, and rituals a *culture*.[1] Reality is not a given; it's a human accomplishment.

---

[1] Similarly, Jim Thomas (1993) defines culture as "the totality of all learned social behavior of a given group; it provides the system of standards for perceiving, believing, evaluating, and acting, and the rules and symbols of interpretation and discourse" (p. 12). David Garland (1990) provides a broader definition: "frameworks of meaning within which social action takes place" (p. 193).

137

Herbert Blumer, a key sociological figure in this strain of thought, said that even tangible objects have different symbolic meanings for different individuals: "A tree will be a different object to a botanist, a lumberman, a poet, and a home gardener" (Blumer, 1969, p. 11). Blumer's statement applies well to a recent experience.

My neighbor cut down several beautiful old locust trees along a property line we share. His action angered me. My reality was *socially constructed* from spending countless hours in the outdoors with co-workers, friends, and family who *defined* trees and brush as "natural habitat" and essential to wildlife and human survival. This reaction would likely confuse my neighbor. From his frame of reference, a locust tree draws lightning strikes, has dangerously heavy limbs that break off easily in the wind, provides no real shade to cattle due to its wispy little leaves, and burns like hard coal in the wood stove. His actions and thinking are filtered through a reality constructed through the experiences and interactions of generations of tobacco and cattle farmers. For my neighbor the locust trees symbolize potential firewood, a hazard, and lost income. For me they symbolize wildlife habitat, a healthy environment, and a few remaining relics of what was once a grand wilderness in the rolling hills of mid-Eastern Kentucky.

Paul Watzlawick (1976), in *How Real Is Real: An Introduction to Communications Theory*, warns us about assuming that our perception of reality is reality.

> Our everyday ideas of reality are delusions which we spend substantial parts of our daily lives shoring up. The most dangerous delusion of all is that there is only one reality. What there are, in fact, are many different versions of reality, some of which are contradictory, but all of which are the results of communication and not reflections of eternal, objective truths. (p. 10)

How does this way of thinking help us understand criminal justice? Applied to crime and justice studies, the social construction of reality framework asks us to pursue the following types of inquiry.

- Investigate the *myths* associated with crime and crime control thinking
- Study the formation and maintenance of occupational cultures
- Scrutinize how certain behaviors and situations come to be defined as "crime"
- Dissect the way in which public and private-based crime control tactics are produced.

Intellectual Foundation: The Interpretive School

The intellectual foundation upon which this orientation rests is most commonly known as the interpretive school (Einstadter & Henry, 1995;

May, 1996; Waters, 1994).[2] *Language, culture, myth, symbols, meaning, social interaction, rituals,* and *defining situations and objects* are key concepts in the interpretive tradition. "Interpretive" refers to theoretical models that assume that humans, by actively interpreting the world around them, create systems of meaning; interpretive theorists make sense of those meaning systems and expose their inner workings. The interpretive school encompasses different areas of theorizing in academics, including symbolic interactionism, social constructionism, cultural anthropology, rhetorical studies, institutional theory, ethnomethodology, and phenomenology.

Our field of study has a rich tradition of applying the socially constructed reality orientation to the study of crime and criminal justice. Indeed, the sociological school of thought known as "symbolic interactionism" has been a forceful influence in the study of crime and deviance. Howard Becker (1963) provided criminology with a symbolic interactionist insight that turned our thinking about crime and deviance on its head. As opposed to taking the definition of crime as a given (as do the rational/ legal and systems orientations), Becker asserted that it "is not the quality of the act the person commits, but rather a consequence of the application by others of rules and sanctions to an *offender*" (Becker, 1963, p. 30). Truly understanding law-breaking, therefore, requires us to question: 1) the process of how certain behaviors are defined as "illegal"; and 2) the reaction of the criminal justice system. Other academics working in the interpretive tradition observed firsthand the occupational workings and culture found in the police, courts, and corrections—much like a cultural anthropologist might study the tribal culture of an indigenous group of people (see, for example, Cicourel, 1968; Skolnick, 1966; Sundow, 1965; Sykes, 1958).

Starting in the early 1970s, and continuing through the mid-1980s, the social construction of reality orientation fell out of favor.[3] It cut across the grain of the predominant theoretical framework in our field, the systems orientation, and the strong emphasis on quantitative-based research. Since the late 1980s, however, it has had a growing influence on our understanding of crime, crime control, and the criminal justice system. Its renewed popularity is partly due to our discipline's realization that politicians, bureaucrats, and the media promote numerous beliefs—crime is

[2] Einstadter and Henry (1995) actually label these as "Interpretive Social Process" theories. Others have called it the interactionist/constructionist paradigm. Academics in our field seem to be most comfortable with the label "social constructionism," but this is actually only one strain of thought within the interpretive school.

[3] Part of the reason for this may have been the misperception that social constructionist thinking is aligned only with radical or Marxist criminology. As Rafter (1990, p. 378) points out, Marxist criminology actually rejected this approach. "Richard Quinney had this vision in his early work, *The Social Reality of Crime,* which was strongly epistemological in approach, emphasizing the 'formulation of criminal definitions' and the 'portrayal of crime in personal and mass communications.' But by the mid-1970s, Quinney had rejected this emphasis, criticizing 'social constructionist thought' for a 'failure to provide an image of what a new world should look like.'"

ever-worsening, drug use causes violence, law violators are often set free due to technical loopholes, or tougher sentencing laws such as "three strikes" reduce crime—that do not square with our field's research findings. A developing interest in how and why these false beliefs (myths) come about helped prompt a resurgence of interest in interpretive perspectives.[4] We will next explore the variety of forms this theoretical orientation has assumed in crime and justice studies.

Criminal Justice as Drama

Peter Manning, the author of the first reading, has spent much of his career studying the interpretive dimension of policing. The early foundation for his work is Erving Goffman's (1959) *dramaturgical analysis*—a complicated-sounding concept that simply means viewing "policing as if it were a great, persuasive drama" (Manning, 1997, p. 36). *Dramaturgy* studies the culture of groups; applied to criminal justice, it gazes at the system's bureaucracies as if they were a theatrical play complete with a team of *actors*, a *stage*, and an *audience*. Criminal justice actors adopt and perform certain *roles*, and in doing so, present to the audience an impression of themselves. An actor, or a *team of actors*, work hard to construct and maintain an effective impression of themselves through the orchestration of *appearances*. Goffman (1959) labeled this status-building and maintenance process as *impression management*.

Manning's article examines how the police institution engages in impression management through the construction and maintenance of appearances. Manning (1999) theorizes that because the police have an "impossible mandate" they have struggled throughout their history for legitimacy. In order to overcome their ambiguous status

> the police have followed the course of most other bureaucratic institutions in society, responding to their problems by merely giving the appearance of facing them while simultaneously promoting the trained incapacity to do otherwise. (p. 109)

Manning discusses the impression-management strategies the police employ— *myths* of police "professionalism"—to maintain their precarious legitimacy.

A related, but more recent line of criminal justice scholarship, known as *institutional theory*, focuses on the powerful influence of shared ideas, beliefs, and values (culture) within an organization's institutional environment (Crank, 1994; Crank & Langworthy, 1992; Meyer & Rowan, 1977). In opposition to the systems orientation, which assumes that CJ agencies pursue certain actions and policies for purposes of enhancing their rationality and

---

[4] Another, perhaps even more important reason, has to do with the renewed interest in interpretive approaches in all the social sciences. Ethnography—a type of cultural description and analysis that studies culture from within the group—continues to attract adherents who reject positivistic approaches (see Clifford Geertz's interview with Olson, 1991).

effectiveness, institutional theory sees organizations as constructing their own social reality—referred to as *myths*—for purposes of maintaining their legitimacy, managing their image, or giving the appearance of competency.

John Crank (1994) argues, for example, that community policing provides the police institution the *mythic images* of grassroots democracy and close-knit communities so that "police organizations can ceremonially regain the legitimacy that was ceremonially withdrawn in the 1960s" (p. 347). John Rosecrance (1986) has documented the same phenomenon in probation agencies, where the myth of individualized justice is sustained through the ceremonial use of probation presentence reports. My research has examined police paramilitary units (SWAT teams), concluding that their explosive growth during the government's latest drug war had more to do with these units' high cultural appeal—the myths of the warrior, the elite special operations soldier, and waging a "war" on crime and drugs—as opposed to a rational reaction to worsening crime (Kraska & Cubellis, 1997).

Criminal Justice as Moral Panic

In the summer of 2001, U.S. society was gripped by shark attacks. Nearly every week it seemed another person was killed or mauled by these marauding beasts; newspapers dubbed the phenomenon "the revenge of the sharks." Beaches closed, attendance at open beaches dropped dramatically, and shark hunters were hired to eliminate the threat. The panic continued even after scientists reported that the number of shark attack casualties and deaths were actually lower in the summer of 2001 than in previous years.

Social constructionism focuses on the process by which a *social problem*, like shark attacks, is constructed (Spector & Kitsuse, 1977). Social constructionism has established itself as a highly influential presence in our field (Best, 1987; Brownstein, 1999; Cohen, 1972; Goode & Ben-Yehuda, 1994; Jenkins, 1994; Kappeler, Blumberg, & Potter, 2000; Rafter, 1990; Robinson, 2000).[5] In article 12, Marjorie Zatz relies heavily on this approach in her examination of the criminal justice system's handling of an alleged Chicano youth gang crisis.

Zatz centers her analysis on a key social constructionist concept, *moral panic*.[6] Stanley Cohen's (1972) original definition remains the standard.

> Societies appear to be subject, every now and then, to periods of moral panic. A condition, episode, person or groups of persons emerges to become defined as a threat to societal values and interests; its nature is presented in a stylized and stereotypical fashion by the mass media;

---

[5] See Rafter (1990) for an excellent overview of the application of social constructionist thinking to the study of criminal justice.

[6] Erich Goode and Nachman Ben-Yehuda (1994) have written a book on the intricacies and usefulness of the moral panic concept. See Ungar (2001) as well for an interesting linkage of moral panic with Beck's *risk society* (chapter 9).

> the moral barricades are managed by editors, bishops, politicians, and other right-thinking people; socially accredited experts pronounce their diagnoses and solutions; ways of coping are evolved or (more often) resorted to; the condition then disappears, submerges or deteriorates and become more visible. (p. 9)

The key here is that social problems such as "dangerous Chicano youth gangs" are actively constructed through a complex process involving the media, governmental officials, the public, politicians, and other interested parties. Zatz asserts that *moral entrepreneurs*—key players actively involved in the construction process—succeeded in painting a mythical portrait of Latino gang violence, justifying the criminal justice system's punitive reaction.

> It was the social imagery of Chicano youth gangs, rather than their actual behavior, that lay at the root of the gang problem in Phoenix. The imagery of gangs as violent converged with that of Mexicans as *different*. The potential threat of disorder and of contempt for the law escalated to the point at which a *moral panic* ensued. (pp. 153–154)

Zatz's emphasis on race, as an important factor in the social construction process, highlights an important development in social constructionism. As will be discussed in chapter 8 (oppression), the social construction of reality orientation is adopted routinely by academics studying the nexus of race and criminal justice as well as gender and criminal justice (see, for example, Rafter, 1990; Robinson, 2000).[7]

Myths and Criminal Justice

Article 13 by Victor Kappeler provides a nice overview of the primary concepts and ideas associated with criminal justice as a socially constructed reality. It is based on the ideas developed in the book that has, more than any other single work, brought social constructionism into the mainstream of criminal justice studies—*The Mythology of Crime and Criminal Justice*. Kappeler's article effectively exposes the deep-seated mythological beliefs that underlie overly punitive and ineffective crime laws and criminal justice policy. The section that identifies the various players in the myth construction process—the media, government officials, politicians, and the public—is particularly instructive.

A Point of Departure

The concepts and ideas discussed here—criminal justice as a theatrical play, social problems as humanly constructed moral panics, and myth used

---

[7] In "The Construction and Reinforcement of Myths of Race and Crime," Matthew Robinson details the creation and reinforcement of numerous race myths and their harmful effect on criminal justice practice.

as a tool to gain bureaucratic legitimacy—are not easily digested. Interpretive school thinking is abstract, philosophically and sociologically. Yet we all can relate to the core notion that differing views of reality can exist simultaneously, and those realities, even if we appreciate that they are human constructions, seem real, accurate, and beyond dispute.

Some readers may have already noticed the connection between the social construction of reality theoretical orientation and the organizing framework for this book. Using the metaphors of system, crime control vs. due process, oppression, or politics, I am employing a social constructionist tactic. The social construction of reality metaphor, though, might make some readers uncomfortable. It lies in opposition, for the most part, to rational/legal or systems thinking. In fact, it represents a point of departure in this book: the first four orientations represent more conventional ways of thinking about criminal justice, and the final four are decidedly *more critical*. Being more critical means that the last four orientations

- are quite skeptical about: governmental power and control, punitive crime-control activities, "official" versions of the truth, calls for enhanced criminal justice growth, or the erosion of human freedoms in the name of security and safety;
- focus on the role of power differentials—whether rooted in economic disparities, political access, or gender and race—as a major driving force in the character and functioning of the criminal justice apparatus; and
- are similar to "open system" thinking in that they focus on the big picture (macro-structural forces driving the entire CJA) even when their analysis focuses on the micro-processes of reality construction or power differentials.

We can think of the eight orientations as a continuum; the final four orientations lie further down the continuum of questioning and being skeptical of the criminal justice apparatus. All the orientations contribute to our critical thinking skills. Awareness of the insights of each orientation help us assess where we fall on the continuum.

References

Becker, H. (1963). *Outsiders: Studies in the sociology of deviance*. New York: Free Press.

Best, J. (1987). Rhetoric in claims-making: Constructing the missing children problem. *Social Problems, 34*(2), 101–121.

Blumer, H. (1969). *Symbolic interactionism*. Englewood Cliffs: Prentice-Hall.

Brownstein, H. (1999). *The social reality of violence and violent crime*. New York: Allyn and Bacon.

Cicourel, A. V. (1968). *The social organization of juvenile justice*. New York: John Wiley.

Cohen, S. (1972). *Folk devils and moral panics: The creation of the mods and rockers*. London: McGibbon and Kee.

Crank, J. P. (1994). Watchman and community: Myth and institutionalization in policing. *Law and Society Review, 28*(2), 325–351.

Crank, J. P., & Langworthy, R. (1992). An institutional perspective of policing. *Journal of Criminal Law and Criminology, 83*(2), 338–362.

Einstadter, W., & Henry, S. (1995). *Criminological theory: An analysis of its underlying assumptions*. New York: Harcourt Brace.

Garland, D. (1990). *Punishment and modern society*. Chicago: University of Chicago Press.

Goode, E., & Ben-Yehuda, N. (1994). *Moral panics*. Oxford: Blackwell.

Goffman, E. (1959). *The presentation of self in everyday life*. London: Allen Lane.

Jenkins, P. (1994). The ice age: The social construction of a drug panic. *Justice Quarterly, 11*(1), 7–31.

Kraska, P. B., & Cubellis, L. (1997). Militarizing Mayberry and beyond: Making sense of American paramilitary policing. *Justice Quarterly, 14*(4), 607–629.

Kappeler, V. E., Blumberg, M., & Potter, G. (2000). *The mythology of crime and criminal justice* (3rd ed.). Prospect Heights, IL: Waveland Press.

Manning, P. K. (1999). The police: Mandate, strategies, and appearances. In V. E. Kappeler (Ed.), *The police and society* (pp. 94–122). Prospect Heights, IL: Waveland Press.

May, T. (1996). *Situating social theory*. Philadelphia: Open University Press.

Meyer, J. W., & Rowan, B. (1977). Institutionalized organizations: Formal structure as myth and ceremony. *American Journal of Sociology, 83*(2), 340–368.

Olson, G. A. (1991). Clifford Geertz on ethnography and social construction. http://jac.gsu.edu/jac/11.2/Articles/geertz.html

Rafter, N. H. (1990). The social construction of crime and crime control. *Journal of Research in Crime and Delinquency, 27*(4), 376–389.

Robinson, M. (2000). The construction and reinforcement of myths of race and crime. *Journal of Contemporary Criminal Justice, 16*(2), 133–156.

Rosecrance, J. (1986). Maintaining the myth of individualized justice: Probation presentence reports. *Justice Quarterly, 5*(2), 235–256.

Skolnick, J. (1966). *Justice without trial*. New York: Wiley.

Spector, M., & Kitsuse, J. I. (1987). *Constructing social problems*. New York: Aldine de Gruyter.

Sykes, G. (1958). *Society of captives*. Princeton: Princeton University Press.

Sundow, D. (1965). Normal crimes: Sociological features of the penal code in a public defender office. *Social Problems, 12*(3), 255–270.

Thomas, J. (1993). *Doing critical ethnography*. Newbury Park, CA: Sage.

Ungar, S. (2001). Moral panic versus the risk society: The implications of the changing sites of social anxiety. *British Journal of Sociology, 52*(2), 271–291.

Waters, M. (1994). *Modern sociological theory*. Thousand Oaks, CA: Sage.

Watzlawick, P. (1976). *How real is real? An anecdotal introduction to communications theory*. New York: Vintage Books.

The Police
Mandate, Strategies, and Appearances

Peter Manning

The "Impossible" Mandate

The police in modern society are in agreement with their audiences—which include their professional interpreters, the American family, criminals and politicians—in at least one respect: they have an "impossible" task. Certainly, all professionals have impossible tasks insofar as they try to surmount the problems of collective life that resist easy solutions. The most "successful" occupations, however, have managed to construct a mandate in terms of their own vision of the world. The police officer's mandate, on the other hand, is defined largely by the public—not, at least at the formal level, in his or her own terms.

Several rather serious consequences result from the public's image of the police. The public is aware of the dramatic nature of a small portion of police work, but it ascribes the element of excitement to all police activities. To much of the public, the police are seen as alertly ready to respond to citizen demands, as crime-fighters, as an efficient, bureaucratic, highly organized force that keeps society from falling into chaos. Police officers consider the essence of their roles to be the dangerous and heroic enter-

Originally published in *Policing: A View from the Street* (1978), edited by Peter K. Manning and John Van Maanen. Republished in Kappeler, V. E. (Ed.), *The Police and Society* (1999, pp. 94–122), Waveland Press, Inc. Used by permission of the author.

prise of crook-catching and the watchful prevention of crimes.[1] The system
of positive and negative sanctions from the public and within the department encourages this heroic conception. The public wants crime prevented
and controlled; that is, it wants criminals caught. Headlines herald the
accomplishments of G-Men and FBI agents who often do catch dangerous
people, and the reputation of these federal authorities not infrequently rubs
off on local police officers who are much less adept at catching criminals.

In an effort to gain the public's confidence in their ability, and to
insure thereby the solidity of their mandate, the police have encouraged
the public to continue thinking of them and their work in idealized terms,
terms, that is, which grossly exaggerate the actual work done by police.
They do engage in chases, in gunfights, in careful sleuthing. But these are
rare events. Most police work resembles any other kind of work: it is bor-
ing, tiresome, sometimes dirty, sometimes technically demanding, but it is
rarely dangerous. Yet the occasional chase, the occasional shootout, the
occasional triumph of some extraordinary detective work have been seized
upon by the police and played up to the public. The public's response has
been to demand even more dramatic crook-catching and crime prevention,
and this demand for arrests has been converted into an index for measuring how well the police accomplish their mandate. The public's definitions
have been converted by the police organization into distorted criteria for
promotion, success, and security. Most police departments promote officers from patrol to detective work, a generally more desirable duty, for
"good pinches"—arrests that are most likely to result in convictions.[2] The
protection of the public welfare, however, including personal and property
safety, the prevention of crime, and the preservation of individual civil
rights, is hardly achieved by a high pinch rate. On the contrary, it might
well be argued that protection of the public welfare could best be indexed
by a low arrest rate. Because their mandate automatically entails mutually
contradictory ends—protecting both public order and individual rights—
the police resort to managing their public image and the indexes of their
accomplishment. And the ways in which the police manage their appearance are consistent with the assumptions of their occupational culture,
with the public's view of the police as a social-control agency, and with the
ambiguous nature of our criminal law.

The Efficient, Symptom-Oriented Organization

The Wickersham report, the Hoover administration's report on crime
and law enforcement in the United States, was published in 1931. This pre-
cursor of the Johnson administration's *The Challenge of Crime in a Free Society* became a rallying point for advocates of police reform. One of its central
themes was the lack of "professionalism" among the police of the time—their
lack of special training, their corruption, their brutality, and their use of illegal procedures in law enforcement. And one of its results was that the police,
partly in order to demonstrate their concern with scientific data gathering on

crime and partly to indicate their capacity to "control" crime itself, began to stress crime statistics as a major component of professional police work.

Crime statistics, therefore—and let this point be emphasized—became a police construction. The actual amount of crime committed in a society is unknown—and probably unknowable, given the private nature of most crime. The *crime rate*, consequently, is simply a construction of police activities. That is, the crime rate pertains only to "crimes known to the police," crimes that have been reported to or observed by the police and for which adequate grounds exist for assuming that a violation of the law has, in fact, taken place. (The difference between the *actual* and *known crimes* is often called the "dark figure of crime.") Of course, the construction of a crime rate placed the police in a logically weak position in which they still find themselves. If the crime rate is rising, they argue that more police support is needed to fight the war against crime; if the crime rate is stable or declining, they argue that they have successfully combated the crime menace—a heads-I-win-tails-you-lose proposition.

In spite of their inability to control the commission of illegal acts (roughly, the actual rate), since they do not know about all crime, the police have claimed responsibility for crime control, using the crime rate as an index of their success. This use of the crime rate to measure success is somewhat analogous to the use of a patrol officer's arrest rate as an indication of personal success in law enforcement. Questions about the actual amount of crime and the degree of control exercised are thus bypassed in favor of an index that offers great potential for organizational or bureaucratic control. Instead of grappling with the difficult issue of defining the ends of police work and an operational means for accomplishing them, the police have opted for "efficient" law-enforcement defined in terms of fluctuations of the crime rate. They transformed concern with undefined ends into concern with available means. Their inability to cope with the causes of crime—which might offer them a basis for defining their ends—shifts their "organizational focus" into symptomatic concerns, that is, into a preoccupation with the rate of crime, not its reasons.

This preoccupation with the symptoms of a problem rather than with the problem itself is typical of all bureaucracies. For one characteristic of a bureaucracy is goal-displacement. Bureaucratic organizations tend to lose track of their goals and engage in ritual behavior, substituting means for ends. As a whole, bureaucracies become so engrossed in pursuing, defending, reacting to, and, even, in creating immediate problems that their objective is forgotten. This tendency to displace goals is accelerated by the one value dear to all bureaucracies—efficiency. Efficiency is the be-all and end-all of bureaucratic organizations. Thus, they can expend great effort without any genuine accomplishment.

The police are burdened with the "efficiency problem." They claim to be an efficient bureaucratic organization, but they are unable to define for themselves and others precisely what it is they are being efficient about. In this respect, they do not differ from other paper-shuffling organizations. The police's problem is that the nature of their work is uncertain and negatively defined. It is uncertain in the absence of a consensus not only between the police and the public but also among themselves as to what the goals of a police department should be. It is defined in the negative because the organization punishes its members—patrol officers—for violating departmental procedures but offers no specifications on what they should do or how they should do it.

What do the police do about the problematic nature of law, about the problems arising from their involvement with politics, about their preoccupation with the symptoms of crime rather than the causes? Do they selectively adopt some strategies at the expense of others? Do they vacillate? Are the roles of the organization's members blurred? Before answering these questions, let us examine how the police, through various strategies, manage their appearance before the public. The questions will then be easier to answer.

Major Strategies of the Police

The responsibilities of the police lead them to pursue contradictory and unattainable ends. They share with all organizations and occupations, however, the ability to avoid solving their problems. Instead, they concentrate on managing them through strategies. Rather than resolving their dilemmas, the police have manipulated them with a professional eye on just how well the public accepts their dexterity. Thus, law enforcement becomes a self-justifying system. It becomes more responsive to its own needs, goals, and procedures than to serving society. In this section, we will show the ways in which the police have followed the course of most other bureaucratic institutions in society, responding to their problems by merely giving the appearance of facing them while simultaneously promoting the trained incapacity to do otherwise.

The two primary aims of most bureaucracies, the police included, are the maintenance of their organizational autonomy and the security of their members. To accomplish these aims, they adopt a pattern of institutional action that can best be described as "professionalism. "This word, with its many connotations and definitions, cloaks all the many kinds of actions carried out by the police.

The guise of professionalism embodied in a bureaucratic organization is the most important strategy employed by the police to defend their mandate and thereby to build self-esteem, organizational autonomy, and occupational solidarity or cohesiveness. The professionalization drives of the police are no more suspect than the campaigns of other striving, upwardly mobile occupational groups. However, since the police have a monopoly on legal violence, since they are the active enforcers of the public will, serving theoretically in the best interests of the public, the consequences of their yearnings for prestige and power are imbued with far greater social ramifications than the relatively harmless attempts of florists, funeral directors, and accountants to attain public stature. Disinterested law enforcement through bureaucratic means is an essential in our society and in any democracy, and the United States police are certainly closer to attaining this ideal than they were in 1931 at the time of the Wickersham report. Professionalism qua professionalism is unquestionably desirable in the police. But if in striving for the heights of prestige they fail to serve the altruistic values of professionalism, if their professionalism means that a faulty portrait of the social reality of crime is being painted, if their professionalism conceals more than it reveals about the true nature of their operations, then a close analysis of police professionalism is in order.

Police professionalism cannot be easily separated in practice from the bureaucratic ideal epitomized in modern police practice. The bureaucratic ideal is established as a means of obtaining a commitment from personnel to organizational and occupational norms. This bureaucratic commitment is designed to supersede commitments to competing norms, such as obligations to friends or kin or members of the same racial or ethnic group. Unlike medicine and law, professions that developed outside the context of bureaucracies, policing has always been carried out, if done on a full-time basis, as a bureaucratic function.

Modern police bureaucracy and modern police professionalism are highly articulated, although they contain some inherent stresses that are not our present concern. The strategies employed by the police to manage their public appearance develop from their adaptation of the bureaucratic ideal. These strategies incorporate the utilization of *technology* and *official statistics* in law enforcement, of *styles of patrol* that attempt to accommodate the community's desire for public order with the police department's preoccupation with bureaucratic procedures, of *secrecy* as a means of controlling the public's response to their operations, of *collaboration* with criminal elements to foster the appearance of a smoothly run, law-abiding community, and of a *symbiotic relationship* with the criminal justice system that minimizes public knowledge of the flaws within this largely privately operated system.

The Effectiveness of Police Strategies

The police have developed and utilized the strategies outlined above for the purpose of creating, as we have said, the appearance of managing their troublesome mandate. To a large extent, they are facilitated in the use of these strategies, in being able to project a favorable impression, by a public that has always been apathetic about police activity. Moreover, what activity the public does observe is filtered through the media with its own special devices for creating a version of reality. The public's meaning of police action is rarely gathered from first-hand experience, but from the constructed imagery of the media—which, in turn, rely upon official police sources for their presentation of the news. The police for their part, understandably, manipulate public appearances as much as they possibly can in order to gain and maintain public support. The specific strategies used by the police to create a publicly suitable image are: the guise of professionalism; the implementation of the bureaucratic ideal of organization; the use of technology, official statistics, and various styles of patrol; secrecy; collaboration with corrupt elements; and the establishment of a symbiotic relationship with the courts. . . .

Professionalism and the Bureaucratic Ideal

The assumptions of professionalism and of a bureaucratic organization include a devotion to rational principles and ends that may then be translated into specific work routines having predictable outcomes. The police are organized in a military command fashion, with rigid rules and a hierarchy governing operations. However, the patrol officer, the lowest ranking in the hierarchy—and usually the least well-trained and educated—is in the key position of exercising the greatest amount of discretion on criminal or possibly criminal activities. Especially in peace-keeping roles and in dealing with minor infractions (misdemeanors), patrol officers have wide discretionary power concerning if, when, why, and how to intervene in private affairs.

Police work must both rely on discretion and control it. Excessive inattention and excessive attention to infractions of the law are equally damaging to a community. However, the complexity of the law, its dynamic and changing properties, the extensiveness of police department regulations, policies, and procedures, and the equivocal, relativistic nature of crime in regard to certain situations, settings, persons, and groups make it impossible to create a job description that would eliminate the almost boundless uncertainty in police patrol.

Neither professionals nor bureaucrats, however, have yet found an effective means of controlling discretion. If an organization cannot control those of its members with the greatest opportunity to exercise discretion, it flounders in its attempts to accomplish its stated purposes. Two general principles suggest why the police have not been able to control discretion. The first has to do with the general problem of control and the second with the specific nature of police work.

People are unwilling to submit completely to the will of organizational superiors. They will always attempt to define and control their own work. Control means the right to set the pace, to define mistakes, to develop standards of "good" production and efficiency. But as surely as superiors seek to control the quality and the extent of work performed by their subordinates in a hierarchy, just as surely will they encounter attempts to reshape and subvert these controls.

In the specific instance of police bureaucracies, patrol officers conceive of themselves as able to make on-the-spot decisions of guilt or innocence.

They do not think of themselves as bureaucratic functionaries nor as professionals. Further, since the police organization itself has become far more interested in efficiency than in purpose, since it is unable to specify its overall objectives, patrol officers find it difficult, if not impossible, to demonstrate that necessary devotion to rational ends required of professionalism and bureaucratic organizations. Until police departments are able to control the amount and kind of discretion exercised by their members, and until the police are able, with the help of lawyers and other citizens, to develop positive means of motivation and reward in line with clear, overall policy directives, the failure of what we have called the professionalism-bureaucracy strategy is an absolute certainty.

Technology, Statistics, and the Crime Rate

This section will evaluate the strategy of technology in the control and prevention of crime, the use of statistics, and the significance of the so-called crime rate. Given the sociological nature of crime, let it be said immediately that present technology deals with unimportant crime and that the FBI index of crimes, by which we base judgments of police effectiveness, is biased and an unrealistic reflection of the actual crime rate.

One of the striking aspects of the President's crime commission report is the thoroughly sociological nature of the document. The discussion of the causes of crime in the first two chapters points to the growth of urbanism, anonymity, the breakdown in social control, and the increasing numbers of frustrated and dissatisfied youth who have always constituted the majority of known lawbreakers. There are no labels such as "evil people," "emotionally disturbed," "mentally ill," or "criminally insane." The first set of recommendations under prevention in the summary pages of the report are "sociological": strengthen the family, improve slum schools, provide employment, reduce segregation, construct housing. All these matters are patently and by definition out of the control of the police.

There is every evidence that the police themselves subscribe to a thoroughly social, if not sociological, definition of the causes of crime—that is, that crime is the manifestation of long-established social patterns and structures that ensnare and implicate the police and the criminals as well as the general public. And they are doubtless correct.

Surveys done by the President's crime commission revealed that there are always contingencies in the information police receive about a crime even before they are able to investigate it. These contingencies involve such matters as the nature of the relationship between the victim and the offender and whether or not the victim believes the police are competent to investigate and solve the crime. Computer technology depends on informational "input." On that point, the police seem both unable to define what sort of information would be useful and unable to obtain, and probably never can obtain in a democratic society, information that would make them better able to enforce the law.

The facts in the problem of "crime prevention" overwhelmingly doom the present professionally based notion that the application of science and technology will begin to ease the distress the police feel as they face the escalating demands of their audiences. Also, it would be easier to assess the value of the technology strategy if we were able to define exactly to what end the technology would be applied and in what ways it could be expected to work.

Styles of Patrol

Police strategy is subject to many contingencies. It is a basic principle of public administration that policy made at the higher echelons of an organization will be effective only if each successively lower level of the organization complies with that policy and is capable of carrying it out. It is also a truism that participants at the lowest level in the hierarchy are the most "difficult" to mobilize and integrate into the organization. A style of patrol is basically the manner in which an administrative police policy is executed. The policy may prescribe that the patrol officer overlook certain types of illegal acts; it may order that he or she minimally enforce particular laws or be sensitive to and strictly enforce others. If the administrative order setting a patrol style does not win the cooperation of the patrol officer, it is certain to fail. Thus, the success of any high-echelon policy that involves the performance of patrol officers is contingent on compliance with that policy. If the administrator's orders are not binding on the patrol officers, no distinctive style of patrol will result; all that will be demonstrated will be the responses of the officers to other aspects of the social environment, especially, how fellow patrol officers perform.

The success of this strategy depends on the capacity of the administrator to create loyalty to internal policies. With the rise of police unions, the discontent of black patrol officers, low pay, and relatively less security for the officers, organizational control is a major problem in all the large police departments. . . .

The effectiveness of the watchman, legalistic, and service styles of patrol will also depend on the degree of political consensus among the community groups patrolled, the clarity of the boundaries of community neighborhoods, competition between the police and self-help or vigilante groups, and the relative importance of nonoccupational norms in enforcement practice—that is, the importance of racial or ethnic similarities between the patrol officers and the people in their neighborhoods. If a clear social consensus on the meaning of the law and what is expected of the police can be established within a community, a well-directed policy of control over police patrol is the most logical and rational approach to police work. In some communities, largely suburban and middle class, the police can carry out what their public demands and a degree of harmony exists. This consensus is absent in our inner cities.

Secrecy and Collaboration

The use of secrecy by the police is, as we have pointed out, a strategy employed not only to assist them in maintaining the appearance of political neutrality but to protect themselves against public complaints. Secrecy also helps to forestall public efforts to achieve better police service and to secure political accountability for police policy. Police collaboration with criminal elements—corruption, in other words—has much the same effect since it decreases the pressure to enforce "unenforceable" laws against certain segments of the police's clientele. . . .

There are several reasons why the police strategies of secrecy and collaboration will continue in force: (1) as long as the client—the public—is seen as the enemy, the police will treasure their secrecy and use it to engineer public consent to their policies and practices; (2) as long as a new political consensus is not formed on the nature and type of police control necessary in society as a whole, the organized, self-serving survival aims of police organizations will emerge victorious. Any well-organized consensual, secretive organization can resist the efforts of an unorganized public, managed by rhetoric and appearances, to reform it; (3) as long as there remains a lack of consensus on the enforcement of our "moralistic" laws, police corruption and selective law enforcement will continue. Collaboration to reduce adversary relationships with the criminal segment of society will always be an effective strategy—providing a sudden upsurge in public morality doesn't temporarily subject the police to a full-scale "housecleaning." Replacements would, of course, be subject to the same pressures and would, in all likelihood, eventually take the same line of least resistance.

One solution to corruption is said to be better educated, more professional police officers. By recruiting the better educated, the more professionalized police departments also seek to diminish the expression of political attitudes on the job and the tendency of police officers to form political power groups based on their occupation. . . . There is, however, no evidence that college-educated or better-paid police officers are "better police officers"; nor is there any evidence that "better officers" alone will solve the essentially structural problems of the occupation.

We can tentatively conclude from this review that corruption will remain with us as long as laws remain that stipulate punishments for actions on which a low public consensus exists. It will remain when there is likely to be a low visibility of police performance, and it will remain while there is a high public demand for illegal services—gambling, prostitution, abortion—and the concomitant need of the police for information on these services from the practitioners themselves.

Symbiosis and Justice

Although the police have the principal discretion in the field with reference to the detection, surveillance, and appraisal of alleged offenders, the final disposition of a criminal case must be made in the courts. The police are thus dependent on the courts in a very special way for their successes. The ideal model of the criminal justice system makes the police essentially the fact gatherers and apprehenders, while the courts are to be the decision-makers.

The police attempt to appear efficient has led them as we have noted before to seek the good pinch, the arrest that will stand up in court. With victimless crimes, such as those involving gambling or drugs or prostitution, the police control the situation since they alone decide whether an offense has been committed and whether they have a legal case against the offender. To control the success rate in these cases, the police create a gaggle of informants, many of whom are compelled to give the police evidence in order to stay free of a potential charge against themselves for a violation similar to the one they are providing information about. In the case of more serious crimes, the problems are more complex; in these cases the police must rely on other informants, and their discretion on arrests and charges are more often exercised by administrators and prosecuting attorneys.

In the prosecution stage, the bureaucratic demands of the court system are paramount. Abraham Blumberg describes these demands and the tension between efficiency and "due process":

> The dilemma is frequently resolved through bureaucratically ordained shortcuts, deviations and outright rule violations by the members of the courts, from judges to stenographers, in order to meet production norms. Because they fear criticism on ethical as well as legal grounds, all the significant participants in the court's social structure are bound into an organized system of complicity. Patterned, covert, informal breaches, and evasions of "due process" are accepted as routine—they are institutionalized—but are nevertheless denied to exist.[3]

The net effect of this strain within the court system is to produce a higher rate of convictions by means of encouraging a plea of guilty to a lesser charge. As far as the police are concerned, then, the strategy of symbiosis is sound.

There are several undesirable effects of this symbiosis. First, it encourages corruption by permitting the police to make decisions about the freedom of their informants; it gives them an illegal hold and power over them, and thus it undercuts the rule of law. Second, many offenders with long criminal records are either granted their freedom as informants or allowed to plead guilty to lesser charges in return for the dismissal of a more serious charge. Skolnick calls this the "reversal of the hierarchy of penalties," because the more serious crimes of habitual criminals are prosecuted less zealously than the minor violations of first offenders. Third, it helps blur the distinction between the apprehension and prosecution aspects of our criminal-justice system.

Notes

[1] Although the imagery of the police and their own self-definition coincide on the dangers of being a police officer, at least one study has found that many other occupations are more dangerous. Police officers kill six times as many people as police officers are killed in the line of duty. In 1955, Robin found that the rate of police fatalities on duty, including accidents, was 33 per 100,000, less than the rate for mining (94), agriculture (55), construction (76), and transportation (44). Between 1950 and 1960, an average of 240 persons were killed each year by police officers—approximately six times the number of police officers killed by criminals. Gerald D. Robin, "Justifiable Homicide by Police Officers," *Journal of Criminal Law, Criminology and Police Science*, 54 (1963), 225–231.

[2] Arthur Niederhoffer, *Behind the Shield* (Garden City, NY: Doubleday, 1967), 221.

[3] Abraham Blumberg, *Criminal Justice* (Chicago: Quadrangle Press, 1967), 69.

Chicano Youth Gangs and Crime

The Creation of a Moral Panic

Marjorie S. Zatz

In the summer of 1978 newspaper accounts relying on information provided by the police depicted a serious flare-up of gang violence in the city of Phoenix. These accounts led almost immediately to the allocation of $40,000 to the police for development of a computerized information-retrieval system on gang members and their delinquent acts. Funds for personnel and equipment were authorized in September 1978, with the city council also authorizing application for a grant from the Law Enforcement Assistance Administration to form a six-member juvenile gang crime unit. At that time, police estimated that the number of gangs in the city had grown over the past 18 months from 5 or 6 to about 35, with each gang consisting of 12 to 18 identifiable members (Arizona Republic 1978). Funding from LEAA was obtained, with the first of three $153,000 grants arriving in February 1979.

Nine months later, the head of the Phoenix police gang unit was quoted as saying:

> The number of youth gangs in the city has doubled in the last six months . . .
>
> There used to be 50 to 60 gangs but now there are between 100 and 120 . . .
>
> The number of gang members totals 3,000 to 4,000 (*Tucson Citizen* 1979).

Zatz, Marjorie S., *Chicano Youth Gangs and Crime: The Creation of a Moral Panic* (pp. 129–158). Copyright © 1987. Reprinted with kind permission from Kluwer Academic Publishers.

Thus, the scope of the problem was depicted by the police as increasing at an alarming rate. The number of gangs reputedly went from 5 or 6 to 35 in 18 months, then to 50 or 60 in the next three months, and then to between 100 and 120. Similarly, police estimates had the number of gang members, most of whom were young Chicano men, increasing from at most 630 (35 gangs of 18 members) to between 3,000 and 4,000 within about 27 months.

How and why the police, media, and elected officials of Phoenix suddenly discovered that the city had a Chicano youth gang problem is the subject of this article. More specifically, I use a variety of qualitative and quantitative data to examine how and why young Chicano men, clustered together in age-sex groupings that are traditional in the Mexican culture, became defined by social control agents as so serious a threat to the community that they were perceived, to use Steven Spitzer's (1975) colorful imagery, as "social dynamite" ready to explode at any minute.

I suggest that the *social imagery* of Chicano youth gangs, rather than their actual *behavior*, lay at the root of the "gang problem" in Phoenix. The convergence of a set of factors, each of which had socially accepted stereotypic characteristics, raised the threat potential to the point at which a "moral panic" ensued and drastic action by social control agents became justified (Cohen 1972, Hall et al. 1978). The key factors which converged in creating the social imagery of Chicano youth gangs as volatile social dynamite were: (1) the interests of the police in acquiring federal funding for specialized functions; (2) the imagery of gangs, and especially of Chicano gangs, as violent; and (3) the imagery of Mexicans and Chicanos as "different." These images joined together to create a vision of disorder that was useful to the police and advantageous to the media.

The Basis for a Moral Panic

The alleged rapid increase in the number of gangs and gang members between about 1977 and 1983 is on the surface suspect. When placed in their demographic context, these police estimates become even more questionable. According to the 1980 Census, there were 6,358 Spanish-origin males between the ages of 10–14 living in the city of Phoenix. Another 6,821 Spanish-origin males were between the ages of 15–49, for a total of 13,179 Spanish-origin teenagers and young adults, including those too old for juvenile court processing (U.S. Department of Commerce 1983).[1] That means that approximately *one-quarter* of the young Chicano males in the city were identified by police as violence prone gang members. Given such a scenario, one would expect violent crime to have escalated dramatically during this period. In contrast, however, incidents of violent crime in Phoenix increased slightly in the late 1970s and then decreased in the early 1980s (U.S. Department of Justice, 1976–1985 reports; gender and age breakdowns by ethnicity not available). Moreover, this local pattern was quite consistent with national trends for violent crime by juvenile males.[2] Since the Uniform Crime Reports do not provide a basis for the fear of increased violence, we must search for alternative explanations for the growing fear of violence by Chicano youths. . . .

The Convergence of Social Images

At the most visible level, social problems, problem populations, and the responses to them are created, at least in part, by the media. As Young (1979) argues, the media confirm, distort, and structure the conflict between police and members of the deviant group. Through the use of crime themes, the media keep public attention focused on the "gang problem" and contribute to a definition of Chicano youths, and their behaviors, as problematic. So doing heightens public awareness of a problem in the community and contributes to a particular ideology of crime (Fishman 1978, Christensen et al. 1982). By allocating resources in the form of a "gang squad" to combat gang-related crime and by supplying the media with the raw material for stories about gangs and their delinquent acts, the police also enhance the perceived threat to the community from this group. Thus, the police do not only respond to crime problems—they also help to create public consciousness of crime and to escalate the perceived threat from marginalized groups (Michalowski 1985: 169, Reiman 1984).

At a less visible level, rooted deeper in the structuring of society and the organization of power relations, defining certain groups as deviant and requiring the intervention of the state control apparatus depoliticizes the process by which powerful groups within society maintain control over less powerful groups (Pfohl 1985).[3] Then, otherwise questionable police responses become legitimized. What might have been viewed as harassment of poor Chicano youths is depicted instead as the legitimate use of the state apparatus to control troublesome behavior. As a consequence, the exercise of complex forms of social control by an expanded police force is also legitimized (Harring 1983, Michalowski 1985).

The Image of Youth Gangs as Violent

The term *gang* has established linguistic meaning and evokes powerful and threatening imagery. Gang members flash scary tattoos as well as knives. They dress in strange garb. Gangs connote violence, guns, and mayhem in the streets. Dating from Thrasher's (1927) study of youths in Chicago's ethnic communities, sociologists have evidenced a keen interest in juvenile gangs. According to Miller (1975), contemporary youth gangs pose a greater threat to public order and safety than even before because of their use of guns.

In addition to this sociological interest, law enforcement agencies and policy makers in recent years have directed an increasing amount of personnel and financial resources to controlling youth gangs. Research on violent offenders, including youthful gang members, has been a major funding priority of the National Institute of Justice. Its predecessor, the Law Enforcement Assistance Administration, was also concerned about the threat of gang violence. It authorized funds for creation of specialized "gang squads" in cities across the U.S. to assist police in identifying gang members and reducing gang violence (see Miller 1975). By freeing up a detail of police officers from other duties so that they could attend to gang youths and by increasing the number of plain-clothed officers in slums and barrios, police work was redesigned in a way which increasingly widened the net of youngsters who fit the police criteria for gang membership. In Phoenix, this national priority translated into the establishment in April of 1979 of an LEAA-funded gang squad. This squad was composed largely, if not totally, of bilingual officers. It also translated into the procurement of additional funds over the next few years from LEAA and the local city council for personnel and computer equipment used to track gang-identified youths.

National and local fears did not just focus on violent gangs, however. Rather, violence by gangs became incorporated into wider concerns with violence by youths. For example, Fagan et al. (1984) conducted a large-scale study of violent offenders in 1982–83 in six cities, including Phoenix. They found, however, that many juveniles initially classified on the basis of arrests as serious violent offenders were really not violent. Indeed, 33 percent of the petitions filed in juvenile court for violent offenses were dropped or dismissed, and another 19 percent resulted in adjudications for lesser offenses, not the serious violent offenses initially charged. Similarly, the Violent Offender Program, a $4 million research and treatment program funded by the Office of Juvenile Justice and Delinquency Prevention, was designed to identify chronic juvenile offenders and test intervention strategies. This program floundered, however, because a sufficient number of chronically violent juveniles could not be found, even though the eligibility criteria were continually expanded (see Bortner 1987, especially chapter 7 for a further discussion of these and other programs).

If, as all of the evidence presented here suggests, gangs did not engage in much violent crime, why was the gang problem so distorted and overstated? Downes (1966: 536) suggests that the gang myth "makes adolescents' occasional delinquencies appear much more purposeful and systematic than they in fact are," thereby exaggerating their differences from conventional society and minimizing their similarities. Secondly, the gang myth deflects attention from the realities facing these poor and minority youths: poor job opportunities, poor schools, and "the social hypocrisy they sense when the rhetoric of equality in our society clashes blatantly with their sole experience of inequality" (1966: 536). This inequality and powerlessness may be especially odious for poor and minority males living in a culture that emphasizes maleness and dominance, and they may view violence as a means of expressing power (Schwendinger and Siegel-Schwendinger 1985). In turn, the combination of male exclusivity, poverty, and ethnic minority status, all of which coalesce to form the imagery of urban youth gangs, also converge into the imagery of those who are different and physically threatening.

The ideological message perpetuated by the myth of gang violence forms part of the larger ideological function of a marginalized population in advanced capitalist societies. By emphasizing the threat from below and associating crime with poverty and ethnic minorities, discontent is funneled into hostility and fear of the poor and minorities, and away from the social structures and institutions that create and perpetuate inequality and injustice (see Reiman 1984, especially chapter 4).

The Image of Mexicans and Chicanos as Different

The concept of "outsiders," of those who are in some important way "different" from the mainstream, has been recognized by sociologists at least since publication of Becker's (1963) monograph by that title. Those who are different, those who cannot be understood, are feared. Differences in culture and language that threaten, by their very difference, the presumed naturalness of the established hegemonic economic and cultural order become symbolic of larger differences. In response, attempts are made to remove, or silence, that difference. Two recent examples in the United States are the social movements to make English the official language of the nation and to pass legislation designed to halt the flow of undocumented, primarily Mexican, workers into the country. The laws that resulted from these movements reduce the extent to which "different" people, with different cultures and languages, can threaten the established hegemony. It is quite predictable, then, that groups of Chicano youths are feared. White middle-class youths may be viewed as deviant within the dominant Anglo culture, but they are culturally and linguistically understandable. They are not "different." In contrast, dark-skinned, Spanish-speaking young men congregating in urban ghettos are "different," and thus, potentially threatening.

Within the Mexican and Chicano culture, however, youthful groupings based on age and gender play traditional and accepted roles in the community. Indeed, they form a central part of the internal dynamics of the community organization. As Moore observes:

> The "gang" in Mexican and Mexican American life is not necessarily delinquent. . . . In the 1930s the precursors of the three Los Angeles gangs we have studied were respectable groups of young men. . . . Then, in the 1940s, the gangs developed a style which soon evoked a sharp reaction from the Anglo community. It was the first clear instance of ascriptive labeling. This was the *pachuco* fad. . . . But the gangs did not seem to be deviant. To be sure, there were fights, occasional serious wounds, and even deaths. But this was in the tradition of aggressive barrio-based youth groups (1985: 5).

Chicano gangs are quite distinct from other gangs (Erlanger 1979, Horowitz 1983, Moore et al. 1978, 1983, Maxson et al. 1985, Zatz 1985).

The extended real and fictive (i.e., compadrazgo) family structure which typifies Chicano barrios links the boys in a wide network of mutual support and obligation. In many ways, the Chicano gang is indistinguishable from the community of which it forms a part. Indeed, the name of the gang is often the same as that of the barrio. The borrowing of the barrio name for the name of the gang is symbolic of the strong social ties linking neighborhood youths and their integration into the wider Chicano culture.

Convergence: Chicano Youth and the Threat of Disorder

Latinos constitute the second largest, and the most rapidly growing, racial/ethnic minority in the United States. The Mexican culture and Spanish language are continually reinvigorated by an ongoing migration from Mexico and Central America. The marginality stemming from the conflict between cultures and from social and economic disadvantage, however, is also reaffirmed, as is the political threat to Anglo domination raised by the growing Latino population, particularly in the Southwestern part of the United States. Vigil (1983) suggests that the Chicano gang, as a phenomenon, developed as an outgrowth of the problems of adaptation from traditional Mexican cultural, social and economic patterns to those of Anglo-America. Over several decades, a Chicano gang subculture evolved, with its own enculturation and socialization patterns. The conflicts between Chicano youths and social control agents, including school officials and police, contributed to their reputation as a source of urban disorder. As Moore (1985) notes, however, it was not until the Sleepy Lagoon murder case and the Zoot-Suit Riots between Chicano youths and Anglo sailors in 1943 that Chicano youth gangs were defined as "problematic" by social control agents and the media. These events were important for two reasons. First, the negative stereotyping of Mexicans by the sheriff's office and judge hearing the murder case portrayed all members of this ethnic group as bloodthirsty savages who were biologically prone to violence (Morales 1972). This social imagery contributed to the perception of Mexicans as "different" and threatening. Second, the Zoot-Suit Riots were a series of direct and violent confrontations between Chicano youths and a branch of the state's legitimate use of force—the navy.

Chicano gangs are collectivities of young men who come together for mutual support and who, individually and as a group, form an integral part of the community's internal organization. As alienated, marginalized youths fighting with the state's control apparatus for guardianship of the barrios, they appear particularly volatile. Where the police are viewed as hostile outsiders who not only fail to protect, but who actually threaten the autonomy of the community and its members, confrontations between the police and groups of young men are likely to ensue. This battle for control over the community calls into question the ability of the state's social control apparatus to maintain order. Perhaps as a response to this threat of disorder and the perceived disrespect for the authority of the state, the legal system has long been used to control Chicano youths:

> law enforcement and barrio relationships are often antagonistic. . . . In
> large part, this hostility stems from the historical legacy of police/com-
> munity relations that started and has persisted on a confrontational
> route . . . this situation has bred an over-policing barrio pattern, *often
> leading to the labeling of even law abiding residents as antisocial and
> criminal.* As a result, many who appear to be cholo are inaccurately
> perceived as gang members and *any youngster living in the barrio is apt
> to be considered a gang member* (Vigil 1983: 58; my emphasis).

By defining all, or even many, barrio youths as antisocial and criminal
gang members, the police escalate the potential threat from the barrio. As
a consequence, the *perceived* threat, and the reaction to it, may far surpass
the *actual* threat, both in the number of youths involved and in the extent
to which they engage in violent or disorderly conduct. That is, the police
and media definition of these youths as "social dynamite" appears to
reflect and articulate fears that extend beyond a reasonable concern for
safety and social peace. This disjuncture between a perceived and an
actual threat has been called a moral panic:

> When such discrepancies appear between threat and reaction,
> between what is perceived and what this is a perception of, we have
> good evidence to suggest we are in the presence of an ideological dis-
> placement. We call this displacement a *moral panic* (Hall 1978: 29)[4]

As is common in other studies of crime waves (e.g., Fishman 1978) the
threatening group in this situation was poor, young, minority, and male.[5]
This set of characteristics forms part of the imagery of Chicano youths as
politically volatile "social dynamite" whose acts, or the fear of their potential acts, engender "moral panics." The social imagery of gangs as violent,
fear-inducing gun-slingers combines with that of Mexicans and Chicanos
as "different" from the Anglo mainstream linguistically and culturally.

Latinos and Anglos have always viewed one another as "different" and
not fully understandable. Recent demographic changes in the Southwest
have forced Latinos and Anglos to take greater notice of one another, however, as an increasing number of Anglos moved to Phoenix and other sun-
belt cities in search of jobs and a comfortable climate at the same time that
economic hardships and political strife led ever larger numbers of Mexicans and Central Americans north in search of jobs and political refuge. As
a consequence, Anglos came into greater contact with people who were
dark, Indian in appearance, Spanish-speaking, and who practiced different
customs. The Anglo response to the presence of larger numbers of "different" people was to try to silence that difference through legislation that
would make English the official language of the country . . . [27 states
have such statutes] and that would close off the southern borders and
reserve jobs for U.S. citizens, preferably Anglos. Where the cultural differences could not be silenced, the Anglo response was fear, particularly of
violence at the hands of the young men.

When we add to this scenario a national law-and-order campaign aimed primarily at youthful offenders which funded specialized police gang squads, increased fear that Los Angeles gangs would spread to Phoenix, and antipathy between the police and the judiciary, we have the ingredients for discovery of the "Chicano youth gang problem." Chicano youths became defined as disorderly, contemptuous of authority, defiant, and violent. This combination of social images into something more threatening than each of its parts would suggest has been called convergence:

> "Convergence" occurs when two or more activities are linked in the process of signification so as to implicitly or explicitly draw parallels between them. Thus, the image of "student hooliganism" links "student" protest to the separate problem of "hooliganism"—whose stereotypical characteristics are already part of socially available knowledge (Hall 1978: 223).[6]

Like student protest and hooliganism in England, youth gangs, Chicanos, and crime waves are socially known to the general public of the United States. By setting the new problem of a perceived growth in violent crimes by Chicano youths in the old context of gangs, the threat-potential to society was amplified. This threat far surpassed the reality of gang violence as evidenced by the statistical data. In reality, violence by young Chicano men was not a major problem in Phoenix, nor was youthful violence a significant problem in the nation as a whole. Indeed, violent crime by young men decreased during the period under study. However, gang violence became *perceived* as a serious problem, and social control agencies and the media *responded* to it as a serious problem. The result of this perceived threat was an increase for the police in federal funds, for the media in thematic stories, for the Anglo community in the need for law-and-order, and for the Chicano community in police harassment.

Conclusions

During the late 1970s and continuing into the early 1980s, the "Chicano youth gang problem" was discovered by the Phoenix police and media. Tied to this discovery was acquisition of federal funds to create and maintain a gang squad within the Phoenix police department. The extensiveness of the problem, however, was disputed by the community and by some social service agencies and counselors working with Chicano youth. It is not at all clear that Phoenix truly faced a major problem of gang-related crime. What is clear, however, is that Chicano youth gangs became defined as a serious social problem—a problem to which the media and law enforcement agencies responded vociferously and vigorously. In so doing, a "moral panic" (Cohen 1972) was created.

Based on analyses of a variety of data sources, I conclude that it was the social imagery of Chicano youth gangs, rather than their actual behavior, that lay at the root of the gang problem in Phoenix. The imagery of gangs as violent converged with that of Mexicans as "different." With the convergence of these images, the potential threat of disorder and of contempt for law escalated to the point at which a "moral panic" ensued. This is not to say that there were no Chicano youth gangs and no gang-related crimes. There were and are. But there was also the usual gamut of regular street crime, corporate crime, and so forth, without any specialized "squads" in place to combat them.

The gang problem emerged concurrent with demographic changes in the Southwest which catapulted Phoenix into one of the ten largest cities in the U.S., a national law-and-order campaign designed to combat lawlessness and aimed particularly at youthful offenders, and rising nationalism and xenophobia. Within this context, the youthful groupings that play a traditional role in the Mexican culture became viewed as problematic, and the youths as "social dynamite" (Spitzer 1975) that would explode if actions were not taken quickly. Increased legal repression and control over the escalating menace of gang violence was enhanced by intensified media coverage of the gang problem. By defining Chicano youths as the source of community disorder, the increased presence of social control agents in the lives of barrio residents became viewed as necessary. As a consequence, legal control over the resistive behavior of this economically and politically subordinate group, and the threat that it posed to the state, was legitimized.

Notes

[1] Extending analysis to the county, the 1980 Census shows a total of 22,963 Spanish-origin mates between the ages of 10–19, 10,903 of whom were between 10–14 years of age (U.S. Department of Commerce, 1983).

[2] See Bortner (1987) for a more general discussion of the overdramatization of violence by adolescents, both in Phoenix and nationally.

[3] As Pfohl has observed, the categorization of groups and acts as deviant is a complex political act located within a particular framework of social, economic, and political power relations. By creating the impression that those without power are the source of community tension, "a systemic control over the resistive behaviors of the have-nots would appear natural or necessary. . . . This, of course, is exactly what happens when power-resistive people or groups of people are categorized as deviant" (1985: 334).

[4] Hall et al. further argue that the cycle of moral panics led to a "law-and-order society" (1978: 29, 323). The state became more coercive as a response to the crisis of hegemony—a crisis that was symbolized in their study by the problem of mugging, and the official response to which was legitimized by the potentiality of a mugging crime wave and a general breakdown of law and order.

[5] Harring (1983:245–246) argues that crime waves, and law-and-order campaigns more generally, exhibit a strong anti-working-class bias, contribute to socially delineating the boundaries between respectable and unacceptable working class behavior, and legitimate police intervention in working-class communities. He argues further that although some elements of the working class may join in once a crime-related issue emerges politically, "their participation cannot obscure the class interests that law and order issues serve" (1983: 227–28). An anti-minority and anti-working-class bias in selectively labeling individuals and groups as criminal or deviant and in setting the limits of the law and of legitimate police behavior has been noted by others as well (e.g., Black 1976, 1984, Michalowski 1985, Pfohl 1985).

[6] Convergence is an integral part of what Hall et al. (1978) call a "signification spiral." This refers to a situation in which some deviant event or activity takes on special meaning, or significance, which makes it appear even more threatening than it was initially. The signification spiral is modeled after Wilkins' deviance amplification spiral in which "less tolerance leads to more acts being defined as crimes leads to more action against criminals" (1965: 90).

References

Arizona Republic (1978) "City will use computer in war on teen gangs." 9 September: B1–2.

Becker, Howard S. (1963) *Outsiders: Studies in the Sociology of Deviance*. New York: The Free Press.

Black, Donald (1976) *The Behavior of Law*. New York: Academic Press.

Black, Donald (1984) "Social control as a dependent variable." Pp. 1–36 in: Donald Black (ed.) *Toward a General Theory of Social Control* Volume 1. New York: Academic Press.

Bortner, M. A. (1987) *Delinquency and Justice: An Age of Crisis*. New York: McGraw-Hill.

Cohen, Stanley (1972) *Folk Devils and Moral Panics: The Creation of the Mods and Rockers*. London: McGibbon and Kee.

Christensen, Jon, Janet Schmidt, and Joel Henderson (1982) "The selling of the police: Media, ideology, and crime control." *Contemporary Crises* 6: 227–239.

Downes, David (1966) "The gang myth." *The Listener* 75: 534–537.

Erlanger, Howard S. (1979) "Estrangement, machismo and gang violence." *Social Science Quarterly* 60: 235–248.

Fagan, Jeffrey, Eliot Hartstone, Cary Rudman, and Karen Hansen (1984) "System processing of violent juvenile offenders: An empirical assessment." Pp. 117–136 in: Robert A. Mathias. Paul DeMuro, and Richard S. Allinson (eds) *Violent Juvenile Offenders. An Anthology*. San Francisco: National Council on Crime and Delinquency.

Fishman, Mark (1978) "Crime waves as ideology." *Social Problems* 25: 531–543.

Hall, Stuart, Chas Critcher, Tony Jefferson, John Clarke, and Brian Roberts (1978). *Policing the Crisis: Mugging, The State, and Law and Order*. New York: Holmes and Meier.

Harring, Sidney L. (1983) *Policing a Class Society: The Experience of American Cities, 1865–1915*. New Brunswick: Rutgers University Press.

Horowitz, Ruth (1983) *Honor and the American Dream: Culture and Identity in a Chicano Community*. New Brunswick: Rutgers University Press.

Maxson, Cheryl L., Margaret A. Gordon and Malcolm W. Klein (1985) "Differences between gang and nongang homicides." *Criminology* 23: 209–221.

Michalowski, Raymond J. (1985) *Order, Law, and Crime: An Introduction to Criminology*. New York: Random House.

Miller, Walter B. (1975) *Violence By Youth Gangs and Youth Groups as a Crime Problem in Major American Cities*. Office of Juvenile Justice and Delinquency Prevention, U.S. Department of Justice. Washington: U.S. Government Printing Office.

Moore, Joan W., Robert Garcia, Carlos Garcia, Luis Cerda, and Frank Valencia (1978) *Homeboys: Gangs, Drugs, and Prison in the Barrios of Los Angeles*. Philadelphia: Temple University Press.

Moore, Joan W. (1985) "Isolation and stigmatization of an underclass: The case of Chicano gangs in East Los Angeles." *Social Problems* 33:1–12.

Morales, Armando (1972) *Ando Sangrando: A Study of Mexican American Police Conflict*. La Puente, CA: Perspectiva Publications.

Pfohl, Stephen J. (1985) *Images of Deviance and Social Control: A Sociological History*. New York: McGraw-Hill.

Reiman, Jeffrey H. (1984) *The Rich Get Richer and the Poor Get Prison: Ideology, Clan, and Criminal Justice*, second ed. New York: John Wiley and Sons.

Schwendinger, Herman and Julia R. Siegel-Schwendinger (1985) *Adolescent Subcultures and Delinquency*. New York: Praeger.

Spitzer, Steven (1975) "Toward a Marxian theory of deviance." *Social Problems* 22: 638–651.

Thrasher, Frederic (1927) *The Gang: A Study of 1313 Gangs in Chicago*. Chicago: University of Chicago Press.

Tucson Citizen (1979) "Gangs proliferate." 28 November.

U.S. Commission on Civil Rights (1970) *Mexican Americans and the Administration of Justice in the Southwest*. Washington: U.S. Government Printing Office.

U.S. Department of Commerce, Bureau of the Census (1983) *1980 Census of Population and Housing Census Tracts*. Washington: U.S. Government Printing Office.

U.S. Department of Justice, Federal Bureau of Investigation (1976–1985) *Uniform Crime Reports 1975–1984*. Washington: U.S. Government Printing Office.

Vigil, James Diego (1983) "Chicano gangs: One response to Mexican urban adaptation in the Los Angeles area." *Urban Anthropology* 12: 45–75.

Wilkins, Leslie T. (1965) *Social Deviance. Social Policy, Action, and Research*. Englewood Cliffs, NJ: Prentice-Hall.

Yablonsky, Lewis (1959) "The delinquent gang as a near-group." *Social Problems* 7: 108–117.

Young, Jock (1979) "Drugs and the role of the police as amplifiers of deviancy." Pp. 96–108 in: Victoria L. Swigert and Ronald A. Farrell (eds.) *The Substance of Social Deviance*. Sherman Oaks, CA: Alfred Publishing Co.

Zatz, Marjorie S. (1985) "Los cholos: Legal processing of Chicano gang members." *Social Problems* 33: 13–30.

Inventing Criminal Justice
Myth and Social Construction

Victor E. Kappeler

The phrase "criminal justice" invokes powerful images and under-standings. It conjures images of uniformed police officers pursuing dangerous criminals down dark alleys or detectives meticulously combing over crime scenes collecting evidence for criminal identification. The phrase can prompt dramatic courtroom scenes where magistrates sit in black flowing robes high above courtroom participants, dispensing equal justice for all. Or it can evoke darker images of crowded places of confinement where dangerous jumper-clad inmates pay their debts to society and pass the time planning new crimes or violent escapes. We might even think of criminal justice as a unified and seamless system that responds to the threat of crime through various agencies dedicated to making society safer and administering justice in a fair and impartial fashion. All these images, however, are constructed mystifications of the reality of criminal justice in U.S. society.

When we think of criminal justice, we usually don't think of police officials falsifying crime statistics to secure resources for their agencies. We don't think about detectives clearing stacks of unsolved cases by pinning crimes on their latest suspect despite no evidence of guilt. Seldom does the image of prosecutors and defense attorneys bargaining to dispose of entire dockets of criminal cases in the backrooms of courthouses come to mind. Nor do we think of attorneys trading the futures of defendants to enhance

Victor Kappeler wrote this article expressly for this book.

the possibility of a judicial appointment or magistrates handing down sentences for purposes of political advancement. Seldom do we think about the children left behind when inmates are sentenced to prison for drug possession or whether inmates really emerge from prison rehabilitated. Our attention is directed away from these alternative images of criminal justice by an array of social actors and myths.

Images of justice are not happenstance. While it is comforting to think of criminal justice as a fixed reality void of political and ideological influences, nothing could be further from the truth. Criminal justice, like crime, is a social construction that shifts with intellectual perspective, political influence, social sentiment, cultural values, and the interests of powerful groups in society. The very notion that criminal justice constitutes a "system" distinct from the larger social context in which it operates is a powerful myth that masks vested interests and contradictions. Likewise, to think of the criminal justice system as protecting us from criminals and evildoers is to misunderstand the powerful forces that construct our reality of justice. By merely invoking the phrase "criminal justice system," we limit our conception of justice. In doing so, we reduce social harm to the behaviors defined as criminal. Likewise, the phrase compels us to view criminal justice as a naturally occurring or even organic functional response to crime. Alternative conceptions of justice are blocked from consideration by preconceived notions.

Learning Criminal Justice Myths

Where do myths come from and how are they learned? Criminal justice myths are collective presentations of reality. Everyone we come into contact with can add a bit of myth to our understanding of criminal justice. We learn about crime myths from our parents, when we are in church, socializing with friends, and from our teachers. Many of our criminal justice practices are based on false conceptions created by the mass media, urban legend, ideology, or pure political power. The process of producing this unified vision is social construction. The largest and most powerful contributors to the social construction of criminal justice are the mass media and government.

The media have a vested interest in the promotion of criminal justice myths. First, the public is fascinated by sensational crime. Crime has become a media product that sells perhaps better than any other media commodity. Attracting a larger audience translates into more advertising dollars. Simply put, the more viewers or readers, the more money a television station or newspaper makes. Second, alternative explanations of criminal justice rarely resonate with the viewers—and a loss of viewers equals a loss of dollars. Third, expression of views that contradict official government positions can lead to enhanced regulation of the industry and a loss of news sources. Media depictions of criminal justice are intertwined with government, money, and ideology. The media are therefore compelled to present a very simplistic, standardized view of justice that does not alienate those who either control or consume it.

The government makes a significant contribution to the social construction of criminal justice. The government is a powerful mythmaker with a vested interest in maintaining the existing definitions of crime, protecting the current operation and public perception of criminal justice, and extending formal social control to groups and behaviors that are perceived to be a threat to the existing social order. These interests extend to seeing that the current response to crime is not significantly altered in purpose or function. Dramatic changes in criminal justice are never implemented because the status quo serves the interests of government, crime-control agencies, and social elites. We build more prisons, mete out longer prison terms, reinstate the death penalty, and move more offenders through the criminal justice system at faster speeds.

The government controls, directs, and molds messages about criminal justice for public consumption. The government can suppress information for national security reasons; it can punish "obscenity"; and it can reward the media for presenting official versions of crime myths. Shaping the content of messages and rewarding the media for myth presentation are frequently done under the guise of public service announcements, controlled press briefings, and the release of state-sponsored research reports.

The government is also a form of media. The government controls extensive print publication resources, commissions and funds research, operates radio stations, and exposes the television-viewing audience to government-sponsored messages. With great regularity governmental agencies like the Federal Bureau of Investigation (FBI), the Bureau of Justice Statistics (BJS), and the National Institute of Justice (NIJ) distribute press releases about criminal justice to the media. One must remember that these press releases are written by the same people who fund the research and decide what statistics should be collected and shared with the public. While much of the research that these agencies release provides basic and needed information, it is often oversimplified and sometimes designed to elicit social concern—at a minimum, it is filtered through a process shaped and controlled by political interests.

In addition to providing the media and public with distorted statistics on crime, the government also disseminates a highly selective ideology of crime and justice. The media need constant sources of information to feed their demand for news products. Convenient sources like police officials and political leaders respond eagerly to media inquiries. Favorite sources for journalists' inquiries are often those who are readily available or those who reliably provide quotable statements.

In this pipeline to the media, governmental officials, criminal justice practitioners, and politicians have a distinct advantage over researchers and scholars. Michael Welch, Melissa Fenwick, and Meredith Roberts

(1998) examined the sources major newspapers used to craft their feature crime stories. These researchers found a striking ideological difference between governmental and academic sources. Generally, governmental spokespersons were more likely to advance a crime-control ideology, whereas academics were more likely to discuss crime causation. Likewise, politicians and criminal justice practitioners were more likely to construct crime in terms of deterrence and the personal pathology of criminals, whereas academics were more likely to discuss the social factors that contribute to crime. Additionally, governmental spokespersons were more likely to advocate stringent crime-control efforts packaged in slogans like "three strikes and you're out" and "get-tough-on-crime," while their academic counterparts subscribed to crime-control measures like education, the provision of social services, and reducing economic disparity and racism. "Reporters' dependence on authorities makes them—and by extension media consumers—particularly vulnerable to deliberate attempts to mislead by governments and agencies" (Hynds, 1990, p. 6).

Media depictions of criminal justice in the United States represent a form of knowledge construction where crime and the response to it is a hybrid product of governmental ideology and media distortion. The media and the government, whether independently or in concert, focus public attention on criminal justice problems, but perhaps more importantly they set the boundaries of thinkable solutions. These two powerful entities establish the seriousness of problems and inform the public of viable solutions. In the process, they sow the seeds of criminal justice myths and teach us how to think about crime and criminal justice.

Myths, Contradictions, and Criminal Justice

Many of our views of criminal justice are based on myths that either hide or attempt to reconcile social contradictions. Myths are conceptual schemes that assist us in interpreting reality and organizing our thoughts and beliefs about reality. Myths let us make sense of the world, reconcile contradictions, and explain processes and events we cannot readily understand. Myths tend to support the status quo by organizing the way we see reality. Myths, in this sense, are sources of authority and power because they allow us to adhere steadfastly to contrived belief systems even when reality contradicts them.

Myths tell us where in society problems reside, where we should look to find solutions, and what solutions are acceptable. Most of us learn that stealing is wrong. When people take property that does not belong to them, it is much easier to remember our early lessons and to label anyone who violates those teachings as criminals and wrongdoers than it is to question an economic system in which many live in poverty. It is comforting to attribute theft to individual greed without ever questioning the role culture and socialization play in creating the powerful desire to accumulate wealth. In this construction, criminal justice becomes the system that protects us from greedy and evil people rather than a system that maintains the economic order.

All myths contain fictions but are used as if they were true accounts of issues or events. The power of myths comes not from their ability to reflect reality accurately but from their repeated presentations. Myths gain power and take on new meanings as they are told and retold—and at some point evolve into truth for many people. The fiction in criminal justice myth comes not only from the fabrication of events but also from the transformation and distortion of ideas about criminal justice into common-sense truths. Crime myths are so powerful and can become so compounded in their public presentations that they shape our thoughts about and reactions to almost any issue related to criminal justice (Kappeler, Blumberg, & Potter, 2000). A lifetime's exposure to criminal justice myths make them seen reasonable and natural—just plain common sense.

Myths provide a conceptual framework from which to identify behaviors needing a criminal justice response, to develop our personal opinions about justice, and to apply ready-made solutions to problems. Myths support and maintain prevailing views of criminal justice and strengthen the tendency to rely on established conceptions of crime. Myths reinforce the current designation of conduct as criminal, support criminal justice practices, and provide the background assumptions for our social response to crime. In a sense, society becomes intellectually blinded by the mythology of criminal justice (Kappeler et al., 2000).

Myths can be restricted to specific criminal events, always presented as occurring regularly or with increasing frequency. Many myths cluster around stalkers, serial killers, or murderers who hide in the back seat of cars at shopping malls. They can tell us about mythical gang initiation rights that require members to victimize innocents (Best and Hutchinson, 1996), they may instruct us about depraved people who dispense poisonous candy to children at Halloween, or they may recount the bravery of cops on mean streets. Myths can broaden their scope by explaining the reasons people commit crime or by supporting our social response to crime. Depraved and evil people commit crime because our criminal justice system is too soft on criminals; the failure to prevent crime is the result of too few laws, police, judges, or prisons.

Myths of Crime and Human Nature

Myths of criminal justice are related to broader social myths about human behavior and society. These broad social myths make our constructions of criminal justice and response to crime seem all the more reasonable and unchallengeable. The way we construct and understand criminal justice is by promoting a series of powerful myths that guide us in interpreting reality in a very narrow fashion. Let's consider some of the broad myths that organize our thoughts about human behavior and criminal justice. These myths create a collective belief system—a powerful ideology—that hides contradictions.

Perhaps the most powerful and sustained social construction of criminal justice is the myth of the "divine lawgiver" and the "sanctity of law." This myth and its derivatives can be traced throughout recorded history from the pharaohs of ancient Egypt, through the divine rights of kings, and even to the founding fathers' declaration of independence. The myth holds that law is not the product of men; it is imbued with a divine quality, making it unquestionable and infallible. Transgressors against divine law are, if not evil, at least sinners in need of redemption, correction, or punishment. The truth, regardless of one's religious beliefs, is that law has no divine source. People just as fallible as the rest of us create law.

Modern mystifications of the law in this fashion include assertions like "the law protects us and grants us our freedom," and "we live in a nation of laws not men." Law has little to do with divinity and freedom. Law is a man-made social construction that protects vested interests and limits, not expands, freedom. The atrocities committed by the Nazis during World War II, the racism of apartheid in South Africa, and the treatment of women under the Taliban in Afghanistan were legally sanctioned. The myth of the divinity of lawgivers and law, however, masks this fact and begs for unquestioned obedience. When the state, its leaders, and their legislation are constructed as something greater than a human product, questioning becomes unthinkable.

Another equally powerful myth explains criminal behavior. According to the myth of human rationality, criminal behavior is a matter of individual choice; criminals are solely responsible for their actions. Crime is not the product of social, political, or economic conditions nor is it the product of the laws that have been passed defining crime. This construction of criminality ignores the fact that society is not just an aggregate of individuals who voluntarily engage in uninfluenced behavior. We all make decisions, think, and behave in a social context. The criminal justice system, especially in the courtroom, goes to great pains to exclude any consideration of the social, historical, political, or economic influences on people.

Some laws are created for the purpose of constructing the "impartiality of the state judiciary and preserving the appearance of the impartiality of the state judiciary . . . because it preserves public confidence in the judiciary" (see *Republican Party of Minnesota v. White*, 2002, p. 9). Likewise, criminal behavior is isolated to the moment in which it occurs and to the individual criminal. The myth focuses our attention on criminal "events" and directs our criminal justice response to these events. The view of individuals as having free will to make rational choices means criminals are also rational social actors who must face the consequences for deliberately violating the law. However, most media presentations of crime, and the vast majority of political speech on crime, are not about rational calculating criminals; they are about senseless random acts of violence. In essence everyone who commits a crime is a rational actor for purposes of punishment. For purposes of generating fear of crime and building the criminal justice system, society is painted as beset by irrational acts of violence.

The myth of human rationality is more about the generation and maintenance of social order than it is about the empirical reality of human behavior. It has very little to do with why people behave the way they do. The myth doesn't explain atrocities, but it does allow us to punish all transgressors without questioning the fundamental fairness or acceptability of the model from which punishment is generated. Breaking the law is the sole criterion. We seldom ask why some socially harmful acts are regulated, some criminalized, and others not addressed at all.

A related myth of rationality and criminal justice is the notion that crime can be deterred by the threat and administration of punishment. In this line of reasoning, it follows that the more certain and severe the punishment, the less likely people are to commit crime. This myth focuses once again on the individual rather than on the social order and reinforces punishment as the most appropriate criminal justice response. The myth is contradictory even if we accept its premise. If criminals are rational actors, then they will not commit crime because of fear of punishment. The high recidivism rates reported in nearly every study of punishment highlight the glaring inaccuracy of this construction of human behavior. The myth has another inherent contradiction. If everyone is individually responsible for their behaviors and social influences and conditions do not direct human behavior, how can punishment—determined and administered by society—prevent crime? In addition, the myth ignores the fact that the threat of punishment is not the reason most people abstain from crime. Ask yourself this question: If all the laws, police, and courts were abolished tomorrow would you go out and murder, rob, steal, or rape? It is not the threat of punishment that makes us conform.

Although most myths deny the role of social influences, one contemporary myth about the causes of crime is that crime is related to a deterioration or breakdown in certain social institutions. The sustained and frequent commission of crime is said to be a product of the failure of the family, religious institutions, the poor socialization of youth, or even moral decay. This myth contradicts the construction of crime as the product of individual choice and the construction of criminals as free-willed, rational actors who are uninfluenced by their social conditions, and it ignores the fact that criminality is the product of how crime is defined by people with the power to affect laws. Myths divert our attention to street crime and to crimes by strangers, while simultaneously evoking laudatory images of family and religious institutions. Given the number of crimes often committed within these institutions—domestic violence; child abuse, rape, and murder; sexual abuse by the clergy—this type of myth hides one reality while attempting to explain another. The myth is that no social institution is responsible for the social conditions in which we live or the failure of the justice system to adequately address social harm. While we can assign individual blame for criminal conduct, we ignore the social conditions and institutions that generate crime. In this myth, justice is something other than the collective decisions of legislators, judges, police officers and corrections officials, and the public accepts the system as it is constructed—contradictions and all.

A Convergent Core Myth

A vast majority of the public believes that the criminal justice system generally and judges specifically are soft on crime and criminals. According to a national survey, the vast majority of respondents subscribe to the view that their local courts do not deal harshly enough with criminals (National Opinion Research Center, 2001). This myth is predicated on the myth of deterrence. It is often argued that if the police caught more criminals, if more people were convicted of crimes, and if judges handed down longer prison sentences, criminal behavior would be reduced. It is, however, a myth that the criminal justice system in the United States is soft on crime. We have the highest rate of citizens convicted of crime by the courts, and we incarcerate and kill more of our citizens than any other Western industrialized democracy (United Nations Survey, 2000). We imprison over 686 persons for every 100,000 residents in the population (Harrison & Beck, 2002). This is a rate more than 7 times greater than that of England, France, and Germany; around 11 times greater than Sweden; 14 times higher than Japan and almost twice the rate of South Africa (United Nations Survey, 2001). The United States has one of the highest rates of incarceration in the entire world surpassing even Russia. The United States has become even more severe in its treatment of offenders in recent years, even while crime is declining. The trend toward increased incarceration is not a universal phenomenon. Both Denmark and England have developed policies that are designed to reduce the number of prison inmates. Yet these countries have considerably lower crime rates than the United States. Still, we continue to move in the opposite direction. In fact almost 6.6 million people are under the control of the criminal justice system (BJS, 2002)—awaiting death, incarcerated in prison or jail, or under probation or parole.

The United States is the only Western industrial nation that continues to execute criminals. Canada, Great Britain, Australia, New Zealand, and all the nations of Western Europe have halted this practice. In many societies, capital punishment was abolished long ago. Most jurisdictions in the United States, however, have not followed suit. It is hard to believe that a society that incarcerates and kills more of its citizens than any other Western industrialized nation is soft on crime. The myth seems to persist because of a continued and unfounded belief in the logic of deterrence and its reinforcement by government officials, the media, and political leaders. So the solution to crime continues to be a system built on flawed logic and contraction that supports the existing social and economic order.

The Costs of Justice Myths

The construction of a social reality of criminal justice based on myths has consequences. While some myths are harmless, myths associated with the criminal justice system have profound consequences for individuals and society at large. Myths direct our attention toward certain social problems and solutions. They also obscure reality and direct our attention away from other social problems and solutions that could have a more meaningful impact on the human condition. The major detriment of myths isn't even that cherished traditions and beliefs have unintended consequences. The problem is that myths hide or help us ignore consequences. Instead of rethinking the premise, energies are directed to explain why appearances to the contrary do not attack the foundation.

Myths hide contradictions in logic and reality, and they obscure the role of powerful groups in society to protect their vested interests. We hire more police officers to detect criminals, employ more judges and lawyers to administer justice, and build more prisons to punish those we deem criminal based on a flawed ideology. We conceptualize criminality not as the presence or absence of poverty, not as the presence or absence of racism in our social institutions, and not as the political construction of those with power but as individual deviation. Because of these myths, changes to the current system seem unthinkable or even unpatriotic. We don't want to admit that a hallowed symbol can be flawed; therefore, we ignore the complications that inevitably accompany implementation. Myths simplify issues that are too complex—that involve reflections we don't want to make and risks we aren't willing to take—whether we don't want to engage in the rigorous, extensive reflection required to confront problems or don't want to sacrifice personal gain to protect someone else's human rights.

All the myths we've discussed give rise to perhaps the most important myth for sustaining the criminal justice practice. This is the myth that no one is responsible for the social conditions in which we live or the failure of the justice system to adequately address social harm. While we assign individual responsibility for criminal conduct, we ignore responsibility for the social conditions that generate crime, the failures of the criminal justice system to prevent crime, and crimes linked to our social institutions. In this myth, criminal justice is something other than the decisions of legislators, judges, police officers, and corrections officials—and the public that participates in and accepts the social construction of the system as an immutable given. The ultimate power of the social construction of criminal justice by myth is its ability to determine what is and is not thinkable.

References

Best, J., & Hutchinson, M. M. (1996). The gang initiation rite as a motif in contemporary crime discourse. In G. W. Potter & V. E. Kappeler (Eds.), *Constructing crime: Perspectives on making news and social problems* (pp. 113–135). Prospect Heights, IL: Waveland Press.

Bureau of Justice Statistics (2002). Key facts at a glance: The number of adults in the correctional population has been increasing. Available at http://www.ojp.usdoj.gov/bjs/glance/corr2.htm

Harrison, P. M., & Beck, A. J. (2002). *Prisoners in 2001*, Bulletin NCJ 195189. Washington, DC: U.S. Department of Justice.

Hynds, P. (1990). Balance bias and critical questions. *Media & Values*, 50, 5–7.

Kappeler, V. E., Blumberg, M., & Potter, G. W. (2000). *The mythology of crime and criminal justice* (3rd ed.). Prospect Heights, IL: Waveland Press.

National Opinion Research Center. General Social Surveys, 1972–2000. Storrs, CT: The Roper Center for Public Opinion Research, University of Connecticut.

Republican Party of Minnesota et al. v. White, Chairperson, Minnesota Board of Judicial Standards, et al. No. 01–521. 536 U. S. (2002) Argued March 26, 2002—Decided June 27, 2002.

United Nations (2001). Surveys of crime trends and operations of criminal justice systems, covering the period 1990–2000. United Nations Crime Reduction and Analysis Branch Office for Drug Control and Crime Prevention.

Welch, M., Fenwick, M., & Roberts, M. (1998). State managers, intellectuals, and the media: A content analysis of ideology in experts' quotes in feature newspaper articles on crime. In G. W. Potter & V. E. Kappeler (Eds.), *Constructing crime: Perspectives on making news and social problems* (pp. 87–110). Prospect Heights, IL: Waveland Press.

7

Criminal Justice as Growth Complex

Chapter 6 taught us that police, courts, and corrections agencies promote myths and ceremonies for the purpose of establishing and maintaining their legitimacy. The growth complex theoretical orientation makes a similar assumption: *a bureaucracy's most basic instinct is to survive and grow.* Compare this assumption to the one made in the rational/legal orientation—bureaucracies are motivated by a desire to maintain the public good. As skeptical as it may seem at first glance, the view that bureaucracies tend to devolve into institutions that best serve themselves is common in our society. For example, many people believe that the medical industry is more interested in its own growth, profits, and protecting itself than in a commitment to prevent and heal illness and injury (Ritzer, 2000).

The Notion of a Growth Complex

As emphasized throughout this book, making theoretical sense of criminal justice requires us to provide explanations of its recent and remarkable growth in size and power. If we examine only the direct criminal justice expenditures (excluding private sector growth for example), spending on police, courts, and corrections between the years 1982–1999 has increased by over 350 percent (Bureau of Justice Statistics, 2002). The United States incarcerates five times more people per capita today than it did just thirty years ago (from 110 per 100,000 to 680 per 100,000) (Garland, 2001). And in the year 2000, the U.S. incarcerated well over 2,000,000 persons, roughly a quarter of all the world's prisoners combined (Justice Policy Institute, 2001).

A number of scholars do not see this growth as merely a forced or rational reaction to a worsening crime problem (rational/legal and systems), or a pendulum swing toward retributive values (crime control/due process), or even the result of shifts in politics (chapter 5). Their position, while acknowledging a partial role for these forces in the initial stages of development, stresses that today's criminal justice apparatus constitutes a *growth complex*, an entity that has taken on a life and logic of its own, for its own sake. Its original objectives—administering justice and controlling crime—are useful to the complex only to the extent that they can further the cause of increased size and power.

As article 14 points out, a former U.S. president and four-star general popularized the idea of a growth complex. In his farewell speech delivered in 1960, Dwight D. Eisenhower warned of the "disastrous rise of misplaced power" at the hands of what he termed the *military-industrial complex*. Articles 14 and 15 both discuss the major elements of an *industrial complex*, in which private sector involvement and influence blends with public sector organizations and objectives. While some of the companies mentioned in article 14 may have been subsumed by others and the people who left public service in the early 1990s may have retired, the process is ongoing. The research by Robert Lilly and Paul Knepper provides an excellent model for current investigations.

After the Cold War ended in 1989, a number of crime and justice analysts raised the same concerns as Eisenhower about the rise of an industrial complex—although this time they were referring to the post-Cold War era's new growth complex (Christie, 1993; Donziger, 1996; Kraska, 1993; Nadelman, 1993).

> Fear of crime drives investment, and crime control is a source of profit. We call this corner the "prison-industrial-complex." Like the military-industrial-complex that dominated defense policy during the Cold War, this crucible of private companies and government, exercises a powerful influence on crime control policy. The government and private security companies now spend almost as much money on crime control each year as the Pentagon spends on national defense. (Donziger, 1996, p. 85)

Nils Christie's path-breaking work in 1993 solidified the usefulness of the industrial-complex concept for making sense of a rapidly expanding criminal justice apparatus.

> The crime control industry provides profit and work while at the same time producing control of those who otherwise might have disturbed the social process. Compared to other industries, the crime control industry

is in a privileged position. There is no lack of raw-material, crime seems to be in endless supply. Endless are also the demands for the service, as well as the willingness to pay for what is seen as security. . . .

The whole institution of crime control in itself is a part of the system of production. The system is of great economic interest to both owners and workers. It is a system of production of vital importance to modern societies. It produces control. In this perspective, the problem arises: when is enough, enough? There is a built-in drive for expansion in industrialization. (Christie, 1993, pp. 13, 168)

More recently, a Pulitzer Prize-winning journalist from the *Wall Street Journal* argued that prisons have become a "self-perpetuating prison-industrial complex" (Hallinan, 2001). He concludes in his book, *Going Up the River: Travels in a Prison Nation*, that correctional facilities are being built more for economic gain than ameliorating the crime problem, creating a system "so lucrative that its founders have become rich men."

Each of these observers is viewing criminal justice through macroscopic lenses, analogous to the systems framework discussed in chapter 3. The criminal justice growth complex is an entity comprised of numerous interrelated and interdependent parts—an intricate structural matrix of CJ and non-CJ governmental bureaucracies, politicians, private companies, media agencies, academic institutions, and myriad interests. While not operating in harmony necessarily by design or even by intent, the net effect is nonetheless a complex of loosely and tightly connected organizations and interests that generate a synergy ideal for expansion.

In the quest for survival, growth, and influence building, the overall goal of pursuing the public interest through democratic processes and values (participation, accountability, fairness, and a concern for human dignity) is relegated to the back burner. The growth complex orientation, thus, views the criminal justice apparatus as an entity that seeks out and constructs new problems for its solution, actively pursues its own self-serving agenda as opposed to working toward the "public good," and is increasingly influenced by the private sector objectives of profit and growth. In its simplest terms, garnering power and size becomes not a means to a laudable end but an end in and of itself.

The Growth Complex Explained

They have warned us. Max Weber, the Frankfurt School, scholars studying the Holocaust, and numerous sociologists and public administrative theorists throughout the years have cautioned us about the propensity of bureaucracies, whether public or private, to lose sight of their original purpose and to pursue self-serving ends of survival, growth, and power (see, for example: Adams & Balfour, 1998; Jay, 1973; Mommsen, 1977). The next section will explore why this phenomenon occurs. In a book purporting to theorize, it is not enough for us to describe the nature of the criminal justice growth complex—we must also examine some reasons for this propensity. An additional benefit of reviewing these possible causal factors is that beyond explaining growth, they also demonstrate how the growth complex framework helps us to understand why the crime control enterprise sometimes pursues and adopts irrational and/or counterproductive policies and procedures.

Means Over Ends: The Negative Consequences of Technical Rationality

Humans come together in groups to accomplish goals, whether those goals are as basic as an indigenous tribe of Athabaskans surviving in the Alaskan wilderness in 40 degrees below zero or as technologically complex as the U.S. Air Force sending satellites into space to support our Global Positioning System (GPS). Communal effort carried out in various forms of organization defines, in large part, our existence as humans. Large, formal organizations, such as the U.S. Military, the U.S. Department of Justice, and multi-national corporations, dominate the landscape of modern societies. While the functional benefits of the rise of the modern *rational-bureaucratic model* of organization are clear (there is little chance I will ever get lost again in the woods using my GPS), numerous analysts have also examined its dysfunctional tendencies.

The irony, according to this line of thinking, is that those features so well-regarded in the rational-bureaucratic organization—high emphasis placed on hierarchical chain of command, neutrality, uniform rules and regulations, rational/scientific decision-making, and efficient goal attainment—have throughout modern history led to numerous bureaucratic pathologies. The most often discussed dysfunction driving the growth complex goes by numerous phrases. A few include:

- *ascendance of technical rationality over substantive reason*
- *fetish for efficiency*
- *means over ends syndrome*
- *bureaupathology*
- *irrationality of rationality*
- *goal displacement*

The thinking behind each of these phrases begins with the concept of *technical rationality*. Technical rationality is an ideology and set of practices that emphasizes the application of *the most efficient means, determined ideally through scientific methods, for the accomplishment of given organizational ends*. These means, once determined, are then institutionalized into rules, routines, and regulations so that organizational members behave in a consistently "rational" (technically efficient) manner. An unintended consequence of this approach is the cultivation of a technocratic mind-set, where organizational members become myopically fixated on technique and the means for the efficient accomplishment of ends. The means of the organization—its processes, rules, regulations, routines, techniques, and protocols—supplant its original purpose for being, a condition sociologist Robert K. Merton referred to as *goal displacement* (Merton, 1957).

Herman Goldstein (1979), the father of problem-oriented-policing, centered his critique of the police institution on what he termed the *means over ends syndrome*, referring to the pathology where police organizations concentrate on technical activities that give the appearance of technical competence (their means), while losing sight of the more difficult issue of what they should actually be accomplishing (their ends). Similar examples are plentiful in criminal justice: probation departments fixating on the processing of probationers' paperwork efficiently while losing sight of their mandate to help their clients become productive citizens; correctional institutions striving to warehouse inmates safely and efficiently while not considering whether their experience in prison helps or hurts society; the plea-bargaining of felony cases in the courts resulting in either too lenient sentences for serious crimes or innocent citizens being coerced into a plea-agreement, all in order to keep the dockets clear. In each case, fixating on efficiency leads to inefficiency; rational decision-making triggers irrational outcomes; and an overemphasis on means transforms them into ends.

When means become ends, an organization not only suffers from goal displacement, it also loses its moral compass. The technocratic spirit is narcissistic. It has an internal focus. External objectives (ends) of the organization—controlling crime, administering justice in a democracy, upholding human rights—are overshadowed by the self-interested objectives of survival, favorable appearance, and sustained growth in size and power. The adoption of technical rationality as the central decision-making filter relegates other, perhaps more important filters, to the back burner.

> Technical efficiency is itself a value, the selection of which may preclude other values. Having chosen efficiency as a central value, other values such as those of justice, equality, human rights, or participation necessarily assume less importance. Reason gives way to rationality. (Denhardt, 1981, p. 30)

Similarly, Eugene Dvorin and Robert Simmons (1972) posit that "human dignity as a decision-making criterion has taken a back seat to securing public financing, efficiency, and bureaucratic survival" (p. 54).

Several prominent academics, such as Max Horkheimer (1974), Jürgen Habermas (1970), George Ritzer (2000), and Zygmunt Bauman (1989) have pointed to the worst-case scenario arising from the ascendance of technical rationality and the loss of a bureaucracy's moral grounding: Nazi Germany's extermination of millions of Jews and other "undesirables." Nils Christie, in drawing from Bauman's *Modernity and the Holocaust,* establishes the prominent role technical rationality played in the Holocaust. His analysis centers on the tendency of rational-bureaucracies to become "morally indifferent." He then cautiously draws parallels with the runaway crime control industry in the United States.

> The extermination camp was a product of industrialization, one product among others of a combination of thought-patterns, social organization, and technical tools. My contention is that the prison system in the USA is rapidly moving in the same direction. To some, the very idea that criminal policy in industrial democratic societies could bear the slightest resemblance to Nazi times and extermination camps sounds absurd. . . . I do not think prisons in modern industrial societies will end up as carbon copies of the camps. Even if the worse comes to the worst, most prisoners will not intentionally be killed in modern prison systems. Gulags are, therefore, a more relevant term for what might come than concentration camps. My gloomy suggestion is limited to saying that a large proportion of males from the lower classes may end up living the most active part of their lives in prisons or camps [resembling gulags]. (Christie, 2000, p. 182)

Dynasty Building: The Quest for Immortality

Another key causal factor in the growth complex phenomenon, according to this theoretical orientation, is the human drive to build dynasties that extend a person's power and that will outlive themselves. Beginning with the early Mayan, Egyptian, Chinese, and Roman civilizations, leaders and bureaucrats have always had a penchant for building bigger and more powerful organizations, complete with impressive physical structures that symbolize their influence and status. Indeed, even in modern times we reward the most successful bureaucracy builders by naming a building after them, immortalizing their place in history.

One of the more well-known examples of shrewd dynasty building in the criminal justice system was first brought to our attention by Howard Becker (1963) in his classic, *Outsiders: Studies in the Sociology of Deviance*. Becker documented the powerful role Commissioner Harry Anslinger and his Federal Bureau of Narcotics (now the Drug Enforcement Administration) played in constructing marijuana use as a serious public harm, lobbying hard for punitive legislation and effectively situating their bureaucracy for another 60 years of remarkable expansion. Many critics of today's war on drugs observe that the same type of irrational bureaucracy building continues. To these observers, the DEA and local police bureaucrats still perpetuate disinformation and fear in the construction of a problem for the ever-expanding war on drugs solution (Gaines & Kraska, 2002; Inciardi, 2000).

Christian Parenti (2001), drawing from insights originally developed by Jeffery Reiman (2001), notes that even when criminal justice bureaucracies fall short of their public interest goals, they often turn the lemons of their failure into bureaucratic lemonade.

> All these predictable failures, like many law enforcement defeats, serve the bureaucracy of control better than victory ever could. . . . Mayhem in prison is parlayed into empire-building. . . . As in the pages of Max Weber, the corrections "officialdom" becomes a parasitic interest group that expands and strengthens the bureaucracy upon which it feeds. This dynamic converts the purported ends ("public safety") into means for the bureaucrats' self-perpetuation. (p. 209)

The Profit Factor

Articles 14 and 15 both demonstrate effectively the final growth factor: the effect the private sector is having on the criminal justice system. Both articles detail how the traditional governmental functions of law enforcement, security, and punishment are being integrated with private corporate influence and thinking. While privatized corrections and police agencies pursuing enhanced profits is a clear formula for unrestrained growth, the private/profit factor also has a more subtle dimension. Several prominent academics have commented on the increasing popularity of the for-profit business model being used for the administration and management of criminal justice agencies (see, for example, Garland, 2001; Kappeler, 1999; Manning, 1992).

One example of the encroaching for-profit outlook in criminal justice bureaucracies is the police practice of civil asset forfeiture. Worrall (2001) finds that drug asset forfeiture money has become institutionalized in modern policing—to the point that police agencies are so dependent on these self-generated funds they actively seek out those cases likely to yield undocumented cash vulnerable to forfeiture. The original goal of crippling large drug organizations, according to Worrall, is displaced by the pursuit of profit.

Merging Complexes

The growth complex theoretical orientation casts the criminal justice apparatus in a critical light: a massive entity with an intricate matrix of organizations, interests, and resources pursuing its own survival, status, and growth in power and size. Lest the reader conjure up conspiratorial images, it is important to emphasize again that authors working within this framework do not see this as some person's or organization's well-designed grand scheme. The notion of a "growth complex" is instead an after-the-fact heuristic device that helps us to make sense of the net effect of a hodgepodge of some loosely and some tightly connected agencies, processes, and ways of thinking that generate a synergistic model ideal for runaway growth.

It is also worth noting that the three causal factors highlighted—technical rationality, dynasty building, and profit—are to be considered only bureaucratic *potentialities*, not inevitable determinants leading to self-interested, self-perpetuating organizations. What makes the study of criminal justice so fascinating is that its organizations, possibly even those that are privatized, also harbor the potential for restraint, a serious focus on laudable ends, and the ardent pursuit of the public interest through rational decision-making (as seen in chapters 2 and 3). The side of the dialectic one chooses to emphasize will depend partly on a person's own theoretical framework, empirical research findings, and the research evidence to which they are exposed.

We began this overview by mentioning Eisenhower's warning about the emergence of the "military-industrial complex" and an examination of the thinking that argues we now have a new growth complex—the criminal justice apparatus. I would like to conclude by suggesting an emerging trend, similar to the public/private blending discussed above, that ties the military and criminal justice complexes together (Kraska, 2001).

The criminal justice system's expansion in the last few decades seems to have few boundaries. Despite the long-standing democratic tradition of clearly separating the U.S. military and its external security function from the police institution and its focus on internal security, the line between the armed forces and the criminal justice system has become increasingly blurred. The military-industrial complex and the criminal justice enterprise share many ideological and material features, including a common government. In the post-Cold War era, it may seem logical to share data and weaponry, cross-train, engage in joint exercises, and borrow from each other's expertise. From a bureaucracy-building perspective, both players benefit in this scenario. The military is able to broaden its mandate from large-scale wars protecting our sovereignty to a host of internal security problems. The criminal justice enterprise gains by tapping into the advanced technology and large budget of the military complex, as well as by shrouding itself in the assumed competence, efficiency, and effectiveness of the military model.

References

Adams, G. B., & Balfour, D. L. (1998). *Unmasking administrative evil*. Thousand Oaks, CA: Sage.

Becker, H. S. (1963). *Outsiders: Studies in the sociology of deviance*. New York: The Free Press.

Bureau of Justice Statistics. (2002). BJS expenditure trends. Retrieved September 7, 2001, from http://www.ojp.usdoj.gov/bjs/glance/exptyp.html

Bauman, Z. (1989). *Modernity and the holocaust*. Cambridge: Polity Press.

Christie, N. (1993). *Crime control as industry: Toward GULAGS, Western style*. New York: Routledge.

Christie, N. (2000). *Crime control as industry: Toward GULAGS, Western style* (3rd ed.). New York: Routledge.

Denhardt, R. B. (1981). *In the shadow of organization*. Lawrence: University Press of Kansas.

Donziger, S. (1996). *The real war on crime: The report of the national criminal justice commission*. New York: Harper Perennial.

Dvorin, E. P., & Simmons, R. H. (1972). *From amoral to humane bureaucracy*. San Francisco: Canfield Press.

Garland, D. (2001). Introduction: The meaning of mass imprisonment. *Punishment and Society, 3*(1), 5–7.

Garland, D. (2001). *The culture of control: Crime and social order in contemporary society*. Chicago: University of Chicago Press.

Habermas, J. (1970). *Toward a rational society*. Boston: Beacon Press.

Hallinan, J. T. (2001). *Going up the river: Travels in a prison nation*. New York: Random House.

Horkheimer, M. (1974). *Eclipse of reason*. New York: The Seabury Press.

Jay, M. (1973). *The dialectical imagination*. Boston: Little Brown.

Justice Policy Institute. (2001). Nation's incarcerated population went up, not down in 1999–2000. Retrieved September 7, 2001, from http://www.cjcj.org/jpi/prisoners2000.html

Kappeler, V. E. (1999). Reinventing the police and society: The spectacle of social control. In V. E. Kappeler (Ed.), *The police and society: Touchstone readings* (pp. 481–493). Prospect Heights, IL: Waveland Press.

Kraska, P. B. (2001). *Militarizing the American criminal justice system: The changing roles of the armed forces and the police*. Boston: Northeastern University Press.

Manning, P. K. (1992). Economic rhetoric and policing reform. *Criminal Justice Research Bulletin, 7*(4), 1–8.

Merton, R. K. (1957). *Social theory and social structure*. New York: Free Press.

Mommsen, W. J. (1977). *The age of bureaucracy: Perspectives on the political sociology of Max Weber*. New York: Harper Torchbooks.

Reiman, J. (2001). *The rich get richer and the poor get prison: Ideology, class, and criminal justice*. Boston: Allyn and Bacon.

Ritzer, G. (2000). *The McDonaldization of society*. Thousand Oaks, CA: Pine Forge Press.

Worrall, J. L. (2001). Addicted to the drug war: The role of civil asset forfeiture as a budgetary necessity in contemporary law enforcement. *Journal of Criminal Justice, 29*(2), 179–187.

Article 14

The Corrections-Commercial Complex

J. Robert Lilly
Paul Knepper

The Military-Industrial Complex

President Eisenhower coined the term "military-industrial complex" in 1961. In his Farewell Radio and Television Address to the American People, Eisenhower (1985, p. 748) warned that government "must guard against the acquisition of unwarranted influence, whether sought or unsought, by the military-industrial complex. The potential for the disastrous rise of misplaced power exists and will persist." Eisenhower was concerned that university researchers would become captives of government lured by the desire for project allocations. At the same time, he worried that a "scientific-technological elite" immune from accountability would dictate national policy. "Only an alert and knowledgeable citizenry," he insisted, "can compel the proper meshing of the huge industrial and military machinery of defense with our peaceful methods and goals, so that security and liberty may prosper together" (Eisenhower 1985, p. 748). . . .

Subgovernments

The military-industrial complex is the most visible pattern of interrelationships otherwise known as a "policy network," "iron triangle," or "sub-

Crime & Delinquency, Vol. 39 No. 2: 150–166. © 1993 by Sage Publications. Reprinted by permission of Sage Publications.

government." Subgovernments are not a legally recognized form of government, but they often exert greater influence over public policy than formal structures of government. Subgovernments are defined as "clusters of individuals that effectively make most of the routine decisions in a given substantive area of policy" (Ripley and Franklin 1984, p. 9). Decision making within a given policy arena rests within a closed circle or elite of government bureaucrats, agency heads, interest groups, and private interests that gain from the allocation of public resources. Congressional committee members, interest groups, and bureaucrats comprise the largest portion of subgovernments although anyone interested in the many benefits that flow from a policy domain may join the circle. These include bureau chiefs, administrators, university academics, private contractors, and members of state and local governments (Palumbo 1988, p. 51).

The military subgovernment, for example, shows a triangular pattern of interaction between a federal agency (the Pentagon), its constituent group in American society (defense contractors), and those in Congress with a special interest in that part of the federal budget (members of armed services committees, defense appropriations committees, and members from congressional districts and states with concentrations of defense spending) (see Adams 1984, p. 326). This is not to say that subgovernments are limited to the military sector. They exist in many arenas of national policy-making, including agriculture, banking, organized labor, education, international business, and scientific research (see Knott and Miller 1987, pp. 131–32; Ripley and Franklin 1984, pp. 97–135). They also operate at both the state and national levels, with stable alliances between legislators, state agencies, private enterprises, and other interest groups (Palumbo 1988, p. 51).

Several characteristics may be identified of subgovernmental control in national policy-making:

First, the participants in a subgovernment share a close working relationship. The subgovernmental participants do not constitute a "power elite" capable of enforcing any policy or interest, but within the policy arena under subgovernmental control no single actor is powerful enough to stop the alliance when the major participants are united (Knott and Miller 1987, p. 130). This participants' alliance becomes stable over time and is characterized by cooperation and compromise. The continued existence and success of this relationship depends on the steady flow of information, access, influence, personnel, and money (Ripley and Franklin 1984, p. 11; Adams 1984, p. 326).

Second, each subgovernment features a distinct overlap between the societal interest and the government bureaucracy in question. Close ties between industry and government are reinforced by a steady flow of personnel. Government policymakers and agency administrators move freely between the two arenas and tend to share common values, interests, and perceptions. The line between the public good and private interest becomes blurred as governmental and nongovernmental institutions become harder to distinguish (Ripley and Franklin 1984, p. 9; Adams 1984, p. 326).

Third, subgovernments operate with a low level of visibility and a high degree of effectiveness from the point of view of those inside the subgovernment. Because most of the policy-making within a subgovernment is routine, subgovernments operate for extended periods without interference or control from outside forces. Decision making is normally invisible and noncontroversial. The closed, low-profile operations of a subgovernment are not noticed by the public, the media, nor other governmental agencies (Ripley and Franklin 1984, p. 10, 105).

Fourth, the subgovernment has the tendency to become a fixture within a given policy arena. Subgovernmental participants work to isolate the mutually beneficial alliance from other arenas. Subgovernments have been called "iron triangles" to convey the idea that they become "iron" by exercising control over the policy-making process for long periods of time. Subgovernmental disintegration is rare (Ripley and Franklin 1984, p. 106). Eventually, policymakers and private participants come to share the assumption that they are not only acting in their own interests, but in the general public interest as well (Ripley and Franklin 1984, p. 9, 105; Adams 1984, p. 327).

Participants in the Corrections Subgovernment

Prompted by such factors as the rapid rise in correctional populations during the 1980s (the nation's prison population more than doubled), a corrections subgovernment of national proportion appears to have emerged.[1] The key participants in the national corrections-commercial complex are (a) private corporations devoted to profiting from imprisonment (b) government agencies anxious to maintain their continued existence, and (c) professional organizations that sew together an otherwise fragmented group into a powerful alliance. These national-level players are in turn linked to corrections subgovernments within states to form a massive policy-making alliance.

Private Concerns

During the 1980s, a number of firms have emerged as players in the national corrections market. A few firms have become quite visible in the ongoing debate about privatization. These firms specialize in the management and ownership of corrections facilities, including Corrections Corporation of America (CCA), and United States Corrections Corporation (USCC) [purchased by CCA in 1998]. CCA is backed by the Massey-Burch Investment group (Massey-Burch owns Kentucky Fried Chicken and Hospital Corporation of America), and it achieved national notoriety in its attempt to purchase the entire Tennessee prison system in 1985 (see Egerton 1984; Tolchin 1985). USCC used an initial investment of $1.9 million to convert an old seminary in St. Mary, Kentucky, into a corrections facility, and became the first private company to build, own, and manage a corrections facility (Logan 1990, p. 25). But alongside these novel, high-profile operations, there are many more companies profiting from the routine, low-profile world of providing prison services.

Private interests profit from imprisoning lawbreakers in various ways . . . including food service design and management, consulting and personnel management, architecture and facilities design, vocational assessment, medical services, drug detection, and transportation. And that is not all. There are companies that sell protective vests for guards, closed-circuit television systems, mechanical and electronic locks, perimeter security and motion detection systems, fencing, flame-retardant bedding, furniture, footwear, lighting, and linen along with shatterproof plastic panels, tamper-proof fasteners, and clog-proof waste disposal systems. . . .

Federal Agencies

Federal agencies joined the corrections-commercial alliance following the creation of the Law Enforcement Assistance Administration (LEAA). LEAA was launched by the Omnibus Crime Control and Safe Streets Act of 1968 and during its massive campaign to restructure the justice system during the 1970s, it doled out $8 billion to state and local justice agencies. LEAA's policy stance was ambiguous; it seemed to many that the agency threw money at the crime problem without sense or strategy. But whatever else LEAA accomplished or failed to accomplish, the agency served to initiate a nationalization of crime policy. In the early years, LEAA gave money to police for hardware (helicopters, tanks, riot gear, and so forth), but in later years the agency developed an emphasis on community corrections and diversion programs. The existence of a central grant-making presence in Washington increased the flow of information between jurisdictions and fostered a sense of common participation (Gordon 1990, p. 200–203).

When LEAA was abolished in 1982, the Office of Justice Programs (OJP) stepped in. OJP is a branch of the Justice Department that began when President Ronald Reagan signed into the law the Justice Assistance Act of 1984 as part of the Comprehensive Crime Control act of 1984. This act amended the Omnibus Crime Control and Safe Streets Act, and created five interrelated bureaus to promote research, collect statistics, and provide financial and technical assistance to state and local governments. The bureaus include the Bureau of Justice Assistance (BJA), the Bureau of Justice Statistics (BJS), the Office of Juvenile Justice and Delinquency Prevention (OJJDP), the Office for Victims of Crime (OVC), and the National Institute of Justice (NIJ). NIJ is the "research branch" of the Justice Department devoted to "targeting resources, assuring their effective allocation, and developing new means of cooperation between the public and private sector" (DeWitt 1988, p. i).

Professional Organizations

Professional organizations comprise the third side of the corrections-commercial triangle. Professional groups such as the American Bar Association (ABA) and the American Correctional Association (ACA) exert considerable influence over correctional policy.[2]

The ABA is the foremost nationwide attorney organization. It exercises enormous influence over corrections policy through criminal code revision. Whereas a professional association of lawyers might naturally be expected to be interested in criminal law reform, the ABA is no ordinary interest group. The ABA's influence over criminal justice policy might be thought of as a "working criminal justice elite" (Melone 1983). From 1971, when initial congressional testimony began on revision of the federal criminal code to its final testimony in 1979, ABA representatives testified on a wide range of topics. These topics included criminal sentencing, probation, the death penalty, and bail jumping. Curiously, it was not the ABA's section on criminal law that offered initial testimony on criminal code reform. Rather, business-oriented sections, such as the Section on Corporation, Banking, and Business Law and the Section on Taxation, were the first to testify before the Senate Judiciary Committee. These sections offered repeated testimony over the years (Melone 1985, p. 38).

The ACA was founded in 1870 as the National Prison Association and became the American Correctional Association in 1954. Composed of about 40,000 correctional professionals, the ACA is involved "in the entire spectrum of correctional activities"; it publishes corrections-related materials, trains personnel, sponsors the annual Congress of Correction, and accredits agencies and programs. The ACA has been described as being to correctional officers and prisons what the American Medical Association (AMA) is to doctors and hospitals, or as one California prison official explained, the ACA is "a lobby, professional standards-setter, peer review group, public relations mill, seller of prison-related junk, and a place where people pop-off and retire" (DiIulio 1987, p. 83). Since its beginning, the ACA has worked to shape national and international policy and has recently expanded its role to uniting public government and private business.

The Corrections-Commercial Complex

The pattern of interaction among the participants in the corrections-commercial complex fits the subgovernmental model. The national corrections subgovernment displays each of the features of subgovernments in other national policy-making arenas.

Each of the participants in the corrections subgovernment shares a close working relationship supported by the flow of information, influence, and money. Just as protecting the nation from foreign enemies is a major industry, punishing people in this country is big business. . . .

There is a distinct overlap between the interests of for-profit companies and professional organizations and the interests of the federal agencies maintained by the flow of influence and personnel. As with the military-industrial complex, there is a constant flow of personnel between the public and private correctional governments. ABA representatives are high-status lawyers often having prestigious individuals and organizations for clients. Many ABA leaders are associated with large private law firms with some of the most successful business enterprises in the United States for clients (Melone 1985, p. 40).

The revolving door so characteristic of the defense industry also characterizes the corrections subgovernment. The heads of private prison firms are often former government officials or corrections administrators who have left public service for private interest. Ted Nissen, president and founder of Behavior Systems Southwest Incorporated (BSS), a private prison firm, is a former employee of the California Corrections Department (Ryan and Ward 1989, p. 13). Tamara S. Lindholm, vice president of BSS, also had a long career in the California Department of Corrections (Logan 1990, p. 22). Craig Dobson, a 20-year veteran of the U.S. Bureau of Prisons, operates a detention facility in Aurora, Colorado, owned by Wackenhut Corrections Corporation (WCC), a company that expanded its operation from private security to prison incarceration. Dobson is also the founder and first director of the National Institute of Corrections Jail Center in Denver (Logan 1990, p. 24). T. Don Hutto, executive vice-resident of Corrections Corporation of America (CCA), is a former commissioner of corrections in Arkansas and Virginia. Hutto also served as president of the American Correctional Association from 1984 to 1986 (Logan 1990, p. 23; Ryan and Ward 1989, p. 37). Richard Mulcrone, former chairman of the Minnesota State Corrections Authority, manages a corrections system division of Control Data Corporation. Maurice Sigler, former chair of the Federal Parole Commission, serves on the Corrections Corporation of America's board of directors (Becker and Stanley 1985, p. 728–29). . . .

Any issue of *Corrections Today*, the official publication of the ACA, contains many examples of the triangular arrangement between government, commerce, and this organization. In ACA's July 1990 "Annual Security and Buyers Guide Issue," employees of private firms published articles describing technological and product developments, and a special section described the products and services of several hundred companies that profit from the deprivation of liberty. Each year at the annual congress of corrections, sellers meet buyers at the American Correctional Association Show. . . .

Along with the ACA, the NIJ has done its part to boost the corrections industry. A 1987 study publicized by this federal agency claimed that society spends an average of $25,000 a year to confine an inmate, while it costs $430,000 for that individual to remain free to commit crimes. The NIJ also calculated that the average crime costs society a whopping $2,300. Although the accuracy of these figures remains questionable, the implication was clear: Every available dollar should be spent on prisons. The NIJ distributed this study to the public by Associated Press and United Press International; it provided valuable support for states rapidly building prisons. California's Governor George Deukmejian cited the study in a 1989 speech justifying the state's $1.5 billion prison operating budget. Assistant Attorney General Richard B. Abell used it in a letter mass-mailed to policymakers across the country. Abell argued that "the costs to society of nonimprisonment are significantly higher than the costs of prison construction" (Barrett and Greene 1989, p. 19). James K. Stewart, while NIJ director, also took the message of merging corrections with private enterprise directly to the public. In a 1985 *New York Times* article, Stewart claimed that the private sector was able to meet the demand for correctional institutions quicker than the government and that the private sector could build and maintain a prison for about 10% to 20% less than the government (Stewart 1985, p. 22).

The corrections-commercial complex operates without public scrutiny and exercises enormous influence over corrections policy. Neither the ABA nor the ACA have any official power to make policy decisions. The fact is, however, that these organizations effectively make many of the decisions that affect the lives of lawbreakers in this country.

Because the activities of subgovernmental participants are by definition low profile, they are difficult to document. But on occasion, these activities come to light. When Professor Emeritus Livingston Hall of Harvard Law School and chairman of the ABA committee of Reform of the Criminal Law gave extensive testimony on diverse issues ranging from conspiracy to federal jurisdiction, Senator Roman Hruski (R-Neb), a ranking member of the Senate Subcommittee holding the hearings, said to Hall: "We are gratified at the number of instances when we conform to your recommendations of today. We will take under advisement those instances where we have not conformed." Professor Hall later commented of the ABA committee's work, "Our committee believes that its work . . . was well worth the time and effort that it spent, because we are very pleased to see that a substantial number of our recommendations have been adopted in both bills" (quoted in Melone 1985, p. 41).

Likewise, the ACA is not an agency of government but it probably has as much to do with the experience of prisoners in this country as the agencies of government with nominal control. One of the ways the ACA exerts major influence is in the setting of standards. Published ACA standards cover such areas as security and control, food service, sanitation and hygiene, medical and health care, inmate rights, work programs, educational programs, recreational activities, library services, records, and personnel issues. ACA also sets standards that relate to crowding, including the size of cells, recreational space, and the total floor space per unit.

Reliance on ACA standards by government agencies and private contractors promotes a close working relationship between the ACA, government agencies, and private companies. Essentially, this arrangement means that the policy adhered to is made by a private organization rather than public officials. Contracts for the operation of private prisons often include a requirement to adhere to ACA standards. This may be stipulated by the government agency involved, or by the contractor (Logan 1990, pp. 128–29). Compliance with these standards is necessary to receive accreditation from the Commission on Accreditation for Corrections. While accreditation is seldom required, it often paves the way for increased funding. It also has been recognized by the courts as one indicator of the acceptability of an institution's conditions that provides an excellent defense against civil suits by inmates for violations of constitutional rights (Clear and Harris 1987, p. 44; DiIulio 1987, p. 215). Recently, Thomas Boshell of Liberty Healthcare Corporation attributed his company's growth to correctional officials' fear of litigation. Contracting with private health care services affords prison officials some protection against malpractice suits by prisoners (Asinof 1988, p. 1).

The corrections-commercial complex shows signs of becoming a fixture within the national policy area of punishing lawbreakers as the participants define their activities in the public interest. Like the military-industrial complex Eisenhower worried about, the alliance of private profit and public punishment seems to have been forged. . . .

Private companies and professional organizations are unabashed in their claim to be operating in the public interest. Private prison officials do not claim to be operating in their own interest while not interfering with the public good, rather, they claim to provide a public good. Defending the activities of Behavior Systems Southwest, Ted Nissen published in *Nation* the opinion that private corrections management gets the public involved as citizens, taxpayers, and concerned Americans. According to Nissen, the prison system is a disaster that he wants to make better and to do it at a profit (Nissen 1985, p. 194) Hugh J. Swink, national director of a management consulting division of the accounting firm of Touche Ross specializing in corrections, has said of private financing of prison construction, "Where it's done right, you're going to see a great benefit to government and a chance for the private sector to make money" (Bacas 1984, p. 62). Tom Beasley, founder of the Corrections Corporation of America (CCA), expressed this unity of interest somewhat more eloquently: "There are rare times when you get involved in something that is productive and profitable and humanistic. We're on the verge of a brand new industry" (Egerton 1984, p. 19). . . .

The Future of the Corrections-Commercial Complex

Will the corrections-commercial complex follow the same road as the military-industrial complex? Will policy analysts uncover soaring corrections budgets, disturbing amounts of waste and inefficiency, massive defects in new corrections construction and prison services?

There is mounting evidence to suggest that this will be the case. Spending for corrections is monumental and growing. The nation's prison and jail population passed the one million mark in 1990 and is rising at a 13% annual growth rate. At this rate it will cost at least $100 million *per week* just for construction of new facilities ("Officials Aim" 1990, p. 1). Connecticut, California, and Ohio have cut millions from their public education budgets while increasing their corrections budgets at unprecedented levels (Barrett and Greene 1989, p. 18). Waste and inefficiency color the delivery of correctional services. Despite doubling the number of imprisoned lawbreakers in the past decade, the recidivism rate remains high. Prisoners in at least one state prison system have come to view prison services—rehabilitation programs and the like—as no more than gimmicks to bring money into the institutions (Kroll 1984, p. 20). As well, there are reports of major defects in new prison construction. A national survey of the design and construction of new jails and prisons has uncovered design blunders that have resulted in facilities that are difficult to keep secure, conducive to inmate suicide, and vulnerable to conditions-of-confinement lawsuits ("Surveyed Officials" 1990, pp. 2–3).

Several questions pose issues for immediate attention: Does a national corrections subgovernment influence incarceration and recidivism rates? When did the national corrections subgovernment begin? What factors led to its formation? What is the relationship between the national and state corrections subgovernments? Is there a connection between get-tough-on-crime politics and the profit-seeking interests of the corrections industry? How rapidly is the international corrections subgovernment developing (Lilly and Knepper 1992)? These questions and others await further research.

Notes

[1] From 1925 to 1974, the record high prison population was in 1961, when 220,149 persons were in prison. Every year since 1975, a new record high has been set. During the 1980s, the prison population more than doubled from 320,821 inmates in 1980 to 710,054 in 1989. Given current population projections, it is conservatively estimated that the U.S. prison population will reach 771,000 inmates by 1993 (U.S. Department of Justice, Bureau of Justice Statistics 1988; Travisono 1990). [The actual figure in 1993 was 909,381; in 2001, the number was 1,330,980.]

[2] The ACA is openly in favor of private corrections facilities. The ACA policy on private sector involvement states: "Profit and nonprofit organizations have resources for the delivery of services that are unavailable from the public correctional agency. . . . For its most effective operation, corrections should use all appropriate resources, both public and private" (*Corrections Today* 1990, p. 173). The ABA has neither embraced nor condemned the privatization of corrections. The Prison and Jail Problems Committee of the ABA Criminal Justice Section did resolve to study the legality of privatization, particularly contracting for the total operational responsibility for a prison or jail—and appointed Ira P. Robbins to draft a model contract and model statute (Robbins 1989).

References

Adams, Gordon. 1984. "The Department of Defense and the Military-Industrial Establishment: The Politics of the Iron Triangle." Pp. 320–34 in *Critical Studies in Organization and Bureaucracy,* edited by F. Fischer and C. Siranni. Philadelphia: Temple University Press.

Asinof, Lynn. 1988. "The Prison Market Gets More Attention From a Variety of Businesses." *Wall Street Journal*, August 4, p. 1.

Bacas, Harry. 1994. "When Prisons and Profits Go Together." *Nation's Business*, October, pp. 62–63.

Barnett, Katherine and Richard Greene. 1989. "Prisons: The Punishing Cost." *Financial World*, April 18, pp. 18–22.

Becker, Craig and Amy Dru Stanley. 1985. "The Downside of Private Prisons." *The Nation*, June 15, pp. 728–30.

Bowditch, Christine and Ronald S. Everett. 1987. "Private Prisons: Problems Within the Solution." *Justice Quarterly* 4:441–53.

Clear, Todd and Patricia M. Harris. 1997. "The Costs of Incarceration." Pp. 37–55 in *America Correctional Crisis*, edited by S. Gottfredson and S. McConville. New York: Greenwood.

Conley, John. 1984. "Prisons, Production, and Profit: Reconsidering the Importance of Prison Industries." *Journal of Social History* 4:257–75.

Corrections Today. 1990. July. Laurel, MD: American Correctional Association.

DeWitt, Charles B. 1988. *National Directory of Corrections Construction*. College Park, MD: American Correctional Association.

DiIulio, John J. 1987. *Governing Prisons: A Comparative Study of Correctional Management*. New York: Free Press.

Durham Alexis. 1989. "The Privatization of Punishment: Justifications, Expectations, and Experience." *Criminal Justice Policy Review* 3:48–73.

Eisenhower, Dwight D. 1985. "Farewell Radio and Television Address to the American People." Pp. 747–49 in *Free Government in the Making*, edited by A. Mason and G. Baker. New York: Oxford University Press.

Egerton, John. 1984. "The Tennessee Walls." *Progressive*, September, p. 19.

Gordon, Diana R. 1990. *The Justice Juggernaut: Fighting Street Crime, Controlling Citizens*. New Brunswick, NJ: Rutgers University Press.

Knepper, Paul. 1990. "Converting Idle Labor into Substantial Wealth: Arizona's Convict Lease System." *Journal of Arizona History* 31:79–96.

Knott, Jack H. and Gary J. Miller. 1987. *Reforming Bureaucracy: The Politics of Institutional Choice*. Englewood Cliffs, NJ: Prentice-Hall.

Kroll, Michael A. 1984. "Prisons for Profit." *Progressive*, September, pp. 18–22.

Lilly, J. Robert and Paul Knepper. 1992. "An International Perspective on the Privatization of Corrections." *The Howard Journal of Criminal Justice* 31:174–91.

Logan, Charles. 1990. *Private Prisons: Cons and Pros*. New York: Oxford University Press.

McDonald, Douglas C. 1990. *Private Prisons and the Public Interest*. New Brunswick, NJ: Rutgers University Press.

Melone, Albert P. 1983. "The American Bar Association Antitrust Legislation and Interest Group Coalitions." *Policy Studies Review* 11:684–98.

———. 1985. "Criminal CODE Reform and the Interest Group Politics of the American Bar Foundation." Pp. 37–56 in *The Politics of Crime and Criminal Justice*, edited by E. S. Fairchild and V. J. Webb. Beverly Hills, CA: Sage.

Nissen, Theodore. 1985. "Free-Market Prisons." *Nation*, September 14, p. 194.

"Officials Aim to 'Fill the Gap' Between Probation and Prison." 1990. *Criminal Justice Newsletter*, September 17, p. 1.

Palumbo, Dennis J. 1988. *Public Policy in America: Government in Action*. San Diego, CA: Harcourt Brace Jovanovich.

Robbins, Ira P. 1988. "Privatization of Corrections: Defining the Issues." *Vanderbilt Law Review* 40:813–28.

———. 1989. "The Legal Dimensions of Private Incarceration." *American University Law Review* 38:531–854.

Ripley, Randall and Grace Franklin. 1984. *Congress, the Bureaucracy, and Public Policy.* Homewood, IL: Dorsey.

Ryan, Mick and Tony Ward. 1989. *Privatization and the Penal System: The American Experience and the Debate in Britain.* Milton Keynes: Open University Press.

Stewart, James K. 1985. "Breaking Up Government's Monopoly on Prison Cells." *New York Times*, March 3, p. 22E.

"Surveyed Officials Cite Errors in Design of Prisons and Jails." 1990. *Criminal Justice Newsletter*, May 1, pp. 2–3.

Tolchin, Martin. 1985. "Company Offers to Run Tennessee's Prisons." *New York Times*, September 13.

Travisono, Diana. 1990. *Directory of Juvenile and Adult Correctional Departments, Institutions, Agencies and Paroling Authorities.* Laurel, MD: American Correctional Association.

U.S. Department of Justice, Bureau of Justice Statistics. 1988. *Historical Statistics on Prisoners in State and Federal Institutions, Yearend 1925–86.* Washington, DC: Author.

———. 1990. *Justice Expenditure and Employment, 1988.* Washington, DC: Author.

The Crime Control Industry and the Management of the Surplus Population

Randall G. Shelden
William B. Brown

Introduction

The criminal produces not only crime but also the criminal law; he produces the professor who delivers lectures on this criminal law; and even the inevitable textbook in which the professor presents his lectures as a commodity for sale in the market. . . . Further, the criminal produces the whole apparatus of the police and criminal justice, detectives, judges, executioners, juries, etc. . . . Crime takes off the labour market a portion of the excess population, diminishes competition among workers, and to a certain extent stops wages from falling below the minimum, while the war against crime absorbs another part of the same population. The criminal therefore appears as one of those natural "equilibrating forces" which establish a just balance and open up a whole perspective of "useful" occupations. (Marx 1993: 52–53)

While arrests and convictions are steadily on the rise, profits are to be made—profits from crime. Get in on the ground floor of this booming industry now! (An advertising brochure from an investment firm, World Research Group, cited in Silverstein 1999: 156)

Critical Criminology, Vol. 9, No. 1–2, (Autumn 2000), pp. 39–52, 54–55; 59–62. Copyright © The Division on Critical Criminology. All rights reserved.

It's like a hotel with a guaranteed occupancy. (Ron Garzini, private
prison booster, quoted in Parenti 1999: 211)

The "war on crime" (including the "war on drugs") has become a
booming business, with literally hundreds of companies, large and small,
eager for a share of the growing profits. Employment in this industry offers
careers for thousands of young men and women, with college degrees in
"criminal justice" now available at more than 3,000 colleges and universities. The criminal justice system provides a steady supply of career possibilities (police officers, correctional officers, etc.), with good starting pay
and benefits, along with job security. Many of these occupations now have
powerful unions.

During the past thirty years a "criminal justice industrial complex" (one
part of a much larger "crime control industry") has emerged to play a similar role as the "military industrial complex." The police, the courts, and the
correctional system have become huge, self-serving and self-perpetuating
bureaucracies with a vested interest in keeping crime at a minimal level.
They need victims and they need criminals, even if they have to invent
them, as they have throughout the "war on drugs" and "war on gangs."[1]

The intent of this article is to provide an overview of the many dimensions of what we are calling a "crime control industry," an industry that
consists of much more than merely the criminal justice system itself. As we
will show, the crime control industry includes a number of businesses that
profit either directly or indirectly from the existence of crime and attempts
to control crime. Examples include private security firms (which provide
not only security police but also an abundance of security hardware), a
"prison industrial complex" (providing plenty of investment opportunities
as well as profits from hundreds of businesses), drug testing firms, and
gun manufacturers, plus colleges and universities that offer "criminal justice" degrees, and a media that thrive on stories about crime and criminals
(ranging from stories on the 11 o'clock news to "real cop stories" on television and major motion pictures). This article addresses one important, but
often neglected, question: why has a "crime control industry" emerged at
this point in American history? In order to answer this question we explore
the overall social context of the emergence and growth of this industry.
Our contention is that the crime control industry has emerged as an inevitable by-product of the normal workings of capitalism: that is to say, it is
driven by a need to make a profit anywhere possible and the need to control an inevitable and growing "surplus population."

The Crime Control Industry

Recognition of the existence of a crime control industry is not of
recent origins. Richard Quinney draws attention to this phenomenon as a
problem in *Class, State and Crime*, first published in 1977. In this book he
identifies what he termed a "social-industrial complex," of which a "crimi-

nal justice industrial complex" is part. This much larger complex is "an involvement of industry in the planning, production, and operation of state programs. These state-financed programs (concentrating on education, welfare, and criminal justice), as social expenses necessary for maintaining social order, are furnished by monopolistic industries" (Quinney 1980: 133). Large corporations, Quinney suggests, have found a new source of profits in this industry, with the criminal justice industry leading the way. Private industry, in short, has found that there is much profit to be made as a result of the existence of crime.

Part of the reason for the growth of the crime control industry is that policy makers have come to advocate a technocratic solution to the crime problem. This perspective, which is almost identical to the perspective taken toward the Vietnam War, suggests that the solution to crime requires a combination of science and technology. Such a position was stated well by the President's Crime Commission in 1967. This Commission wrote:

> More than 200,000 scientists and engineers have applied themselves
> to solving military problems and hundreds of thousands more to inno-
> vation in other areas of modern life, but only a handful are working to
> control the crimes that injure or frighten millions of Americans each
> year. Yet the two communities have much to offer each other: Science
> and technology is a valuable source of knowledge and techniques for
> combating crime; the criminal justice system represents a vast area of
> challenging problems. (President's Commission on Law Enforcement
> and Administration of Justice, 1967: 1)

The government took up this challenge and, as a consequence, the crime control industry has become enormous. The crime control industry is now so huge and complex that it is difficult, if not impossible, to accurately estimate the amount of money spent and the profits generated. However, here we provide preliminary estimates of the size of this industry, by looking at annual expenditures of the three main components of the formal "criminal justice system": police, courts, and corrections. Table 1 shows expenditures covering the years 1982 and 1996 (the latest figures available from the Department of Justice). As shown in Table 1, in 1996 total expenditures exceeded $120 billion, an increase of 235% over 1982. The largest increase went toward the correctional system, at 356% (Maguire and Pastore 1999). At least two writers estimate that total expenditures as of 1999 were in excess of $150 billion (Dyer 2000; Chambliss 1999). Chambliss estimates that by 2005 annual expenditures will be more than $200 billion (Chambliss 1999: 5).

Employment within the crime control industry is growing rapidly, providing many career opportunities for both college students and high school graduates. The most recent data show that in the 1993 fiscal year there were just over 1.8 million employed within this system, a 65% increase from 1982. As of October, 1995—the most recent data available—there were 584,925 sworn police officers, up 27% from 1980 (Maguire and Pastore 1999). The largest component is within the corrections category, with just over 1.4 million employees, representing an increase of over 90% from 1982. The U.S. Census reports that the hiring and training of correctional officers is the "fastest-growing" of all government functions. As of 1992 there were more people working in corrections than all those employed in any *Fortune 500* company except General Motors (Meddis and Sharp 1994). Given that the correctional system is growing more rapidly than any other component of the crime control industry, and that it is perhaps the most lucrative branch, below we discuss the "prison industrial complex."

Table 1
Criminal Justice Expenditures, Fiscal Years 1982 and 1996 (millions of dollars).

	1982	1996	Percent Increase
Police	19,022	53,007	179
Judicial	7,771	26,158	236
Corrections	9,047	41,029	356
Total	$35,839	$120,194	235

Source: McGarrell and Flanagan 1986: 2; Maguire and Pastore 1995, Table 1.2

The Prison Industrial Complex

As of December 31, 1999, there were 1,982,084 adults in jails and prisons in the U.S.A. This figure translates into an incarceration rate of 725 per 100,000 population, which placed the United States number one in the world. At that time it was predicted that by February 15, 2000, the prison population would top 2 million (Ziedenberg and Schiraldi 1999), a prediction which subsequently has come true (Ziedenberg and Schiraldi 2000a). We are far ahead of other industrial democracies, whose incarceration rates tend to cluster in a range from around 55 to 120 per 100,000 population. Some fell well below that figure, with Japan's rate for example reported at 36 per 100,000 population. The average incarceration rate for *all countries of the world* was around 80 per 100,000 population. Within this perspective the incarceration rate in the U.S. is around nine times greater than the global average (Currie 1998: 15). It should also be noted that these figures do not include all of those persons incarcerated in various community-based facilities (for example, those in work-release centers) or incarcerated juveniles. It should further be noted that the number of individuals on probation and parole has also increased during the past 20 years. The number of individuals on probation jumped by 206%, while and the number on parole increased by 220% (Irwin and Austin 2001: 4).

At the same time, the actual number of prisons has increased, along with, in some cases, the capacity within the prison. Some "megaprisons" can hold from 5,000 to 10,000 inmates. As of January 1, 1997, there were a total of 53,928 prisoners locked up in segregation within "super-max" prisons, constituting about 7% of all prisoners nationwide (Irwin and Austin 2001: 118). Prison building has become a booming industry in itself. Whereas in 1990 there were a total of 1,287 prisons (80 federal and 1,207 state prisons), by 1996 there were a total of 2,499 state prisons and 385 federal prisons, for a grand total of 2,883. This figure represents an increase of 124%. Also, there were an additional 2,297 state and 98 federal juvenile correctional facilities (125 federal and 1,375 state prisons) (Rush 1997: 157).

Texas provides a classic example of the prison industrial complex, with most of its prisons having been built since 1980 (at least 80 were built in the 1990s), most located in remote rural areas. An example of the rural nature of most of these facilities can be seen by sampling some of the towns where they are located (population according to the 1990 census):[2] Iowa Park (6,072), Teague (3,268), Dilley (2,632), Brazoria (2,717), Kennedy (3,763), Dalhart (6,246), Marlin (6,386), Rusk (4,366), Richmond (9,801), Woodville (2,636), Navasota (6,296), Fort Stockton (8,524), Childress (5,055), Cuero (6,700). A check of the *Rand McNally Road Atlas* reveals that several Texas prisons and other facilities are located in towns not recorded on the map. Examples include Lovelady, Midway, Tennessee Colony (with three separate prisons each housing over 3,000 inmates), Rosharon (with no less than four prisons housing over 6,000 inmates) and a privately run prison in a town called Venus (with 1,000 inmates). These types of institutions are found in literally every part of the state, from the far eastern regions (Woodville, located a few miles north of Beaumont along U.S. Route 190) to Lamesa (in the Texas "Panhandle" area about 30 miles south of Lubbock where U.S. Route 180 meets 87) and Fort Stockton (about 100 miles southwest of Odessa along Interstate 10).

The Texas prison system has more than 42,000 employees. It operates its own heath services system (with more than 8,000 personnel, including 200 doctors) and employs 35 lawyers. Farming is big business, with control over more than 134,000 acres (about 200 square miles), operating the largest horse and cattle herds in the entire state (more than 10,000 head of cattle and around 1,500 horses). The system also operates 42 factories within 32 prisons under its own "Texas Correctional Industries" (Rush 1997: 157). As of December 31, 1999, there were 706,600 individuals under some form of supervision in the criminal justice system, with a total prison and jail population of 207,526. These figures translate into an incarceration rate of 1,035 per 100,000 population (Louisiana ranks first); this rate is higher than the overall U.S. rate of 682 and Russia's rate of 685. The total prison population was 149,684, up from 92,669 in 1994 (Ziedenberg and Schiraldi 2000b). . . .

Aside from firms who build and operate correctional systems (discussed below), there are several types of businesses that benefit directly from the imprisonment of offenders. These businesses include firms that provide several different kinds of services, such as food, medical services, drug detecting, personnel management, architecture and facilities design, transportation, etc. There are also companies that sell a variety of products, such as protective vests for guards, fencing, furniture, linen, locks, and many more. The amount of money that flows into the coffers of the correctional industrial complex from tax dollars alone is quite substantial. The total operating budget for both state and federal correctional institutions came to almost $30 billion in the 1996 fiscal year. Total expenditures surpassed $35 billion. These figures suggest that it costs about $20,000–$40,000 per year to house one inmate in the U.S. prison system. This does not include the costs of building prisons. A detailed summary is provided in a recent Bureau of Justice Statistics study on expenditures at the state level. State expenditures in constant dollars tripled from 1984 to 1996, from just under $7 billion to more than $22 billion (Stephan 1999).

Prison construction has become a booming business. During the past decade about 92,000 new beds were added each year. These beds are very expensive, ranging from $70,000 each in a maximum-security prison to $29,000 in a minimum-security prison. As of 1998, the total cost of new prison construction was $3.88 billion—this figure including only the cost for the cells. For every 92,000 beds added, there is an estimated cost of $1.3 billion per year. The construction of new prisons has become such a big business that there is a special newsletter called *Construction Report*, its purpose solely to update vendors on new prison projects. Recent issues report the simultaneous construction of dozens of new prisons; in 1996 alone construction was begun on 27 federal prisons and 96 state prisons (Dyer 2000: 13). . . .

The extent of advertising in journals related to this industry provides a good illustration of how companies are "cashing in" on the boom in corrections. Examples come from two major journals serving the correctional industry, *Corrections Today* and *The American Jail*, as well as the American Correctional Association's annual *Directory*. *Corrections Today* is the leading prison trade magazine and the amount of advertising in this magazine tripled in the 1980s. Companies whose products are advertised include the following:

> Prison Health Services, Inc., a company that has, since 1978, "delivered complete, customized healthcare programs to correctional facilities only. The first company in the U.S. to specialize in this area, we can deliver your program the fastest, and back it up with services that are simply the best"; Southwest Microwave, Inc., manufactures fence security, with their latest invention known as "Micronet 750" which is "more than a sensor improvement," it is "a whole new paradigm in fence detection technology"; Acorn Engineering, Inc., with their stainless steel fixtures known as "Penal-Ware" (lavatories, toilets, showers, etc.) and "Master-Trol" electronic valve system; Rotondo Precast, Inc.

boasting "over 21,000 cells . . . and growing"; Nicholson's "BesTea" with "tea for two or . . . two thousand. . . . Now mass-feeding takes a giant stride forward"; Northwest Woolen Mills, manufacturing blankets with the slogan "We've got you covered"; and "Prison on Wheels" from Motor Coach Industries, with their "Inmate Security Transportation Vehicle" (all from *Corrections Today*, August 1996).

We found more than 200 different companies listed in these sources. As well, there is now a Web site on the Internet known as "corrections yellow pages" with at least 1000 different ads on this site.[3]

In the state of California the prison system has grown so fast in recent years that the number of employees has increased by 169% between 1984 and 1992, compared to an 8.7% *decrease* in the number of employees in higher education during the same time period. A more recent study found that during the 1995/96 fiscal year, student fee increases generated $85 million, while that state's "Three Strikes" law cost the taxpayers $75 million (Dyer 2000: 256). Working for the California prison system is very rewarding, since prison guards earn about 58 percent more than the average guard nationally. The California Correctional Peace Officer's Association (the union representing prison guards) has become a potent political force in that state. In 1980 there were 22,500 prisoners, the average salary of a prison guard was $14,400 annually, and the budget for the California Department of Corrections was $300 million. By 1996 there were more than 140,000 prisoners, the average annual salary of guards stood at $44,000 . . . (more than $10,000 above teachers—a very telling statistic)—while the budget was $3 billion. Prison jobs constituted almost half of the growth in state jobs during this time. While the union had only 5,600 members in 1980, currently it has around 23,000 members and collects about $8 million in dues annually. This union contributed $101,000 toward Proposition 184 that created the "Three Strikes and You're Out" law (Pens and Wright 1998). In 1992 this group was the second largest contributor to Political Action Committees, contributing just over $1 million to various candidates. In 1990 it gave almost $1 million to Pete Wilson's successful campaign for governor. The total contributions given in 1990 was 10 times that given by the California Teachers' Association (Schiraldi 1994).

The Privatization of Prisons: More Profits for Private Industry

A recent development in the criminal justice field, related specifically to the prison system, is the trend toward privatization, the process through which private corporations take over the operation of jails and/or prisons. Several years ago Spitzer and Scull warned about the tremendous growth in privatization in general, and within the private police industry specifically. They quoted one source that called this phenomenon "creeping capitalism" or the transfer of "services and responsibilities that were once monopolized by the state" to "profit-making agencies and organizations"

(Spitzer and Scull 1977: 18). It should be noted that privatization is a trend that includes more than the criminal justice system. As noted by Laursen, contracting out, as it is often termed, involves a number of services formerly provided by state and local governments, such as public education, health care, waste collection and so on. Laursen points out that "at least 18 categories of government services" experienced an increase in private-sector involvement between 1987 and 1995 (Laursen 1996: 45–50).

Privatization has become, in the words of Edward Herman (1997: 10), "one of the mantras of the New World Order. Economic, political and media elites assume that privatization provides undeniable benefits and moves us toward a good society." The movement toward privatization stems from the spread of corporate power. This increased power has contributed to the emergence of neoliberal ideology. The core beliefs of this ideology include "the efficiency of the private market, the inefficiency of government, and the dual menaces of inflation and budget deficits." Herman also notes that: "Part of the design of neoliberal politicians and intellectuals has been to weaken the state as a power center that might serve ordinary citizens and challenge the rule of the market" (Herman 1997: 11). Contributing to this trend is the increase in capital flow away from urban centers, leaving these centers in dire financial straits, as governments "have had to limit business taxes and spending on social benefits in order to provide a 'favorable investment climate,' leaving them under financial stress" (Herman 1997: 11–12).

The extent of privatization has not yet been adequately documented, nor do we have any estimates of the amount of money involved. As of 1995, there were private correctional systems either operational or under construction in at least 17 states. They housed prisoners in at least 22 states, which represents about 2% of all prisoners in the country (Stolz 1997: 93). The 1995 annual report of one such corporation, Corrections Corporation of America (CCA), gives some indication of the extent of privatization and the amount of money involved. We are told, first, that CCA is the "leading private sector provider of detention and corrections services to federal, state and local governments." There is also a subsidiary, CCA International, which provides similar "services" in foreign countries. Still another subsidiary is TransCor America, which "is the nation's largest and most experienced prisoner extradition company." CCA is an extensive corporation, trading stock on the New York Stock Exchange. It presently operates 46 correctional facilities, including one in England, two in Australia, and two in Puerto Rico. It is a growth corporation, indicating an obvious vested interest in a relatively high rate of incarceration. Revenues went from $13 million in 1986 to $207 million in 1995 (an increase of 1492%), while assets increased from $8 million to almost $47 million (an increase of 488%) and stockholder equity went from $24 million to $96 million (up 300%). More recent data about CCA have been provided in *The Nation*. For the first nine months of 1998 CCA's net income rose by

63% over 1997 ($63 million). Also, in 1998 CCA purchased one of its leading competitors, U.S. Corrections Corporation. More interesting, however, is that CCA presently exists only as a "brand name" because it merged with a special real estate trust CCA had formed, Prison Realty Corporation. This trust "essentially operates as a tax shelter, enabling the company to evade paying any corporate income taxes." This scheme saves the trust around $50 million per year in taxes (Bates 1999).

A number of serious problems have occurred with respect to the privatization of prisons and jails. Brayson (1996) notes that private profit is the driving force in the privatization of the correctional system. In "Crime Can Pay," a report by Equitable Securities in March, 1996, investors were issued "strong buy" advice. The report concluded: "We consider the industry very attractive. There is substantial room for continued private-prison growth" (Brayson 1996: 34). The potential for profits has not escaped Wall Street. Ted Goins, of Branch, Cabell and Co., compiled a list of "theme stocks" for the 1990s. His highest investment recommendation was Corrections Corporation of America. A Prudential Securities vice president, who is part of a "prison-financing team," is quoted as saying that "We try to keep a close eye on all the crime bills" (Thomas 1994). Wall Street is indeed eager to back the growth in "crime control stocks" with such companies as Merrill Lynch, Prudential Securities, Smith Barney Shearson, and Goldman Sachs among the leaders in support of privatization. As Brayson (1996: 34) notes: "Between 1982 and 1990 California voters approved bonds for prison construction totaling $2.4 billion. After interest is paid to lenders, the total cost will be $4.1 billion. Now the big investors are bullish on private prisons." The firm of Raucher, Pierce and Refsnes of Dallas are the underwriters and investment bankers for Wackenhut Corrections.[4] This company is reported to do about $5–7 million worth of business each year, mostly "buying bonds and securities from the private prison companies or the state entities which issue them and reselling them to investors. That securities market is now a 2–3-billion dollar industry, up from nothing eight years ago . . ." So enthralled about the profits, such securities firms have already launched the "next phase" of such development. This next phase will have private companies financing their own construction, with help from securities firms (Brayson 1996: 34). Such an industry obviously depends upon a steady supply of prisoners and they just as obviously do not have a vested interest in reducing crime and protecting victims.

As noted in a *Wall Street Journal* story, some of the same companies that produced technology used in the Vietnam War are manufacturing and selling high-tech weaponry to fight the "war on crime" (Thomas 1994). A new "iron triangle" (consisting of politicians, small communities, and businesses) similar to the one used in fighting the Vietnam War has been forged and businesses, large and small, are lining up to reap the enormous profits. Wall Street financial giants such as Goldman Sachs, Merrill Lynch, Prudential, etc. are competing to underwrite prison construction with private, tax-exempt bonds that require no voter approval. Such defense industries as Westinghouse Electric Corp., Minnesota Mining and Manufacturing Co., and GDE Systems, Inc. (a division of the old General Dynamics) are also involved, as are many lesser-known companies. Among them are Esmore Correctional Services, which is the largest U.S. maker of police electronics; they cashed in on a contract to build and manage a 1,000 bed prison in Eloy, Arizona (population 7,200, located between Phoenix and Tucson).

During their annual meeting, the American Jail Association advertised many new products. The annual meeting of the American Correctional Association has an even greater display of advertisers. Advertising included such lines as "Tap into the Sixty-Five Billion Local Jails Market" and "Jails are BIG BUSINESS" (Donziger 1996: 93). Correctional Medical Services provides medical care to around 150,000 inmates, three times as many as they "served" in 1987 (reported in USA Today, in an article appropriately titled "Prison Business Is a Blockbuster"; Meddis and Sharpe 1994).

A boom in prison construction in rural areas has resulted in one interesting fact: five percent of the population increase in rural areas during the 1980s was accounted for by the growth in inmates. In those rural counties that built a prison or jail, the new inmate population accounted for almost half of the population growth in the 1980s (Donziger 1996: 94). A total of 213 new rural prisons were built in the 1980s, up from only 40 built in the 1970s; in fact, between 1900 and 1980 only 146 new rural prisons were built in the entire country. Many rural towns have begun to solicit state governments to build a prison nearby. In Texas some towns "bombarded the [Texas Department of Prison] with incentives that range from country club memberships for wardens to longhorn cattle for the prison grounds" (Donziger 1996: 94).

Another example is the Pelican Bay State Prison in Crescent City, California. Built at a cost of $277 million, it has become the largest employer in the county. Before it was built, Crescent City was a dying town, with most of its population living in poverty or near-poverty (20% unemployment rate). Of the county's 17 sawmills, only four were operating, while the fishing industry was dead. During the 1980s a total of 164 businesses went broke. In typical corporate-welfare fashion, local supporters, seeing a way out of their predicament, practically gave away land, water, and power to get the prison built. The prison now provides around 1,500 jobs, a payroll of over $50 million, and a budget of more than $90 million. The prison also indirectly creates more business, such as a $130,000 contract to haul the garbage, a new hospital, a K-Mart, and a new Safeway. Housing starts have doubled, as did the value of real estate while collecting $142 million in real estate taxes, up from $73 million ten years earlier (Parenti 1999: 212).

Politicians often seek assistance from private enterprise when it comes to building prisons. Faced with severe overcrowding in the 1980s, liberal New York Governor Mario Cuomo found that real estate near the city of

New York, where the majority of inmates are from, was costly. He received help from a Republican state senator from the northern part of New York, who in turn arranged for low prices on land for prisons. The result? While 25 years ago this area had only two prisons, today it has 18, with one under construction. . . . These prisons bring in about $425 million in annual payroll and operating expenses; this amounts to an annual "subsidy" of more than $1,000 for each person in the area. The annual salary for a correctional officer in this area is around $36,000, more than 50% higher than the average salary for the state as a whole (Schlosser 1998: 57–58). Clearly, prisons are good for business and for job creation. One downside, however, is the fact that hundreds of families of inmates have to make the long bus ride in order to visit their relatives.[5]

Institutions for young offenders also comprise a profitable industry. A report by Equitable Securities Research in 1997 is illustrative. The title tells it all: "At Risk Youth: A Growth Industry." This industry currently involves around 10,000 to 15,000 private service providers offering everything from education programs to wilderness camps. These services represent a $50 billion per year market (Dyer 2000: 17). A cursory review of a trade magazine, *Juvenile Offenders*, provides many examples of these programs. One of the biggest specific markets relates to the "war on gangs," a metaphor that tends to create a sharp division between "us" and "them" while dehumanizing "them." In this case, "them" includes primarily racial minorities and the poor.

Another method of "cashing in on crime" is through court fees and charges leveled against inmates. For example, in 1995 the state of Virginia collected $36 million in court fees for trials alone. In 1994 Michigan collected $400,000 for inmates' bank accounts and pensions. Each year the Michigan Department of Corrections collects as much as $1 million in rent from inmates of halfway houses and prison work camps. That state passed a law in 1994 that charges inmates up to $60 per day, and prisoners are required pay for doctor visits. Here it is important to note that when a county in Kentucky began to charge inmates for doctors' visits, monthly visits dropped from 1,125 to 225. A similar program in Mobile, Alabama reported similar results. Nevada collects between $800,000 to $1 million per year in room and board (Parenti 1996). A new Missouri law will make failure to pay incarceration-related debts a violation of parole. This charge will no doubt increase the recidivism rate.

A variation of this general theme is found in so-called "joint ventures" between private companies and the state prison system that have made millions in profits through prison labor. It is especially tempting for the state of California which, because of "Three Strikes You're Out" legislation will see prison costs exceed $5.5 billion annually. Many private companies are taking advantage of cheap inmate labor and the tax breaks provided by California's Joint Venture Program. With the passage of Proposition 139 in 1990, private companies are able to use inmate labor to make products to be sold on the open market. One company employs 18 inmates at San Quentin to do data entry work for firms such as Chevron, Bank of America, and Macy's. Inmates in Ventura make phone reservations for TWA at $5 an hour; on the outside with unionized labor, this job would pay $18 per hour. Low wages are common. In Arizona, 10% of the inmates work for private companies and make less than the minimum wage. Many benefits accrue to private companies, including the fact that they do not have to pay benefits. In Oregon, $4.5 million worth of "Prison Blues," the registered trademark for a line of jeans, were sold (Parenti 1995). A Web site, www.prisonblues.com, advertises these jeans, providing the location of an "authorized retailer" and an 800 number.

Among the more recent developments in the prison industry is the entrance of long-distance phone companies. Such industry giants as AT&T, Bell South and MCI have found prisons to be an excellent market for long distance business given that inmates all over the country spend countless hours on the telephone talking with relatives. Of course this practice requires a collect call, which brings these companies into prison for the huge profits to be made. AT&T has an ad that reads: "How he got in is your business. How he gets out is ours." MCI, not wanting to miss out, went so far as installing, for free, pay phones throughout the California prison system. They levy a $3 surcharge for each phone call made, paid by the inmates' relatives. MCI offered the Department of Corrections 32 percent of the profits (Schlosser 1998: 63).

Finally, there are people known as "bed brokers." These individuals act like travel agents; in this case they help locate jail and prison beds. An example is Dominion Management, of Edmond, Oklahoma. For a fee, they will search for a correctional facility with an empty bed, offering a sort of "rent-a-cell" program. Areas suffering from overcrowding are often in desperate need for additional space, the cost of which can run between $25 to $60 per "man-day." Bed brokers earn a commission of around $2.50 to $5.50 per man-day (Schlosser 1998: 65–66). The emergence of this practice can be traced to Texas. In the 1980s the state of Texas began to use county jails to provide temporary housing to ease overcrowding in the prison system (the District of Columbia began the same thing). They began calling county jails looking for beds. A company known as N-Group Securities in Houston saw a profit. Texas towns were short on jobs and developers began to approach these towns with plans to build more jails. Wall Street investment firms like Drexel Burnham Lambert offered to underwrite some "junk bonds" for the project. However, the state of Texas soon started building prisons—$1.5 billion worth—and hiring about 12,000 guards. With this surplus of beds, they called other states for the purposes of renting cells. The result is business from 13 states, from Hawaii to Massachusetts (Pens and Wright 1998).

We have seen numerous instances of serious problems with the privatization of prisons and other components of the criminal justice system.

Given that tax dollars support it, "in theory" the criminal justice system is accountable to the public. With privatization there is no accountability. Numerous scandals demonstrate this, such as escapes, cost over-runs, etc. Russell Clemens, an economist with the Department of Research for the American Federation of State, County, and Federal Employees, put the problem in perspective when he noted that the various "problems regarding security, staffing, and quality of services have plagued prison privatization from its inception." He pointed out that, in addition to numerous escapes, there have been problems pertaining to both health care and food service which characterize "the low quality of service in privately operated prisons" (Dyer 2000: 203). The riot at a private prison in New Jersey operated by Esmor Corrections Corporation is illustrative. This riot generated a lot of media coverage. As a result Esmor's stock went from $20 to $7 per share. Since this riot, numerous private prison corporations have been caught failing to report problems within their prisons. The reason is simple: such secrecy protects shareholders "from adverse market reactions that would likely occur if a problem were to be reported." This secrecy has been called the "Esmor effect" (Dyer 2000: 204). . . .

Other Components of the Crime Control Industry

There are other components of the crime control industry. One important component is the educational system, especially the thousands of criminal justice programs within colleges and universities. There are currently about 3,000 such programs in this country. Nationwide, the average budget of each department or program offering degrees in criminal justice varies considerably, and no firm estimates are available. However, if we take $1 million (which is the annual budget for the department in which the lead author of this article works), the total annual expenditures come to around $3 billion. Additional expenditures have come in the form of grants from various government agencies (e.g., National Institute of Justice). Like the Cold War, the war on crime requires huge amounts of technical research (as Quinney noted over 20 years ago). Researchers, especially those seeking grants from the Department of Justice, are eager to reap the financial benefits of such state-supported research. Total funding for research on the problem of crime in fiscal year 1993 came to $997,023, an increase of almost 700% over 1983.

Other components of this industry that might be included are: (1) the profits made by hospitals and insurance companies (from, for instance, hospital emergency room visits, doctor's fees, insurance premiums on auto and other insurance covering crime, etc.) and the salaries of those who deal with victims (e.g., doctors, nurses, paramedics, insurance adjusters); (2) the profits from the sale of books (e.g., college textbooks, trade books), magazine and journal articles, newspaper coverage (and the advertisers who profit from crime stories), television crime shows (and their advertisers) and movies about crime (with the enormous salaries paid to actors and actresses who star in them); (3) the money collected by courts through various fines (especially traffic tickets), special courses defendants can enroll in as a condition of (or in lieu of) their sentence (e.g., traffic schools, petty larceny programs); (4) the money collected by bailbondsmen.

Two additional categories are worth mentioning separately. One is drug testing which, as a result of the "war on drugs," has become a booming industry. One recent estimate is that over 15 million Americans were tested in 1996, double the figure from five years earlier; the total cost was $600 million. The American Management Association estimated that drug testing in the private sector alone increased by 305% between 1987 and 1994. In their 1994 report this group also claims that 90% of all manufacturing companies tested their employees in 1993 (Staples 1997: 93–94). The leading tester of hair samples (one of the most common methods of drug testing) boasted that more than 500 corporations use this method. Another method of drug testing is the "Drug Alert" tester, of SherTest Corporation, which targets family members. One of the representatives of this company claimed that this device can be used to increase love and care between parents and children by "breaking down the barriers of denial between parent and child." Another company, Barringer Technologies, Inc., makes "particle detection devices" for the police, claiming it has sold thousands of $35 "testing kits." Still another company, Psychometrics Corporation, introduced a new kit selling for $75; the day after it hit the market, the company's stock went from $3.00 per share to $10.50 (Staples 1997: 97). Finally, drug testing is used constantly in jails and prisons all over the country, with plenty of federal dollars to study the results (many studies are conducted by criminologists in criminal justice programs—including the senior author's department), known as the ADAM program. . . .

Concluding Thoughts

The work of Noam Chomsky seems relevant here, as he has examined attempts by the U.S. government to build up a global economy dominated by big business (Chomsky 1994, 1996). The operating principle is one of "economic freedom"—meaning that big business is "free" to invest, sell, and appropriate all profits. To do so business requires a "favorable business climate" and a stable local environment (meaning free of political turmoil, such as citizens trying to seek some form of democracy). Getting the support of the American public is of vital importance. To garner such support, the state historically has used the threat of an external enemy. For about 40 years the enemy was "Communism" and the Soviet Union via the "Cold War." With external enemies diminishing, the state has been forced to invent new, internal threats, including "crime," "gangs," and especially "drugs." Just as anti-communism helped mobilize the American people to support massive war expenditures to guarantee a "stable business climate" overseas, anti-crime, anti-gang, and anti-drug hysteria has helped mobilize a frightened public to support massive, almost military-like expenditures for the "war on crime." The main targets for this war continue to be those groups deemed "superfluous" to the creation of wealth and profit as we move from a manufacturing to a service/information economy. As Marx noted, capitalism creates a "surplus labor force." The state, in turn, must develop ways to control this population. As big business continues to reap enormous profits, and as increasing numbers of people are inevitably relegated to the surplus population (especially inner-city minorities), the potential for the disruption of "normal business activities" increases, whether through radical democratic grass-roots activities or through criminal activity. As long as such a potential exists so will the potential for the increase in the "crime control industry."

Notes

[1] For further discussion of the "war on drugs" see Baum (1997) and Gordon (1994) and Shelden (2001); for a discussion of the "war on gangs" see Shelden, Tracy, and Brown (2001).

[2] The location of these prisons was found in the American Correctional Association's annual Directory of 1997.

[3] See (http://www.correctionsyellow.com) as well as (http://www.correcfions.com).

[4] Wackenhut Corporation has had a very suspect history. This company was founded in 1954 by former FBI agent George Wackenhut. Board members have included several top people in the intelligence industry, including many former CIA figures, such as Frank Carlucci (National Security Advisor for Reagan), William Raborn (former CIA head) and Bobby Ray Inman (former CIA Deputy Director). Even former CIA head William Casey was once Wackenhut's outside counsel. The current head of Wackenhut, George Canosa, was once part of the right-wing Cuban-American Foundation (Brayson 1996: 34). Wackenhut was at one time heavily involved in "security checks" for many corporations during the height of the Cold War. During the 1960s it had files on as many as 2.5 million "suspected dissidents" and, through its publication *Security Review*, regularly attacked the anti-war movement. One investigation by *The Nation* found that several employees of Wackenhut in El Salvador were involved in an unsuccessful plot, with ultra right-wing members of the Salvadoran Militia, to kidnap U.S. Ambassador Pat Cannon. Wackenhut denies the charge, but admits it still has employees in El Salvador. Wackenhut was named in a 1991 lawsuit alleging involvement in the manufacturing and selling of weapons and explosives to the Contras of Nicaragua. Also, a Congressional Committee recently found that the company may have broken some laws in its surveillance work for oil companies on the Alaskan pipeline (Brayson 1996: 30).

[5] Ironically, this fact has created yet another business, founded 1973 by an ex-convict, Operation Prison Gap, which operates a bus service for these families. They now have 35 buses and vans traveling on weekends and holidays (Schlosser 1998: 58).

References

Baum, D. 1997. *Smoke and Mirrors: The War on Drugs and the Politics of Failure.* Boston: Back Bay Book.

Bates, E. 1999. "CCA: The Sequel," *The Nation.* June 7: 22–23.

Brayson, C. 1996. "Crime Pays for Those in the Prison Business," *The National Times*, September: 28–35

Chambliss, W. 1999. *Power, Politics, and Crime.* Boulder, CO: Westview.

Chomsky, N. 1994. *Keeping the Rabble in Line.* Monroe, WI: Common Courage Press.

———. 1996. *Powers and Prospects: Reflections on Human Nature and the Social Order.* Boston: South End Press.

Currie, E. 1998. *Crime and Punishment in America*. New York: Metropolitan Books.

Donziger, S. 1996. *The Real War on Crime*. New York: Harper/Collins.

Dyer, J. 2000. *The Perpetual Prisoner Machine*. Boulder, CO: Westview Press.

Gordon, D. 1994. *The Return of the Dangerous Classes: Drug Prohibition and Policy Politics*. New York: W. W. Norton.

Herman, E. 1997. "Privatization: Downsizing Government for Principle and Profit," *Dollars and Sense*, (March/April): 10–37.

Irwin, J. and J. Austin. 2001. *It's About Time: America's Imprisonment Binge* (3rd ed.). Belmont, CA: Wadsworth.

Laursen, E. 1996. "A Tale of Two Communities," *Z Magazine*, (October): 45–50.

McGarrell, E. F. and T. J. Flanagan (eds.). 1986. *Sourcebook of Criminal Justice Statistics—1985*. Washington, DC: U.S. Department of Justice.

Maguire, K. and A. L. Pastore (eds.). 1995. *Sourcebook of Criminal Justice Statistics—1994*. Washington, DC: U.S. Department of Justice.

———. 1999. *Sourcebook of Criminal Justice Statistics—1998*. Washington, DC: U.S. Department of Justice, on-line version.

Marx, K. 1993. "The Usefulness of Crime." Pp. 52–53 in D. Greenberg (ed.), *Crime and Capitalism* (2nd ed.). Philadelphia: Temple University Press.

Meddis, S. V. and D. Sharp. 1994. "Prison Business is a Blockbuster," *USA Today*, (December): 13.

Parenti, C. 1996. "Pay Now, Pay Later: States Impose Prison Peonage," *The Progressive*, 60: 26–29.

———. 1995. "Inside Jobs: Use of Prison Labor in the U.S.," *New Statesman and Society*, 8: 20–21.

———. 1999. *Lockdown America: Police and Prisons in the Age of Crisis*. New York: Verso.

Pens, D., and P. Wright, eds. 1998. *The Ceiling of America: An Inside Look at the US Prison Industry*. Monroe, ME: Common Courage Press.

President's Commission on Law Enforcement and Administration of Justice. 1967. *Task Force Report: Science and Technology*. Washington, DC: U.S. Government Printing Office.

Quinney, R. 1980. *Class, State and Crime* (2nd ed.). New York: Longman.

Rush, G. E. 1997. *Inside American Prisons and Jails*. Incline Village, NV: Copperhouse.

Schiraldi, V. 1994. *The Undue Influence of California's Prison Guards' Union: California's Correctional-Industrial Complex*. San Francisco: Center on Juvenile and Criminal Justice.

Schlosser, E. 1998. "The Prison-Industrial Complex," *The Atlantic Monthly* (December): 51–77.

Shelden, R. G. 2001. *Controlling the Dangerous Classes: A Critical Introduction to the History of Criminal Justice*. Boston: Allyn and Bacon.

Shelden, R. G., S. K. Tracy, and W. B. Brown. 2001. *Youth Gangs in America* (2nd ed.). Belmont, CA: Wadsworth.

Silverstein, K. 1999. "America's Private Gulag." Pp. 156–163 in D. Burton-Rose (ed.), *The Ceiling of America: An Inside Look at the U.S. Prison Industry*. Monroe, ME: Common Courage Press.

Spitzer, S. and A. T. Scull. 1977. "Privatization and Capitalist Development: The Case of Private Police," *Social Problems*, 25: 18–29.

Staples, W. G. 1997. *The Culture of Surveillance: Discipline and Social Control in the United States*. New York: St. Martin's Press.

Stephan, J. J. 1999. *State Prison Expenditures, 1996.* Washington, DC: U.S. Department of Justice.

Stolz, B. A. 1997. "Privatizing Corrections: Changing the Corrections Policy-Making Subgovernment," *The Prison Journal*, 77 (1): 92–111.

Thomas, P. 1994. "Making Crime Pay: Triangle of Interests Creates Infrastructure to Fight Lawlessness," *Wall Street Journal*, May 12: A1, A6.

Ziedenberg, J. and V. Schiraldi. 2000a. *Poor Prescription: The Costs of Imprisoning Drug Offenders in the United States.* Washington, DC: Justice Policy Institute (www.cjcj.org/drug).

———. 2000b. *Texas Tough? An Analysis of Incarceration and Crime Trends in the Lone Star State.* Washington, DC: Justice Policy Institute.

———. 1999. *The Punishing Decade: Prison and Jail Estimates at the Millennium.* Washington, DC: Justice Policy Institute.

8

Criminal Justice
as Oppression

We established in the first chapter that the most recognized theoretical work in our field focuses on the why of crime. One branch of criminological theory is an exception to this tradition. The area of scholarship referred to as *critical criminology* has for the past thirty-five years targeted the government's construction of, and reaction to, crime versus the approach of accepting the established definitions of crime and theorizing why people break laws. Although this perspective is included in all crime theory textbooks, it concentrates far more on analyzing criminal justice/governmental behavior than it does criminal behavior.[1] Put differently, its center of attention is on "state" behavior: from the state defining certain acts as criminal, to the criminal justice system's administration of the criminal law.

Jeffrey Reiman's (2001) well-known book, *The Rich Get Richer and the Poor Get Prison*, is an excellent example of critical scholarship that theorizes the behavior of the criminal justice system and how the government defines what we call crime (see also Arrigo, 1999; Christie, 2000; Garland,

[1] In my experience some critical criminologists might not care for their work being characterized as "theorizing criminal justice," despite their concentration on legal system and crime control behavior and the fact that less attention is given to positing formal theories of crime. This resistance is showing signs of weakening, however, as found in the recent scholarship cited in this overview. Quinney's *Critique of Legal Order* (1974) was the first comprehensive study of the CJA from a radical orientation, and still stands, along with Duffee's (1980) work, as a unique contribution to criminal justice studies.

215

2001; Miller, 1996; Parenti, 1999; and Simon, 1993). Randall Shelden (2001) has recently devoted an entire book to examining CJA behavior, concentrating on the history of oppression and built-in biases against minorities, women, and the poor. As will be discussed in the section on feminist scholarship, research from this perspective has greatly furthered our theoretical understanding of the criminal justice apparatus by focusing on gender and patriarchy.

The oppression orientation views criminal justice, in its simplest terms, as an apparatus of *oppression*. When observing the history and current functioning of law-making, police, court, and corrections, its lens focuses our attention on the *oppression* of the disadvantaged and less powerful in society. The term oppression is derived from the word *oprimere*, meaning to *press against*. Its meaning today is the unjust or excessive use of power or authority. The oppression orientation concentrates, therefore, on class, race, and gender biases in the construction and administration of criminal law prohibitions. In a society characterized by acute inequalities, the major function of the criminal justice apparatus has historically been, and continues to be, the control of those defined as a threat to the stability of the dominant economic and cultural order.

Intellectual/Historical Context

We established in chapter 3 that the system framework began its ascent to prominence in the 1960s. During this period of social unrest, a number of academics began to develop an alternative orientation—a way of thinking that was generically referred to as the "conflict model" (as opposed to the "consensus model"). Applied to the legal system, the *conflict model* held that society was best characterized by the existence of conflict: criminal laws and the way in which they were administered resulted from power struggles between competing groups and opposing interests. By contrast, system thinking viewed the law and its administration emanating from a shared set of interests—a collective normative order shared by most of society's members. The system framework, stemming from Parsons's structural functionalism, is a *consensus model*.[2]

Pluralist and Radical Conflict Theory

There are two branches of scholarly works rooted in the conflict tradition.[3] The first is referred to as pluralist conflict theory, meaning that society consists of multiple groups and interests struggling for power and influence over the process of defining what constitutes crime and the manner in which these laws are administered (notice the similarity to criminal

---

[2] Most theorists now view this debate as misguided, and conflict and consensus are seen as co-existing in a type of dialectic relationship.

[3] See Einstader and Henry (1995) for a clear review of conflict theory's development.

justice as socially constructed reality). Pluralists see conflict stemming from economics, religion, ideology, culture, race, gender, or status. The groups and interests that attain the most political, economic, and cultural power guide the legal apparatus's behavior.

The second branch sees all conflict rooted in the *economics* of class-divided societies—radical conflict theory. It is the free-market, capitalist economic order that creates a class of privileged elites (the haves or the bourgeoisie) and a marginalized class known as the "surplus population." The threat posed by the victims of the free-market system, the economically disenfranchised, is contained by both social welfare measures and the criminal justice system. As discussed below, this branch of critical criminology has evolved significantly. Early theorists adopted a simplistic view where oppression of the poor was directly and intentionally controlled by the economically powerful (*instrumental thinking*) (Quinney, 1974). More contemporary work, however, views class oppression as a structural event where the state attempts through numerous measures to sustain the viability of a contradictory capitalist order that inherently produces high levels of inequality (*structural thinking*) (Beirne, 1979; Chambliss & Seidman, 1982; Michalowski, 1985; Parenti, 1999; Reimann, 2001; Spitzer, 1975).

Feminist Scholarship: Patriarchy, Gender, and the Law

Not all critical criminologists focus primarily on class conflict. An impressive area of scholarship has emerged, based in feminist theory, that employs different lenses. Gender and patriarchy are, according to Caulfield and Wonders (1994), "the central organizing principle of contemporary life, shaping human actions in every sphere, including the criminal justice system" (p. 215).

The feminist gaze directs our attention to the effects that stereotypical constructions of masculinity and femininity (gender) and a male-dominated hierarchical social arrangement (patriarchy) have on: 1) how the state defines crime; and 2) how women are treated by the criminal justice system as victims, offenders, and workers.

In Western thought, men's experiences have been taken as the norm and generalized to the population. The experiences of men have dominated explanations of difference and superiority. A seventeenth-century writer, Poulain de la Barre, observed, "All that has been written about women by men should be suspect, for the men are at once judge and party to the lawsuit" (cited in de Beauvoir, 1961, p. xxi). One consequence of male-centered (andocentric) systems of knowledge is inaccurate readings of human history, evolution, and behavior. The one-sided interpretations are presented as objective and authoritative depictions of the human condition. In the conclusion of article 16 (not included in the excerpt reprinted here), Kathleen Daly and Meda Chesney-Lind point out that regardless of age, race, class, or nationality, men are more likely to be involved in serious crime. They point out that most theories of crime consider the "normalcy" of crime as a result of social processes and structures, yet theorists rarely examine patriarchal structures for forms and expressions of masculinity, such as controlling others and wielding uncompromising power. They suggest that gender differences in crime may signal that crime may not be so normal after all—and that cause for hope lies in that gender difference.

Aside from impacting our field's theories of crime, the feminist literature has contributed substantially to our theoretical understanding of the CJA (see for example Chesney-Lind, 2001; Daly, 1994; Danner, 1998; Mann, 1995; Martin & Jurik, 1996; Miller, 1998; Price & Sokoloff, 1995; Renzetti & Goodstein, 2001). Through feminist lenses we can see how and why:

- the CJA has neglected to take seriously various forms of violence against women, such as domestic violence and rape;
- female criminal justice workers suffer harassment and discrimination in the fields of police and corrections;
- female arrestees and offenders are treated unfairly by the criminal justice system; and
- stereotypical notions of masculinity embedded in rational/legal criminal justice ideology and policy lead to unethical and counterproductive practices.

Minorities and Criminal Justice

The criminal justice scholarship centered around class and gender is vast. The literature focusing on race and criminal justice, while only in its early stages of development, has expanded significantly in the last five years. Feminist and class-oriented criminologists are focusing more intensely on race and CJA behavior as part of their class and gender-based analyses. Moreover, numerous scholars, such as Katheryn Russell (the author of article 18), are concentrating predominantly on race, crime, and criminal justice (see, for example, Gabbidon, Greene, & Young, 2001; Lusane, 1991; Mann, 1993; Miller, 1996; Milovanovic & Russell, 2001; Robinson, 2000; Websdale, 2001).

The bulk of this literature is targeted at documenting the disparate treatment certain racial and ethnic minorities receive at the hands of the criminal justice apparatus and sensitizing readers to the inequities in the system. Russell (2001) and Hawkins (2001) have started the process of developing this literature into theoretical models of race and legal system behavior.

Expansive and Diverse Coverage

For many, critical criminology still conjures up an image of Marxist theorists holding out hope for a socialist revolution. This is a remnant of the outdated criticisms levied nearly two decades earlier against early critical scholarship. Such characterizations have no doubt played a role in keeping this orientation somewhat segregated from the rest of the discipline. An updated assessment, however, would likely convince even the most cynical that this literature constitutes an expansive and highly diverse body of scholarship. The following key themes are essential to this perspective.

Intersections: Race, Gender, and Class

Being poor, an ethnic minority, and a woman is often said to be a triple disadvantage in our society. Combining feminist and race scholarship allows an expanded framework for analyzing criminal justice. Rather than the single lens of class, as found in early conflict scholarship, the triple lenses of class, race, and gender create a prism. Gregg Barak, Jeanne Flavin, and Paul Leighton (2001) summarize this way of thinking:

> We strive to portray the social realities of justice in America, vis-à-vis an examination of class, race, and gender and the administration of criminal justice. Although class, race, and gender are viewed here as interconnecting systems of difference, and as belonging to a larger system of privilege and inequality, we still appreciate the uniqueness of these categories and the importance of viewing them both alone and in combination. (p. 23)

This framework stresses, therefore, the presence of multiple inequalities in operation simultaneously. Recurring patterns of discrimination and ill treatment in how crime is defined and how laws are enforced emanate from the social and power relations of gender, class, and race.

Dangerous and Threatening Groups

One only has to watch a few episodes of the popular television show *Cops* to observe accurately that the bulk of the activities of the CJA concentrate on controlling and containing the poor and marginalized members of society. In 2002, the criminal justice system had over three percent of the U.S. population under direct correctional supervision—up from less than one-half percent in 1982. Most of this three percent comes from the surplus population, and an over-representative number from poor minorities.

A key theme of oppression thinking is that this unfortunate state of affairs is not a *forced reaction* to an ever-worsening crime problem (the rational/legal theoretical orientation). Rather, they see our government and society choosing to respond to the fallout of racism, patriarchy, and an unjust economic system with criminal justice-based solutions designed to control "dangerous" or "threatening" groups. By defining and reacting to marginalized group behavior as individual acts of criminality, the structural contradictions and social maladies underlying our social problems go unexamined (Reiman, 2001). Likewise, a society intent on using lower-class crime as a scapegoat will overlook the significant social harms produced by the "corporate-caste" (Parenti, 1999).

Conspiracy vs. Structural Thinking

Early critical criminologists wrote during a time when the government was being critiqued passionately on many fronts. The criminal justice system was no exception. In a chapter titled, "Preservation of Domestic Order by the Ruling Class," Quinney (1974) forthrightly claimed that "law has become the ultimate means by which the state secures the interests of the ruling class" (p. 52). These types of statements implied an intentional and concerted effort by the power elite to oppress the "rabble" that threaten the capitalist order.

Oppression literature has worked hard to combat the criticism that it is premised on simplistic conspiratorial logic. Of the numerous works I reviewed for this section, including those from feminist and race studies, a large percentage of them went out of their way to clarify that race, gender, and class bias/oppression is not generally the result of a conscious design or program of oppression by a few controlling elites. What they articulate in its place is a structural explanation (referred to above as "structural thinking").

The growth orientation (chapter 7) also employed structural thinking. From this perspective, criminal justice growth emanated not from a grand scheme but from agencies, processes, and ways of thinking that generated a synergistic model leading to exponential growth. It is the patterned ways of thinking, organizing, and acting—all of which revolve around producing and sustaining the economic and cultural status quo—that drives the creation of oppressive laws and criminal justice activities. The power elite, and especially criminal justice practitioners, need not consciously oversee and manipulate the oppression of the downtrodden and marginalized; the construction of the crime problem and oppressive measures to address it are guided by the capitalist economic order, patriarchy, and racism. The net-effect can be gender, race, and class bias and oppression—even if this is not the intent of individual members of the media, legislature, criminal justice system, or the corporate world.

Dialectical and Historical Thinking

Most critical scholars stress that these structural forces and their effects on the oppressed must be placed in historical context. Understanding what exists requires an examination of its historical development. Consequently, critical scholars have examined the history of class, race, and gender bias in the making of drug laws, the formation of police, the development of parole and probation, juvenile justice, prisons, and the courts. An example of the power of historical context is found in the literature on lynching. During the late 1800s and early 1900s nearly 3,500 young African Americans were lynched across the southern United States. Several scholars have demonstrated the importance of connecting this gruesome historical practice with the disproportionate numbers of African-American men executed today by the criminal justice system in the South (Dray, 2001; Miller, 1996).

To study history is to study social change. A key feature of *critical* historical analysis is an approach to understanding change known as "dialectics." Dialectical thinking sees societal transformation as flowing from the tensions that arise between opposites and contradictions. Karl Marx, borrowing from the German philosopher Hegel (who borrowed from eastern Taoist philosophy), demonstrated that economic and social contradictions form the basis for society's self-transformation. Marx emphasized the internal contradiction and tension created by an economic system that generates high rates of poverty among some and enormous material wealth among others.

Oppression theorists note other tensions and contradictions as well. Ferrell (1993) examines the dialectic between the criminal justice system and graffiti artists, noting how the interplay between the two has generated an ongoing process of state control and cultural resistance. This pattern undermines the state's initial attempts at control by cultivating a stronger counter-control effort. Feminists have traced how the internal contradictions found in patriarchy have led to a powerful resistance movement, intense conflict, and sweeping social transformations.

Socialism, Critique and Praxis: A New Eclecticism

Probably the two most diametrically opposed frameworks discussed in this book are the systems and the oppression orientations. Ironically, both share a strong commitment to linking their scholarship and research to social change. Obviously they differ significantly in the types of changes sought. Recall that the systems orientation strives to bring about a more efficient and effective criminal justice system. The stereotype of critical criminologists is that the only change they seek is a socialist revolution. Although a few theorists 20 years ago espoused this position, the changes advocated today by those working within this orientation vary tremendously, ranging from slowing criminal justice growth, to altering gendered socialization practices, to child welfare solutions (Christie, 2000; Currie, 1998; Lynch & Stretesky, 1999). Today's oppression theorists even discuss specific reforms within the criminal justice system, although they tend to favor non-criminal justice solutions to the crime problem. A growing number of critical theorists employ critical thinking only as a tool of scholarly analysis and do not advocate specific strategies for social change.

Still, the oppression orientation has a strong tradition of being committed to social praxis. In praxis, thought and action, or theory and practice, are dialectically related. Their mutual interaction with one another reinforces and sometimes transforms the other (referred to as a *mutually transformative process*). The development of theory for critical criminologists is seen as a practical endeavor—it can inform and transform practice just as practice can inform and transform theory. At the heart of this process is the activity of *critique*. Through a socio-historical critique of *what is*, oppression theorists aspire to move toward a more just, free, and peaceful society.

Bias and Subtlety

The oppression orientation's commitment to critique and praxis is seen by some observers as evidence that it is "biased." While it may be true that critical criminology operates from an ideological frame of reference, this is true with all of the orientations discussed in this book. Morgan (1986) makes the same point in his book on organizations:

> The criticism has merit in that the critical perspective is ideological, but it is certainly no more ideological than any other. The chapters in this book show that all theories of organization are inherently ideological in that they tend to give us rather one-sided views. Thus although the domination [oppression] metaphor may lead us to focus on organizations in an extreme way, it is really no more extreme than any other viewpoint, including the highly orthodox. (p. 319)

Not all oppression thinking comes from feminist, race, or class-based scholarship. Although not written by critical criminologists, the authors of a recent article in the journal *Criminology* conclude their study on police behavior by stating, "even controlling for various types of suspect behavior, these police do appear to replicate several larger societal tendencies to distribute disrespect disproportionately to those of low or peripheral status" (Mastrofski, Reisig, & McCluskey, 2002, p. 540). Oppression thinking is embedded in this guarded language. A critical theorist would use more pointed language: the disrespectful treatment of the poor and powerless by the state is a reflection of gender, race, and class biases endemic to our society.

References

Arrigo, B. A. (1999). *Social justice/criminal justice: The maturation of critical theory in law, crime, and deviance*. Boston: Wadsworth.

Barak, G., Flavin, J. M., & Leighton, P. S. (2001). *Class, race, gender, and crime: Social realities of justice in America*. Los Angeles: Roxbury Publishing.

Beirne, P. (1979). Empiricism and the critique of Marxism on law and crime. *Social Problems, 26*(4), 373–385.

Carr, W., & Stephens, K. (1986). *Becoming critical: Education, knowledge and action research*. London: The Falmer Press.

Caulfield, S., & Wonders, N. (1994). Gender and justice: Feminist contributions to criminology. In G. Barak (Ed.), *Varieties of criminology: Readings from a dynamic discipline*. Westport, CT: Praeger.

Chambliss, W., & Seidman, R. B. (1982). *Law, order, and power*. Reading, MA: Addison-Wesley.

Chesney-Lind, M. (2001). Out of sight out of mind: Girls in the juvenile justice system. In C. M. Renzetti & L. Goodstein (Eds.), *Women, crime, and the criminal justice: Original feminist readings*. Los Angeles: Roxbury.

Christie, N. (2000). *Crime control as industry: Toward GULAGS, western style* (3rd ed.). New York: Routledge.

Daly, K. (1994). *Gender, crime, and punishment*. New Haven: Yale University Press.

Danner, M. (1998). Three strikes and it's women who are out: The hidden consequences for women of criminal justice policy reforms. In S. L. Miller (Ed.), *Crime control and women: Feminist implications of criminal justice policy*. Thousand Oaks, CA: Sage.

Dray, P. (2002). *At the hands of persons unknown: The lynching of black America*. New York: Random House.

Duffee, D. E. (1980, 1990). *Explaining criminal justice: Community theory and criminal justice reform*. Prospect Heights, IL: Waveland Press.

Einstadter, W., & Henry, S. (1995). *Criminological theory: An analysis of its underlying assumptions*. New York: Harcourt Brace.

Ferrell, J. (1993). *Crimes of style: Urban graffiti and the politics of criminality*. New York: Garland.

Gabbidon, S. L., Greene, H. T., & Young, V. D. (2001). *African American classics in criminology and criminal justice*. Thousand Oaks, CA: Sage.

Garland, D. (2001). *The culture of control: Crime and social order in contemporary society*. Chicago: The University of Chicago Press.

Hawkins, D. F. (2001). Beyond anomalies: Rethinking the conflict perspective on race and criminal punishment. In S. L. Gabbidon, H. T. Greene, & V. D. Young (Eds.), *African American classics in criminology and criminal Justice*. Thousand Oaks, CA: Sage.

Jurik, N., & Martin, S. (2001). Femininities and masculinities, and organizational conflict: Women in criminal justice occupations. In C. M. Renzetti & L. Goodstein (Eds.), *Women, crime, and the criminal justice: Original feminist readings*. Los Angeles: Roxbury.

Lusane, C. (1991). *Pipe dream blues: Racism and the war on drugs*. Boston: South End Press.

Lynch, M. J., & Stretesky, P. (1999). Marxism and social justice: Thinking about social justice, eclipsing criminal justice. In B. A. Arrigo (Ed.), *Social justice/criminal justice: The maturation of critical theory in law, crime, and deviance*. Boston: Wadsworth.

Mann, C. R. (1993). *Unequal justice: A question of color*. Bloomington: Indiana University Press.

Mann, C. R. (1995). Women of color and the criminal justice system. In B. R. Price & N. J. Sokoloff (Eds.), *The criminal justice system and women: Offenders, victims, and workers*. New York: McGraw-Hill.

Martin, S. E., & Jurik, N. C. (1996). *Doing justice, doing gender: Women in law and criminal justice occupations*. Thousand Oaks, CA: Sage.

Mastrofski, S., Reisig, M. D., & McCluskey, J. D. (2002). Police disrespect toward the public: An encounter-based analysis. *Criminology, 40*(3), 519–552.

Michalowski, R. J. (1985). *Order, law, and crime: An introduction to criminology.* New York: Random House.

Miller, J. (1996). *Search and destroy: African-American males in the criminal justice system.* Cambridge: University of Cambridge Press.

Miller, S. L. (1998). *Crime control and women: Feminist implications of criminal justice policy.* Thousand Oaks, CA: Sage.

Milovanovic, D., & Russell, K. (2001). *Petit apartheid in the U.S. criminal justice system.* Durham, NC: Carolina Academic Press.

Morgan, G. M. (1986). *Images of organization.* Newbury Park, CA: Sage.

Parenti, C. (1999). *Lockdown America: Police and prisons in the age of crisis.* New York: Verso Press.

Price, B. R., & Sokoloff, N. J. (1995). *The criminal justice system and women: Offenders, victims, and workers.* New York: McGraw-Hill.

Quinney, R. (1974). *Critique of legal order: Crime control in capitalist society.* Boston: Little, Brown.

Reiman, J. (2001). *The rich get richer and the poor get prison: Ideology, class, and criminal justice.* Boston: Allyn and Bacon.

Renzetti, C. M., & Goodstein, L. (2001). *Women, crime, and the criminal justice: Original feminist readings.* Los Angeles: Roxbury.

Robinson, M. (2000). The construction and reinforcement of myths of race and crime. *Journal of Contemporary Criminal Justice, 16*(2), 133–156.

Russell, K. (2001). Toward developing a theoretical paradigm and typology for petit apartheid. In D. Milovanovic & K. Russell (Eds.), *Petit apartheid in the U.S. criminal justice system.* Durham, NC: Carolina Academic Press.

Shelden, R. (2001). *Controlling the dangerous classes: A critical introduction to the history of criminal justice.* Needham Heights, MA: Allyn and Bacon.

Simon, J. (1993). *Poor discipline: Parole and the social control of the underclass, 1890–1990.* Chicago: University of Chicago Press.

Spitzer, S. (1975). Toward a Marxian theory of deviance. *Social Problems, 22,* 638–651.

U.S. Correctional Population at All-Time High (2002). CNN News Report: August 25, 2002.

Websdale, N. (2001). *Policing the poor: From slave plantation to public housing.* Boston: Northeastern University Press.

Feminism and Criminology

Kathleen Daly
Meda Chesney-Lind

Defining Feminism

What Is Feminism?

In their introduction to *What Is Feminism?* Mitchell and Oakley (1986:3) suggest that it is "easier to define feminism in its absence rather than its presence." Delmar (1986) offers a "baseline definition" on which feminists and nonfeminists might agree: a feminist holds that women suffer discrimination because of their sex, that they have needs which are negated and unsatisfied, and that the satisfaction of these needs requires a radical change. "But beyond that," Delmar says, "things immediately become more complicated" (1986:8).

This complication arises because feminism is a set of theories about women's oppression *and* a set of strategies for social change. Cott (1987) identifies the paradoxes of first-wave feminism[1] (the "woman movement" in the nineteenth and early twentieth centuries), which reflect the merging of these theoretical and political impulses. These paradoxes include acknowledging diversity among women but claiming women's unity, requiring gender consciousness but calling for an eradication of gender-based distinctions and divisions, and aiming for individual freedom and autonomy by mobilizing a mass-based movement. The same paradoxical elements are seen in second-wave feminism (the contemporary women's

Justice Quarterly, 5(4): 502–505; 524–526. © 1988. Reprinted with permission of the Academy of Criminal Justice Sciences.

movement beginning in the 1960s). Unfriendly interpretations of these
contrary tendencies include, "These women don't know what they want"
or "They want it both ways." Yet as Harding (1986:244) suggests, "The
problem is that we [feminists] do not know and should not know just what
we want to say about a number of conceptual choices with which we are
presented—except that the choices themselves create no-win dilemmas for
our feminisms." The task of describing *and* changing a spectrum of
women's experiences, which have been formed by particular and often
competing allegiances to class, race, and other social groups, is not
straightforward but a blurred and contingent enterprise.

Distinguishing Feminist from Nonfeminist Analyses

It is not easy to know when a work or action is feminist. Delmar asks,
for example, "Are all actions and campaigns prompted or led by women,
feminist?" (1986:11). "Can an action be 'feminist' even if those who perform it are not?" (1986:12). She contrasts several views of feminism. It
may be diffuse activity, any action motivated out of concern for women's
interests, whether or not actors or groups acknowledge them as feminist.
This view empties feminism of any meaning because all actions or analyses
having women as their object fall into the same category. Delmar opts
instead for another approach, which is to "separate feminism and feminists from the multiplicity of those concerned with women's issues." Feminism can be defined as a field—even though diverse—but feminists can
"make no claim to an exclusive interest in or copyright over problems
affecting women" (1986:13).

Neither a scholar's gender nor the focus of scholarship—whether
women, gender difference, or anything else—can be used to distinguish
feminist, nonfeminist, or even antifeminist works. Scholars' theoretical
and methodological points of view are defined by the way in which they
frame questions and interpret results, not by the social phenomenon
alone. Thus to Morris's (1987:15) question—"Does feminist criminology
include criminologists who are feminist, female criminologists, or criminologists who study women"—we reply that research on women or on
gender difference, whether conducted by a male or a female criminologist,
does not in itself qualify it as feminist. Conversely, feminist inquiry is not
limited to topics on or about women; it focuses on men as well. For criminology, because most offenders and criminal justice officials are men, this
point is especially relevant; allied social institutions such as the military
have not escaped feminist scrutiny (Enloe 1983, 1987). When feminist,
nonfeminist, or not-really-feminist distinctions are drawn, the main source
of variation is how in exclusively scholars (or activists) define a continuum
of feminist thought.

Pateman (1986), for example, compares theories addressing "women's
issues" with those that are "distinctly feminist." She terms the former
"domesticated feminism" and sees it in liberal and socialist thought when

scholars try to fit women or gender relations into existing theories, making "feminism . . . safe for academic theory" (1986:4). Such efforts deny that "sexual domination is at issue, or that feminism raises a problem [patriarchy], which is repressed in other theories" (1986:5). A more distinctive feminist approach assumes that individuals are gendered, and that "individuality is not a unitary abstraction but an embodied and sexually differentiated expression of the unity of humankind" (1986:9).

The implications of a distinctive feminist approach are profound—in Pateman's and others' words, "subversive"—for social, political, criminological, and other theories. It is one thing to say that women have been excluded from general theories of social phenomena. It is another matter to wonder how theories would appear if they were fashioned from women's experiences and if women had a central place in them. In addition, it is equally important to query the gender-specific character of existing theories fashioned from men's experiences.

Although some scholars (typically, liberal and Marxist feminists who do not accord primacy to gender or to patriarchal relations) assume that previous theory can be corrected by including women, others reject this view, arguing that a reconceptualization of analytic categories is necessary. Working toward a reinvention of theory is a major task for feminists today. Although tutored in "male-stream" theory and methods,[2] they work within and against these structures of knowledge to ask new questions, to put old problems in a fresh light, and to challenge the cherished wisdom of their disciplines. Such rethinking comes in many varieties, but these five elements of feminist thought distinguish it from other types of social and political thought:

- Gender is not a natural fact but a complex social, historical, and cultural product; it is related to, but not simply derived from, biological sex difference and reproductive capacities.

- Gender and gender relations order social life and social institutions in fundamental ways.

- Gender relations and constructs of masculinity and femininity are not symmetrical but are based on an organizing principle of men's superiority and social and political-economic dominance over women.

- Systems of knowledge reflect men's views of the natural and social world; the production of knowledge is gendered.

- Women should be at the center of intellectual inquiry, not peripheral, invisible, or appendages to men.

These elements take different spins, depending on how a scholar conceptualizes gender, the causes of gender inequality, and the means of social change. Generally, however, a feminist analysis draws from feminist theories or research, problematizes gender, and considers the implications of findings for empowering women or for change in gender relations.

Finally, we note that scholars may think of themselves as feminists in their personal lives, but they may not draw on feminist theory or regard themselves as feminist scholars. For personal or professional reasons (or both), they may shy away from being marked as a particular kind of scholar. . . .

Gender Equality in the Criminal Justice System

In the early days of second-wave feminism, calls for legal equality with men were apparent everywhere, and the early feminist critics of criminal law and justice practices reflected this ethos. Today feminist legal scholars are more skeptical of a legal equality model because the very structure of law continues to assume that men's lives are the norm, such that women's legal claims are construed as "special treatment." Alternatives to thinking about equality and difference have been proposed in view of women's social and economic subordinate status and gender differences in paid employment, sexuality, and parenthood; see, e.g., *International Journal of the Sociology of Law* 1986; MacKinnon 1987; Rhode 1987; Vogel forthcoming; *Wisconsin Women's Law Journal* 1987. Feminist dissensus over what should be done partly reflects different perspectives on gender, but increasingly one finds that strategies for change reflect lessons learned from engaging in the legal process. As feminists have moved to change the law, so too has the law changed feminism.[3]

Questioning Equality Doctrine and the Equal Treatment Model

Feminist analyses of criminal justice practices reflect a similar shift by moving away from a liberal feminist conceptualization of gender discrimination as a problem of equal treatment. This recent change is more pronounced in British than in American criminology (related, no doubt, to the preponderance of statistical approaches in the United States). It is seen in studies and literature reviews by Allen (1987), Chesney-Lind (1986, 1987), Daly (1987a, 1987b, forthcoming), Eaton (1983, 1985, 1986, 1987), Heidensohn (1986, 1987), Smart (1985), and Worrall (1987). Unlike previous statistical studies of gender-based disparities in court outcomes (for reviews see Nagel and Hagan 1983; Parisi 1982), more recent qualitative studies of legal processes analyze the interplay of gender, sexual and familial ideology, and social control in courtroom discourse and decision making at both the juvenile and the adult levels. This work addresses how gender relations structure decisions in the legal process, rather than whether men and women are treated "the same" in a statistical sense. Eaton (1986:15) sums up the limitations of analyzing sentencing as an equal treatment problem in this way: "The [discrimination] debate is conducted within the terms of legal rhetoric—'justice' and 'equality' mean 'equal treatment,' existing inequalities are to be ignored or discounted." Thus, just as feminist legal scholars are critiquing equality doctrine, feminist criminologists now are questioning how research on discrimination in the courts is conducted.

While feminist scholars are identifying the limitations of an equal treatment model in law or in research on legal practices, that model, and the statistical evidence on which it is based, are the centerpiece of sentencing reforms in the United States. Although these reforms are taking shape in different ways (Blumstein, Cohen, Martin, and Tonry 1983; Shane-DuBow, Brown, and Olsen 1985; Tonry 1987), they aim to reduce sentencing disparity by punishing "like crimes" in the same way. A major problem is that sentencing reforms are designed to reduce race- and class-based disparities in sentencing men. Their application to female offenders may yield equality with a vengeance: a higher rate of incarceration and for longer periods of time than in the past.[4] Like reforms in divorce (Weitzman 1985) and in child custody (Fineman 1988), devised with liberal feminist definitions of equality, sentencing reform also may prove unjust and may work ultimately against women.

The limitations of current equality doctrine are also apparent for changing the prison (or jail) conditions of incarcerated women. Litigation based on equal protection arguments can improve conditions for women to some degree (e.g., training, educational, or work release programs), but such legal arguments are poorly suited to the specific health needs of women and to their relationships with children (Leonard 1983; Resnik and Shaw 1980). Indirectly they may also make it easier to build new facilities for female offenders than to consider alternatives to incarceration. Historical studies of the emergence of women's prisons in the United States suggest that separate spheres notions, which were applied to penal philosophy, may have offered somewhat better conditions of confinement for women (notably white, not black women; see Rafter 1985) than an equality-with-men model (Freedman 1981; SchWeber 1982). Therefore equality defined as equal treatment of men and women, especially when men's experiences and behavior are taken as the norm, forestalls more fundamental change and in some instances may worsen women's circumstances.

Reflections

We are in a time of transition in which gender equality (or equality for other social groups), founded on legal principles of equal access to and due process in social institutions, offers a limited prospect for changing the panoply of inequalities in daily life. In the case of gender relations we cannot retreat to separate spheres, nor can we embrace equality doctrine uncritically. Criminologists, especially those involved in the formation of policy, should be aware that equal treatment is only one of several ways of redressing discrimination and of moving toward a more humane justice system.

Notes

[1] [Moved from the first page of the article to explain "first-wave feminism."] First-wave feminism (termed "the woman movement") arose in the United States and in some European countries in conjunction with the movement to abolish slavery. Its beginning in the United

230 States is typically marked by the Seneca Falls, New York, convention (1848), and its ending by the passage of the 19th Amendment to the United States Constitution (granting women's suffrage)

States is typically marked by the Seneca Falls, New York, convention (1848), and its ending by the passage of the 19th Amendment to the United States Constitution (granting women's suffrage), coupled with the falling-out among women activists over the Equal Rights Amendment proposed in the early 1920s. See DuBois (1981) for the nineteenth-century context, Cott (1987) for the early twentieth-century context when the term "feminist" was first used, Giddings (1984) for black women's social movement activity, Kelly-Gadol (1982) for "pro-woman" writers in the four centuries before the nineteenth century, and Kimmell (1987) for men's responses to feminism. Second-wave American feminism emerged in the mid-1960s in conjunction with the civil rights movement, the new left, and a critical mass of professional women (see Evans 1979; hooks 1981, 1984). It has not ended (but see Stacey 1987 for an analysis of "postfeminist" consciousness). Note that the conventional dating of the first- and second-wave is rightly challenged by several scholars who find greater continuity in feminist consciousness and action (Cott 1987; Delmar 1986; Kelly-Gadol 1982).

[2] We are uncertain who introduced the concept "male-stream" because citations vary. *The Feminist Dictionary* (Kramarae and Treichler 1985:244) says "coined by Mary Daly," but does not say where.

[3] This observation paraphrases a remark made by Martha Fineman at the Feminism and Legal Theory Conference, University of Wisconsin Law School, July 1988. Feminist analyses of law and strategies for change are prodigious; see Graycar (1987) for a summary of some themes. Majury (1987), Rights of Women, Family Law Subgroup (1985), and Schneider (1986) illustrate dilemmas in legal strategy.

[4] For example, California's determinate sentencing law may have had an impact on increasing the length of prison sentences for women (Blumstein et al. 1983, volume 1:114, 213–14). To our knowledge, evidence on the impact of sentencing reform in changing the rates of incarceration for women is not yet available. We note, however, that the female share of the jail and prison population has increased in the last decade. Of those in jail, women were 6 percent in 1978 and 8 percent in 1986 (Bureau of Justice Statistics 1987:5) [11.6% in 2001]; of those in state and federal prisons, women were 4 percent in 1978 (Flanagan and McCleod 1983:545) and 5 percent in 1987 (Bureau of Justice Statistics 1988:3) [6.6% in 2001.

References

Allen, Hilary (1987) "Rendering Them Harmless: The Professional Portrayal of Women Charged with Serious Violent Crimes." In Pat Carlen and Anne Worrall (eds.), *Gender, Crime and Justice*. Philadelphia: Open University Press, pp. 81–94.

Blumstein, Alfred, Jacqueline Cohen, Susan E. Martin, and Michael H. Tonry, eds. (1983) *Research on Sentencing. The Search for Reform*. Vols. 1 and 2. Washington, DC: National Academy Press.

Bureau of Justice Statistics, U.S. Department of Justice (1987) "Jail Inmates 1986," NCJ-107123. Washington, DC: U.S. Government Printing Office.

——— (1988) "Prisoners in 1987," NCJ-110331. Washington, DC: U.S. Government Printing Office.

Chesney-Lind, Meda (1986) "Women and Crime: The Female Offender." *Signs: Journal of Women in Culture and Society* 12(1):78–96.

——— (1987) "Female Offenders: Paternalism Reexamined." In Laura L. Crites and Winifred L. Hepperle (eds.), *Women, the Courts, and Equality*. Newbury Park, CA: Sage, pp. 114–39.

Cott, Nancy (1987) *The Grounding of Modern Feminism*. New Haven: Yale University Press.

Daly, Kathleen (1987a) "Structure and Practice of Familial-Based Justice in a Criminal Court." *Law and Society Review* 21(2):267–90.

——— (1987b) "Discrimination in the Criminal Courts: Family, Gender, and the Problem of Equal Treatment." *Social Forces* 66(l):152–75.

——— (1988) "The Social Control of Sexuality: A Case Study of the Criminalization of Prostitution in the Progressive Era." In Steven Spitzer and Andrew T. Scull (eds.), *Research in Law, Deviance, and Social Control.* Volume 9. Greenwich, CT: JAI, pp. 171–206.

——— (1989) "Rethinking Judicial Paternalism: Gender, Work-Family Relations, and Sentencing." *Gender and Society* 3:9–36.

Delmar, Rosalind (1986) "What Is Feminism?" In Juliet Mitchell and Ann Oakley (eds.), *What is Feminism?* New York: Pantheon, pp. 8–33.

DuBois, Ellen Carol (1981) *Elizabeth Cady Stanton/Susan B. Anthony: Correspondence, Writings, and Speeches.* New York: Schocken.

Eaton, Mary (1983) "Mitigating Circumstances: Familiar Rhetoric." *International Journal of the Sociology of Law* 11:385–400.

——— (1985) "Documenting the Defendant: Placing Women in Social Inquiry Reports." In Julia Brophy and Carol Smart (eds.), *Women in Law: Explorations in Law, Family, and Sexuality.* Boston: Routledge and Kegan Paul, pp. 117–38.

——— (1986) *Justice for Women? Family, Court and Social Control.* Philadelphia: Open University Press.

——— (1987) "The Question of Bail: Magistrates' Responses to Applications for Bail on Behalf of Men and Women Defendants." In Pat Carlen and Anne Worrall (eds.), *Gender, Crime and Justice.* Philadelphia: Open University Press, pp. 95–107.

Enloe, Cynthia H. (1983) *Does Khaki Become You? The Militarization of Women's Lives.* Boston: South End.

——— (1987) "Feminists Thinking about War, Militarism, and Peace." In Beth B. Hess and Myra Marx Feree (eds.), *Analyzing Gender.* Newbury Park, CA: Sage, pp. 526–47.

Evans, Sarah (1979) *Personal Politics: The Roots of Women's Liberation in the Civil Rights Movement and the New Left.* New York: Knopf.

Fineman, Martha (1988) "Dominant Discourse, Professional Language, and Legal Change in Child Custody Decisionmaking." *Harvard Law Review* 10(4):727–74.

Flanagan, Timothy J. and Maureen McLeod, eds. (1983) *Sourcebook of Criminal Justice Statistics–1982.* Bureau of Justice Statistics, U.S. Department of Justice. Washington, DC: U.S. Government Printing Office.

Freedman, Estelle B. (1981) *Their Sisters' Keepers: Women's Prison Reform in America, 1830–1930.* Ann Arbor: University of Michigan Press.

Giddings, Paula (1984) *When and Where I Enter: The Impact of Black Women on Race and Sex in America.* New York: Morrow.

Graycar, Regina (1986) "Yes, Virginia, There is a Feminist Legal Literature: A Survey of Some Recent Publications." *Australian Journal of Law and Society* 3:105–35.

Harding, Sandra (1986) *The Science Question in Feminism.* Ithaca: Cornell University Press.

Heidensohn, Frances M. (1968) "The Deviance of Women: A Critique and an Enquiry." *British Journal of Sociology* 19(2):160–76.

hooks, Bell (1981) *Ain't I a Woman?* Boston: South End.

——— (1984) *Feminist Theory: From Margin to Center.* Boston: South End.

Kelly-Gadol, Joan (1977) "Did Women Have a Renaissance?" Reprinted 1987 in Renate Bridenthal, Claudia Koonz, and Susan Stuard (eds.), *Becoming Visible: Women in European History.* 2nd edition. Boston: Houghton Mifflin, pp. 175–201.

Kimmel, Michael S. (1987) "Men's Responses to Feminism at the Turn of the Century." *Gender and Society* 1(3):261–83.

Kramarae, Cheris and Paula A. Treichler (1985) *A Feminist Dictionary.* Boston: Pandora/Routledge and Kegan Paul.

Leonard, Eileen B. (1983) "Judicial Decisions and Prison Reform: The Impact of Litigation on Women Prisoners." *Social Problems* 31(l):45–58.

Majury, Diana (1987) "Strategizing in Equality." *Wisconsin Women's Law Journal* 3:169–87.

Mitchell, Juliet and Ann Oakley, eds. (1986) *What is Feminism?* New York: Pantheon.

Morris, Allison (1987) *Women, Crime and Criminal Justice.* New York: Blackwell.

Nagel, Ilene H. and John Hagan (1983) "Gender and Crime: Offense Patterns and Criminal Court Sanctions." In Michael H. Tonry and Norval Morris (eds.), *Crime and Justice: An Annual Review of Research.* Volume 4. Chicago: University of Chicago Press, pp. 91–144.

Parisi, Nicolette (1982) "Are Females Treated Differently? A Review of the Theories and Evidence on Sentencing and Parole Decisions." In Nicole Hahn Rafter and Elizabeth A. Stanko (eds.), *Judge, Lawyer, Victim, Thief.* Boston: Northeastern University Press, pp. 205–20.

Pateman, Carole (1986) "The Theoretical Subversiveness of Feminism." In Carole Pateman and Elizabeth Gross (eds.), *Feminist Challenges: Social and Political Theory.* Boston: Northeastern University Press, pp. 1–10.

Resnik, Judith and Nancy Shaw (1980) "Prisoners of Their Sex: Health Problems of Incarcerated Women." In Ira Robbins (ed.), *Prisoners' Rights Sourcebook: Theory, Litigation and Practice.* Volume 2. New York: Clark Boardman, pp. 319–413.

Rights of Women, Family Law Subgroup (1985) "Campaigning around Family Law: Politics and Practice." In Julia Brophy and Carol Smart (eds.), *Women in Law: Explorations in Law, Family, and Sexuality.* Boston: Routledge and Kegan Paul, pp. 188–206.

Schneider, Elizabeth M. (1986) "Describing and Changing: Women's Self-Defense Work and the Problem of Expert Testimony on Battering." *Women's Rights Law Reporter* 9(3-4):195–225.

SchWeber, Claudine (1982) "'The Government's Unique Experiment in Salvaging Women Criminals: Cooperation and Conflict in the Administration of a Women's Prison—The Case of the Federal Industrial Institution for Women at Alderson." In Nicole Hahn Rafter and Elizabeth A. Stanko (eds.), *Judge, Lawyer, Victim, Thief.* Boston: Northeastern University Press, pp. 277–303.

Shane-DuBow, Sandra, Alice P. Brown, and Erik Olsen (1985) *Sentencing Reform in the United States: History, Content, and Effect.* National Institute of Justice, U.S. Department of Justice. Washington, DC: U.S. Government Printing Office.

Smart, Carol (1985) "Legal Subjects and Sexual Objects: Ideology, Law and Female Sexuality." In Julia Brophy and Carol Smart (eds.), *Women in Law: Explorations in Law, Family and Sexuality.* Boston: Routledge and Kegan Paul, pp. 50–70.

Stacey, Judith (1987) "Sexism by a Subtler Name? Postindustrial Conditions and Postfeminist Consciousness in the Silicon Valley." *Socialist Review* 17(96):7–28.

Tonry, Michael H. (1987) *Sentencing Reform Impacts.* National Institute of Justice, U.S. Department of Justice. Washington, DC: U.S. Government Printing Office.

Weitzman, Lenore J. (1985) *The Divorce Revolution: The Unexpected Social and Economic Consequences for Women and Children in America.* New York: Free Press.

Worrall, Anne (1987) "Sisters in Law? Women Defendants and Women Magistrates." In Pat Carlen and Anne Worrall (eds.), *Gender, Crime and Justice.* Philadelphia: Open University Press, pp. 108–24.

Feminist Theory, Crime, and Justice

Sally S. Simpson

Feminism: Perspectives and Methods

Feminism is best understood as both a worldview and a social movement that encompasses assumptions and beliefs about the origins and consequences of gendered social organization as well as strategic directions and actions for social change. As such, feminism is both analytical and empirical. In its incipient form, feminist research almost exclusively focused on women—as a way of placing women at the center of inquiry and building a base of knowledge. As it has matured, feminism has become more encompassing, taking into account the gendered understanding of all aspects of human culture and relationships (Stacey and Thorne, 1985:305).

It would be a mistake, however, to think of feminism as a single theory. Feminism has expanded into a diverse set of perspectives and agendas, each based on different definitions of the "problem," competing conceptions of the origins and mechanisms of gender inequality/oppression, and divergent strategies for its eradication. Collectively, these perspectives share a concern with identifying and representing women's interests, interests judged to be insufficiently represented and accommodated within the mainstream (Oakley, 1981:335).

Criminology, Vol. 27, No. 4 (November 1989): 606–609; 612–617. Copyright © 1989 by the American Society of Criminology. Reprinted with permission.

Liberal Feminism

Liberal feminism was conceived within a liberal-bourgeois tradition that called for women's equality of opportunity and freedom of choice (Eisenstein, 1981). For the most part, liberal feminists see gender inequality[1] emerging from the creation of separate and distinct spheres of influence and traditional attitudes about the appropriate role of men and women in society (Pateman, 1987). Such attitudes are reinforced by discrimination against women in education, the work place, politics, and other public arenas.

Liberals do not believe the system to be inherently unequal; discrimination is not systemic. Rather, men and women can work together to "androgynize" gender roles (i.e., blend male and female traits and characteristics; Bem, 1974) and eliminate outdated policies and practices that discriminate against women. Affirmative action, the equal rights amendment, and other equal opportunity laws/policies are advocated as redistributive measures until a meritocratic gender restructuring of society occurs.

Socialist Feminism

For socialists, gender oppression is an obvious feature of capitalist societies. Depending on whether one is a socialist woman (Marxist-feminist) or a socialist-feminist, however, the weight that one gives to capitalism as a necessary and/or sufficient cause of that oppression will vary (Eisenstein, 1979). If one is the former, gender (and race) oppression is seen as secondary to and reflective of class oppression.

Socialist-feminists attempt a synthesis between two systems of domination, class and patriarchy (male supremacy). Both relations of production and reproduction are structured by capitalist patriarchy (Beauvoir, 1960; Hartmann, 1979; Mitchell, 1971). Gender difference, as a defining characteristic of power and privilege in a capitalist society, can only be attacked by constructing a completely different society, one that is free of gender and class stratification (Oakley, 1981).

Radical Feminism

The origins of patriarchy, and the subordination of women therein, are seen by radical feminists to rest in male aggression and control of women's sexuality. Men are inherently more aggressive than women, who, because of their relative size disadvantages and dependency on men during childbearing years, are easy to dominate and control. The arguments of radical feminists (e.g., Atkinson, 1974; Barry, 1979; Firestone, 1970; Rich, 1980) bring sexuality to the analytical fore. The "personal" is "political" (Millett, 1971). Sex not gender is the crucial analytical category; male domination, not class, is the fundamental origin of female subordination. Radical feminists' political and social agendas encompass lesbian separatism (Atkinson, 1974) and technological control of reproduction (Firestone, 1970).

Women of Color

In her eloquent "Ain't I a woman" speech, Sojourner Truth (1851) informed white suffragists of their myopia about race by highlighting how as a black woman her experience was different from theirs. Joseph and Lewis (1981) remind us that Truth's commentary is no less relevant today. Many women of color see the women's liberation movement as hopelessly white and middle class, immune to their concerns. As hooks (1987:62) observed,

> Most people in the United States think of feminism . . . as a movement
> that aims to make women the social equals of men. . . . Since men are
> not equals in white supremacist, capitalist, patriarchal class structure,
> which men do women want to be equal to?

The alternative frameworks developed by women of color heighten feminism's sensitivity to the complex interplay of gender, class, and race oppression. Patriarchy permeates the lives of minority women, but it does not take the same form that it does for whites (Brittan and Maynard, 1984). Though these contributions may not have coalesced yet into a coherent theoretical framework, radical, socialist, and Marxist women of color have provided possible points of integration with theories of race oppression (e.g., Joseph, 1981a, 1981b; Wellman, 1977).

In sum, feminist theory is not one perspective; it is a cacophony of comment and criticism "concerned with demystifying masculine knowledge as objective knowledge" (Brittan and Maynard, 1984:210) and offering insights from a women's perspective.

Feminist Methods

> The male epistemological stance, which corresponds to the world it
> creates, is objectivity; the ostensibly uninvolved stance, the view from
> a distance and from no particular perspective, apparently transparent
> to its reality. It does not comprehend its own perspectivity, does not
> recognize what it sees as subject like itself, or that the way it appre-
> hends its world is a form of its subjection and presupposes it. (MacKin-
> non, 1982:23–24)

Concern over the nonobjective consequences of so-called objective normal science (Kuhn, 1970) has led some feminists to challenge the scientific enterprise. Keller (1982) arranges these challenges on a political spectrum from slightly left of center (liberal feminists) to the more radical left. The liberal critique takes an equal employment opportunity approach by observing the relative absence of women from the scientific community. This view "in no way conflicts either with traditional conceptions of science or with current liberal, egalitarian politics" (p. 114).

From this point, however, the criticisms become increasingly fundamental to the way knowledge is produced; they range from charges of bias in selecting research topics and interpreting results to rejecting rationality and objectivity as purely male products. More radical feminists have adopted a methodological strategy that is in direct opposition to the scientific method. In order to "see" women's existence (which has been invisible to objective scientific methods) "feminist women must deliberately and courageously integrate . . . their own experiences of oppression and dis-crimination . . . into the research process" (Miles, 1983:121). *Feminist methods* are necessarily subjectivist, transdisciplinary, nonhierarchical, and empowering.

Where one falls along Keller's feminist-political spectrum will determine one's choice of methods (i.e., quantitative versus qualitative) and whether one sees methods and theory as interrelated as opposed to separate and distinct. Thus, methods used by feminists are more diverse than typically credited (for examples, see Jayarate, 1983; Reinhartz, 1983; Stacey and Thorne, 1985).

Together, the above theoretical and methodological points form a feminist perspective. All have been incorporated into criminology, but some have had a greater impact than others. . . .

Gender and Justice Processing

Comedian Richard Pryor once called attention to discrimination in the U.S. criminal justice system by defining justice as "just us." His concern with differential sentencing practices is one shared by feminists who primarily study the conditions under which criminal justice is gendered and with what consequences. Although liberal approaches typically dominate the gender-and-justice research, other feminist perspectives are gaining ground—especially in research on courts and corrections.

There are many stages in the criminal justice system at which gender may have an impact on decision making. The findings of some of the better-known studies of several strategic points in the decision-making process are summarized below.

Police.   Arguments about whether and how justice is gendered must begin with police behavior. That police decisions to arrest can be influenced by extralegal factors such as the demeanor of the offender (Black, 1980) has been established. It is less clear how gender, either alone or in conjunction with other characteristics, may consciously or inadvertently influence police behavior.

In the liberal "equal treatment" tradition, Moyer and White (1981) test police bias in response decisions under "probable" responses to hypothetical situations. Neither gender nor race had an effect on police behavior once crime type, especially as it interacts with demeanor of the offender, was controlled. On the other hand, Freyerhern's (1981) comparison of juvenile male and female probabilities of transition from self-report incident to police contact and arrest, finds males to be more likely to incur police contact and arrest than females. Both of these studies are methodologically problematic, however. Moyer and White cannot generalize their findings to real police encounters and Freyerhern (1981:90) does not calculate transition probabilities across individual offense categories, nor does he include status offenses. Avoiding some of these methodological traps but still working within a liberal tradition, Visher (1983) finds the interaction between race and gender to be a key factor influencing arrest decision. Visher finds police chivalry only toward white females once "legal" factors are controlled. She hypothesizes that black females are treated more harshly than their white counterparts because they are less apt to display expected (i.e., traditional) gender behaviors and characteristics when they encounter a mostly white and male police force.

Race and gender are also found to interact through victim characteristics (Smith et al., 1984). An analysis of 272 police-citizen encounters, in which both a suspected offender and victim were present, revealed that white female victims received more preferential treatment from police than black female victims. Thus, although chivalry may be alive and well for white women, it appears to be dead (if it ever existed) for blacks.

Courts. Police contact is not the only point in justice processing at which discrimination can occur. Women have been found to receive more lenient treatment in the early stages of court processing (i.e., bail, release on own recognizance, and/or cash alternatives to bail; Nagel, 1983) and further into the process, e.g., conviction and sentencing (Bernstein et al., 1977; Nagel and Weitzman, 1972; Simon, 1975). Other studies find no gender bias when controlling for crime seriousness and prior record (Farrington and Morris, 1983) or little effect from extralegal factors when legal factors and bench bias are controlled (Nagel, 1983). Variation in sentencing may be related to so-called countertype offenses, that is, women are treated more harshly when processed for nontraditional female crimes, like assault (Bernstein et al., 1977; Nagel and Weitzman, 1972), or when they violate female sexual norms (Chesney-Lind, 1973; Schlossman and Wallach, 1978). Given variable-specification problems, however, some of these findings are potentially spurious.

Once again, race may confound these effects. Spohn et al. (1982) address the issue of paternalism in sentencing, especially for black women. Controlling for prior record and attorney type, they found that black women are incarcerated significantly less often than black men, but about as often as white men. They conclude that the apparently lenient treatment of black women is not due to paternalism in their favor but rather to the racial discrimination against black vis-à-vis white men.

Studies of court processing are not entirely dominated by liberal perspectives. More critical perspectives emphasize social power and patriarchal control as the primary mechanisms through which justice is gendered (Kruttschnitt, 1982, 1984). Eaton (1986:35) argues that magistrate courts in Great Britain (the lower courts) reinforce the dominant imagery of justice (i.e., courts are ostensibly fair and just) while they maintain the status quo: "It is in these courts that the formal rules of society—the laws—are endorsed; it is here, too, that the informal, unwritten rules regulating social relations [e.g., gender, class, and race] are re-enacted."

When are females apt to be subjected to formal mechanisms of control? When other, more informal, constraints are lacking or disrupted. Kruttschnitt (1982, 1984) suggests that sentencing outcomes are affected by a woman's social status and/or her respectability. Differential sentencing among women is tied to the degree to which women are subjected to formal versus informal social control in their everyday lives.

Daly (1987a, 1989b) and Eaton (1986, 1987) offer convincing evidence that the most important factor determining sentence outcome, once prior record and offense seriousness are controlled, is marital and/or familial status.[2] Marital status has been found to matter for women (married receive more lenient sentences) but not for men (Farrington and Morris, 1983; Nagel, 1981) or to be as important for both (Daly, 1987a, 1987b).

Pretrial release and sentencing are seen to be both "familied" and "gendered." They are familied in that court decisions regarding the removal of men and women from families "elicit different concerns from the court" (Daly 1987a:154). They are gendered in that women's care of others and male economic support for families represent "different types of dependencies in family life" (p. 154). Men and women without family responsibilities are treated similarly, but more harshly than familied men and women. Women with families, however, are treated with the greatest degree of leniency due to "the differing social costs arising from separating them from their families" (Daly, 1987b:287). The economic role played by familied men can, more easily, be covered by state entitlement programs, but it is putatively more difficult to replace the functional role of familied women. Judges rationalize such sentencing disparities as necessary for keeping families together (Daly, 1989b).

As these latter studies suggest, much of the observed gender bias in processing may not be a case of overt discrimination for or against women relative to men. Instead, judicial decisions may be influenced by broader societal concerns about protecting nuclear families (Daly, 1989b) and the differing roles and responsibilities contained therein (Eaton, 1986). It is not clear that such forms of justice are overtly paternalistic, nor are they necessarily racist. Rather, in a society that stratifies other rights and privileges by gender, race, and class, "equality" in sentencing may not be just (Daly, 1989a).

Eaton (1986:10–11) takes a somewhat different view of familied justice. In her opinion, the courts reflect the needs and interests of patriarchy and capitalism, in which attendant inequities are reproduced. "Family-based" justice is a visible manifestation of the patriarchal and capitalist need to maintain and protect the nuclear family—within which gender and productive/reproductive relations first emerge.

Corrections. As it became clear that, compared with males, female prisoners were treated differently (in some cases more leniently and in others more harshly), liberal feminist perspectives came to dominate research questions and policy considerations (see, Haft, 1980; Heide, 1974; Simon, 1975).

The linkages between female incarceration and male control of female sexuality are developed by radical feminists (Chesney-Lind, 1973; Smart, 1976). Rasche (1974), for example, describes how prostitutes with venereal disease were prosecuted and institutionalized, with the "cure" as a condition of release. Nondiseased prostitutes were less likely to go to jail or prison. Certain prison practices, such as checking for evidence of a hymen during forced physical examinations and vaginal contraband searches, have been used as techniques to control the sexuality of youthful offenders and to humiliate and degrade female inmates (Burkhart, 1973; Chesney-Lind, 1986).

Socialist feminists emphasize how prison tenure and treatment vary by class and race (Freedman, 1981; French, 1977, 1978; Lewis, 1981; Rafter, 1985). In her historical accounting of the development of women's prisons, Rafter (1985:155) observes how race determined whether and where a woman was sent to prison.

> Comparison of incarceration rates and in-prison treatment of black women and white women demonstrates that partiality was extended mainly to whites. Chivalry filtered them out of the prison system, helping to create the even greater racial imbalances among female than male prisoner populations. And partiality toward whites contributed to the development of a bifurcated system, one track custodial and predominantly black, the other reformatory and reserved mainly for whites.

The bifurcated system of women's corrections emerges in part from two competing images of female nature. In one view, women are seen as fragile and immature creatures, more childlike than adult. Consequently, the female offender is perceived as a "fallen woman," in need of guidance but not a true danger to society (Rasche, 1974). The reformatory is perfectly suited to such an offender. Primarily staffed by reform-minded middle-class women, reformatory training programs emphasized skills that would turn the white, working-class misdemeanants into proper (and class-appropriate) women, that is, good servants or wives (Rafter, 1985:82).

In custodial prisons, however, a different archetype dominated. Women's "dark side," their inherent evil and immorality (Smart, 1976) shaped prison philosophy. Here, the predominantly black felons (who were perceived as more masculine, more self-centered, volatile, and dangerous) were treated like men—only, given the conditions of their incarceration (i.e., fewness of numbers and at the mercy of violent male offenders), their equality was tantamount to brutal treatment and often death (Rafter, 1985:181).

The degree to which prisons function as something other than just plates of punishment and/or treatment is a popular theme in neo-Marxist literature. Extending this interpretation to women, Marxist-feminists (e.g., Wilson, 1985; Hartz-Karp, 1981) argue that prisons, like other institutions of social control (e.g., mental health facilities), retool deviant women for gender-appropriate roles in capitalist patriarchal societies:

> If deviant women are more frequently assigned to the mental health system for social control than to the criminal justice system, it is perhaps because of the superior ability of the mental health system to "retool" worn-out or rebellious domestic workers. (Wilson, 1985:18)

Societal control of female deviance serves the needs of capital. When those needs change, so too will the mechanisms and directions of social control.[3]

In this vein, Carlen (1983) demonstrates how "down, out and disordered" women in Scotland are disciplined through medical and judicial apparatuses. Most of the imprisoned are poor women; many have histories of alcohol and drug abuse, and a large number come from violent homes. These life experiences combine, setting into motion a cycle of deviance, imprisonment, and patriarchal and class discipline that is tenacious and defeating:

> Being seen as neither wholly mad nor wholly bad, [women] are treated to a disciplinary regime where they are actually infantalised at the same time as attempts are made to make them feel guilty about their double, triple, quadruple, or even quintuple refusal of family, work, gender, health, and reason. (Carlen, 1983:209)

Where to Go from Here?

In 1976, Carol Smart suggested a number of topics for feminist research.[4] A decade later, feminist criminology has amassed a considerable body of knowledge in most of these areas—so much so in fact that feminists now are more self-critical—especially in the areas of policy and legislative changes (see Daly and Chesney-Lind, 1988). This is a positive step. It suggests not only that a feminist voice is being heard, but that it is loud enough to produce disagreement and intellectual exchange.

Notes

[1] Phillips (1987) argues that the choice of terms describing gender relations imply particular views of what the problem is. So, inequality (a term favored by liberals and some women of color) suggests that women deserve what men and/or whites are granted. Oppression (socialists and women of color) implies a complex combination of forces (ideological, political, and economic) that keep woman in her place. Subordination is a term favored by radical feminists and some women of color who identify the holder of power as the culprit (men and whites respectively).

[2] These effects appear to be strongest for black defendants (Daly, 1989a).

[3] Cloward and Piven (1979) and Box (1983) assert that female deviance is handled by the medical community, in part, because women are more likely to direct their deviance

inward (i.e., they privatize it into self-destructive behaviors, like depression and suicide). Such behavior is conceptualized as sickness (like "hysteria" earlier) and is thus subject to the formal control of the psychiatric community.

[4] The relevant topics are the female offender and the attitudes of criminal justice personnel toward her; criminal justice processing; gender and corrections; and the structure and purpose of law.

References

Atkinson, T-G. (1974). Radical feminism and love. In *Amazon odyssey*. New York: Links Books.

Barry, K. (1979). *Female sexual slavery*. New York: Avon Books.

Beauvoir, S. de (1960). *The second sex*. London: Four Square Books.

Bem, S. (1974). The measurement of psychological androgyny. *Journal of Consulting and Clinical Psychology, 42*,155–162.

Bernstein, I. N., Kick, E., Leung, J., & Schulz, B. (1977). Charge reduction: An intermediary stage in the process of labeling criminal defendants. *Social Forces, 56*, 362–384.

Black, D. (1980). *On the manners and customs of the police*. New York: Academic Press.

Box, S. (1983). *Power, crime, and mystification*. London: Tavistock.

Brittan, A., & Maynard, M. (1984). *Sexism, racism and oppression*. Oxford: Basil Blackwell.

Burkhart, K. W. (1973). *Women in prison*. Garden City, N.Y.: Doubleday.

Carlen, P. (1983). *Women's imprisonment: A study in social control*. London: Routledge & Kegan Paul.

Chesney-Lind, M. (1973). Judicial enforcement of the female sex role. *Issues in Criminology, 8*, 51–69.

Chesney-Lind, M. (1986). Women and crime: The female offender. *Signs, 12*, 78–96.

Cloward, R. A., & Piven, F. F. (1979). Hidden protest: The channeling of female innovation and resistance. *Signs, 4*, 651–669.

Daly, K. (1987a). Discrimination in the criminal courts: Family, gender and the problem of equal treatment. *Social Forces, 66*, 152–175.

Daly, K. (1987b). Structure and practice of familial-based justice in a criminal court. *Law and Society Review, 21*, 267–290.

Daly, K. (1989a). Neither conflict nor labeling nor paternalism will suffice: Intersections of race, ethnicity, gender, and family in criminal court decisions. *Crime and Delinquency, 35*, 136–168.

Daly, K. (1989b). Rethinking judicial paternalism: Gender, work-family relations, and sentencing. *Gender and Society, 3*, 9–36.

Daly, K., & Chesney-Lind, M. (1988). Feminism and criminology. *Justice Quarterly, 5*, 497–538.

Eaton, M. (1986). *Justice for women? Family, court, and social control*. Philadelphia: Open University Press.

Eaton, M. (1987). The question of bail: Magistrates' responses to applications for bail on behalf of men and women defendants. In P. Carlen & A. Worrall (Eds.), *Gender, crime and justice*. Philadelphia: Open University Press.

Eisenstein, Z. (1979). *Capitalist patriarchy and the case for socialist feminism*. New York: Monthly Review Press.

Eisenstein, Z. (1981). *The radical future of liberal feminism*. New York: Monthly Review Press.

Farrington, D., & Morris, A. (1983). Sex, sentencing and reconviction. *British Journal of Criminology, 23*, 229–248.

Firestone, S. (1970). *The dialectic of sex: The case for feminist revolution.* New York: Bantam.

Freedman, E. (1981). *Their sisters' keepers: Women's prison reform in America, 1830–1930.* Ann Arbor: University of Michigan Press.

French, L. (1977). An assessment of the black female prisoner in the South. *Signs, 3*, 483–488.

French, L. (1978). The incarcerated black female: The case of social double jeopardy. *Journal of Black Studies, 8*, 321–335.

Freyerhern, W. (1981). Gender differences in delinquency quantity and quality. In L. H. Bowker (Ed.), *Women and crime in America.* New York: Macmillan.

Haft, M. G. (1980). Women in prison: Discriminatory practices and some legal solutions. In S. Datesman & F. R. Scarpitti (Eds.), *Women, crime, and justice.* New York: Oxford University Press.

Hartman, H. (1979, Summer). The unhappy marriage of Marxism and feminism: Toward a more progressive union. *Capital and Class*, 1–13.

Hartz-Karp, J. (1981). Women in constraints. In S. K. Mukherjee & J. A. Scutt (Eds.), *Women and crime.* Sydney: Australian Institute of Criminology with Allen and Unwin.

Heide, W. S. (1974). Feminism and the "fallen woman." *Criminal Justice and Behavior, 1*, 369–373.

hooks, bell. (1987). Feminism: A movement to end sexist oppression. In A. Phillips (Ed.), *Feminism and equality.* Oxford: Basil Blackwell.

Jayarate, T. E. (1983). The value of quantitative methodology for feminist research. In G. Bowies & R. D. Klein (Eds.), *Theories of women's studies.* Boston: Routledge & Kegan Paul.

Joseph, G. I. (1981a). The incompatible ménage a trois: Marxism, feminism, and racism. In L. Sargent (Ed.), *Women and revolution.* Boston: South End Press.

Joseph, G. I. (1981b). White promotion, black survival. In G. I. Joseph & J. Lewis (Eds.), *Common differences: Conflicts in black and white feminist perspectives.* Boston: South End Press.

Joseph, G. I., & Lewis, J. (Eds.). (1981). *Common differences: Conflicts in black and white feminist perspectives.* Boston: South End Press.

Keller, E. F. (1982). Feminism and science. In N. O. Keohane, M. Z. Rosaldo, & B. C. Gelpi (Eds.), *Feminist theory.* Chicago: University of Chicago Press.

Kruttschnitt, C. (1982). Respectable women and the law. *The Sociological Quarterly, 23*, 221–234.

Kruttschnitt, C. (1984). Sex and criminal court dispositions: The unresolved controversy. *Journal of Research in Crime and Delinquency, 21*, 213–232.

Kuhn, T. (1970). *The structure of scientific revolutions* (2nd ed.). Chicago: University of Chicago Press.

Lewis, D. (1981). Black women offenders and criminal justice: Some theoretical considerations. In M. Warren (Ed.), *Comparing female and male offenders.* Beverly Hills, CA: Sage.

MacKinnon, C. A. (1982). Feminism, Marxism, method, and the state: An agenda for theory. In N. O. Keohane, M. Z. Rosaldo, & B. C. Gelpi (Eds.), *Feminist theory*, Chicago: University of Chicago Press.

Miles, M. (1983). Toward a methodology for feminist research. In G. Bowles & R. D. Klein (Eds.), *Theories of women's studies.* Boston: Routledge & Kegan Paul.

Millett, K. (1971). *Sexual politics*. London: Rupert Hart-Davis.

Mitchell, J. (1971). *Woman's estate*. New York: Random House.

Moyer, I. L., & White, G. F. (1981). Police processing of female offenders. In L. H. Bowker (Ed.), *Women and crime in America*. New York: Macmillan.

Nagel, I. H. (1981). Sex differences in the processing of criminal defendants. In A. Morris & L. Gelsthorpe (Eds.), *Women and crime*. Cambridge: Cambridge Institute of Criminology.

Nagel, I. H. (1983). The legal/extra-legal controversy: Judicial decisions in pretrial release. *Law and Society Review, 17*, 481–515.

Nagel, S., & Weitzman, L. J. (1972). Double standard of American justice. *Society, 9*, 18–25, 62–63.

Oakley, A. (1981). *Subject women*. New York: Pantheon.

Pateman, C. (1987). Feminist critiques of the public/private dichotomy. In A. Phillips (Ed.), *Feminism and equality*. Oxford: Basil Blackwell.

Phillips, A. (Ed.). (1987). *Feminism and equality*. Oxford: Basil Blackwell.

Rafter, N. H. (1985). *Partial justice: Women in state prisons, 1800–1935*. Boston: Northeastern University Press.

Rasche, C. (1974). The female offender as an object of criminological research. *Criminal Justice and Behavior, 1*, 301–320.

Reinhartz, S. (1983). Experimental analysis: A contribution to feminist research. In G. Bowles & R. D. Klein (Eds.), *Theories of women's studies*. Boston: Routledge & Kegan Paul.

Rich, A. (1980). Compulsory heterosexual and lesbian existence. *Signs, 5*, 631–660.

Schlossman, S., & Wallach, S. (1978). The crime of precocious sexuality: Female juvenile delinquency in the progressive era. *Harvard Educational Review, 48*, 65–94.

Simon, R. (1975). *Women and crime*. Lexington, MA: D.C. Heath.

Smart, C. (1976). *Women, crime and criminology: A feminist critique*. London: Routledge & Kegan Paul.

Smith, D., Visher, C., & Davidson, L. (1984). Equity and discretionary justice: The influence of race on police arrest decisions. *Journal of Criminal Law and Criminology, 75*, 234–249.

Spohn, C., Gruhl, J., & Welch, S. (1982). The effect of race on sentencing: A reexamination of an unsettled question. *Law and Society Review, 16*, 71–88.

Stacey, J., & Thorne, B. (1985). The missing feminist revolution in sociology. *Social Problems, 32*, 301–316.

Truth, S. (1851). Cited in G. I. Joseph & J. Lewis (Eds.), *Common differences: Conflicts in black and white feminist perspectives*. Boston: South End Press.

Visher, C. (1983). Gender, police arrest decisions, and notions of chivalry. *Criminology, 21*, 5–28.

Wellman, D. (1977). *Portraits of white racism*. New York: Cambridge University Press.

Wilson, N. K. (1985). *Witches, hookers, and others: Societal response to women criminals and victims*. Paper presented at the annual meeting of the American Society of Criminology, San Diego.

Affirmative Race Law

Katheryn K. Russell

. . . Existing laws act to further racial disparity, and more laws are needed that sanction racial harms. "Affirmative race law" is the term given to legislation that seeks to address overt and covert racial discrimination. Affirmative race law acknowledges American racial history and acts as a bulwark against existing racial subordination and discrimination. Failing to adopt more affirmative race law promises a range of potentially negative consequences, including alienation, criminal violence, community unrest, health risks, and paranoia.

Racial Disparities under Existing Law: Two Examples

Explicit racial double standards have been excised from the American criminal law. Yet, race still affects today's criminal justice system. For example, police department policies that target particular crimes and particular communities may result in unintended racial disparities in arrest and conviction rates. Police crackdowns on drug sales are an example of this. It is widely acknowledged that it is easier for police to uncover drug activity in open-air drug markets than in office suites. People engaged in drug trafficking on the street are thus more likely to be arrested than those who operate from an office. For a number of reasons, minorities engage in street-level drug dealing more than Whites, and Whites engage in office-level drug dealing more than Blacks. A police department's decision to target street-level drug offenders may be based upon efficiency and not race. It also may be based upon a decision to target violence associated with street-level drug offending. Whether driven by these or other concerns, such policies result in arrest patterns and sentences that are racially disparate. This means that police policies and practices can result in one kind of law enforcement for Blacks and another for Whites. The federal crack-cocaine law is a more specific example of this problem.

Crack v. Powder Cocaine

In 1986, immediately following the death of college basketball star Len Bias, Congress enacted the federal crack cocaine law. It was believed that Bias, who had just signed a million-dollar contract to play for the Boston Celtics, died from an overdose of crack cocaine. Later it was learned that he died from ingesting powder cocaine.[1]

Crack v. Powder Cocaine under Federal Law

	Quantity	Sentence
Powder cocaine	500 grams	5 years
Crack cocaine	5 grams	5 years

Crack cocaine is made by mixing powder cocaine with baking soda and water. These ingredients are heated until the water evaporates and all that remains are crack-cocaine rocks. The federal crack statute mandates a five-year prison term for possession of five grams of crack cocaine. Under the same federal law, possession of five hundred grams of powder cocaine is required for a five-year prison term. Prison sentences are mandatory under the federal law. In 1995, 88 percent (12,300) of the people serving sentences under this law were Black.[2] Because the penalty for possession of crack cocaine is one hundred times harsher than the penalty for possession of powder cocaine, the federal law is described as having a "100:1 disparity."

In *U.S. v. Clary,*[3] Edward Clary was convicted under the federal crack law. Clary, who is Black, was convicted of possessing 67.6 grams of crack and faced a mandatory ten-year prison term. He argued that the law was racially discriminatory, in violation of the U.S. Constitution. After reviewing the history of U.S. drug laws, the district court agreed with Clary. It found that drug use that is perceived to be threatening to middle-class Whites tends to result in harsh legislative penalties—particularly where the threat is racialized. For instance, in the early 1900s, widespread animosity toward Asians led to the 1909 Smoking Opium Exclusion Act. The Harrison Act of 1914 was enacted to allay White fears of being harmed by Black heroin addicts.

In addition to reviewing the social and political impetus for drug legislation, the court evaluated the medical evidence. The court found little medical support for the harsh legislative distinctions between powder and crack. The court determined that Congress had enacted the law for symbolic reasons, not because crack is one hundred times more lethal than powder cocaine. The Clary court concluded that racial disparities in the federal crack law were driven primarily by White fear of Black crime. On appeal, the decision was reversed.

Racial disparities in the application of the federal crack law have triggered diverse voices of dissent. In 1995, after reviewing the history of the federal law, its goals, and its application, the U.S. Sentencing Commission recommended that Congress equalize the sentences for crack and powder. The Commission was specifically created to review federal law and eliminate unwarranted sentencing disparity.

The Commission's review of the federal crack law revealed that more Whites use crack cocaine than Blacks and that the medical research does not support the 100:1 disparity. The Commission concluded that the distinctions between crack and powder are primarily social, not physiological. For example, the distribution and marketing of crack are more likely to involve violence, due to "turf" wars and open-air drug sales, than the sale of powder cocaine. In the final analysis, the Sentencing Commission found that the federal law was the "primary cause of growing racial disparity between sentences for Black and White federal defendants."[4]

Congress voted 332–82 to overrule the recommendation of the Sentencing Commission. President Bill Clinton upheld the Congressional vote, thus making it the first time a president rejected the recommendations of the Sentencing Commission.

In *U.S. v. Armstrong*[5] the Supreme Court had a chance to address the crack statute's inequities, or minimally to express alarm about the 100:1 disparity. The Court declined to do either. After reviewing claims that Black crack defendants were being tried in federal court while White crack offenders were being tried in state court (which imposes lighter penalties), the Court found insufficient evidence of selective prosecution.

After Congress voted against equalizing crack and powder cocaine sentences, federal prisoners initiated riots at five correctional facilities. Fires were set, windows and furniture were damaged, and several inmates and prison staffers were injured. The riots led to a nationwide lock-down of federal prisons.

The most unique response to the powder and crack inequities has come from federal judges. Judges at both ends of the political spectrum have actively opposed the statute, arguing that the mandatory sentences do not allow enough judicial elbow room. The law forces judges to impose tough sentences, without due consideration of mitigating circumstances. Some judges have resigned in protest, and others have refused to follow the guidelines.[6] Some of the communities hardest hit by crime associated with crack have also protested the 100:1 disparity.

In November 1996, two psychologists published research results that challenged the medical arguments for the disparity. After reviewing two decades of research on cocaine, they concluded that a 2:1 disparity between crack and powder is medically supportable. The researchers found that some distinction is justified because crack produces a quicker, more intense high and because its cheap price makes it more widely accessible than powder cocaine.[7] In April 1997, the Sentencing Commission altered its position and called on Congress to reduce the crack and powder disparity from 100:1 to 5:1. Three months later Attorney General Janet Reno recommended that Congress consider narrowing the disparity to 10:1.

The Death Penalty and the Race-of-the-Victim Effect

In the landmark case of *McCleskey v. Kemp*,[8] a Black man was convicted of killing a White police officer and sentenced to die. Warren McCleskey argued that the Georgia death penalty was racially biased, in violation of the Equal Protection Clause. The defense introduced the results of a study that analyzed more than two thousand Georgia homicide cases. The research indicated that the victim's race was the most significant factor in determining whether someone convicted of capital murder would be sentenced to death. In 22 percent of the cases involving a Black offender and a White victim, the defendant was sentenced to death. In stark contrast, only 1 percent of the cases involving a Black offender and a Black victim resulted in a death sentence.[9]

Despite these findings, the U.S. Supreme Court upheld the Georgia death penalty. To establish a violation of the Equal Protection Clause, a capital defendant has to prove that there was racial discrimination in his particular case—e.g., that the judge or jury members were motivated by racial bias in their decision to impose a death sentence. Though the Court indirectly acknowledges the existence of unexplained racial disparity, it finds that statistics alone are insufficient to establish a constitutional violation. The Supreme Court failed to offer a convincing rationale for rejecting empirical proof of racial discrimination. In civil cases, such as Title VII race discrimination suits, statistics are routinely used. In practical effect, the *McCleskey* Court sets an impossible standard for proving that the death penalty is racially discriminatory. Today, very few Whites—e.g., jurors, judges, and lawyers—would publicly admit that race affected their legal decision-making. Furthermore, the decision overlooks the fact that race discrimination may not be intentional. All of us are influenced by the negative stereotypes of minorities, and this likely has some impact on the criminal justice system. The *McCleskey* decision is disappointing because the Court failed to address the fact that racial discrimination has newer, subtler forms that cannot be rectified by an intentional discrimination standard.

The federal cocaine statute and the operation of the death penalty challenge the notion that the criminal justice system has sufficient checks against race discrimination built into it. The racial disparities inherent in both of these laws have eluded justice system checks. The federal law remains despite objections by federal judges, doctors, prisoners, and the U.S. Sentencing Commission. It has remained despite its dire social consequences, including the loss of voting rights for huge numbers of Black men.[10] Likewise, attempts to adopt the Racial Justice Act, a clear check on racial discrimination in capital sentencing, were soundly defeated. The Act would have required states to monitor their death sentences to assess what role, if any, race played. In February 1997, the American Bar Association (ABA) issued an unprecedented call for a moratorium on capital punishment. The ABA resolution was motivated by concerns that the death penalty is being administered in an unpredictable, haphazard manner. The ABA's vote for a moratorium, like the Racial Justice Act, if heeded, would have operated as a check and balance on racial disparities in capital sentencing. . . .

Absence of Affirmative Race Law and the Increased Probability of Antisocial Responses

What will happen if more affirmative race law is *not* adopted? There are a range of possible outcomes, including alienation, disdain, anger, and criminal violence. Alienation, a form of social isolation, may be the most common response. Developing affirmative race law is minimally necessary to build Black trust in police, courts, and corrections. The distrust that many Blacks have of the criminal justice system has a number of ramifications. For instance, it strains the relationship between the police and Black communities and may mean that Blacks will be less likely to assist police in crime solving. This is particularly troubling since Blacks are disproportionately likely to be crime victims.

Absence of Affirmative Race Law and Criminal Offending

Affirmative race law is premised on the fact that the low level of trust Blacks have in the criminal justice system may manifest itself in antisocial behaviors, including criminal violence. Violence may be the way that someone responds to racial injustice. An angry, physical response may be the only way the person can be heard. The following incidents illustrate this point.

In an article by law professor Patricia Williams, she recounts a racial incident in which she was denied entrance to a clothing store by a White clerk. Williams, who is Black, states, "I was enraged. At that moment I literally wanted to break all the windows in the store and take lots of sweaters."[11] Williams responded to the racial slight by making a creative public complaint. She typed up a detailed account of the incident, made it into a poster, and attached it to the window of the United Colors of Benneton store where she had been denied entry. In discussing her feelings of outrage about the incident, Williams comments on the direct, causal link between racism and crime. Williams confides, "My rage was admittedly diffuse, even self-destructive, but it was symmetrical."[12] Williams says that her emotional reaction matched the offense against her and that her response was not only reasonable but predictable. In her case, she had a legal, productive medium through which she could express her anger. Further, the combination of her education and public stature allowed her to publicize the incident—which likely produced some measure of vindication.

Such public channels, however, are not available to most Blacks who are subjected to continuing racial assaults. For young Black men in particular, who may be embarrassed and angered by the sting of racism, there is no such outlet. There are numerous incidents that describe how racial assaults can escalate to violence. For instance, in January 1995, four Black teens in Kentucky were arrested for killing a White man. The man was purportedly killed because he hung a confederate flag in the back of his truck.[13] . . .

In November 1995, a Black man set out to murder Stacey Koon, one of the police officers convicted in the Rodney King beating. On the eve of Koon's release from a halfway house, after less than three years behind bars, Randall Tolbert stormed into the correctional facility. He took three hostages when he was unable to locate Koon. Tolbert was killed in a shootout with the police. Tolbert was upset that Koon had served a light sentence in the King beating and also took offense that Koon had been placed in a halfway house in a Black Los Angeles neighborhood. Tolbert's brother commented, "It was like they were trying to slap us in the face by putting [Koon] here."[14]

In February 1995, a White rookie police officer shot and killed an unarmed Black youth in a Paterson, New Jersey, drug bust. In response to the shooting, one young Black man commented, "The [Black] youth of Paterson we don't want to be violent, but we want justice served. . . . [I]f justice is not served, then there will be repercussions."[15] The young man's statement is consistent with Williams's rage and Tolbert's violence. His comments express his view that the New Jersey police acted beyond their legal authority, that the system will not redress this wrong, and that he had no legal way to voice his discontent and be heard.

Community Responses to the Failure of Law

There have been several cases involving a racial assault that have resulted in widespread community protests. In October 1996, after the police-shooting death of a young Black man, a Black community in St. Petersburg, Florida, erupted in hours of violence. Sixty homes and businesses were burned down and damage was estimated in the millions. A month earlier, the Black community in Pittsburgh reacted angrily to the acquittal of a police officer tried in the beating death of Jonny Gammage.

The reaction that followed the acquittal in the first LAPD/Rodney King trial produced the greatest violence in response to a criminal verdict this century. In April 1992, a jury comprised of eleven Whites and one Hispanic returned not-guilty verdicts for all four officers charged in the King beating. The acquittals sparked days of rioting in Los Angeles. There were outbreaks of violence in several other cities across the country. In Los Angeles alone, more than fifty people were killed, hundreds of people were injured, dozens of businesses were burned down, and countless stores were looted. Estimates of property damage were in the billions.

The above examples offer clear links between racial assaults and criminal responses. Incidents of police brutality and harassment create further disillusionment within minority communities. In 1997, the U.S. Commission on Civil Rights completed its review of the conditions in St. Petersburg that led to the rioting. A federal civil rights investigator charged the St. Petersburg police with exacerbating racial tensions. After noting that the department had a gross pattern of misconduct, he urged "special training because [the police] represent the spark that could bring about more disturbances."[16]

For some Blacks, disillusionment with the justice system may become anger, and anger may become rage. Rage may become crime. The concern is whether this rage will cause retaliation, either in the form of intraracial or interracial violence. The latter could take the form of Blacks committing crime in White communities or the targeting of White law enforcement officials.

Physical Tolls

Recent studies have established that exposure to race discrimination and racism may have health consequences. In a 1995 study, Duke University researchers designed a study to measure whether exposure to racist encounters has an effect on heart rates for Black women. Black participants were placed in a setting where controversial racial comments were made and discussed. Participants heard comments including, "It is necessary for police to use force with Blacks, given the inherent hostile and aggressive tendencies Blacks are known to have." Researchers found that after being exposed to racist comments, the participants' heart rates and blood pressure accelerated. They also found that participants had a range of reactions to the racist comments, including cynicism, anger, resentment, and anxiety. The researchers noted that each of these emotions is associated with stress hormones. The findings indicated that the chronic stress of racism may contribute to increased rates of heart disease among Blacks.[17] In another study, published in 1996, two medical researchers looked at the impact of race discrimination on blood pressure. The study is based upon interviews with more than four thousand Blacks and Whites. They found elevated blood pressure levels for those Blacks exposed to multiple incidents of race discrimination and higher levels for those who internalized rather than confronted race discrimination.[18]

The next section examines another, less obvious effect of the law's failure to redress racial harm. "Conspiricizing" addresses how the appeal of genocide theories may increase when the justice system is perceived as illegitimate.

"Conspiricizing"

The Black community has elevated theorizing about government-sanc-tioned conspiracies to an art form.[19] All manner of conspiracies have been offered to answer the question, "What's wrong with this picture?" More to the point, why are Black people in such bad shape? Circulating in the Black community are conspiracy theories offered to explain a host of inex-plicable racial conditions. The ones with the most potency are those related to genocide. These include:

- Plots to infect the Black community with infectious diseases, includ-ing the acquired immune deficiency virus
- Plots to contaminate the Black community through food or commerce
- Plots to destroy the Black man
- Plots to infiltrate poor Black communities with crack cocaine

For years, rumors have circulated that the U.S. government created the acquired immune deficiency virus. According to this conspiracy theory, the virus was placed in Black communities in the United States and African countries to wipe out the world's Black population. Another related theory is that the government already has a vaccine for the virus but has not made it widely available. The popularity of this theory is buttressed by the government-sanctioned Tuskegee syphilis experiment in the 1950s. In this case, close to four hundred Black men with syphilis were recruited to par-ticipate in a medical treatment experiment. The men thought they were being treated. Instead, White doctors were using the Black men as guinea pigs, watching and studying the progression of the syphilis.

Various conspiracy theories have circulated that certain companies with large Black markets sell contaminated goods or are connected to White-supremacist groups. Businesses including Church's Chicken, Coors Beer, and Snapple Beverages have been the focus of some of these rumors.

Perhaps the most popular conspiracy theory is that there is a govern-ment plot to destroy successful Black men. These theories reach their zenith when criminal allegations are leveled against entertainers, athletes, and politicians (e.g., Mike Tyson, Marion Barry, Clarence Thomas, Michael Jackson, and O. J. Simpson). Many Blacks believe that the FBI was behind the assassination of Malcolm X. Some have speculated that the FBI solicited the Nation of Islam to murder Malcolm X. Others have suggested that Mar-tin Luther King's assassination had the fingerprints of the U.S. government.

For more than a decade, it had been rumored that the crack-cocaine epidemic was engineered by the U.S. government. The crack scourge has had a particularly devastating effect on poor, Black communities—sending many of its members to prisons or to graves. In August 1996, this conspir-acy theory was given new legs. Gary Webb's three-part series for the *San Jose Mercury News* indicates a link between the CIA and crack cocaine. According to the article, the Nicaraguan contras were allowed to smuggle crack cocaine and guns into the inner cities. This was done to help the con-tras raise money to overthrow their government.[20] The Congressional Black Caucus, the Rainbow Coalition, and other Black organizations and individuals called for a thorough federal investigation. Attorney General Janet Reno and National Drug Czar Barry McCaffrey have stated that the CIA was not directly involved with introducing crack into poor communi-ties. An official investigation concluded there was no conspiracy.

A recent incarnation of the genocide conspiracy theory is that rap music has been allowed to proliferate as a way to perpetuate negative images of Blacks. According to this theory, Black rappers are encouraged to portray Black men as street hustlers and thugs and Black women as ever-ready sexual objects. Some have questioned whether the government and record executives have enlisted gangster rappers to engage in a form of "psychological warfare."[21] This argument is reminiscent of other con-spiracy theories in which Blacks, knowingly or unwittingly, participate in anti-Black conspiracies with Whites.

Many White eyes glaze over when someone Black insists that the gov-ernment is out to destroy Blacks. These claims are often dismissed as para-noid ramblings or as an unfair attempt to shift blame. However, each time a conspiracy is proven to have some basis in fact, it increases the likelihood that Blacks will believe the next conspiracy theory that circulates.[22] The most recent news about the government's role in introducing crack into Black communities, combined with historical evidence (e.g., Tuskegee experi-ment), underscore the legitimacy of conspiracy theories. It is not surprising that the belief that the government is engaged in an aggressive assault on the Black community is strengthened each time a conspiracy myth turns out to be a conspiracy fact. The prevalence and credence attached to these conspir-acies indicate high levels of social alienation. Many of these theories are directly traceable to the law's failure to provide adequate Black redress.

Critique of Affirmative Race Law

Affirmative race law can be critiqued on a number of grounds. First, some might suggest that it is impractical, especially in today's political cli-mate. In the past decade there has been a steady retrenchment on civil rights for minorities (e.g., affirmative action). It is, therefore, unlikely that politicians would embrace laws designed to explicitly address subtler forms of discrimination against Blacks.

Another concern raised by affirmative race laws is their usefulness. Specifically, how far do they go in addressing the problems of racial dis-crimination in the justice system? It is true that the law cannot reasonably be relied upon to solve the problem of racial injustice. However, more laws can be enacted and applied to more effectively combat these problems.

A third concern is that affirmative race laws would create greater inter-racial tension. Accordingly, rather than legitimizing the fact that Blacks are discriminated against, adopting and enacting more affirmative race law will reinforce for Whites that Blacks are always "crying wolf." It might even increase the probability of "White riots." That is, Whites would be more likely to "leave the cities, go to Idaho, or Oregon . . . and punish the blacks by closing their day care centers and cutting off their Medicaid."[23]

Assuming that each of the above criticisms is legitimate, the harm that will result from the failure to adopt more affirmative race law far outweighs any harm that will result from adopting more affirmative race law. As the discussion in this article makes clear, there are numerous harmful outcomes—political, sociological, physiological and criminological—should we fail to recognize and remedy racial injustices. Law professor Randall Kennedy, who as a general rule rejects color-conscious remedies for race discrimination, acknowledges that more must be done. In his recent book, Kennedy states, "[A]ction will have to be taken to rectify injustices that nourish [Black] feelings of racial aggrievement. To improve the effectiveness of police and prosecutors, high priority should be given to correcting and deterring illegitimate racial practices that diminish the reputation of the law enforcement establishment."[24] The explicit aim of affirmative race law is to rectify injustices. Whatever resentment occurs as a result of enacting more affirmative race laws will be offset by the reduction of other forms of racial tension. . . .

Afterword

The public representation of Blackness is a distorted one. The media as well as the academic community are largely responsible for this caricature. Blacks are routinely portrayed as marginal, deviant members of society. The exceptions to these portrayals have been insufficient to alter the public's perception. These deeply rooted images are clearly holdovers from slavery. Our public language on race and crime makes it difficult to combat these stereotypical images. Specifically, research methods for measuring racial discrimination in the criminal justice system (relying only on the formal stages), a gross underemphasis on White crime, and the failure to require that scientists publicly rebut incorrect statements on race and crime research combine to reinforce skewed, negative impressions of Blacks and Blackness. Some of these concerns may abate as more minorities enter the social science, law, and journalism communities.

The O. J. Simpson case has provided an ongoing national stage to air our racial viewpoints on crime. Among the more salient lessons we can take away from the criminal case is that Blacks and Whites have a perception of the criminal justice system that is tied to their direct and indirect experiences. Other racial groups also have experience-based perceptions of the justice system. Hopefully, more researchers will take on the charge of studying Latinos, Asians, and Native Americans and criminal justice.

The negative opinions that Blacks express about the justice system are partly rooted in the fact that the law continues to provide inadequate redress for racial harms. The law is no racial panacea. However, it could be used more effectively to provide racial redress. Its failure to provide consistent racial remedies may result in greater racial unrest, peaking in violence.

Part of our problem in examining race, crime, and justice is our generally ahistorical analysis of the role the law has played as an agent of repression. The slave codes, Black codes, and Jim Crow attest to this. Blacks will remain steadfast in their distrust of the justice system until the law is used more affirmatively to redress racial wrongs. Addressing racial disparities requires scrutiny of existing law as well as a willingness to ponder what additional laws are necessary. The current criminal justice system offers insufficient checks and balances to correct unexplained racial disparities.

It is odd that in current debates on crime and race we focus little attention on the historical workings of American criminal law. This painful history is roundly dismissed as irrelevant to the operation of the criminal justice system today. However, an analysis of this history indicates that there are aspects of past discrimination that persist today. This history and its vestiges affect current thinking on race, crime, and criminal justice. Any discussion of the legacy of slavery is often characterized as "playing the race card," and consequently not taken seriously. (This sentiment is embodied by statements like, "Slavery ended over a hundred years ago," "I didn't own slaves," or "You weren't a slave.") American racism and criminal justice, which involved the systematic denial of basic human rights to Blacks for more than three hundred years, simply cannot be dismissed as irrelevant to today's criminal justice system.

The contradiction of an ahistorical analysis of race and crime should be readily apparent. For example, two of this country's political founders, Thomas Jefferson and Abraham Lincoln, are regularly lauded for their political savvy and impact upon the principles and future of this nation. At the same time, however, their ideology and actions on slavery are conveniently overlooked. The selective application of historical facts creates a kind of "intellectual chaos" and cannot help us move forward in resolving critical issues regarding the relationship between race, crime, and criminal justice.

Notes

[1] U.S. Sentencing Commission, *Cocaine and Federal Sentencing Policy* 122–123 (1995).

[2] Ronald Smothers, "Wave of Prison Uprisings Provoke Debate on Crack," *New York Times*, October 24, 1995, at A18.

[3] 846 F. Supp. 768 (E.D. Mo. 1994), *rev'd* 34 F.3d 709 (1994)

[4] U.S. Sentencing Commission, *Cocaine* 163. For a detailed analysis of federal cocaine law, see William Spade, "Beyond the 100:1 Ratio: Towards a Rational Cocaine Sentencing Policy," 38 *Arizona Law Review* 1233 (1996).

[5] 116 S.Ct.1480 (1996).

[6] See, e.g., Associated Press, "Judge Is Forced to Lengthen Sentences for Crack," *New York Times*, November 27, 1995 at B5; Toni Locy, "Second Judge Rejects Guidelines for Sentencing in Crack Case: Pressure By D.E.A. Agent Cited as Term Is Reduced," *Washington Post*, July 21, 1994, at B1; Associated Press, "U.S. Judge, Citing Racism, Gives Black Defendant Lesser Sentence," *New York Times*, February 20, 1993, at 8.

7 Dorothy K. Hatsukami and Marian W. Fischman, "Crack Cocaine and Cocaine Hydrochloride: Are the Differences Myth or Reality?" 276 *Journal of the American Medical Association* 1580 (1996).

8 481 U.S. 279 (1987).

9 See, generally, David Baldus, George Woodworth, and Charles Pulaski, *Equal Justice and the Death Penalty* (1990).

10 See, e.g., Marc Mauer, "Intended and Unintended Consequences: State Racial Disparities in Imprisonment," Sentencing Project (1997). (Fourteen percent of all Black men are either permanently or currently ineligible to vote.) For discussion of historical roots of disenfranchisement, see Randall Kennedy, *Race, Crime, and the Law* 87–88 (1997).

11 Patricia Williams, "Spirit-Murdering the Messenger: The Discourse of Fingerpointing as the Law's Response to Racism," 42 *University of Miami Law Review* 127, 129 (1987).

12 Ibid.

13 See, e.g., Carol Castenada, "In Kentucky, Confederate Flag Is Fatal," *USA Today*, January 30, 1995, at 4A; Tony Horwitz, "A Death for Dixie," *New Yorker*, March 18, 1996, at 64.

14 Tom Gorman and Bettina Boxall, "Family Tells of Slain Gunman's Anger at Koon," *Los Angeles Times*, November 25, 1995, at A1.

15 Neil MacFarquhar, "Angry Calm at the Services for Teenager Slain by Police," *New York Times*, February 27, 1995, at B5 (author's emphasis).

16 "Rights Official Sees Danger from Police," *New York Times*, February 28, 1997, at A19 (author's emphasis).

17 Maya McNeilly et al., "Effects of Racist Provocation and Social Support on Cardiovascular Reactivity in African American Women," 2 *International Journal of Behavioral Medicine* 321 (1995).

18 Nancy Kreiger and Stephen Sidney, "Racial Discrimination and Blood Pressure: The CARDIA Study of Young Black and White Adults," 86 *American Journal of Public Health* 1370 (1996).

19 See, generally, Patricia Turner, *I Heard It Through the Grapevine: Rumor in African American Culture* (1993); Regina Austin, "Beyond Black Demons and White Devils: Anti-Black Conspiracy Theorizing and the Black Public Sphere," 22 *Florida State University Law Review* 1021 (1995).

20 Gary Webb, *San Jose Mercury News*, August 18–20, 1996.

21 See, e.g., Ambrose Lane, Sr., "Interview with Earl Ofari Hutchinson," WPFW radio talk show, September 16, 1996. (A caller raised a question about this conspiracy theory. Dr. Hutchinson disagreed that there was such a conspiracy.)

22 See, e.g., Pierre Thomas, "FBI Role in Impeachment Probed," *Washington Post*, February 26, 1997, at A10 (indicating that FBI may have withheld evidence in impeachment hearings of Black former judge Alcee Hastings).

23 Frank Rich, "The L.A. Shock Treatment," *New York Times*, October 4, 1995 (quoting Ben Stein).

24 Kennedy, *Race, Crime, and the Law* 4.

Poverty and the Criminal Process

William J. Chambliss
Robert B. Seidman

. . . The law will differentially reflect the perspectives, values, definitions of reality, and morality of the middle and upper classes while being in opposition to the morality and values of the poor and lower classes. Given this twist in the content of the law, we are not surprised that the poor should be criminal more often than the nonpoor. The systematically induced bias in a society against the poor goes considerably further than simply having values incorporated within the legal system which are antithetical to their ways of life. Since, in complex societies, the decision to enforce the laws against certain persons and not against others will be determined primarily by criteria derived from the bureaucratic nature of the law-enforcement agencies, we have the following propositions which explain what takes place within these agencies and the kinds of decisions they are likely to make:

1. The legal system is organized through bureaucratically structured agencies, some of which are primarily norm-creating agencies and others of which are primarily norm-enforcing agencies.

2. The formal role-expectation for each official position in the bureaucracy is defined by authoritatively decreed rules issuing from officials in other positions who themselves operate under position-defining norms giving them the power to issue such rules.

Pp. 474–477 in *Law, Order and Power* (1971). Permission granted by the authors.

3. Rules, whether defining norm-creating positions or norm-applying positions, necessarily require discretion in the role-occupant for their application.

4. In addition, the rules are for a variety of reasons frequently vague, ambiguous, contradictory, or weakly or inadequately sanctioned.

5. Therefore, each level of the bureaucracy possesses considerable discretion as to the performance of its duties.

6. The decision to create rules by rule-creating officials or to enforce rules by rule-enforcing officials will be determined primarily by criteria derived from the bureaucratic nature of the legal system.

7. Rule-creation and rule-enforcement will take place when such creation or enforcement increases the rewards for the agencies and their officials, and they will not take place when they are conducive to organizational strain.

8. The creation of the rules which define the roles of law-enforcing agencies has been primarily the task of the appellate courts, for which the principal rewards are in the form of approval of other judges, lawyers, and higher-status middle-class persons generally.

9. The explicit value-set of judges, lawyers, and higher-status middle-class persons generally is that which is embodied in the aims of legal-rational legitimacy.

10. Therefore, the rules created by appellate courts will tend to conform to the requirements of legal-rational legitimacy and to the specific administrative requirements of the court organization.

11. The enforcement of laws against persons who possess little or no political power will generally be rewarding to the enforcement agencies of the legal system, while the enforcement of laws against persons who possess political power will be conducive to strains for those agencies.

12. In complex societies, political power is closely tied to social position.

13. Therefore, those laws which prohibit certain types of behavior popular among lower-class persons are more likely to be enforced, while laws restricting the behavior of middle- or upper-class persons are not likely to be enforced.

14. Where laws are so stated that people of all classes are equally likely to violate them, the lower the social position of an offender, the greater is the likelihood that sanctions will be imposed on him.

15. When sanctions are imposed, the most severe sanctions will be imposed on persons in the lowest social class.

16. Legal-rational legitimacy requires that laws be stated in general terms equally applicable to all.

17. Therefore, the rules defining the roles of law-enforcement officials will require them to apply the law in an equitable manner.

18. Therefore, to the extent that the rules to be applied are potentially applicable to persons of different social classes, the role-performance of law-enforcement officials may be expected to differ from the role-expectation embodied in the norms defining their positions.

Taken as a unit, these propositions represent the basis of a theory of the legal process in complex societies. It is a theory derived essentially from the facts of the operation of criminal law—facts gathered by a large number of researchers into the criminal-law process at each level of the operation.

Poverty and the Legal System

The empirical data and the propositions based on them make it abundantly clear that the poor do not receive the same treatment at the hands of the agents of law-enforcement as the well-to-do or middle class. This differential treatment is systematic and complete. It includes the practice by the police and prosecuting attorneys of choosing to look for and impose punishments for offenses that are characteristically committed by the poor and ignoring those committed by the more affluent members of the community. Where offenses are equally likely to be committed by persons from different social classes (such as gambling), the police will look for these crimes in the lower-class neighborhoods, rather than in middle- or upper-class neighborhoods. . . .

That the selective enforcement by policing agencies is not merely a function of what is most pressingly needed by the society is clearly indicated by a comparison of civil rights law-enforcement and the enforcement of laws prohibiting the use of "dangerous drugs." On the one hand, although riots and general discontent are rampant in the urban areas were black ghettos are concentrated, the laws which prohibit discrimination in employment, unions, and housing, consumer fraud, housing violations, and other protections for the poor are effectively ignored at every level of the government, federal, state, and local. By contrast, despite the preponderance of scientific evidence demonstrating that the smoking of marijuana is a relatively harmless pastime (less harmful, most experts agree, than drinking alcohol), laws prohibiting marijuana smoking are enforced vigorously. With respect to unfair employment, housing, and labor practices, enforcement would involve the enforcement agencies in conflicts with politically powerful groups. The federal government, for example, would be involved in serious conflict with the politically powerful trade unions if the section of the National Labor Relations Act prohibiting discrimination in unions were enforced. And if sanctions were inflicted for discrimination in employment, as it can be under Title VII of the Civil Rights Act of 1964, the federal and state governments would be at loggerheads with many of the nation's leading corporations. It is to avoid such clashes that only fourteen of some eight thousand complaints received by the Department of Justice between 1965 and 1968 complaining of discrimination in employment resulted in litigation.[1]

On the other hand, since marijuana smokers were, until quite recently, concentrated among the poor black and Chicano (Mexican-American) populations in the United States, these laws could be enforced at the will of the enforcement agencies and indeed they were. Recently, the spread of marijuana and other "drugs" to middle- and upper-class youths has increased the population of "criminals" substantially. It has also brought into public view some of the problems of selective enforcement which characterize America's legal process. It is possible that this increased visibility of police activities will bring about changes in policy and law. It is unlikely, however, that these changes will substantially alter the tendency of the legal system to select for enforcement laws dealing with acts of the poor. . . .

Notes

[1] William F. Ryan, "Uncle Sam's betrayal," *The Progressive*, May 1968, pp. 25–28.

Crime Control in the Capitalist State

Richard Quinney

The awareness that the legal system does not serve society as a whole, but serves the interests of the ruling class, is the beginning of a critical understanding of law in capitalist society. The ruling class through its use of the legal system is able to preserve a domestic order that allows the dominant economic interests to be maintained and promoted. This class, however, is not in direct control of the legal system, but must operate through the mechanisms of the state. Thus it is to the state that we must turn for further understanding of the nature and operation of the legal order. For the role of the state in capitalist society is to defend the interests of the ruling class, and crime control becomes a major device in that defense.

The Capitalist State

Criminologists and legal scholars generally neglect the state as a focus of inquiry. Failing to distinguish between civil society and the political organization of that society, they ignore the major fact that civil society is secured politically by the state and that a dominant economic class is able by means of the state to advance its own interests. Or, when the state is admitted into a criminological or legal analysis, it is usually conceived of as an impartial agency devoted to balancing and reconciling the diverse interests of competing groups. This view not only obscures the underlying real-

ity of advanced capitalist society but is basically wrong in reference to the
legal order. In a critical analysis of the legal order we realize that the capitalist state is a coercive instrument serving the dominant economic class.

Several observations must be made in a critical analysis of crime control in the capitalist state. First, we must inquire into the nature of the
state, that is, into the complexity of that which we call the state. Second,
we must determine how the dominant economic class relates to the state,
that is, how that class becomes a ruling class and how the state governs in
relation to it. Third, we must observe the development of the state in reference to capitalist economy.

"The state," as Miliband notes, is not a thing that exists as such. "What
'the state' stands for is a number of particular institutions which, together,
constitute its reality, and which interact as parts of what may be called the
state system."[1] Miliband goes on to observe that the state, or state system,
is made up of various elements: (1) the government, (2) the administration, (3) the military and the police, (4) the judiciary, and (5) the units of
sub-central government.[2] The government of the time, with its duly
empowered agents, is invested with state power and speaks in the name of
the state. The administration of the state is composed of a large variety of
bureaucratic bodies and departments concerned with the management of
the economic, cultural, and other activities in which the state is involved.
The directly coercive forces of the state, at home and abroad, are the
police and the military. They form that branch of the state which is concerned with the "management of violence." The judiciary is an integral
part of the state, supposedly independent of the government, which affects
the exercise of state power. Finally, the various units of sub-central government constitute the extension of the central government. They are the
administrative devices for centralized power, although some units may
exercise power on their own over the lives of the populations they govern.

It is in these institutions that state power lies, and it is in these institutions that power is wielded by the persons who occupy the leading positions. Most important, these are the people who constitute the *state elite*,
as distinct from those who wield power outside of state institutions.[3] Some
holders of state power, members of the state elite, may also be the agents
of private economic power. But when members of private economic power
are not members of the state elite, how are they able to rule the state?
Somehow the interests of the dominant economic class must be translated
into the governing process in order for that class to be a true ruling class.

Miliband has observed the essential relation between the dominant
economic class and the process of governing.

> What the evidence conclusively suggests is that in terms of social ori-
> gin, education and class situation, the men who have manned all com-
> mand positions in the state system have largely, and in many cases
> overwhelmingly, been drawn from the world of business and property,

or from the professional middle classes. Here as in every other field, men and women born into the subordinate classes, which form of course the vast majority of the population, have fared very poorly— and not only, it must be stressed, in those parts of the state system, such as administration, the military and the judiciary, which depend on appointment, but also in those parts of it which are exposed or which appear to be exposed to the vagaries of universal suffrage and the fortunes of competitive politics. In an epoch when so much is made of democracy, equality, social mobility, classlessness and the rest, it has remained a basic fact of life in advanced capitalist countries that the vast majority of men and women in these countries has been governed, represented, administered, judged, and commanded in war by people drawn from other, economically and socially superior and relatively distant classes.[4]

The dominant economic class is thus the ruling class in capitalist societies.

Viewed historically, the capitalist state is the natural product of a society divided by economic classes. Only with the emergence of a division of labor based on the exploitation of one class by another, and with the breakup of communal society, was there a need for the state. The new ruling class created the state as a means for coercing the rest of the population into economic and political submission. That the state was termed "democratic" does not alter its actual purpose.

The state, as Engels observed in his study of its origins, has not existed in all societies. There have been societies with no notion of state power. Only with a particular kind of economic development, with economic divisions, did the state become necessary. The new stage of development, Engels observes, called for the creation of the state:

> Only one thing was wanting: an institution which not only secured the newly acquired riches of individuals against the communistic traditions of the gentile order, which not only sanctified the private property formerly so little valued, and declared this sanctification to be the highest purpose of all human society; but an institution which set the seal of general social recognition on each new method of acquiring property and thus amassing wealth at continually increasing speed; an institution which perpetuated, not only this growing cleavage of society into classes, but also the right of the possessing class to exploit the non-possessing, and the rule of the former over the latter.
> And this institution came. The state was invented.[5]

And the state, rather than appearing as a third party in the conflict between classes, arose to protect and promote the interests of the dominant class, the class that owns and controls the means of production. The state continues as a device for holding down the exploited class, the class that labors, for the benefit of the ruling class. Modern civilization, as epitomized by capitalist societies, is thus founded on the exploitation of one class by another, and the state secures this arrangement.

Law has become the ultimate means by which the state secures the interests of the ruling class. Laws institutionalize and legitimate the existing property relations. A legal system, a public force, is established.

> This public force exists in every state; it consists not merely of armed men, but also of material appendages, prisons and coercive institutions of all kinds, of which gentile society knew nothing. It may be very insignificant, practically negligible, in societies with still undeveloped class antagonisms and living in remote areas, as at times and in places in the United States of America. But it becomes stronger in proportion as the class antagonisms within the state become sharper and as adjoining states grow larger and more populous.[6]

It is through the legal system, then, that the state explicitly and forcefully protects the interests of the capitalist ruling class. Crime control becomes the coercive means of checking threats to the existing economic arrangements. The state defines its welfare according to the general well-being of the capitalist economy.

Legislation of Crime Control

Crime control in capitalist society is accomplished by a variety of methods, strategies, and institutions. The government, especially through its legislative bodies, establishes official policies of crime control. Supposedly representing the people, Congress enacts legislation that controls the population according to the interests of the ruling class. The administrative branch of the state, usually in conjunction with the government, establishes and enforces crime control policies. Specific agencies of law enforcement, such as the Federal Bureau of Investigation and the recent Law Enforcement Assistance Administration, have great latitude in determining the nature of crime control efforts. Local police departments enforce national policies of law enforcement, while at the same time creating their own systems of crime control. And on the national level, operating as an administrative unit of the government of the time, there is the Department of Justice. In the name of justice, the state is able through its Department of Justice to officially repress the "dangerous" and "subversive" elements of the population, that is, those who would threaten the state and its supporting economic structure.

All of these state institutions attempt to rationalize the legal system by employing the advanced methods of science and technology. And whenever any changes are to be attempted toward the end of reducing the incidence of crime, rehabilitation of the individual or reform within the institutions is suggested rather than a revolution in the institutions themselves. To drastically alter the society and the crime control institutions would be to alter beyond recognition the existing economic system.

The congressmen who draft and enact crime control policies are of a single mind regarding the need for crime control in the preservation of the capitalist system. Contrary to liberal political theory, political leaders are in agreement on the truly fundamental issues. The governments of capitalist countries, Miliband argues,

> . . . have mostly been composed of men who beyond all their political, social, religious, cultural and other differences and diversities, have at least had in common a basic and usually explicit belief in the validity and virtues of the capitalist system, though this was not what they would necessarily call it; and those among them who have not been particularly concerned with that system, or even aware that they were helping to run a specific economic system, much in the way that they were not aware of the air they breathed, have at least shared with their more ideologically-aware colleagues or competitors a quite basic and unswerving hostility to any socialist alternative to that system.[7]

The commitment to capitalism, therefore, determines the government's policies and, moreover, provides the rationale for social legislation, including crime control legislation. Though legislators may differ on some specific issues, they are in basic agreement on the control, through law, of behavior and activities that threaten the capitalist system—euphemistically referred to as "the American way of life."

In recent years the government has been particularly active in the areas of crime control. This activity reflects in large part the reaction of the government to a crisis in the capitalist system. The solution has been simplistic, but nevertheless consequential: to protect the existing order by controlling crime. Congress has enacted a series of crime bills. The concern of Congress over the challenges to the existing order, a concern reflected in the crime legislation, is documented in the opening statement of the 1968 crime bill:

> Congress finds that the high incidence of crime in the United States threatens the peace, security and general welfare of the Nation and its citizens. To prevent crime and to insure the greater safety of the people, law enforcement efforts must be better coordinated, intensified, and made more effective at all levels of government.
>
> Congress finds further that crime is essentially a local problem that must be dealt with by State and local governments if it is to be controlled effectively.
>
> It is therefore the declared policy of the Congress to assist State and local governments in strengthening and improving law enforcement at every level by national assistance. It is the purpose of this title to (1) encourage States and units of general local government to prepare and adopt comprehensive plans based upon their evaluation of State and local problems of law enforcement; (2) authorize grants to States and units of local government in order to improve and strengthen law enforcement; and (3) encourage research and development directed toward the improvement of law enforcement and the development of new methods for the prevention and reduction of crime and the detection and apprehension of criminals.[8]

Not only was the war on crime intensified by this legislation, but the federal government stimulated local governments to engage in the battle. With the creation of the Law Enforcement Assistance Administration, requiring large amounts of financing and guidance, local governments were enlisted in the crusade to make capitalism survive.

The government's reaction to the crisis of the 1960s—to the riots, assassinations, and "crime in the streets"—was to define the problem as one of insufficient laws and inadequate law enforcement. Rather than acknowledging that the crisis was a result of the contradiction in the capitalist system itself, which would have been against the interests of the government, the government enacted further repressive legislation. . . .

The Technology of Crime Control

The modern era of repression has been realized in the rationalization of crime control. The legal order itself, as a rationalized form of regulation, continues to demand the latest techniques of control. It is only logical, then, that science should come to serve the state's interest in crime control. And this use of science makes the modern legal order the most repressive (and rational) that any society has known.

American society today is well on the way to, or has already reached, what may well be called "the police state." What we are experiencing is the "Americanization of 1984," a police state brought to you with the aid of science and modern techniques of control.

> The enactment of this police state—less conspicuous yet far more threatening than one dominated by the military—is a scientific enterprise. Its low-profiled selective repression is based on surveillance, fear, intimidation, and information control, rather than on the massive deployment of police.
>
> An underlying drive facilitating development of a police state is the historical governmental trend toward centralization. Information-gathering is merely one more example of the federal government's tendency to centralize and coordinate state and local activities. The implications of information concentrated in Washington are clear: Senator Charles Mathias, commenting in 1967 on the government's 3.1 billion records about individual citizens, suggested that "if knowledge is power, this encyclopedic knowledge gives government the raw materials of tyranny."
>
> Technological advances have facilitated the drive to increased concentration of information and power. Computers and Vietnam-perfected hardware applied on the home front are shortening the road to 1984.[9]

The move to apply the latest in science and technology to crime control by the state was made in the mid-1960s with the President's Crime Commission (the Commission on Law Enforcement and Administration of Justice). The state's application of science and technology to crime control was probably inevitable, however, given the tendency to rationalize all systems of management and control. Yet it was with the President's Crime Commission, staffed by scientists, that scientific crime control was justified and presented to the public. The Commission's recommendations were soon made concrete and instituted by the newly created crime control agencies. Science and technology give today's crime control systems their most advanced and insidious character.

The President's Crime Commission included in its coverage of the crime problem a special Task Force Report on *Science and Technology* [see article 5]. The special project was funded by the Office of Law Enforcement Assistance of the Justice Department, which was also responsible for the staff and organization of the task force. The actual work was conducted by the Institute for Defense Analyses (of the Department of Defense). The project was directed by Dr. Alfred Blumstein, a staff member of the Institute for Defense Analyses. The complete study is contained in the Task Force Report, but the recommendations and arguments of the task force are also included in the final report of the Commission, *The Challenge of Crime in a Free Society*. The message of the task force's research and analysis is (1) that crime control must become more scientific, (2) that crime control must utilize the kind of science and technology that already serves the military, and (3) that the federal government must institute and support such a program. The chapter on "Science and Technology" in the Commission's final report begins:

> The scientific and technological revolution that has so radically changed most of American society during the past few decades has had surprisingly little impact upon the criminal justice system. In an age when many executives in government and industry, faced with decision-making problems, ask the scientific and technical community for independent suggestions on possible alternatives and for objective analyses of possible consequences of their actions, the public officials responsible for establishing and administering the criminal law—the legislators, police, prosecutors, lawyers, judges, and corrections officials—have almost no communication with the scientific and technical community.[10]

That there is a science and a technology available for crime control, on a military model, is the good news presented in the opening lines of the task force's own report:

> The natural sciences and technology have long helped the police to solve specific crimes. Scientists and engineers have had very little impact, however, on the overall operations of the criminal justice system and its principal components: police, courts, and corrections. More than 200,000 scientists and engineers have applied themselves to solving military problems and hundreds of thousands more to innovation in other areas of modern life, but only a handful are working to control the crimes that injure or frighten millions of Americans each

year. Yet, the two communities have much to offer each other: science and technology is a valuable source of knowledge and techniques for combating crime; the criminal justice system represents a vast area of challenging problems.[11]

The Science and Technology Task Force goes on to list the kind of equipment and tactics that should be used in the war on crime [see pp. 69–70, article 5]. . . .

The similarities between military operations and domestic crime control are made clear, and the Crime Commission is advised to pursue the militarization of crime control [see pp. 72–73, article 5]. . . .

The stage is reached where military operations abroad and crime control at home have become one—in objective and technique. . . .

Reform, Repression, and Resistance

The contradiction within advanced capitalist society is that a system which violates human sensibilities in turn calls for resistance and rebellion by the population. And the more such resistance occurs, whether in outright political acts or in behavior that otherwise violates the rules of such a society, the more the state must bring its repressive forces to bear on the people. The state's failure to respond would allow changes that would undoubtedly spell the end of the kind of political economy upon which that society rests. Thus today in America we are witnessing the repression of a society that refuses to use its resources to solve its own problems. To protect the system from its own victims, a war on crime is being waged.

The crime control programs . . . have been constructed within the framework of "reform." This is to be expected, since reform is no more than the existing society's way of adjusting the system so that it will survive according to its own terms. Many of the crime control programs have been an integral part of the programs confronting poverty, racial inequality, and campus disorders. Under the guise of working toward "new frontiers," "the great society," and the like, measures have been instituted to preserve the existing social and economic arrangements. At the same time, measures have been developed to control resistance to the reforms and to prevent changes that go beyond them. The state thus activates the option that must accompany reform, namely repression. Reform and repression are not alternative options for the state but complementary ones.

> . . . Faced as they are with intractable problems, those who control the levers of power find it increasingly necessary further to erode those features of "bourgeois democracy" through which popular pressure is exercised. . . . The state must arm itself with more extensive and more efficient means of repression, seek to define more stringently the area of "legitimate" dissent and opposition, and strike fear in those who seek to go beyond it.[12]

The process of repression is cumulative. Further repression can only engender more protest, and further protest necessitates more repression by the state. The transition is to a new kind of control, one that transforms crime control into an expression of a larger system of state authoritarianism. . . .

That we are entering a new kind of America, or rather a modernization of the old one, seems evident from our study of crime control. The state, in its support of advanced capitalism, an economic system that cannot respond to human needs and still exist, must remake itself. The modern state, with its ruling class, maintains its control over internal challenges by developing and institutionalizing the instruments of science and technology. This "new-style" fascism is a complex of modernized control mechanisms. It is a pervasive form of control: indeed, a managed society. As Bertram Gross has described this new order, "A managed society rules by a faceless and widely dispersed complex of warfare-welfare-industrial-communications-police bureaucracies caught up in developing a new-style empire based on a technocratic ideology, a culture of alienation, multiple scapegoats, and competing control networks."[13] Not only will the economy be managed, but the total society will be managed by the modern state.

The police component of the new state will be, as we know from present experience, a network of law enforcement systems decentralized on a geographical basis yet guided by federal agencies. "It will include the Attorney General's office, the FBI, the CIA, the military intelligence agencies, federal-aid crime agencies, and new computer-based dossier facilities tied in with the Internal Revenue Service, the Census Bureau, and credit-rating offices."[14] This control complex will, of course, be integrated into an expanding welfare system which itself malignly controls the population. We will be bound, finally, by a communications network.

> In toto, the warfare-welfare-industrial-communication-police complex would be the supramodern fascist form of what has hitherto been described as "oligopolistic state capitalism." Its products would be: (1) increasingly differentiated armaments (including more outer-space and under-sea instruments of destruction) that in the name of defense and security would contribute to world insecurity; (2) increasingly specialized medical, education, housing, and welfare programs that would have a declining relation to health, learning, community, or social justice; (3) industrial products to serve warfare-welfare purposes and provide consumer incentives for acceptance of the system; (4) communication services that would serve as instruments for the manipulation, surveillance, and suppression—or prettifying—of information on domestic and foreign terrorism; (5) police activities designed to cope with the new "crime" of opposing the system, probably enlisting organized crime in the effort.[15]

Is there an alternative to this future? Certainly the liberal reform solutions are not the answer; they only lead to further repression and open the way for the neo-fascist state. Only a vision that goes beyond reform of the capitalist system can provide us with a humane existence and a world free of the authoritarian state. Crime control in modern America is a crucial indication of the world that can emerge under present images and theories of society and human nature. Only with a critical philosophy of our present condition can we suggest a way out of our possible future. We are capable of an alternative existence, one that frees us and makes us human. We must think and act in a way that will bring about a world quite different from the one toward which we are currently heading. A socialist future is our hope.

Notes

[1] Ralph Miliband, *The State in Capitalist Society* (New York: Basic Books, 1969), p. 49.

[2] *Ibid.*, pp. 49–55.

[3] *Ibid.*, p. 54.

[4] *Ibid.*, pp. 66–67.

[5] Frederick Engels, *The Origin of the Family, Private Property, and the State* (New York: International Publishers, 1942), p. 97.

[6] *Ibid.*, P. 156.

[7] Miliband, *The State in Capitalist Society*, p. 70.

[8] "Omnibus Crime Control and Safe Streets Act," Public Law 90-351, *United States Statutes at Large*, 1968, vol. 82 (Washington, D.C.: U.S. Government Printing Office, 1969), pp. 197–198.

[9] Jeff Gerth, "The Americanization of 1984," *SunDance*, I (April–May, 1972), pp. 64–65.

[10] President's Commission on Law Enforcement and Administration of Justice, *The Challenge of Crime in a Free Society* (Washington, D.C.: U.S. Government Printing Office, 1967), p. 245.

[11] *Science and Technology*, Task Force Report of the President's Commission on Law Enforcement and Administration of Justice, Prepared by the Institute for Defense Analyses (Washington, D.C.: U.S. Government Printing Office, 1967), p. 1.

[12] Miliband, *The State in Capitalist Society*, pp. 271–272.

[13] Bertram Gross, "Friendly Fascism, A Model for America," *Social Policy*, 1 (November–December, 1970), p. 46. Gross goes on to suggest that this "new-style" fascism will differ strikingly from traditional fascism: "Under techno-urban fascism, certain elements previously regarded as inescapable earmarks of fascism would no longer be essential. Pluralistic in nature, techno-urban fascism would need no charismatic dictator, no one-party rule, no mass fascist party, no glorification of the state, no dissolution of legislatures, no discontinuation of elections, no distrust of reason. It would probably be a cancerous growth *within* and *around* the White House, the Pentagon, and the broader political establishment" (p. 46).

[14] *Ibid.*, p. 47.

[15] *Ibid.*, p. 48.

Crisis and Control

Christian Parenti

Much of the current critique of the prison industrial complex relies on showing the *direct involvement* of *specific economic interests*."[1] This "interest group model," the preferred style of muckraking journalists, borrows heavily from the accurate left critique of how the arms lobby created the military industrial complex. Making direct causal links and finding proverbial "smoking guns" is a powerful path of argument. But interest groups go only so far. Ultimately the whole of capitalist society is greater than the sum of its corporate and non-corporate parts. To really understand America's incarceration binge and criminal justice crackdown, we need to move from a narrow interest-group-based model to a more holistic class analysis that looks at the needs of the class system and class society in general."[2]

Even if prison building created no Keynesian stimulus, and there were no private prisons to profit from locking up the poor, and if prison labor were abolished—in other words, if all directly interested parties were removed from the equation—American capitalism would still, without major economic reforms, have to manage and contain its surplus populations and poorest classes with paramilitary forms of segregation, containment, and repression. At the heart of the matter lies the contradiction discussed earlier: capitalism needs the poor and creates poverty, intentionally through policy and organically through crisis. Yet capitalism is also directly and indirectly threatened by the poor. Capitalism always creates surplus populations, needs surplus populations, yet faces the threat of political, aesthetic, or cultural disruption from those populations. Prison and criminal justice are about managing these irreconcilable contradictions.

Consider once more the numbers: while it is true that the recovery of the late nineties drove down official African-American male jobless rates precipitously (from 13.6 percent in 1992 to 8.5 percent in 1997) there remains a barely concealed stratum of suffering below this green statistical turf. After all, "official statistics exclude from the labor force millions of people who don't have jobs, say they want jobs, but are not actively searching for work (according to the government's definition of searching). And if they are not part of the labor force, they are not considered unemployed."[3] When "discouraged workers" who have given up the quest for employment and the incarcerated are added to the equation, the real unemployment rate for African-American men emerges as a brutal 25.2 percent.[4] Among Black youth during the mid-nineties unemployment was twice as high as among white youth.[5] And overall African-American and Latino *poverty* rates are even higher. These two major American ethnic groups together make up 22.8 percent of the U.S. population "but account for 47.8 percent of Americans living in poverty."[6] Overall, 35.6 million Americans—40 percent of whom are children—are impoverished. Despite a momentary buoyancy in the economy, Black and brown poverty has been increasing steadily since the mid-seventies.[7] The trend towards immiseration and isolation accelerated during the eighties and throughout much of the nineties.

Now compare this statistical sketch of the "surplus population" to the numbers on incarceration. According to the Sentencing Project, nearly one-third of all African-American men between the ages of twenty and twenty-nine are "under criminal justice supervision on any given day." In other words they are in prison or jail or on probation or parole. Drug "offenders" make up the bulk of this jailed and semi-jailed population. And while African Americans constitute only 13 percent of all monthly drug users, they represent 35 percent of all drug arrests, 55 percent of all drug convictions, and a staggering 74 percent of drug prisoners. While Black women are not incarcerated at the same rate as Black men, their rate of incarceration on drug charges is accelerating exponentially: the number of Black women in prison rose by 828 percent from 1986 to 1991.[8]

To reiterate how this buildup occurred, recall that politicians in the age of restructuring face a populace racked by economic and social anxiety. The political classes must speak to and harness this anxiety, but they cannot blame the U.S. class structure. So they invent scapegoats: the Black/Latino criminal, the immigrant, the welfare cheat, crackheads, superpredators, and so on. These political myths are deployed, first and foremost, to win elections. But the eventual *policy byproducts* of this racialized anti-crime discourse are laws like three strikes and mandatory minimums. Most important, of course, are the drug laws. Drug offenders constituted more than a third (36 percent) of the increase in state prison populations between 1985 and 1994; in the federal system drug offenders make up more than two-thirds (71 percent) of the prison population.[9]

The question still remains: if capitalism always creates a surplus population, why did it not use criminal justice to absorb, contain, and isolate these groups in the past? To some extent it did. But in each epoch and place capitalist societies have developed specific and unique combinations of co-optation, amelioration, and repression to reproduce the class structure and deal with the contradictions of inevitable poverty. In the nineteenth century in the United States, westward expansion offered a way of harnessing and alleviating the social pressure of poverty; racism directed other pressures, and whatever class struggle was left over was managed with bayonets. Early in the postwar era, profits were high enough to afford an ameliorative compromise: capital bought relative peace with labor in the form of an incipient welfare state and cooperation with organized labor. And in Europe, working class power, democratic political structures, and a cultural ethos of reform have maintained many strong welfare states. But in the U.S., the international crisis of over-production, declining profits, and the domestic challenge of racial and class rebellion required a move away from a politics of the carrot towards a politics of the stick.

To restore sagging profit margins capital launched a multifaceted domestic and international campaign of restructuring. Though the cause of the profit plunge was multifaceted—the rising organic composition of capital, and general over-production and saturation of global markets—*class struggle was also a key part of the equation*. Some on the left wish not to "blame" labor for the profit crisis. But the distribution of surplus value is, at a certain level, a zero-sum game. And by the 1960s popular forces had exacted heavy concessions from capital in the form of an expanded social wage and increased regulation on business. Regardless of the real etiology of the crisis, capital's solution has focused heavily on redisciplining labor: that is, on assaulting the living standards and general power of working people.

In the United States this has meant that older forms of absorbing and co-opting the poor and working classes with welfare and employer concessions had to go. These forms of social democratic and Keynesian intervention—while keeping class struggle contained, providing stimulus, and legitimizing the market system—had the unfortunate side-effect of *empowering* the laboring classes in ways that were destructive for business profits. . . . With strong unions, inexpensive higher education, and ample welfare, the classes that sell their labor had less reason to take poorly paid, dangerous, or dirty work. To truly discipline labor, *all* alternative avenues of sustenance had to be closed. Thus we had the Reagan-Bush-Clinton welfare enclosures, the assaults on environmental regulation, the rights of labor, consumers, and the poor; in short, the near total evisceration of all New Deal and Great Society forms of downward redistribution.

The great business counteroffensive of the eighties and nineties has helped restore profits, but it has also invigorated the perennial problem of how to manage the surplus, excluded, and cast-off classes. This then is the mission of the emerging anti-crime police state. As the class structure polarizes in the interests of restored profitability, the state must step in to deploy and justify police terror, increase surveillance, and overuse incarceration. This politics of punishment works in two ways: it contains and controls those who violate the class-biased laws of our society, but prison also produces a predator class that, when returned to the street, frightens and disorganizes communities, effectively driving poor and working people into the arms of the state, seeking protection. Thus both crime control and crime itself keep people down.

This emerging anti-crime police state, or criminal justice industrial complex, though not necessarily planned as such, is the form of class control currently preferred by elites because it does not entail the dangerous side effects of empowerment associated with the co-optative welfare model. The criminal justice crackdown, and its attendant culture of fear, absorbs the dangerous classes without politically or economically empowering them. The war on poverty and the raft of social democratic reforms associated with it also absorbed surplus populations, but this model of social control ran the risk of subsidizing political rebellion, or at least economic disobedience in the form of proletariat "slacking." . . .

Criminal justice also reproduces racism in a coded and thus ideologically palatable fashion: this updated version of hate has massive retail appeal. In a system of haves and have-nots, divisive infighting among society's lower ranks is preferable to clearly defined struggle between the major classes. . . .

Recommendations

. . . My recommendations, as regards criminal justice, are quite simple: we need less. Less policing, less incarceration, shorter sentences, less surveillance, fewer laws governing individual behaviors, and less obsessive discussion of every lurid crime, less prohibition, and less puritanical concern with "freaks" and "deviants." Two-thirds of all people entering prison are sentenced for non-violent offenses, which means there are literally hundreds of thousands of people in prison who pose no major threat to public safety. These minor credit card fraudsters, joyriders, pot farmers, speed freaks, prostitutes, and shoplifters should not rot in prison at taxpayers' expense.

Notes

[1] See, for example, Terry Kupers, *Prison Madness: The Mental Health Crisis Behind Bars and What We Must Do About It* (San Francisco: Jossey-Bass, 1999), pp. 266–69. Kupers's book is excellent but its short analysis of the prison industrial complex could be broader.

[2] The impulse to focus on interest groups as opposed to the *general logic of class society* is born of the great tradition of American red baiting. A very concrete, journalistic, "anti-corporate" critique is unpopular but politically acceptable. However, a more abstract and organic critique of capitalist *society as a whole* rings the deep emotional, non-rational, bells

of our almost Pavlovian anti-communism. Ironically red baiting, which often uses the trope of economic determinism, forces leftists into a simplistic lobbying and interest-group-focused style of analysis that is itself far more "economistic" than most Marxist class analysis, which takes into account more than the paper trails of campaign contributions.

[3] Robert Cherry, "Black men still jobless," *Dollars & Sense*, November 1, 1998.

[4] Ibid.

[5] William Julius Wilson, *When Work Disappears: The World of the New Urban Poor* (New York: Vintage, 1996), p. 146.

[6] Scot Shepard, "Household incomes up, but troubling gaps remain," *Atlanta Constitution*, September 25, 1998.

[7] US Census 1997 annual report, cited in Jim Lobe, "Economy-U.S.: slight reduction in poverty in 1997," Inter Press Service, September 24, 1998.

[8] Marc Mauer and Tracy Huling, "Young black Americans and the criminal justice system: five years later," Sentencing Project Report, 1995.

[9] Marc Mauer, "Americans behind bars: U.S. and international rates of incarceration, 1995," Sentencing Project Report, 1997.

9

Criminal Justice as Late Modernity

A key objective of this book is to promote the conscious development of a theoretical infrastructure about crime-control practices and the criminal justice system. The final area of theorizing examined—what we'll refer to as the late modern theoretical orientation—comes closest to pursuing this project. Scholars such as David Garland, Jonathan Simon, and numerous others are making theoretical sense of recent trends in criminal justice by situating them within macro-shifts in a rapidly changing "late modern" society. David Garland describes the objective of his book, *The Culture of Crime Control: Crime and Social Order in Contemporary Society* (from which article 22 is excerpted):

> This book sets out to develop a history of the present in the field of crime control and criminal justice. In the process of describing this history, it aims to solve a problem that has been perplexing commentators for much of the last twenty years—the problem of **explaining** how our contemporary responses to crime came to take the form that they did . . . and to **understand** the ensemble of [crime control and criminal justice] practices and policies that has emerged. (Garland, 2001, p. 2) [emphasis added]

The late modern theoretical orientation is our best contemporary example of a community of scholars actively developing criminal justice theory.

Understanding Criminal Justice through Late Modern Lenses[1]

Scholars taking this perspective do not look solely at criminal justice. The theoretical technique they employ involves situating current changes in crime-control practices and the criminal justice system within a larger context. Their analysis begins with the premise that the growth of, and changes in, the criminal justice apparatus are best understood by contextualizing them within macro shifts in society—shifts associated with the current era of human history characterized as "late modernity."[2] They explain changes in criminal justice as adaptations to late modern social conditions.

Late modernity must be understood in relation to what preceded it. Social theorists often conceive of human history as falling into two major eras—the pre-modern and modern. Modernity encompasses empirical science, modern medicine, industry, large-scale societies with a high division of labor, advanced technology, faith in government to provide for the social welfare and security of its citizenry, human reason, and a belief in the virtues of progress. Pre-modernity preceded the Enlightenment and is characterized by belief systems rooted in religion or nature (paganism), hunter/gatherer or agriculturally-based societies, autocratic governments, and simple technologies.

Beginning in the 1950s, and accelerating rapidly by the late-1970s, the modern era has gone into hyper-drive, resulting in a series of changes that are altering society culturally and structurally. While most do not argue that these changes constitute a rupture from the past (i.e., a "post"-modern era), the rapid acceleration of the major tenets of modernity constitute a new social, political, and cultural reality that deserves its own label—late modernity. A few of the more commonly cited features of late modernity include economic globalization, dominance of free-market model, increasing cultural diversity, rise in bureaucratic surveillance, a preoccupation with safety, a fading industrial base replaced with a service/information economy, changing conceptions of gender, complex shifts in political ideology, rapid advancement of high technology, an omnipresent media, and a blurring of traditional distinctions (e.g., public and private, police and military).

It is important to recognize that the process of moving from one era into another is best seen as the gradual overtaking of the old with the new.

---

[1] Approaching this literature as a single category poses some difficulties. There is a good deal of variation and disagreement among scholars working in this area. For the sake of clarity and brevity, our discussion will focus on unifying themes, not the various differences and disagreements.

[2] Late modernity itself is a highly contested term. The debate centers around whether the changes we are seeing recently constitute a continuation of modernity, an acceleration of modernity, or something qualitatively different than modernity. Some scholars prefer the concept postmodernity or postmodernism—viewing society as having radically severed connection with the modern era (Baudrillard, 1976; Best & Kellner, 1997; Jameson, 1991).

Today's society still practices and even values elements of the pre-modern, yet its influence has been replaced in many spheres of social life with the modern. For example, criminal justice policy is often based on the pre-modern notions of crime as evil doing, criminals as immoral hedonists, and justice as lethal vengeance. Yet at the same time modernist notions of crime as social failing, and punishment as rehabilitation, are still with us.

By concentrating on late modern trends, this orientation develops theories of recent historical changes in criminal justice and social control—a pursuit that the renowned French philosopher Michel Foucault termed a "history of the present." Foucault's writings are the central inspiration for this body of work (Burchell, Gordon, & Miller, 1991; Foucault, 1977). Foucault examined the nature of power and control. He demonstrated that as modernity has advanced, the practice of controlling people is increasingly exercised not so much through brute force wielded by the state but through multiple aspects of modern social life, including schools, bureaucratic routines, architecture, language, and the production and use of knowledge.

As an example, the place where I work was originally built in the late 1960s to train police officers in a college classroom setting. The structural make-up and furnishings of the building reinforce a vocational/technical model of education that most criminal justice educators want to put to rest. Despite decades of change, much of it still has the feel of a training academy, as opposed to an institution of higher education, exerting a subtle yet ever-present influence over the daily activities and thinking of its inhabitants.

Power was a central theme of the oppression chapter. Stenson (1991) describes how Foucault's conception of power is different.

> There are no simple engine rooms of power, whether in reified conceptions of the ruling class, patriarchy and so on. Rather, power is dispersed, it exists in the capillaries, the nooks and crannies spread across the whole terrain of society. Instead of a monolith of power, or structure of oppression, we may equally envisage an increasing diversification and pluralization of the circuits of power. (p. 14)

Theorists inspired by Foucault—Rose (2000) labels them "analysts of control practices" (p. 205)—study the total circuitry of control/power in late modern society that includes the criminal justice system. Foucault referred to the intricate set of control practices as various forms of "governing" or "governmentality." Late modern "governmentality" does not refer primarily to state governing; to the contrary, Foucault emphasized the growing circuitry of more mundane forms of rule aside from coercive state control. These softer forms of control are found in schools, Wal-mart, amusement parks, hospitals, transportation systems, credit cards, or banks. At these locales, controls are embedded within the individual's mind and taken-for-granted routines, resulting in voluntarily chosen controls (what governmentalists term "governing through freedom") (see Burchell et al., 1991; Garland, 1997).

The perspective gained through late modern lenses is not only an avenue for better understanding criminal justice, it also informs us about the nature of power, control, and maintaining order in a rapidly changing social world. Its gaze extends beyond the state, and its theoretical framework locates contemporary criminal justice thinking and practices within a broader social, economic, and political context. The following section outlines five key themes of late modernity and their corresponding influence on the criminal justice apparatus.

Five Key Themes

All five of the themes identified below can be found in articles 22 and 23. Although I am presenting them as five separate themes for sake of simplification, they are actually integrated throughout this body of work, comprising an interrelated, complex story of recent criminal justice change.

Actuarial Justice: Risk, Safety, and Control

The rise of the actuarial society is the most common theme discussed in the late modern literature. An actuary is a statistician who computes risks for insurance companies. *Actuarial justice* (also referred to as the *new penology*) refers to how actuarial thinking overshadows modernist notions of administering justice. The actuarial rationale places emphasis on:

- the collection of quantitative data and analysis,
- thinking about problems and people in statistical aggregates,
- basing decisions on statistical analysis,
- a continual assessment of risks, harms, and dangers, and
- concentrating on maximizing safety and minimizing risk.

Jonathan Simon and Malcolm Feeley examine the displacement of the traditional legal precepts of criminal justice—as outlined in Packer's theoretical orientation, for example—with the features of actuarial justice. Modern notions of equity, individualized justice, rights-based processes, and reacting to violations of law are displaced by the late modern emphasis on efficiency, minimizing risk, targeting hot-spots of potential danger, and prevention. Recall that the growth orientation also concerned itself with the rise of actuarial justice, except that it described it as the "ascendance of technical rational thinking over substantive reasoning," resulting in organizations valuing means over ends and efficiency over justice. This same type of "technical managerialism" in late modern CJ organizations is what Simon and Feeley mean by "justice being not understood as a rational system but through the rationality of the system" (also a key theme found in Christie, 2000).

The heart of actuarial reasoning is maximizing certainty in an uncertain world. It is the quest to make human existence more predictable, safe, secure, and orderly. Late modern theorists note that this preoccupation with risk minimization has gone into overdrive in the last fifteen years, resulting in what Garland (2001) calls a "culture of security consciousness," and Bauman (2000) a "safety ethic." These theorists posit the ascendance of a powerful norm in late modern society—safety and security—that relegates other important norms, like individual liberty or tolerance of difference, to the back burner (see also Ericson & Haggerty, 1997; O'Malley, 1992; Pratt, 1998; Young, 1999).[3]

I recently attended a middle-school (grades six through eight) orientation for my daughter that highlighted the actuarial paradigm. Assuring parents that the school was "safe" and that our children were not at "risk" was the most heavily emphasized institutional goal—beyond learning or the physical and social development of our children. The principal proudly announced that for the first time they were able to procure a city police officer to work full-time in their school. Dressed in his uniform, styled after military BDUs (battle-dress-uniform), the officer never spoke of enforcing the law. Rather, he emphasized his role as one of "facilitating a safe, orderly learning environment." He encouraged students and parents to report any disciplinary infractions, particularly at bus stops, where outside of the school's total video and audio surveillance system children are often "picked on." This hyper-concern with safety and control was not evident a mere 15 years earlier.

Neo-Liberal and Neo-Conservative Politics

Thinking of crime and crime control in terms of risk management ties into the next theme emphasized in this perspective. In late modernity, ideological descriptors such as the "left" or "right" have lost their usefulness. The political landscape has become uncertain and disjointed, marked by the appearance of an influential and pervasive political rationality—referred to as "neo-liberal" (Barry, Osborne, & Rose, 1996). Neo-liberal politics has little to do with what we normally associate with liberalism. According to Patrick O'Malley's (1999) extensive writings, it features, instead:

- an attack on state-centered governance, expounding a view that the interventionist welfare state has crippled economic dynamism by over-regulation . . .

- an assault on welfarism [supported by traditional liberalism] which is seen as generating a culture of dependency . . . and as destroying individual freedom and responsibility by inserting technocratic government into all walks of life . . .

- the advocacy of the free market as a model for most social order . . .

---

[3] In the social construction framework we discussed the notion of a "moral panic." The example used involved the fear over shark attacks. Late modern theorists would define these social events not so much in terms of a panic driven by moralism but, rather, by the perception of high risk and breakdown in certainty—a "risk panic."

- an emphasis on cost-effective, results-based government, coupled with accountability at all levels . . .
- the reaffirmation of individual responsibility . . .
- an affirmation of freedom of choice, including choice in relation to consumption. (p. 184)

Notice how these tenets, rooted in a private-sector ethos, run counter to the modernist notion of the government providing for its citizens' welfare and security. Neo-liberal politics, according to theorists such as O'Malley, are the force that has brought about significant changes in crime control and criminal justice in the last 20 years. These include the rapid growth of private sector security, a preoccupation with actuarialism and risk management, the decline of the rehabilitative ideal, and the emergence of punitive and just deserts penalties.

While neo-liberalism may account for the cool calculus of actuarial changes, some criminal justice scholars note that it doesn't explain the expressive, angry, and moralistic dimension of late modern crime-control policies (Garland, 1997; O'Malley, 1999; Simon, 1995). Zero-tolerance policing, boot-camps, chain gangs, and the death penalty are more accurately explained through the other major political rationality noted by O'Malley, "neo-conservatism." Neo-conservatism is a more traditional form of rightist thinking where state-enforced law and order is valued. While neo-liberalism and neo-conservatism politics share important features— such as advocating the free market model and a disdain for social welfarism—their differences lead to contradictory and incoherent crime-control policies.

Contradiction and Incoherence in Criminal Justice Policy

The late modern theoretical framework presupposes a social world characterized by volatility, incoherence, and contradiction. The transition from a pre-modern to modern society took roughly 500 years and was marked by jarring upheavals. Late modernity has sprinted to the forefront in only a few decades. The crime-control apparatus's adaptations to this rapidly changing set of social conditions mirror the volatility and contradiction of the age. It operates in a state of ambivalence between actuarial based justice versus emotive pain delivery, between state-centered versus private sector crime control, and between preventative/proactive measures versus reactionary/punitive policies (Garland, 2001; O'Malley, 1999).

There has been a good deal of discussion about why exactly this state of incoherence and volatility has emerged. Feeley and Simon emphasize the ascendance of actuarial justice, O'Malley points to disjointed political ideologies, Simon posits that late modern negativity is struggling against progressive, modernist policies, and Garland argues that the criminal justice system's inability to control crime has resulted in a legitimacy crisis for the state (O'Malley, 1999). All of these elements likely play a role.

While some theorists take the field's volatility as a given, DeMichelle and Kraska (2001) caution against assuming that criminal justice practitioners cannot transform late modern contradictions into coherent policies. They demonstrate the operational harmony between two seemingly contradictory developments—the simultaneous expansion of community policing (CP) and militarized policing (MP). Even when confronted with the paradox of democratization (CP) versus militarization (MP), police practitioners have managed to construct rationales and practices that exhibit what Rose (2000) calls a "strategic coherence."

> Practitioners have the ability to maneuver through the tensions and pressures of late-modern influences. It is not uncommon for them to have to amalgamate contradictory messages so that their real-world thinking and practice makes sense to them. After all, has not the administration of justice always been fraught with contradictions through which practitioners have had to navigate? It does appear, however, that the rapid pace of change and intense volatility of late modern society will seriously test their abilities. (DeMichelle & Kraska, 2001, p. 98)

The Decline of State Sovereignty

In late modernity, crime control has expanded far beyond the formal criminal justice system. According to Garland, there has been a redistribution of state crime-control responsibilities to the private sector, community organizations, partnerships with private and public social service agencies, and interested citizens. "The criminal justice state is shedding its 'sovereign' style of governing by top-down command and developing a form of rule close to that described by Michel Foucault as 'governmentality'" (Garland, 2001, p. 125). The emphasis on reaching out to form partnerships has resulted in the blurring of traditional distinctions, such as between the public and private sector, and criminal justice and military entities and efforts (Haggerty & Ericson, 2001; Kraska, 2001).

This diminishment of state sovereignty over crime control, however, has not been voluntary; rather, it has been a consequence of neo-liberal politics and the perception that the state cannot control crime or ensure our security. The decline of state sovereignty, therefore, leads to a government that simultaneously redistributes its crime-control responsibilities and reasserts its legitimacy through symbolic law-and-order expenditures, policies, and rhetoric. The point is not that criminal justice spending or size will decrease within a society fixated on safety and security. To the contrary, "the criminal justice state is larger than before, but it occupies a smaller place in the overall field [of crime control] because of the growth of private security and the activities of communities and business" (Garland, 2001, p. 138).

The Socially Exclusive Society

The final trend linked with this perspective is *exclusion*. This concept has two related meanings in the late modern framework.[4] The first has to do with Jock Young's notion of the rise of the "exclusive society" (Young, 1999). A society preoccupied with fear about danger and risk, and guided by free-market neo-liberal ideology, will by default define those members of society that pose a potential danger—and do not fit into the new economy—as the excluded "other." The exclusive society functions from a paradigm that views the bifurcation between those included and those excluded as a permanent state of affairs requiring careful management versus the social welfare model of helping the downtrodden join mainstream society.

The second meaning deals with the exclusive society's effect on crime-control practices: criminal justice behavior revolves around maintaining the barrier between the included and excluded (Bauman, 2000; Cohen, 1985; Rose, 2000; Young, 1999). In other words, criminal justice rationale and action will emphasize solutions such as mass incarceration or aggressive police patrol work targeted at inner-city hot-spots to confine danger and minimize risk. These types of practices insure that populations remain excluded. Crime-control strategies are, of course, also targeted at segregating the "included." Gated communities and the close surveillance of business districts are good examples.

An Intellectual Project

The lens of late modernity helps us make theoretical sense of recent changes in crime control and criminal justice using an informative set of concepts and ideas. The five themes of actuarial justice, neo-liberalism, volatility in purpose, decline in state sovereignty, and the exclusion paradigm are the most recent interpretations of crime-control methods. As noted at the beginning of the chapter, the body of work from the perspective of late modernity is perhaps the best example of scholars theorizing criminal justice. Their intellectual project has as much to do with understanding contemporary society as it does with criminal justice. These academics do not see themselves as policy analysts or change agents—as compared, for example, to those working within the systems or oppression orientation. The outcome they hope to achieve is the development of better theory. Studying crime control and criminal justice is a window through which we can make better sense of shifts in the nature of social control and power in the late modern era.

---

[4] Young actually notes that exclusion operates on three levels: 1) economic exclusion from the legitimate economic opportunity; 2) social exclusion between people in civil society; and 3) the ever-expanding exclusionary activities of the criminal justice system and private security (Young, 1999, p. vi).

References

Baudrillard, J. (1976). *Symbolic exchange and death*. London: Sage.

Barry, A., Osborne, T., & Rose, N. (1996). *Foucault and political reason: Liberalism and rationalities of government*. Chicago: University of Chicago Press.

Bauman, Z. (2000). Social issues of law and order. *British Journal of Criminology, 40*, 205–221.

Best, S., & Kellner, D. (1997). *The postmodern turn: Critical interrogations*. New York: Guilford Press.

Burchell, G., Gordon, C., & Miller, P. (1991). *The Foucault effect: Studies in governmentality*. Hemel Hempstead, England: Harvester Wheatshef.

Christie, N. (2000). *Crime control as industry: Toward GULAGS, Western style* (3rd ed.). New York: Routledge.

Cohen, S. (1985). *Visions of social control*. Cambridge: Polity Press.

DeMichelle, M., & Kraska, P. B. (2001). Community policing in battle-garb: A paradox or coherent strategy. In P. B. Kraska (Ed.), *Militarizing the American criminal justice system: The changing roles of the armed forces and the police*. Boston: Northeastern University Press.

Ericson, R. V., & Haggerty, K. D. (1997). *Policing the risk society*. Oxford: Clarendon Press.

Foucault, M. (1977). *Discipline and punish: The birth of the prison*. Harmondsworth: Penguin.

Garland, D. (1997). Governmentality and the problem of crime: Foucault, criminology, sociology. *Theoretical Criminology, 1*(2), 173–214.

Garland, D. (2001). *The culture of control: Crime and social order in contemporary society*. Chicago: The University of Chicago Press.

Haggerty, K. D., & Ericson, R. V. (2001). The military technostructures of policing. In P. B. Kraska (Ed.), *Militarizing the American criminal justice system: The changing roles of the armed forces and the police*. Boston: Northeastern University Press.

Jameson, F. (1991). *Postmodernism, or the cultural logic of late capitalism*. Durham: Duke University Press.

Kraska, P. B. (2001). *Militarizing the American criminal justice system: The changing roles of the armed forces and the police*. Boston: Northeastern University Press.

O'Malley, P. (1992). Risk, power and crime prevention. *Economy and Society, 21*(3), 252–275.

O'Malley, P. (1999). Volatile and contradictory punishment. *Theoretical Criminology, 3*(2), 175–196.

O'Malley, P. (2000). Criminologies of catastrophe? Understanding criminal justice on the edge of the new millennium. *The Australian and New Zealand Journal of Criminology, 33*(2), 153–167.

Pratt, J. (1998). Towards the "decivilizing" of punishment. *Social and Legal Studies, 7*(4), 487–515.

Rose, N. (2000). Government and control. *British Journal of Criminology, 40*, 321–339.

Simon, J. (1995). They died with their boots on: The boot camp and the limits of modern penalty. *Social Justice, 22*(2), 25–48.

Stenson, K., & Cowell, D. (1991). *The politics of crime control*. London: Sage.

Young, J. (1999). *The exclusive society: Social exclusion, crime and difference in late modernity*. London: Sage.

Crime Control and Social Order

David Garland

. . . Today's world of crime control and criminal justice was not brought into being by rising crime rates or by a loss of faith in penal welfarism, or at least not by these alone. These were proximate causes rather than the fundamental processes at work. It was created instead by a series of adaptive responses to the cultural and criminological conditions of late modernity— conditions which included new problems of crime and insecurity, and new attitudes towards the welfare state. But these responses did not occur outside of the political process, or in a political and cultural vacuum. On the contrary. They were deeply marked by the cultural formation that I have described as the "crime complex"; by the reactionary politics that have dominated Britain and America during the last twenty years; and by the new social relations that have grown up around the changing structures of work, welfare and market exchange in these two late modern societies.

During the 1980s and the 1990s the political culture that articulated these social relations was quite different from that which had prevailed in the heyday of the welfare state. In its emphases if not in every respect, this culture was more exclusionary than solidaristic, more committed to social control than to social provision, and more attuned to the private freedoms of the market than the public freedoms of universal citizenship. The institutions of crime control and criminal justice have shifted in this same general direction. They have adjusted their policies, practices and representations in order to pursue the social objectives and invoke the cultural themes that now dominate in the political domain.

The specific policies and practices that have emerged are adaptations to the world in which crime control now operates and to the practical predicaments that this world creates. As we have seen, these new practices typically emerge as local solutions to the immediate problems encountered by individuals and organizations as they go about their daily routines. But what they add up to is a process of institutional adaptation in which the whole field of crime control gradually adjusts its orientation and functioning. In terms of that bigger picture, the adjustments that have occurred are structural, and concern the relationship between crime control and social order. Over time, our practices of controlling crime and doing justice have had to adapt to an increasingly insecure economy that marginalizes substantial sections of the population; to a hedonistic consumer culture that combines extensive personal freedoms with relaxed social controls; to a pluralistic moral order that struggles to create trust relations between strangers who have little in common; to a "sovereign" state that is increasingly incapable of regulating a society of individuated citizens and differentiated social groups; and to chronically high crime rates that coexist with low levels of family cohesion and community solidarity. The risky, insecure character of today's social and economic relations is the social surface that gives rise to our newly emphatic, overreaching concern with control and to the urgency with which we segregate, fortify, and exclude. It is the background circumstance that prompts our obsessive attempts to monitor risky individuals, to isolate dangerous populations, and to impose situational controls on otherwise open and fluid settings. It is the source of the deep-seated anxieties that find expression in today's crime-conscious culture, in the commodification of security, and in a built environment designed to manage space and to separate people.

I have described how the new crime control developments have "adapted" and "responded" to the late modern world, and to its political and cultural values. But these developments also, in their turn, play a role in *creating* that world, helping to constitute the meaning of late modernity. Crime control today does more than simply manage problems of crime and insecurity. It also institutionalizes a set of responses to these problems that are themselves consequential in their social impact. In America and Britain today, "late modernity" is lived—not just by offenders but by all of us—in a mode that is more than ever defined by institutions of policing, penality, and prevention.[1]

This desire for security, orderliness, and control, for the management of risk and the taming of chance is, to be sure, an underlying theme in any culture. But in Britain and America in recent decades that theme has become a more dominant one, with immediate consequences for those caught up in its repressive demands, and more diffuse, corrosive effects for the rest of us.[2] Spatial controls, situational controls, managerial controls, system controls, social controls, self-controls—in one social realm after another, we now find the imposition of more intensive regimes of regulation, inspection and control and, in the process, our civic culture becomes increasingly less tolerant and inclusive, increasingly less capable of trust.[3] After a long-term process of expanding individual freedom and relaxing social and cultural restraints, control is now being re-emphasized in every area of social life— with the singular and startling exception of the economy, from whose deregulated domain most of today's major risks routinely emerge.

The rise to dominance of this cultural theme has the character of a reaction, a backlash, an attempted undoing of accumulated historical change. The 1950s, 1960s, and 1970s were decades of rapid social and economic change during which families and communities were severely dislocated, even as individuals and social groups enjoyed new freedoms, more varied lifestyles, and an enhanced range of consumer choices. That earlier phase subsequently gave way to a wave of anxiety about the breakdown of family, the relaxation of institutional disciplines, and the collapse of informal norms of restraint. In the closing decades of the twentieth century the pursuit of freedom has come to be overshadowed by a new sense of disorder and of dangerously inadequate controls. As we have seen, a reactionary politics has used this underlying disquiet to create a powerful narrative of moral decline in which *crime* has come to feature—together with teenage pregnancies, single parent families, welfare dependency, and drug abuse—as the chief symptom of the supposed malaise. This call for return to order has led to the imposition of extensive new disciplines and controls, though it has been a feature of these developments that they have been targeted against particular social groups rather than universally imposed. The 1980s and 1990s have seen a return to restraint, a retrofitting of controls, an attempt to put the lid back on a newly disordered world. But despite these efforts, the clocks have not been turned back. There has been no return to a world in which all individuals are more hemmed in by the communal controls of local belonging, steady work, and tight-knit family. What has happened is that the individual freedoms granted by late modern morals and markets have been shored up by a new structure of controls and exclusions, directed against those groups most adversely affected by the dynamics of economic and social change—the urban poor, welfare claimants, and minority communities.

Convinced of the need to reimpose order, but unwilling to restrict consumer choice or give up personal freedoms; determined to enhance their own security, but unwilling to pay more taxes or finance the security of others; appalled by unregulated egoism and antisocial attitudes but committed to a market system which reproduces that very culture, the anxious middle classes today seek resolution for their ambivalence in zealously controlling the poor and excluding the marginal.[4] Above all, they impose controls upon "dangerous" offenders and "undeserving" claimants whose conduct leads some to suppose that they are incapable of discharging the responsibilities of the late modern freedom. The most vehement punishments are reserved for those guilty of child abuse, illegal drug use, or sexual violence—precisely the areas in which mainstream social and cultural norms have undergone greatest change and where middle-class ambivalence and guilt are at their most intense.

Punishment and Welfare in Late Modernity

This study has focused on the effects of the new social relations and political culture in the field of crime control. But the same kinds of effects can also be seen in other areas of social and economic policy, above all, in the treatment of the poor. In political discourse and government policy the poor are once again viewed as undeserving and treated accordingly. Their poverty is attributed to their supposed lack of effort, their feckless choices, their distinctive culture, and chosen conduct.[5] In the increasingly prosperous world of the 1990s and since, these persistently poor populations are easily viewed as "different" and not merely "disadvantaged." Like persistent offenders and "career criminals," they are conveniently regarded as an alien culture, a class apart, a residuum left behind by the fast-paced, high-tech processes of the globalized economy and the information society.[6] The themes that dominate crime policy—rational choice and the structures of control, deterrents, and disincentives, the normality of crime, the responsibilization of individuals, the threatening underclass, the failing, overly lenient system—have come to organize the politics of poverty as well. The same premises and purposes that transformed criminal justice are evident in the programmes of "welfare reform" that have been adopted by governments (and opposition parties) on both sides of the Atlantic and in the restructured social policy to which these have given rise.

Beginning in the 1980s benefits levels have been steadily reduced, even in periods when the numbers of out-of-work claimants greatly increased.[7] The provision of welfare has been skirted round with work conditions and disciplinary restrictions. "Choice" and "responsibility" have been emphasized, "dependency" anathematized, and "the market" has come to be viewed as a providential force of nature rather than a set of social relations that requires careful regulation and moral restraint. The termination of benefits is increasingly used as a means to force claimants off the rolls—usually into low-paid work but no doubt also into the alternative economy of drugs and crime. Unemployed workers have had to demonstrate that they are "active jobseekers" before they can claim benefits. A recognition that social and economic processes can create undeserved hardship has given way to a more moralistic account of labour market success and failure, in much the way that determinist criminologies have been displaced by the moralism of rational choice. Solidarity with the victims of social and economic dislocation has given way to a more condemnatory view of claimants, many of whom are now viewed as members of a culturally distinct and socially threatening "underclass," in which all of the pathologies of late modern life are concentrated. At the same time, chronic unemployment for certain social groups has come to be seen as a normal fact of economic life, quite beyond the reach of government policy or regulatory control. In the new economic order, only entrepreneurial conduct and prudent risk management can offset the threat of insecurity: the state no longer acts as the insurer of last resort; citizenship no longer guarantees security. Like the system of criminal justice, the benefits structure of the welfare state has come to be viewed as a generator of problems and pathologies rather than a cure for them. Reform efforts focus upon reducing costs, strengthening disincentives, surrounding benefit payments with controls and restrictions, and "getting people off welfare." Less effort is directed to addressing the structural sources of unemployment, poverty, and ill-health. The parallels with the new field of crime control are impossible to miss.

During the last twenty years, the combined effect of "neo-liberal" and "neo-conservative" policies—of market discipline and moral discipline—has been to create a situation in which more and more controls are imposed on the poor while fewer and fewer controls affect the market freedoms of the rest. Tax cuts for upper income groups, housing and pensions subsidies for the middle classes, the deregulation of the finance and credit industries, the privatization of major industries, and a prolonged stock market boom—these have ensured that those in well paid work have enjoyed increased living standards, enhanced consumer freedom, and ever fewer state controls on their economic conduct. The widening gap between rich and poor that these policies have created, together with the meanness of state benefits, have prompted those who can afford it to look to private, market-based provision of goods when it comes to housing, health, education, and pensions. A thriving market in commodified services has grown up parallel to the welfare state, in precisely the same way that the new market in private policing and security has appeared alongside the criminal justice system. The predictable consequence has been that the middle classes have become less inclined to view state welfare as a system that works to their benefit. Instead, it comes to be seen as a costly and inefficient government bureaucracy redistributing the hard-earned income of people in employment to an undeserving mass of idle and feckless recipients. With welfare, as with crime, large sections of the middle and working classes see themselves as victimized, by the poor and by a system that reproduces the problem it is supposed to solve.[8] The more punitive, more demanding welfare-to-work structures that have been put in place in recent years are the direct expression of this new sentiment. What Galbraith called a culture of contentment has increasingly given way to an anti-welfare politics in which the market freedoms and economic interests of the middle and upper classes dictate a more restrictive and less generous policy towards the poor.[9] In the prosperous 1990s these policies succeeded in reducing welfare rolls and limiting the growth of social spending. It remains to be seen how they will function once the economy falters and unemployment levels once more begin to rise.

The Dialectic of Freedom and Control

Historians have pointed to a recurring pattern of social development in which the upheaval and disruption characteristic of periods of social change subsequently give way to efforts at consolidation and the reimposition of order and control.[10] This dialectic between freedom and control could be said to have characterized the last thirty years. In certain respects, the social liberation of the 1960s and the market freedoms of the 1980s are now being paid for in the coin of social control and penal repression. Where the liberating dynamic of late modernity emphasized freedom, openness, mobility, and tolerance, the reactionary culture of the end of the century stresses control, closure, confinement, and condemnation. The continued enjoyment of market-based personal freedoms has come to depend upon the close control of excluded groups who cannot be trusted to enjoy these freedoms. So long as offenders and claimants appear as "other," and as the chief source of their own misfortune, they offer occasions for the dominant classes to impose strict controls without giving up freedoms of their own. In contrast to a solidaristic social control, in which everyone gives up some personal freedom in order to promote collective welfare, market individualism is the freedom of some premised upon the exclusion and close control of others.

When we impose control upon offenders today, we take pains to affirm their supposed freedom, their moral responsibility, and their capacity to have acted otherwise. The criminologies and sentencing assumptions that have become influential in the 1980s and 1990s—criminologies of choice and control—are precisely those that echo today's cultural norms and socio-political imperatives. We live in a social world built upon the imperatives of individual choice and personal freedom. Criminological accounts that slight free choice and stress social determinants now lack the kind of resonance and ideological appeal that they exerted in the heyday of the welfare state. Those accounts that highlight rational choice and the responsiveness of offenders to rewards and disincentives chime with today's common sense and with the individualistic morality of our consumer culture. Offenders must be deemed to be free, to be rational, to be exercising choice, because that is how we must conceive of ourselves. "Crime is a decision not a disease" is the new conventional wisdom.[11] More precisely put, crime is taken to be a freely chosen act, a rational decision, except in these cases where it is actually the determined outcome of a constitutional pathology. If individuals are to be deemed irresponsible, if impersonal forces are to account for their actions, then these must be forces that do not act upon the rest of us—causes with their roots in biological, psychological, and cultural difference. If we are to see ourselves as the uncaused causes of our own actions and choices, as the moral individualism of market society teaches us to do, then those not fully in control of their own conduct must appear different in some extra-social sense. Their otherness is a condition of their exculpation. What is missing today, what is actively suppressed by our cultural commitments, is the excluded middle that lies between complete freedom and irresistible compulsion—the old welfarist notion that individual decisions and choices are themselves socially structured, as are the capacities and opportunities for realizing them.

In the middle decades of the last century, the criminal justice system formed part of a broader solidarity project. Its programmatic response to crime was part of the welfare state's programmatic response to poverty and destitution. Criminal justice was shaped by the politics of social democracy, and its ideals were the reintegrative ideals of an inclusive welfare state society. And if its actual practices fell far short of these ideals, as they typically did, they could at least be criticized by reference to these ideals, and reformed in ways that lessened the gap. Today, welfare state institutions still play a supporting role in economic and social life, just as penal-welfare institutions still underpin criminal justice. But that solidarity project no longer dominates the rhetoric of policy or the logic of decision making. The high ideals of solidarity have been eclipsed by the more basic imperatives of security, economy, and control. Crime control and criminal justice have come to be disconnected from the broader themes of social justice and social reconstruction. Their social function is now the more reactionary, less ambitious one of reimposing control on those who fall outside the world of consumerist freedom. If penal welfare conveyed the hubris and idealism of twentieth-century modernism, today's crime policies express a darker and less tolerant message.

The Social Roots of Crime Control

The explanation for some of the more puzzling facts of contemporary crime control can be found if we trace their connections to the kinds of social organization and political culture that dominate in Britain and America today.

Why has the prison moved from being a discredited institution destined for abolition, to become an expanded and seemingly indispensable pillar of late modern social life? Not because it was the centrepiece of any penal programme that argued the need for mass imprisonment. There was no such programme. Imprisonment has emerged in its revived, reinvented form because it is able to serve a newly necessary function in the workings of late modern, neo-liberal societies: the need for a "civilized" and "constitutional" means of segregating the problem populations created by today's economic and social arrangements. The prison is located precisely at the junction point of two of the most important social and penal dynamics of our time: risk and retribution.[12] With the absolutist logic of a penal sanction, it punishes and protects, condemns and controls. Imprisonment simultaneously serves as an expressive satisfaction of retributive sentiments and an instrumental mechanism for the management of risk and the confinement of danger. The sectors of the population effectively excluded from the worlds of work, welfare and family—typically young urban minority males—increasingly find themselves in prison or in jail, their social and economic exclusion effectively disguised by their criminal status. Today's reinvented prison is a ready-made penal solution to a new problem of social and economic exclusion.

Why do governments so quickly turn to penal solutions to deal with the behaviour of marginal populations rather than attempt to address the social and economic sources of their marginalization? Because penal solutions are immediate, easy to implement, and can claim to "work" as a punitive end in themselves even when they fail in all other respects. Because they have few political opponents, comparatively low costs, and they accord with common sense ideas about the sources of social disorder and the proper allocation of blame. Because they rely upon existing systems of regulation, and leave the fundamental social and economic arrangements untouched. Above all, because they allow controls and condemnation to be focused on low-status outcast groups, leaving the behaviour of markets, corporations and the more affluent social classes relatively free of regulation and censure.

Why have we made such massive new investments in private security and created such thriving markets in commodified control? Because the old fashioned sovereign state can deliver punishment but not security, and this has become apparent to economic actors who have a real stake in the process. Because affluent sectors of the population have become accustomed to insuring themselves and their property and are increasingly willing to spend money on the pursuit of personal safety. Because these same groups are acutely aware of the social and racial divisions that characterize today's society and resort to defensive space and fortified property as ways of warding off threatening outsiders. And because in high crime societies, the problems of personal security, crime prevention and penal provision have created commercial opportunities that have been vigorously exploited by the private interests and market forces that neo-liberalism has so effectively liberated.

Why is the emphasis now shifting to situational crime prevention and away from the social reform programmes that used to dominate the field? Because unlike earlier efforts to build social prevention programmes, job creation schemes, and community regeneration, the new situational methods do not appear to benefit the undeserving poor, to imply a social critique, or to disturb market freedoms. Their implementation can proceed outside of a politics of solidarity and collective sacrifice, and in the absence of support for redistributive welfare programmes. Their growing appeal rests on the fact that they can be distributed through the market as customized commodities, rather than delivered by state agencies. Like private policing and commercial security, these methods mesh with the dynamics of market society, adapting themselves to individuated demand, slotting into the circuits of profitable supply and private consumption.

Why is the image of the suffering victim now so central to the crime issue and our responses to it? Because in the new morality of market individualism, public institutions lack compelling force and the state's law lacks independent authority. Whatever mutuality and solidarity exists is achieved through the direct identification of individuals with one another, not with the polity or the public institutions to which they each belong. In a world in which moral sentiments are increasingly privatized along with everything else, collective moral outrage more easily proceeds from an individualized basis than from a public one. A declining faith in public institutions now means that only the sight of suffering "individuals like us" can be relied upon to provoke the impassioned responses needed to supply the emotional energy for punitive policies and a war upon crime. In the individualistic culture of consumer capitalism, the law more and more relies upon identifications of an individual kind. Justice, like the other public goods of the post-welfare society, is increasingly rendered in the currency of consumer society, increasingly adapted to individuated demand. The new importance attributed to the figure of the "victim" is created not by the reality of victimhood—there has always been plenty of that—but by the new significance of visceral identification in a context where few sources of mutuality exist.[13]

Finally, why do contemporary crime policies so closely resemble the anti-welfare policies that have grown up over the precisely the same period? Because they share the same assumptions, harbour the same anxieties, deploy the same stereotypes, and utilize the same recipes for the identification of risk and the allocation of blame. Like social policy and the system of welfare benefits, crime control functions as an element in a broader system of regulation and ideology that attempts to forge a new social order in the conditions of late modernity.

That Future Is Not Inevitable

I have argued that today's crime control strategies have a certain congruence, a certain "fit" with the structures of late modern society. They represent a particular kind of response, a particular adaptation, to the specific problems of social order produced by late modern social organization.[14] But such policies are not inevitable. The social surface upon which crime control institutions are built poses certain problems, but does not dictate how these will be perceived and addressed by social actors and authorities. These responses are shaped by political institutions and cultural commitments. They are the products of a certain style of politics, a certain conjuncture of class forces, a particular historical trajectory. They are the outcome (partly planned, partly unintended) of political and cultural and policy choices—choices that could have been different and that can still be rethought and reversed.[15]

The general explanation that I have set out here necessarily involves two kinds of accounts: a *structural* account that points to the general characteristics, of a certain kind of social organization, and a *conjunctural* account that identifies the choices and contingencies that shaped how particular social groups adapted to these structures and mediated their social consequences. In narrating these historical developments I have tried to distinguish these different levels of analysis, and to differentiate structural characteristics from political or cultural adaptations. I have tried to argue that the reconfigured field of crime control is structurally related to the conditions of late modernity, while emphasizing that "structurally related" is not the same as "strictly determined." But in the real world there is no clear separation between "social structure" and "political response": the two come bundled together. Only comparative analyses allow us to show how the same structural coordinates can support quite different political and cultural arrangements. This study has chosen to consider the United Kingdom and the United States together, in an effort to point up the structural similarities that mark their social, political and penological trajectories. But Britain is not America. Its penal regime is not so repressive, its social and racial divisions are not so deep, its recent history has not been so explosive. Nor are the competing political parties the same in every respect—Clinton is not Bush and Blair is not Thatcher, and the differences that distinguish their governments' policies have had real consequences for people's lives. My claim is not that there are no differences that matter. My claim is that there are now important structural similarities in the patterns of thought and organizational strategies that shape practice in these two late modern societies, no matter which party is currently in power. A more extensive work of international comparison could have shown how other societies, such as Canada, Norway, the Netherlands, or Japan, have experienced the social and economic disruptions of late modernity without resorting to these same strategies and levels of control.[16]

But even if the present study cannot show this conclusively, its analyses do suggest points at which different choices might have been made, different policies pursued, and different outcomes made more likely.[17] As we have seen, political actors in Britain and America have repeatedly chosen to respond to widespread public concern about crime and security by formulating policies that punish and exclude. They have assumed the posture of a sovereign state deploying its monopoly of force to impose order and punish lawbreakers. As I have argued, this attempt to create social order through penal means is deeply problematic, particularly in late modern democracies. Instead of working to build the complex institutions of governance and integration needed to regulate and unify today's social and economic order, these penal policies have set up a division between those groups who can be allowed to live in deregulated freedom, and those who must be heavily controlled. Instead of reversing the processes of economic marginalization and social exclusion that are endemic in today's globalized economy, the new emphasis upon punishment and policing has overlaid and reinforced these very processes. Instead of addressing the difficult problem of social solidarity in a diverse, individuated world, our political leaders have preferred to rely upon the certainties of a simpler, more coercive, Hobbesian solution.

But other possibilities exist for the control of crime and the shaping of orderly conduct. . . . Efforts to share responsibility for crime control, to embed social control into the fabric of everyday life, to reduce the criminogenic effects of economic transactions, to protect repeat victims—these are possibilities that already exist and could be given much more prominence in government policy. As compared to penal solutions, these other possibilities are better adapted to the social arrangements of the late modern world, more realistic about the limits of the sovereign state and its criminal justice mechanisms, and less liable to reinforce existing social divisions.

We have seen that the American and British publics today are highly attuned to the crime issue, and that political actors feel compelled to respond directly to these concerns. To be out of touch with public sentiment on this issue is to invite negative headlines and political disaster. But the emotional involvement that many people now have with this issue need not always result in the expression of punitive sentiments. The public demands that something should be done about crime, that their property and persons should be protected, that offenders should be adequately punished and controlled, and that the system should operate reliably and efficiently. But these recurring concerns are capable of being met in a variety of ways. Public attitudes about crime and control are deeply ambivalent.[18] They leave room for other resolutions. Politicians have tended to take the easy route here, to opt for segregation and punishment rather than try to embed social controls, regulate economic life, and develop policies that will enhance social inclusion and integration. If late modern societies are to uphold the ideals of democracy, equal rights for all, and a minimum of economic security for the whole population, they will need to ensure that moral regulation and social control are extended to the mainstream processes of economic decision making and market allocation—not confined to the world of offenders and claimants.

Nor is it just our politicians who will need to revise their attitudes. As we have seen, the cumulative choices of individuals and households make a difference too, and form the basis upon which social structures emerge. Today's enormous market in private security and defensive space is a consequence of these choices. So too, is the widening gap between those who can afford to protect themselves and those who cannot. Precisely because choices that seem rational from an individual viewpoint can produce irrational outcomes when repeated on a massive scale, the market in security is one that also needs to be subjected to collective regulation and moral restraint. Today's governmental authorities may be obliged to operate alongside this private sector, and in conjunction with it, but they are not obliged to stand back and allow its unregulated consequences to fall where they may.

The New Iron Cage

At the beginning of the twenty-first century, the United States . . . [experienced] an unprecedented economic boom, with low unemployment levels, rising standards of living, a federal surplus and healthy state budgets. The United Kingdom . . . [also enjoyed] an extended economic recovery. Crime rates fell steadily in both places during the 1990s, with the United States recording declines in every year between 1992 and the present, and England and Wales experiencing five consecutive years of decrease until the reported increase of the year ending 1999.[19] Yet despite these positive trends, there is every sign that the shift towards punitive justice and a security build up is continuing unabated.[20] As the market in private security expands, the delivery of penal legislation speeds up, and the crime complex reproduces itself, we face the real possibility of being locked into a new "iron cage." Max Weber long ago described how the capitalist rationality outlived the spiritual vocation that originally gave it impetus and meaning. The new culture of crime control, born of the fears and anxieties of the late twentieth century, could well continue long after its originating conditions have ceased to exist. After all, such arrangements spawn institutional investments and produce definite benefits, particularly for the social groups who are at the greatest distance from them. They entail a way of allocating the costs of crime—unjust, unequal, but feasible none the less. Penal solutions may be expensive, but the last twenty-five years have shown that their financial costs can be borne even where taxpayers are notoriously reluctant to meet the costs of other public expenditure.

The new crime-control arrangements do however involve certain social costs that are, over the long term, less easily accommodated. The hardening of social and racial divisions, the reinforcement of criminogenic processes; the alienation of large social groups; the discrediting of legal authority; a reduction of civic tolerance; a tendency towards authoritarianism—these are the kinds of outcomes that are liable to flow from a reliance upon penal mechanisms to maintain social order.[21] Mass imprisonment and private fortification may be feasible solutions to the problem of social order, but they are deeply unattractive ones. A large population of marginalized, criminalized poor may lack political power and command little public sympathy, but in aggregate terms they would have the negative capacity to make life unpleasant for everyone else. It is no accident that the dystopian images of the 1980s movie *Blade Runner* have had such powerful cultural resonance.[22] Gated communities and the purchase of private security may be options for the rich, but they cannot offer a general social solution to the problems of crime and violence—not least because full private protection is beyond the means of most middle-class households who will continue to rely on the public police and state provision.[23] Mass imprisonment may continue to be affordable for "law and order" states, a provider of much needed jobs for rural communities, and a source of profit for commercial corrections companies. But over the long term it is probable that its conflict with the ideals of liberal democracy will become increasingly apparent, particularly where penal exclusion (and the disenfranchisement it entails) is so heavily focused upon racial minorities. A government that routinely sustains social order by means of mass exclusion begins to look like an apartheid state.

These social and political costs make it less likely that such policies will continue indefinitely. The recent reduction in crime rates has made the issue of crime control slightly less urgent, slightly less prominent in political discourse. The costs of mass imprisonment are beginning to be apparent. In the United States, there is currently a public debate prompted by evidence of faulty convictions in a high percentage of death penalty cases, and at least one governor has called a moratorium on executions pending the results of further inquiries. Some of the most conservative figures in crime policy are beginning to back away from the prospect of continued mass incarceration.[24] The policy is beginning to be the problem, not the solution. If these shifts continue, there is a prospect that current trends will be tempered and perhaps eventually reversed.

But the most fundamental lesson of the twentieth century is not a political one but a structural one. The problem of crime control in late modernity has vividly demonstrated the limits of the sovereign state. The denials and expressive gestures that have marked recent penal policy cannot disguise the fact that the state is seriously limited in its capacity to provide security for its citizens and deliver adequate levels of social control. The lesson of the late twentieth-century experience is that the nation state cannot any longer hope to govern by means of sovereign commands issued to obedient subjects, and this is true whether the concern is to deliver welfare, to secure economic prosperity, or to maintain "law and order." In the complex, differentiated world of late modernity, effective, legitimate government must devolve power and share the work of social control with local organizations and communities. It can no longer rely upon "state knowledge," on unresponsive bureaucratic agencies, and upon universal solutions imposed from above. Social and political theorists have long argued that effective government in complex societies cannot rely upon centralized command and coercion.[25] Instead it must harness the governmental capacities of the organizations and associations of civil society, together with the local powers and knowledge that they contain. We are discovering—and not before time—that this is true of crime control as well.

Notes

[1] On the cultural consequences of America's use of mass imprisonment and the death penalty, see D. Garland (ed), *Mass Imprisonment* (London: Sage, 2001) and A. Sarat (ed), *The Killing State* (New York: Oxford University Press, 1998).

[2] P. Hirst, 'Statism, Pluralism and Social Control', and Z. Bauman, 'The Social Uses of Law and Order', both in D. Garland and J. R. Sparks (eds), *Criminology and Social Theory* (Oxford: Oxford University Press, 2000).

[3] For a wide-ranging essay on the themes of inclusion and exclusion, see J. Young, *The Exclusive Society* (London: Sage, 1999).

[4] '[F]rom everything we know about the opinions of most Americans, they want the benefits of orthodoxy in terms of community and social order, but they do not want to give up any significant amount of personal freedom to achieve these ends. They deplore the loss of family values, but oppose the move away from no-fault divorce; they want friendly mom-and-pop stores but are enamoured of low prices and consumer choice', F. Fukuyama, *The Great Disruption* (New York: Simon and Schuster, 1999), 90. Fukuyama is relying here on the empirical evidence set out in A. Wolfe, *One Nation, After All* (New York: Viking, 1998). Charles Leadbetter makes the same points about contemporary Britain: 'We want a free, diverse, open society but we also want a society that is ordered by older, more traditional virtues of civility, politeness and responsibility', C. Leadbetter, *The Self-Policing Society* (London: Demos, 1996).

[5] See H. Dean and P. Taylor-Gooby, *Dependency Culture* (Hemel Hempstead: Harvester Wheatsheaf, 1992); M. B. Katz, *The Undeserving Poor: From the War on Welfare to the War on the Poor* (New York: Pantheon, 1989); H. J. Gans, *The War Against the Poor: The Underclass and Antipoverty Policy* (New York: Basic Books, 1995).

[6] See L. Morris, *Dangerous Classes: The Underclass and Social Citizenship* (London: Routledge, 1994); R. McDonald (ed.), *Youth, 'the Underclass' and Social Exclusion* (London: Routledge, 1997); C. Jencks and P. E. Peterson (eds.), *The Urban Underclass* (Washington DC: The Brookings Institute, 1991).

[7] See H. Dean and P. Taylor-Gooby, *Dependency Culture* (Hemel Hempstead: Harvester Wheatsheaf, 1992) for an account of how U.K. social policy in the 1980s brought about 'a cut in benefits, a weakening of social welfare entitlement, a harsher regime of surveillance and a real increase in costs of living for [poor people of working age]' (p. 24). On U.S. policies, see S. Danziger and P. Gottschalk, *America Unequal* (Cambridge, MA: Harvard University Press, 1995): 'Simply put, throughout the 1980s, economic growth did little to help poor and low-income workers, and government policies were not reoriented to counter . . . adverse changes in the labor market. Social programs lifted fewer families, especially families with children, out of poverty in the 1980s than the 1970s for two reasons. First, the percentage of the working poor served by the programs declined after Reagan's initial budget reductions. Second, real benefits continued to decline, as nominal benefit levels in many programs did not keep pace with the modest inflation of the 1980s' (p. 29).

[8] M. Gilens, *Why Americans Hate Welfare: Race, Media and the Politics of Antipoverty Policy* (Chicago: University of Chicago Press, 1999).

[9] J. K. Galbraith, *The Culture of Contentment* (London: Sinclair Stevenson, 1992). In his speech of 29 September 1998, Prime Minister Tony Blair set out New Labour's view of the welfare state: 'I challenge each and every one of us over the welfare state. We are spending more but getting less, failing to help those who need it and sometimes helping those who don't. Billions wasted every year through fraud and abuse.'

[10] See, e.g., T. Raab, *The Struggle for Stability in Early Modern Europe* (New York: Oxford University Press, 1975); M. Wiener, *Reconstructing the Criminal* (New York: Cambridge University Press, 1990).

[11] Prime Minister John Major used this phrase in his Speech on 9 September 1994 at Church House London.

[12] Recent attempts in Britain and the U.S.A. to 'reinvent' probation and community penalties try to emulate this combination, but so far with little success. The cost advantages of 'community punishments', as compared with prison, make it likely that these attempts will continue, probably focusing on the penal possibilities of electronic monitoring and similar technologies.

[13] The notion of crime control and criminal justice as commodities to be bought and sold by individual consumers is clearly set out in an Institute of Economic Affairs pamphlet. 'The real problem is that "producers" in the criminal justice system are not directly answerable to their customers (the victims of crime). As a result, they can pursue their own interests which may conflict with those of the victims. The solution will be when the consumer can choose to buy protection in the market-place', D. Pyle, *Cutting the Costs of Crime: The Economics of Crime and Criminal Justice* (London: IEA, 1995), 61. On the criminal justice morality of late modern societies, see H. J. Boutellier, *Crime and Morality—The Significance of Criminal Justice in Post-modern Culture* (Dordrecht, Netherlands: Kluwer Academic, 2000). The other side of this individualized moral dynamic, is that offenders whom we do not recognize as being 'just like us' are more easily condemned to harsh punishment.

[14] For an account of recent developments in Australian crime control and criminal justice, many of which follow the pattern I have described in the U.S. and the U.K., see R. Hogg and D. Brown, *Rethinking Law and Order* (Annandale, NSW: Pluto Press, 1998).

[15] As Wesley Skogan notes in his discussion of crime and disorder: 'it should be clear that many factors that appear to engender disorder or may counter its spread are shaped by conscious decisions by persons in power. These decisions reflect the interests of banks, real-estate developers, employers, governmental agencies, and others playing for large economic and political stakes. None of these decisions are irreversible, although they obviously may be motivated by still larger economic and demographic forces.' W. G. Skogan, *Disorder and Decline* (Chicago: University of Chicago Press, 1990), 179. For an insightful discussion of the importance of place and a detailed case study of how large-scale social forces are experienced (and addressed) in a specific locale, see E. Girling et al., *Crime and Social Change in Middle England: Questions of Order in an English Town* (London: Routledge, 2000).

[16] See S. Snacken et al., 'Changing Prison Populations in Western countries: Fate or Policy?' *European Journal of Crime, Criminal Law and Criminal justice*, vol. 3, no. 1 (1995), 18–53; J. Muncie and J. R. Sparks (eds), *Imprisonment: European Perspectives* (Hemel Hempstead: Harvester Wheatsheaf, 1991); M. Mauer, *Race to Incarcerate* (New York: The New Press, 1999), ch. 2.

[17] Within the U.S.A., research evidence suggests that the most punitive states, as measured by imprisonment rates, are also those with the least generous welfare policies and large racial minority populations. See K. Beckett and B. Western, 'Governing Social Marginality: Welfare, Incarceration and the Transformation of State Policy' in D. Garland (ed), *Mass Imprisonment* (London: Sage, forthcoming). Similar contrasts have been drawn in the U.K. between Scotland, with its stronger welfare traditions and its less punitive penal policies, and England and Wales. See L. McAra, 'The Politics of Penality: An Overview of the Development of Penal Policy in Scotland', in P. Duff and N. Hutton (eds), *Criminal Justice in Scotland* (Aldershot: Ashgate, 1999), 355–80 and D. J. Smith, 'Less Crime Without More Punishment', *Edinburgh Law Review* (1999). The contours of crime control may be socially structured, but the determination of policy is, in the end, a matter of political choice within social and cultural constraints.

[18] For a summary discussion of public opinion and its ambivalence, see M. Tonry, 'Rethinking Unthinkable Punishment Policies in America', *UCLA Law Review* (1999), vol. 46, no. 6, 1751–91.

[19] For U.S. data, see K. Maguire and A. Pa store (eds.), *Sourcebook of Criminal Justice Statistics*, 1995. On England and Wales, see Home Office, *Digest 4: Information on the Criminal Justice System*, ed. G. C. Barclay and C. Travers (London: Home Office, 1999) and D. Povey and J. Cotton, *Recorded Crime Statistics: England and Wales, October 1998 to September 1999* (London: Home Office, 18 January 2000): 'In the twelve months ending September

1999, the police in England and Wales recorded a total of 5.2 million offences. The trend in recorded offences shows a 2.2 per cent increase compared to the previous twelve months. This increase follows five consecutive falls for year ending September figures' (p. 3).

[20] Setting out the re-election campaign themes for 1996, a leading political adviser to President Clinton listed these as follows: 'I came here to make America better. And, by the way we measure a better America, it is better. There are more people working than on the day I took office. There are more people in prison cells than on the day I took office', James Carville, *The New Yorker*, 3 April 1995. While Tony Blair's claim has been to be 'tough on crime, tough on the causes of crime', Bill Clinton's aim is to be 'tough and smart'. 'Violent crime and the fear it provokes are crippling our society, limiting personal freedom and fraying the ties that bind us. The crime bill before Congress gives you a chance to do something about it—to be tough and smart', President Clinton, *State of the Union Address*, 26 January 1994.

[21] Discussing the influence of capital punishment upon American political culture, Austin Sarat notes 'capital punishment is a tool of the powerful against dominated groups. As such, it appears as an enactment of the finality of state power, a finality that is quite at odds with the spirit and substance of democracy. The death penalty always calls us to certainty, and, in so doing, invites us to forget the limits of our reason', A. Sarat (ed), *The Killing State* (New York: Oxford University Press, 1999), 11.

[22] Ridley Scott's film 'Blade Runner' was originally released in 1982. See M. Davis, 'Beyond Blade Runner: Urban Control-the Ecology of Pear', *Open Magazine Pamphlet Series #23* (Open Magazine: Open Media, 1992). On being elected in 1997, Prime Minister Tony Blair talked publicly about the need to avoid a 'Blade Runner' scenario developing in Great Britain.

[23] See P. Hirst, 'Statism, Pluralism and Social Control', p. 130.

[24] See J. J. DiIulio Jr., 'Two Million Prisoners are Enough', *The Wall Street Journal*, 12 March 1999. In January 2000, Governor George H. Ryan of Illinois announced a moratorium on the use of the death penalty in his state, pending an inquiry into why more death row inmates in his state had been exonerated than executed since capital punishment was reinstated in 1977. For details, see J. S. Liebman et al., *A Broken System: Error Rates in Capital Cases, 1973–1995* (New York: The Justice Project, 2000). A Gallup poll conducted shortly after this event, reported that support for capital punishment had declined from 80 per cent in 1994, to 66 per cent-the lowest level in nineteen years. See B. Shapiro, 'Capital Offense', *The New York Sunday Times*, 26 March 2000. *Sourcebook of Criminal Justice Statistics—1998* reports that public concern about crime and violence has fallen off slightly front its peak in 1994 (Table 2.1).

[25] J. C. Scott, *Seeing Like A State* (Yale: Yale University Press, 1998); P. Hirst, *Associative Democracy* (Cambridge: Polity, 1992);P. Selznick, *The Moral Commonwealth* (Berkeley, CA: University of California Press, 1992); J. Kooiman, *Modern Governance: New Social-Governmental Interactions* (London: Sage, 1993).

Article

23

The New Penology
Notes on the Emerging Strategy of Corrections and Its Implications

Malcolm M. Feeley
Jonathan Simon

The outlines of the "old" penology become most visible when one considers what has been shared across the perceived lines of opposition in modern corrections and criminal law. Modern American law, whose concepts still form the core of law school education, concentrates on individuals; the individual is the unit of analysis. This concern is especially emphasized in the criminal process. Criminal law focuses on intention in order to assign guilt. Criminal procedure has erected barriers to conviction to test evidence and protect the accused individual in the face of the powerful state. Criminal sanctioning has been aimed at individual-based theories of punishment.

In contrast, the new penology is markedly less concerned with responsibility, fault, moral sensibility, diagnosis, or intervention and treatment of the individual offender. Rather, it is concerned with techniques to identify, classify, and manage groupings sorted by dangerousness. The task is managerial, not transformative (Cohen, 1985; Garland and Young, 1983; Messinger, 1969; Messinger and Berecochea, 1990; Reichman, 1986; Wilkins, 1973). It seeks to *regulate* levels of deviance, not intervene or respond to individual deviants or social malformations.

Criminology, Vol. 30, No. 4 (November 1992): 449–474. Copyright © 1992 by the American Society of Criminology. Reprinted with permission.

Although the new penology is much more than "discourse," its language helps reveal this shift most strikingly. It does not speak of impaired individuals in need of treatment or of morally irresponsible persons who need to be held accountable for their actions. Rather, it considers the criminal justice *system*, and it pursues systemic rationality and efficiency. It seeks to sort and classify, to separate the less from the more dangerous, and to deploy control strategies rationally. The tools for this enterprise are "indicators," prediction tables, population projections, and the like. In these methods, individualized diagnosis and response is displaced by aggregate classification systems for purposes of surveillance, confinement, and control (Gordon, 1991).

Distinguishing Features of the New Penology

What we call the new penology is not a theory of crime or criminology. Its uniqueness lies less in conceptual integration than in a common focus on certain problems and a shared way of framing issues. This strategic formation of knowledge and power offers managers of the system a more or less coherent picture of the challenges they face and the kinds of solutions that are most likely to work. While we cannot reduce it to a set of principles, we can point to some of its most salient features.

The New Discourse

A central feature of the new discourse is the replacement of a moral or clinical description of the individual with an actuarial language of probabilistic calculations and statistical distributions applied to populations. Although social utility analysis or actuarial thinking is commonplace enough in modern life—it frames policy considerations of all sorts—in recent years this mode of thinking has gained ascendancy in legal discourse, a system of reasoning that traditionally has employed the language of morality and been focused on individuals (Simon, 1988).[1] For instance, this new mode of reasoning is found increasingly in tort law, where traditional fault and negligence standards—which require a focus on the individual and are based upon notions of individual responsibility—have given way to strict liability and no-fault. These new doctrines rest upon actuarial ways of thinking about how to "manage" accidents and public safety. They employ the language of social utility and management, not individual responsibility (Simon, 1987; Steiner, 1987).[2] It is also found in some branches of antidiscrimination law, wherein the courts are less interested in intent (i.e., discrimination based on identifying individuals whose intentions can be examined) than in effects (i.e., aggregate consequences or patterns that can be assessed against a standard of social utility [Freeman, 1990] and corporate misconduct [dan-Cohen, 1986; Stone, 1975]).[3]

Although crime policy, criminal procedure, and criminal sanctioning have been influenced by such social utility analysis, there is no body of commentary on the criminal law that is equivalent to the body of social utility analysis for tort law doctrine.[4] Nor has strict liability in the criminal law achieved anything like the acceptance of related no-fault principles in tort law. Perhaps because the criminal law is so firmly rooted in a focus on the individual, these developments have come late to criminal law and penology.

Scholars of both European and North American penal strategies have noted the recent and rising trend of the penal system to target categories and subpopulations rather than individuals (Bottoms, 1983; Cohen, 1985; Mathieson, 1983; Reichman, 1986). This reflects, at least in part, the fact that actuarial forms of representation promote quantification as a way of visualizing populations.

Crime statistics have been a part of the discourse of the state for over 200 years, but the advance of statistical methods permits the formulation of concepts and strategies that allow direct relations between penal strategy and the population. Earlier generations used statistics to map the responses of normatively defined groups to punishment; today one talks of "high-rate offenders," "career criminals," and other categories defined by the distribution itself. Rather than simply extending the capacity of the system to rehabilitate or control crime, actuarial classification has come increasingly to define the correctional enterprise itself.

The importance of actuarial language in the system will come as no surprise to anyone who has spent time observing it. Its significance, however, is often lost in the more spectacular shift in emphasis from rehabilitation to crime control. No doubt, a new and more punitive attitude toward the proper role of punishment has emerged in recent years, and it is manifest in a shift in the language of statutes, internal procedures, and academic scholarship. Yet looking across the past several decades, it appears that the pendulum-like swings of penal attitude moved independently of the actuarial language that has steadily crept into the discourse.[5]

The discourse of the new penology is not simply one of greater quantification; it is also characterized by an emphasis on the systemic and on formal rationality. While the history of systems theory and operations research has yet to be written, their progression from business administration to the military and, in the 1960s, to domestic public policy must be counted as among the most significant of current intellectual trends. In criminal justice the great reports of the late 1960s, like *The Challenge of Crime in a Free Society* (see note 5), helped make the phrase "criminal justice system" a part of everyday reality for the operatives and students of criminal law and policy.[6]

Some of the most astute observers identified this change near the outset and understood that it was distinct from the concurrent rightward shift in penal thinking. Jacobs (1977) noted the rise at Stateville Penitentiary of what he called a "managerial" perspective during the mid-1970s. The regime of Warden Brierton was characterized, according to Jacobs, by a focus on tighter administrative control through the gathering and distribution of statistical information about the functioning of the prison. Throughout the 1980s this perspective grew considerably within the correctional system. Jacobs presciently noted that the managerial perspective might succeed where traditional and reform administrations had failed because it was capable of handling the greatly increased demands for rationality and accountability coming from the courts and the political system.

The New Objectives

The new penology is neither about punishing nor about rehabilitating individuals. It is about identifying and managing unruly groups. It is concerned with the rationality not of individual behavior or even community organization, but of managerial processes. Its goal is not to eliminate crime but to make it tolerable through systemic coordination.

One measure of the shift away from trying to normalize offenders and toward trying to manage them is seen in the declining significance of recidivism. Under the old penology, recidivism was a nearly universal criterion for assessing success or failure of penal programs. Under the new penology, recidivism rates continue to be important, but their significance has changed. The word itself seems to be used less often precisely because it carries a normative connotation that reintegrating offenders into the community is the major objective. High rates of parolees being returned to prison once indicated program failure; now they are offered as evidence of efficiency and effectiveness of parole as a control apparatus.[7]

It is possible that recidivism is dropping out of the vocabulary as an adjustment to harsh realities and is a way of avoiding charges of institutional failure. . . . However, in shifting to emphasize the virtues of return as an indication of effective control, the new penology reshapes one's understanding of the functions of the penal sanction. By emphasizing correctional programs in terms of aggregate control and system management rather than individual success and failure, the new penology lowers one's expectations about the criminal sanction. . . .

The waning of concern over recidivism reveals fundamental changes in the very penal processes that recidivism once was used to evaluate. For example, although parole and probation have long been justified as means of reintegrating offenders into the community (President's Commission, 1967:165), increasingly they are being perceived as cost-effective ways of imposing long-term management on the dangerous. Instead of treating revocation of parole and probation as a mechanism to short-circuit the supervision process when the risks to public safety become unacceptable, the system now treats revocation as a cost-effective way to police and sanction a chronically troublesome population. In such an operation, recidivism is either irrelevant[8] or, as suggested above, is stood on its head and transformed into an indicator of success in a new form of law enforcement.

The importance that recidivism once had in evaluating the performance of corrections is now being taken up by measures of system functioning.

Heydebrand and Seron (1990) have noted a tendency in courts and other social agencies toward decoupling performance evaluation from external social objectives. Instead of social norms like the elimination of crime, reintegration into the community, or public safety, institutions begin to measure their own outputs as indicators of performance. Thus, courts may look at docket flow. Similarly, parole agencies may shift evaluations of performance to, say, the time elapsed between arrests and due process hearings. In much the same way, many schools have come to focus on standardized test performance rather than on reading or mathematics, and some have begun to see teaching itself as the process of teaching students how to take such tests (Heydebrand and Seron, 1990:190–194; Lipsky, 1980:4–53).

Such technocratic rationalization tends to insulate institutions from the messy, hard-to-control demands of the social world. By limiting their exposure to indicators that they can control, managers ensure that their problems will have solutions. No doubt this tendency in the new penology is, in part, a response to the acceleration of demands for rationality and accountability in punishment coming from the courts and legislatures during the 1970s (Jacobs, 1977). It also reflects the lowered expectations for the penal system that result from failures to accomplish more ambitious promises of the past. Yet in the end, the inclination of the system to measure its success against its own production processes helps lock the system into a mode of operation that has only an attenuated connection with the *social* purposes of punishment. In the long term it becomes more difficult to evaluate an institution critically if there are no references to substantive social ends.

The new objectives also inevitably permeate through the courts into thinking about rights. The new penology replaces consideration of fault with predictions of dangerousness and safety management and, in so doing, modifies traditional individual-oriented doctrines of criminal procedure. This shift is illustrated in *U.S. v. Salerno*,[9] which upheld the preventive detention provision in the Bail Reform Act of 1984. Writing the opinion for the Court, then Associate Supreme Court Justice William Rehnquist reasoned that preventive detention does not trigger the same level of protection as other penal detentions because it is intended to manage risks rather than punish. While the distinction may have seemed disingenuous to some, it acknowledges the shift in objectives we have emphasized and redefines rights accordingly.[10]

New Techniques

These altered, lowered expectations manifest themselves in the development of more cost-effective forms of custody and control and in new technologies to identify and classify risk. Among them are low frills, no-service custodial centers; various forms of electronic monitoring systems that impose a form of custody without walls; and new statistical techniques for assessing risk and predicting dangerousness. These new forms of control are not anchored in aspirations to rehabilitate, reintegrate, retrain, provide employment, or the like. They are justified in more blunt terms: variable detention depending upon risk assessment.[11]

Perhaps the clearest example of the new penology's method is the theory of incapacitation, which has become the predominant utilitarian model of punishment (Greenwood, 1982; Moore et al., 1984). Incapacitation promises to reduce the effects of crime in society not by altering either offender or social context, but by rearranging the distribution of offenders in society. If the prison can do nothing else, incapacitation theory holds, it can detain offenders for a time and thus delay their resumption of criminal activity. According to the theory, if such delays are sustained for enough time and for enough offenders, significant aggregate effects in crime can take place although individual destinies are only marginally altered.[12]

These aggregate effects can be further intensified, in some accounts, by a strategy of selective incapacitation. This approach proposes a sentencing scheme in which lengths of sentence depend not upon the nature of the criminal offense or upon an assessment of the character of the offender, but upon risk profiles. Its objectives are to identify high-risk offenders and to maintain long-term control over them while investing in shorter terms and less intrusive control over lower risk offenders.

Selective incapacitation was first formally articulated as a coherent scheme for punishing in a report by a research and development organization (Greenwood, 1982), but it was quickly embraced and self-consciously promoted as a justification for punishment by a team of scholars from Harvard University, who were keenly aware that it constituted a paradigm shift in the underlying rationale for imposing the criminal sanction (Moore et al., 1984).[13]

The New Penology in Perspective

The correctional practices emerging from the shifts we identified above present a kind of "custodial continuum." But unlike the "correctional continuum" discussed in the 1960s, this new custodial continuum does not design penal measures for the particular needs of the individual or the community. Rather, it sorts individuals into groups according to the degree of control warranted by their risk profiles.

At one extreme the prison provides maximum security at a high cost for those who pose the greatest risks, and at the other probation provides low-cost surveillance for low-risk offenders. In between stretches a growing range of intermediate supervisory and surveillance techniques. The management concerns of the new penology—in contrast to the transformative concerns of the old—are displayed especially clearly in justifications for various new intermediate sanctions.

What we call the new penology is only beginning to take coherent shape. Although most of what we have stressed as its central elements— statistical prediction, concern with groups, strategies of management— have a long history in penology, in recent years they have come to the fore, and their functions have coalesced and expanded to form a new strategic approach. Discussing the new penology in terms of discourse, objective, and technique, risks a certain repetitiveness. Indeed, all three are closely linked, and while none can be assigned priority as the cause of the others, each entails and facilitates the others.

Thus, one can speak of normalizing individuals, but when the emphasis is on separating people into distinct and independent categories the idea of the "normal" itself becomes obscured if not irrelevant.[14] If the "norm" can no longer function as a relevant criterion of success for the organizations of criminal justice, it is not surprising that evaluation turns to indicators of internal system performance. The focus of the system on the efficiency of its own outputs, in turn, places a premium on those methods (e.g., risk screening, sorting, and monitoring) that fit wholly within the bureaucratic capacities of the apparatus.

But the same story can be told in a different order. The steady bureaucratization of the correctional apparatus during the 1950s and 1960s shifted the target from individuals, who did not fit easily into centralized administration, to categories or classes, which do. But once the focus is on categories of offenders rather than individuals, methods naturally shift toward mechanisms of appraising and arranging groups rather than intervening in the lives of individuals. In the end the search for causal order is at least premature.

In the section below we explore the contours of some of the new patterns represented by these developments, and in so doing suggest that the enterprise is by now relatively well established.

New Functions and Traditional Forms

Someday perhaps, the new penology will have its own Jeremy Bentham or Zebulon Brockway (Foucault, 1977:200; Rothman, 1980:33), some gigantic figure who can stamp his or her own sense of order on the messy results of incremental change. For now it is better not to think of it so much as a theory or program conceived in full by any particular actors in the system, but as an interpretive net that can help reveal in the present some of the directions the future may take. The test of such a net, to which we now turn, is not its elegance as a model but whether it enables one to grasp a wide set of developments in an enlightening way (in short, does it catch fish?). Below we reexamine three of the major features of the contemporary penal landscape in light of our argument—the expansion of the penal sanction, the rise of drug testing, and innovation within the criminal process—and relate them to our thesis.

The Expansion of Penal Sanctions

During the past decade the number of people covered by penal sanctions has expanded significantly.[15] Because of its high costs, the growth of prison populations has drawn the greatest attention, but probation and parole have increased at a proportionate or faster rate. The importance of these other sanctions goes beyond their ability to stretch penal resources; they expand and redistribute the use of imprisonment. Probation and parole violations now constitute a major source of prison inmates, and negotiations over probation revocation are replacing plea bargaining as modes of disposition (Greenspan, 1988; Messinger and Berecochea, 1990).[16]

Many probation and parole revocations are triggered by events, like failing a drug test, that are driven by parole procedures themselves (Simon, 1990; Zimring and Hawkins, 1991). The increased flow of probationers and parolees into prisons is expanding the prison population and changing the nature of the prison. Increasingly, prisons are short-term holding pens for violators deemed too dangerous to remain on the streets. To the extent the prison is organized to receive such people, its correctional mission is replaced by a management function, a warehouse for the highest risk classes of offenders.

From the perspective of the new penology, the growth of community corrections in the shadow of imprisonment is not surprising.[17] The new penology does not regard prison as a special institution capable of making a difference in the individuals who pass through it. Rather, it functions as but one of several custodial options. The actuarial logic of the new penology dictates an expansion of the continuum of control for more efficient risk management. For example, the various California prisons are today differentiated largely by the level of security they maintain and, thus, what level risk inmate they can receive. Twenty years ago, in contrast, they were differentiated by specialized functions: California Rehabilitation Center, for drug users; California Medical Prison at Vacaville, for the mentally ill; Deuel Vocational Institute, for young adults.

Thus, community-based sanctions can be understood in terms of risk management rather than rehabilitative or correctional aspirations. Rather than instruments of reintegrating offenders into the community, they function as mechanisms to maintain control, often through frequent drug testing, over low-risk offenders for whom the more secure forms of custody are judged too expensive or unnecessary.[18]

The new penology's technique of aggregation has been incorporated in a number of sentencing reforms. Minnesota and, more recently, the U.S. Sentencing Commission have made population an explicit concern. The U.S. Sentencing Guidelines, which provide for "fixed" sentences as determined by a 238-cell grid, specifies that the presumptive sentence is a function of prior record and seriousness of offense, but as Alschuler (1991) has shown, although these guidelines have been defended as a step toward providing equal justice, in fact they are based upon "rough aggregations and statistical averages," which mask significant differences among offenders and offenses. The guidelines movement, he observes, marks "a changed attitude toward sentencing—one that looks to collections of cases and to social harm rather than to individual offenders and punishments they deserve . . . [and rather than] the circumstances of their cases" (p. 951).

Drugs and Punishment

Drug use and its detection and control have become central concerns of the penal system. No one observing the system today can fail to be struck by the increasingly tough laws directed against users and traffickers, well-publicized data that suggest that a majority of arrestees are drug users, and the increasing proportion of drug offenders sent to prison.[19]

In one sense, of course, the emphasis on drugs marks a continuity with the past 30 years of correctional history. Drug treatment and drug testing were hallmarks of the rehabilitative model in the 1950s and 1960s. The recent upsurge of concern with drugs may be attributed to the hardening of social attitudes toward drug use (especially in marked contrast to the tolerant 1970s),[20] the introduction of virulent new drug products, like crack cocaine, and the disintegrating social conditions of the urban poor.

Without dismissing the relevance of these continuities and explanations for change, it is important to note that there are distinctive changes in the role of drugs in the current system that reflect the logic of the new penology. In place of the traditional emphasis on treatment and eradication, today's practices track drug use as a kind of risk indicator. The widespread evidence of drug use in the offending population leads not to new theories of crime causation but to more efficient ways of identifying those at highest risk of offending. With drug use so prevalent that it is found in a majority of arrestees in some large cities (Flanagan and Maguire, 1990:459), it can hardly mark a special type of individual deviance. From the perspective of the new penology, drug use is not so much a measure of individual acts of deviance as it is a mechanism for classifying the offender within a risk group.

Thus, one finds in the correctional system today a much greater emphasis on drug testing than on drug treatment. This may reflect the normal kinds of gaps in policy as well as difficulty in treating relatively new forms of drug abuse. Yet, testing serves functions in the new penology even in the absence of a treatment option. By marking the distribution of risk within the offender population under surveillance, testing makes possible greater coordination of scarce penal resources.

Testing also fills the gap left by the decline of traditional intervention strategies. One of the authors spent a year observing parole supervision in California, where drug testing was the predominant activity for agents (Simon, 1990). If nothing else, testing provided parole (and probably probation) agents a means to document compliance with their own internal performance requirements. Agents are supposed to meet with their parolees twice a month on average, but with few parolees working, they can often be hard to find. When they are located, there is often little to do or talk about since the agent cannot offer them a job or coerce them to take one.[21] Testing provides both an occasion for requiring the parolee to show up in the parole office and a purpose for meeting. The results of tests have become a network of fact and explanation for use in a decision-making process that requires accountability but provides little substantive basis for distinguishing among offenders.

Innovation

Our description may seem to imply the onset of a reactive age in which penal managers strive to manage populations of marginal citizens with no concomitant effort toward integration into mainstream society. This may seem hard to square with the myriad new and innovative technologies introduced over the past decade. Indeed the media, which for years have portrayed the correctional system as a failure, have recently enthusiastically reported on these innovations: boot camps, electronic surveillance, high security "campuses" for drug users, house arrest, intensive parole and probation, and drug treatment programs.

Although some of the new proposals are presented in terms of the "old penology" and emphasize individuals, normalization, and rehabilitation, it is risky to come to any firm conviction about how these innovations will turn out. If historians of punishment have provided any clear lessons, it is that reforms evolve in ways quite different from the aims of their proponents (Foucault, 1977; Rothman, 1971). Thus, we wonder if these most recent innovations won't be recast in the terms outlined in this paper. Many of these innovations are compatible with the imperatives of the new penology, that is, managing a permanently dangerous population while maintaining the system at a minimum cost.

One of the current innovations most in vogue with the press and politicians are correctional "boot camps." These are minimum security custodial facilities, usually for youthful first offenders, designed on the model of a training center for military personnel, complete with barracks, physical exercise, and tough drill sergeants. Boot camps are portrayed as providing discipline and pride to young offenders brought up in the unrestrained culture of poverty (as though physical fitness could fill the gap left by the weakening of families, schools, neighborhoods, and other social organizations in the inner city).

The camps borrow explicitly from a military model of discipline, which has influenced penality from at least the eighteenth century.[22] No doubt the image of inmates smartly dressed in uniforms performing drills and calisthenics appeals to long-standing ideals of order in post-Enlightenment culture. But in its proposed application to corrections, the military model is even less appropriate now than when it was rejected in the nineteenth century; indeed, today's boot camps are more a simulation of discipline than the real thing.

In the nineteenth century the military model was superseded by another model of discipline, the factory. Inmates were controlled by making them work at hard industrial labor (Ignatieff, 1978; Rothman, 1971). It was assumed that forced labor would inculcate in offenders the discipline required of factory laborers, so that they might earn their keep while in custody and join the ranks of the usefully employed when released. One can argue that this model did not work very well, but at least it was coherent. The model of discipline through labor suited our capitalist democracy in a way the model of a militarized citizenry did not.[23]

The recent decline of employment opportunities among the populations of urban poor most at risk for conventional crime involvement has left the applicability of industrial discipline in doubt. But the substitution of the boot camp for vocational training is even less plausible. Even if the typical 90-day regime of training envisioned by proponents of boot camps is effective in reorienting its subjects, at best it can only produce soldiers without a company to join. Indeed, the grim vision of the effect of boot camp is that it will be effective for those who will subsequently put their lessons of discipline and organization to use in street gangs and drug distribution networks. However, despite the earnestness with which the boot camp metaphor is touted, we suspect that the camps will be little more than holding pens for managing a short-term, mid-range risk population.

Drug testing and electronic monitors being tried in experimental "intensive supervision" and "house arrest" programs are justified in rehabilitative terms, but both sorts of programs lack a foundation in today's social and economic realities. The drug treatment programs in the 1960s encompassed a regime of coercive treatment: "inpatient" custody in secured settings followed by community supervision and reintegration (President's Commission, 1967). The record suggests that these programs had enduring effects for at least some of those who participated in them (Anglin et al., 1990). Today's proposals are similar, but it remains to be seen whether they can be effective in the absence of long-term treatment facilities, community-based follow-up, and prospects for viable conventional life-styles and employment opportunities.[24] In the meantime it is obvious that they can also serve the imperative of reducing the costs of correctional jurisdiction while maintaining some check on the offender population.

Our point is not to belittle the stated aspirations of current proposals or to argue that drug treatment programs cannot work. Indeed, we anticipate that drug treatment and rehabilitation will become increasingly attractive as the cost of long-term custody increases. However, given the emergence of the management concerns of the new penology, we question whether these innovations will embrace the long-term perspective of earlier successful treatment programs, and we suspect that they will emerge as control processes for managing and recycling selected risk populations. If so, these new programs will extend still further the capacity of the new penology. The undeniable attractiveness of boot camps, house arrest, secure drug "centers," and the like, is that they promise to provide secure custody in a more flexible format and at less cost than traditional correctional facilities. Indeed, some of them are envisioned as private contract facilities that can be expanded or reduced with relative ease. Further, they hold out the promise of expanding the range of low- and mid-level custodial alternatives, thereby facilitating the transfer of offenders now held in more expensive, higher security facilities that have been so favored in recent years. Tougher eligibility requirements, including job offers, stable residency, and promises of sponsorship in the community can be used to screen out "higher risk" categories for noncustodial release programs (Petersilia, 1987). Thus, despite the lingering language of rehabilitation and reintegration, the programs generated under the new penology can best be understood in terms of managing costs and controlling dangerous populations rather than social or personal transformation.

Social Bases of the New Penology

The point of these reinterpretations is not to show that shifts in the way the penal enterprise is understood and discussed inexorably determine how the system will take shape. What actually emerges in corrections over the near and distant future will depend on how this understanding itself is shaped by the pressures of demographic, economic, and political factors. Still, such factors rarely operate as pure forces. They are filtered through and expressed in terms in which the problems are understood. Thus, the strategic field we call the new penology itself will help shape the future.

The New Discourse of Crime

Like the old penology, traditional "sociological" criminology has focused on the relationship between individuals and communities. Its central concerns have been the causes and correlates of delinquent and criminal behavior, and it has sought to develop intervention strategies designed to correct delinquents and decrease the likelihood of deviant behavior. Thus, it has focused on the family and the workplace as important influences of socialization and control.

The new penology has an affinity with a new "actuarial" criminology, which eschews these traditional concerns of criminology. Instead of training in sociology or social work, increasingly the new criminologists are trained in operations research and systems analysis. This new approach is not a criminology at all, but an applied branch of systems theory. This shift in training and orientation has been accompanied by a shift in interest. A concern with successful intervention strategies, the province of the former, is replaced by models designed to optimize public safety through the management of aggregates, which is the province of the latter.

In one important sense this new criminology is simply a consequence of steady improvements in the quantitative rigor with which crime is studied. No doubt the amassing of a statistical picture of crime and the criminal justice system has improved researchers' ability to speak realistically about the distribution of crimes and the fairness of procedures. But, we submit, it has also contributed to a shift, a reconceptualization, in the way crime is understood as a social problem.[25] The new techniques and the new language have facilitated reconceptualization of the way issues are framed and policies pursued. Sociological criminology tended to emphasize crime as a relationship between the individual and the normative expectations of his or her community (Bennett, 1981).[26] Policies premised on this perspective addressed problems of reintegration, including the mismatch among individual motivation, normative orientation, and social opportunity structures. In contrast, actuarial criminology highlights the interaction of criminal justice institutions and specific segments of the population. Policy discussions framed in its terms emphasize the management of high-risk groups and make less salient the qualities of individual delinquents and their communities.

Indeed, even the use of predictive statistics by pioneers like Ernest Burgess (1936) reflected sociological criminology's emphasis on normalization. Burgess's statistics (and those of most other quantitative criminologists before the 1960s) measured the activity of subjects defined by a specifiable set of individual or social factors (e.g., alcoholism, unemployment, etc.). In the actuarial criminology of today, by contrast, the numbers generate the subject itself (e.g., the high-rate offender of incapacitation research). In short, criminals are no longer the organizing referent (or logos) of criminology. Instead, criminology has become a subfield of a generalized public policy analysis discourse. This new criminal knowledge aims at rationalizing the operation of the systems that manage criminals, not dealing with criminality. The same techniques that can be used to improve the circulation of baggage in airports or delivery of food to troops can be used to improve the penal system's efficiency.

The Discourse of Poverty and the "Underclass"

The new penology may also be seen as responsive to the emergence of a new understanding of poverty in America.[27] The term *underclass* is used today to characterize a segment of society that is viewed as permanently excluded from social mobility and economic integration. The term is used to refer to a largely black and Hispanic population living in concentrated zones of poverty in central cities, separated physically and institutionally from the suburban locus of mainstream social and economic life in America.

In contrast to groups whose members are deemed employable, even if they may be temporarily out of work, the underclass is understood as a permanently marginal population, without literacy, without skills, and without hope; a self-perpetuating and pathological segment of society that is not integratable into the larger whole, even as a reserve labor pool (Wilson, 1987). Conceived of this way, the underclass is also a dangerous class, not only for what any particular member may or may not do, but more generally for collective potential misbehavior.[28] It is treated as a high-risk group that must be managed for the protection of the rest of society. Indeed, it is this managerial task that provides one of the most powerful sources for the imperative of preventive management in the new penology. The concept of "underclass" makes clear why correctional officials increasingly regard as a bad joke the claim that their goal is to reintegrate offenders back into their communities.

Reintegration and rehabilitation inevitably imply a norm against which deviant subjects are evaluated. As Allen (1981) perceived more than a decade ago, rehabilitation as a project can only survive if public confidence in the viability and appropriateness of such norms endures. Allen viewed the decline of the rehabilitative ideal as a result of the cultural revolts of the 1960s, which undermined the capacity of the American middle classes to justify their norms and the imposition of those norms on others. It is this decline in social will, rather than empirical evidence of the failure of penal programs to rehabilitate, that, in Allen's analysis, doomed the rehabilitative ideal.

Whatever significance cultural radicalism may have had in initiating the breakup of the old penology in the mid-1970s, the emergence of the new penology in the 1980s reflects the influence of a more despairing view of poverty and the prospects for achieving equality (views that can hardly be blamed on the Left). Rehabilitating offenders, or any kind of reintegration strategy, can only make sense if the larger community from which offenders come is viewed as sharing a common normative universe with the communities of the middle classes—especially those values and expectations derived from the labor market. The concept of an underclass, with its connotation of a permanent marginality for whole portions of the population, has rendered the old penology incoherent and laid the groundwork for a strategic field that emphasizes low-cost management of a permanent offender population.

The connection between the new penality and the (re)emergent term *underclass* also is illustrated by recent studies of American jails. For instance, Irwin's 1985 book, *The Jail*, is subtitled *Managing the Underclass in American Society*. His thesis is that "prisoners in jails share two essential characteristics: detachment and disrepute" (p. 2). For Irwin, the function of jail is to manage the underclass, which he reports is also referred to as "rabble," "disorganized," "disorderly," and the "lowest class of people."

In one rough version of Irwin's analysis, the jail can be viewed as a means of controlling the most disruptive and unsightly members of the underclass. But in another version, it can be conceived of as an emergency service net for those who are in the most desperate straits. As other social services have shrunk, increasingly this task falls on the jail.

Whichever version one selects, few of those familiar with the jails in America's urban centers find it meaningful to characterize them only as facilities for "pretrial detention" or for serving "short-term sentences." Although not literally false, this characterization misses the broader function of the jail. The high rates of those released without charges filed, the turnstile-like frequency with which some people reappear, and the pathological character- istics of a high proportion of the inmates lead many to agree with Irwin that the jail is best understood as a social management instrument rather than an institution for effecting the purported aims of the criminal process. . . .

In providing an explanation . . . there is a danger that the terms will reify the problem, that they will suggest the problem is inevitable and permanent. Indeed, it is this belief, we maintain, that has contributed to the lowered expectations of the new penology—away from an aspiration to affect individ- ual lives through rehabilitative and transformative efforts and toward the more "realistic" task of monitoring and managing intractable groups.

The hardening of poverty in contemporary America reinforces this view. When combined with a pessimistic analysis implied by the term *underclass*, the structural barriers that maintain the large islands of third world misery in America's major cities can lead to the conclusion that such conditions are inevitable and impervious to social policy intervention. This, in turn, can push corrections ever further toward a self-understanding based on the imperative of herding a specific population that cannot be disaggregated and trans- formed but only maintained[29]—a kind of waste management function. . . .[30]

Conclusion

Our discussion has proceeded as if the new penology—the new way of conceiving of the functions of the criminal sanction—has contributed to the recent rise in prison populations. Although we believe that it has, we also acknowledge that the new penology is both cause and effect of the increases. We recognize that those conditions we referred to at the outset as "external" have placed pressures on criminal justice institutions that, in turn, have caused them to adapt in a host of ways. The point of our paper, how- ever, has been to show just how thorough this adaptation has been. It has led to a significant reconceptualization of penology, a shift that institutional- izes those adaptive behaviors. It embraces the new forms that have arisen as a result of this adaptation. As such, the new language, the new conceptual- ization, ensures that these new forms will persist independently of the pres- sures. They appear to be permanent features of the criminal justice system.

Notes

[1] A number of influential scholars have commented on this process, often calling attention to what they regard as the shortcomings of traditional individual-based legal language when applied to the problems of the modern organization-based society. See, e.g., dan-Cohen (1986), Stone (1975).

[2] In contrasting the "old" and the "new" tort law, Steiner (1987:8) observes: "They [judges with the new tort law] visualize the parties before them less as individual persons or dis- crete organizations and more as representatives of groups with identifiable common char- acteristics. They understand accidents and the social losses that accidents entail less as

unique events and more as statistically predictable events. Modern social vision tends then toward the systemic-group-statistical in contrast with the vision more characteristic of the fault system, the dyadic-individual-unique."

[3] There has been considerable resistance to the actuarial logic in this area as well. See *McCleskey v. Kemp*, 107 S. Ct. 1756 (1987).

[4] But even here there are signs that this is changing. Although they do not frame their discussion in our terms, a number of scholars have observed that many of the provisions in the Racketeer Influenced and Corrupt Organizations (RICO) statute run counter to the traditional individual-based orientation of the criminal law and in fact are designed to facilitate regulation of organizational behavior, not individual conduct.

[5] A good example of this is the President's Commission on Law Enforcement and Administration of Justice, created in 1966. Its report, *The Challenge of Crime in a Free Society* (1967), combined a commitment to the rehabilitative ideal with a new enthusiasm for actuarial representation. Indeed, that document represents an important point of coalescence for many of the elements that make up the new penology.

[6] Not everyone believes that this has been a positive change. For a critical perspective see Kelling (1991).

[7] This is especially true for a number of new, intensive parole and probation supervision programs that have been established in recent years. Initially conceived as a way to reintegrate offenders into the community through a close interpersonal relationship between agent and offender, intensive supervision is now considered as an enhanced monitoring technique whose ability to detect high rates of technical violations indicates its success, not failure.

[8] This does not mean that recidivism ceases to be a meaningful concept, but only that in its new mode of operation the penal system no longer accords it the centrality it once had. Recidivism remains a potent tool of criticism of the system, especially given its former significance. See, e.g., the California Legislative Analyst's *Report to the 1989/1990 Budget* (Sacramento), which contains a strong attack on the parole process for emphasizing the high rate of recidivism.

[9] 107 S. Ct. 2045, 2101–2 (1987).

[10] There is a rapidly growing literature on the Supreme Court's shift away from individual rights in the area of criminal procedure. See, e.g., the Supreme Court's finding that forced medication for a mentally ill prisoner is subject to diminished procedural review because it is essentially a risk-management decision on the part of custodial managers rather than a punitive deprivation, *Washington v. Harper*, 110 S. Ct. 1028, 1039–40 (1990). For a discussion of shifts in criminal procedure more generally, see Greenspan (1988).

[11] One of the authors has spent time with corrections officials in Japan and Sweden as well as the United States and found that significantly different language is used to characterize penal policies. In Sweden he heard the language of therapy and rehabilitation (the offender is not properly socialized and requires rehabilitative therapy). In Japan he heard the language of moral responsibility (the offender is morally deficient and needs instruction in responsibility to the community). In the United States, he heard the language of management (in a high-crime society, we need expanded capacity to classify offenders in order to incapacitate the most dangerous and employ less stringent controls on the less dangerous). Juxtaposed against each other, the differences are dramatic.

There is a similarity in approach between the new penology and the views expressed by Soviet legal theorist Eugenii Pashukanis (1978). He predicted that under socialism, law would "wither away" and be replaced with management based upon considerations of social utility rather than traditional individualized considerations. See, e.g., Sharlet (1978).

[12] Incapacitation then is to penology what arbitrage is to investments, a method of capitalizing on minute displacements in time; and like arbitrage it has a diminished relationship to the normative goal of enhancing the value of its objects.

[13] Throughout the book the authors acknowledge the significance of their approach. They warn, "When one holds these tests [use of correlates to serious criminal activity as a basis for formulating sentences] to a more exacting standard emphasizing individual justice, however, the proposed tests have greater difficulty; inaccuracy, resulting in false positives,

and the inclusion of variables that are not entirely under the control of individuals and are not in themselves dangerous criminal conduct" (p. 76).

Throughout the book, they repeatedly express similar warnings, e.g., "A . . . question is whether narrowing the focus of the system weakens the power and stature of the criminal law." (p. 90); "At the foundation of selective incapacitation is the distinctly illiberal view that people differ in their capacity for evil and that these differences are not the result of broad social processes but of something inherent in the individual" (p. 91). Ultimately, they conclude, "In our view the threshold objections to selective incapacitation do mark out important areas of vulnerability and uncertainty, but none stands as an absolute barrier to further consideration on the issue" (p. 92).

[14] The mean of a multinomial variable is incoherent.

[15] In 1988, 3.7 million adults were under some form of correctional sanction in the United States, a 38.8% increase since 1984 (Bureau of Justice Statistics, 1989:5). [In 2002, 6.7 million people were under some form of correctional supervision (http://www.ojp.usdoj.gov/bjs/glance/corr2.htm).]

[16] In 1988 there were 14 states in which more than a quarter of all prison admissions came from parole revocation (Bureau of Justice Statistics, 1989:69). In California, in 1988, 59% of admissions were from parole revocations (ibid.). [In 2002, 14% of adults leaving probation returned to incarceration; 41% of parolees returned to incarceration (http://www.ojp.usdoj.gov/bjs/pub/pdf/ppus02.pdf).]

[17] The importance of supervisory sanctions is all the more interesting given the effort of recent sentencing reform to remove discretion from corrections offices and establish juridical control through legislatures, judges, and prosecutors (Zimring and Hawkins, 1991).

[18] The public remains interested in punishment for its own sake, and the expansion of parole and probation is tied in some degree to the ability of penal managers to convince the public that these supervisory sanctions can be punitive as well as managerial.

[19] Incarceration for drug offenses grew at twice the rate of other offenses between 1976 and 1984 (Zimring and Hawkins, 1991:164). [In 1984, there were 31,700 state incarcerations for drug offenses; in 2001, there were 246,100 (http://www.ojp.usdoj.gov/bjs/glance/tables/corrtyptab.htm); in 2001, 20.4% of state inmates were serving a sentence for a drug violation (http://www.ojp.usdoj.gov/bjs/pub/pdf/p02.pdf).]

[20] Support for the legalization of marijuana, e.g., peaked among first year college students in 1977 at 52.9% and has since declined, reaching 16.7% in 1989 (Flanagan and Maguire, 1990:195). [28% of the general population in 1977 favored legalizing marijuana, the percentage dropped to 23 in 1985 and reached 34% in 2001 (http://www.usatoday.com/news/nation/2001/08/23/marijuana-poll.htm).]

[21] The law no longer requires that parolees be employed, and jobs are not available in the communities where many parolees reside.

[22] The prison borrowed from the earlier innovations in the organization of spaces and bodies undertaken by the most advanced European military forces. See, e.g., Rothman (1971:105–108).

[23] The model of industrial discipline was rarely fully achieved in prisons, but at least it had a clear referent in the real world, one that provided a certain coherence and plausibility to the penal project. The boot camp, like so much else in our increasingly anachronistic culture, is a signifier without a signified.

[24] In his important 1966 essay "Work and Identity in the Lower Class," Rainwater suggested that members of the lower class often choose "expressive" life-styles of deviance in the absence of opportunities for the most prestigious and desirable roles in the occupational structure. But he argued they also predictably burn out and accept the identification offered by even low-level employment of the good worker and provider. Rainwater urged that keeping entry-level employment available and tolerable was essential to fostering that transition. Today, when entry-level employment has shrunk to levels not imagined in the mid-1960s, the transition of those who are dissuaded or simply burn out on crime cannot be assumed (Duster, 1987).

[25] Again, we would point to the 1967 President's Commission report as a critical point of emergence for the actuarial criminology that dominates today, especially the Task Force report on "Science and Technology" (Ch. 11).

[26] The research relied on ethnography and life histories. See, e.g., the work of Blumstein et al. (1986), Burgess (1974), Shaw (1931), Sutherland (1934).

[27] Although in this paper we emphasize recent significant shifts, a management approach is not wholly unprecedented. For instance, during the formative years of the development of the modern criminal justice system, the late eighteenth and the early nineteenth century, the term "dangerous classes" was used widely in discussions of English criminal justice policies. Influenced in part by Malthusian thinking and burgeoning urban populations, policy analysts of the time often treated criminal justice policy in aggregate management terms, treating crime as an indicator of the dangerousness of a larger group, rather than of individuals. For instance, transportation of convicted felons was often regarded as but one of several interrelated policies to export the dangerous classes. Other policies accomplishing similar ends were voluntary emigration and indentured servitude, both of which were actively promoted by the government. The invention of the large-scale prison helped to individualize crime policy.

[28] A recent study estimated that on any one day in 1988 roughly one in every four young (between ages 20 and 29) black males was under some form of correctional custody (Mauer, 1990). More recently, a similar study calculated that on a given day in 1990 some 42% of all young black males in Washington, D.C., were in custody. The growing visibility of the link between penality and race is likely to reinforce the sense that crime is the product of a pathological subpopulation that cannot be integrated into the society at large, as well as the perception that the penal system can do no better than maintain custody over a large segment of this population. [In a five-year follow-up study, The Sentencing Project found that 1 in 3 black males between the ages of 20 and 29 were in custody (http://www.sentencingproject.org/pdfs/9070smy.pdf).]

[29] However, those who work in corrections, whether they want to do social work or enforce laws, resist such deterministic ideas and resist conceiving of their jobs as recycling human beings from one level of custodial management to another with little reference to justice or social reintegration.

[30] This term is more than metaphor. In 1989, then Governor Deukmejian of California proposed that prison inmates be used to process toxic wastes.

References

Allen, Francis. (1981). *The Decline of the Rehabilitative Idea*. New Haven: Yale University Press.

Alschuler, Albert. (1991). The failure of sentencing guidelines: A plea for less aggregation. *University of Chicago Law Review, 58*, 901–951.

Anglin, Douglas, George Speckhart, Elizabeth Piper Deschenes. (1990). *Examining the Effects of Narcotics Addiction*. Los Angeles: UCLA Neuropsychiatric Institute, Drug Abuse Research Group.

Bennett, James. (1981). *Oral History and Delinquency: The Rhetoric of Criminology*. Chicago: University of Chicago Press.

Blumstein, Alfred, Jacqueline Cohen, Jeffrey A. Roth, and Christy A. Visher (eds.). (1986). *Criminal Careers and "Career Criminals."* Washington, D.C.: National Academy Press.

Bottoms, Anthony. (1983). Neglected features of contemporary penal systems. In David Garland and Peter Young (eds.), *The Power to Punish*. London: Heinemann.

Bureau of Justice Statistics. (1989). *Correctional Populations in the United States, 1988*. Washington, D.C.: U.S. Department of Justice.

Burgess, Ernest W. (1936). Protecting the public by parole and parole prediction. *Journal of Criminal Law and Criminology, 27*, 491–502.

Burgess, Ernest W. (1974). *The Basic Writings of Ernest W. Burgess*, ed. Donald Bogue. Chicago: University of Chicago Press.

Cohen, Stanley. (1985). *Visions of Social Control: Crime, Punishment and Classification*. Oxford: Polity Press.

dan-Cohen, Meir. (1986). *Persons, Rights and Organizations*. Berkeley: University of California Press.

Doyle, James M. (1992). "It's the Third World down there!": The colonialist vocation and American criminal justice. *Harvard Civil Rights-Civil Liberties Law Review, 27*, 711–726.

Duster, Troy. (1987). Crime, youth unemployment and the black urban underclass. *Crime and Delinquency, 33*, 300–316.

Foucault, Michel. (1977). *Discipline and Punishment*. New York: Pantheon.

Foucault, Michel. (1978). *The History of Sexuality. Vol. I, An Introduction*. New York: Random House.

Foucault, Michel. (1982). The subject and power. In Hubert L. Dreyfus and Paul Rabinow (eds.), *Michel Foucault: Beyond Structuralism and Hermenuetics*. Chicago: University of Chicago Press.

Freeman, Alan. (1990). Antidiscrimination law: The view from 1989. In David Kaiyrs (ed.), *The Politics of Law*. New York: Pantheon.

Garland, David. (1985). *Punishment and Welfare*. Aldershot: Gower.

Garland, David and Peter Young (eds.). (1983). *The Power to Punish: Contemporary Penality and Social Analysis*. London: Heinemann.

Gordon, Diana R. (1991). *The Justice Juggernaut: Fighting Street Crime, Controlling Citizens*. New Brunswick: Rutgers University Press.

Greenspan, Rosanne. (1988). The transformation of criminal due process in the administrative state. Paper prepared for delivery at the annual meeting of the Law and Society Association, Vail, CO, June 1988.

Greenwood, Peter. (1982). *Selective Incapacitation*. Santa Monica, CA: Rand.

Habermas, Jurgen. (1974). *Communication and the Evolution of Society*. Boston: Beacon Press.

Habermas, Jurgen. (1985). Law as medium and law as institution. In Gunther Teubner (ed.), *Dilemmas of Law in the Welfare State*. Berlin: de Gruyter.

Hay, Douglas. (1975). Property, authority and the criminal law. In Douglas Hay, Peter Linebaugh, and Edward P. Thompson (eds.), *Albion's Fatal Tree*. New York: Pantheon.

Heydebrand, Wolf and Carroll Seron. (1990). *Rationalizing Justice: The Political Economy and Federal District Courts*. New York: State University of New York Press.

Ignatieff, Michael. (1978). *A Just Measure of Pain: The Penitentiary in the Industrial Revolution, 1750–1850*. London: Macmillan.

Irwin, John. (1985). *The Jail: Managing the Underclass in American Society*. Berkeley: University of California Press.

Jacobs, James B. (1977). *Stateville: The Penitentiary in Mass Society*. Chicago: University of Chicago Press.

Kelling, George L. (1991, Autumn). Crime and metaphor: Toward a new concept of policing. *The City Journal*, pp. 65–71.

Krygier, Martin. (1989). Law as tradition. *Law and Philosophy, 5*, 237–262.

Lipsky, Michael. (1980). *Street Level Bureaucrats*. New York: Russell Sage Foundation.

Maguire, Kathleen and Timothy J. Flanagan. (1990). *Sourcebook of Criminal Justice Statistics 1989*. U.S. Department of Justice, Bureau of Justice Statistics, Washington, D.C.: U.S. Government Printing Office.

Maltz, Michael. (1984). *Recidivism*. Orlando, FL: Academic Press.

Mathieson, Thomas. (1983). The future of control systems—The case of Norway. In David Garland and Peter Young (eds.), *The Power to Punish*. London: Heinemann.

Mauer, Marc. (1990). *Young Black Men and the Criminal Justice System*. Washington, D.C.: The Sentencing Project.

Messinger, Sheldon. (1969). Strategies of control. Ph.D. dissertation, Department of Sociology, University of California at Los Angeles.

Messinger, Sheldon and John Berecochea. (1990). Don't stay too long but do come back soon. Proceedings, Conference on Growth and Its Influence on Correctional Policy, Center for the Study of Law and Society, University of California at Berkeley.

Moore, Mark H., Susan R. Estrich, Daniel McGillis, and William Spelman. (1984). *Dangerous Offenders: The Elusive Target of Justice*. Cambridge, MA: Harvard University Press.

National Institute of Justice. (1990). *Research in Action—Drug Use Forecasting*. Washington, D.C.: U.S. Department of Justice.

Nelken, David. (1982). Is there a crisis in law and legal ideology? *Journal of Law and Society, 9*, 177–189.

Pashukanis, Eugenii. (1978). *Law and Marxism: A General Theory*, trans. Barbara Einhurn. London: Ink Links.

Petersilia, Joan. (1987). *Expanding Options for Criminal Sentencing*. Santa Monica, CA: Rand.

President's Commission on Law Enforcement and the Administration of Justice. (1967). *The Challenge of Crime in a Free Society*. Washington, D.C.: Government Printing Office.

Rainwater, Lee. (1966). Work and identity in the lower class. In Sam B. Warner (ed.), *Planning for a Nation of Cities*. Cambridge, MA: MIT Press.

Reichman, Nancy. (1986). Managing crime risks: Toward an insurance-based model of social control. *Research in Law, Deviance and Social Control, 8*, 151–172.

Rothman, David. (1971). *The Discovery of the Asylum: Social Order and Disorder in the New Republic*. Boston: Little, Brown.

Rothman, David. (1980). *Conscience and Convenience: The Asylum and its Alternative in Progressive America*. Boston: Little, Brown.

Sharlet, Robert. (1978). Pashukanis and the withering away of law in the USSR. In Sheila Fitzpatrick (ed.), *Cultural Revolution in Russia: 1928–1931*. Bloomington: Indiana University Press.

Shaw, Clifford. (1931). *The Natural History of a Delinquent Career*. 1968. Westport, CT: Greenwood Press.

Simon, Jonathan. (1987). The emergence of a risk society: Insurance law and the state. *Socialist Review, 95*, 61–89.

Simon, Jonathan. (1988). The ideological effect of actuarial practices. *Law and Society Review, 22*, 771–800.

Simon, Jonathan. (1990). From discipline to management: Strategies of control in parole supervision, 1890–1990. Ph.D. dissertation, Jurisprudence and Social Policy Program, University of California at Berkeley.

Steiner, Henry J. (1987). *Moral Vision and Social Vision in the Court: A Study of Tort Accident Law*. Madison: University of Wisconsin Press.

Stone, Christopher. (1975). *Where the Law Ends*. New York: Harper & Row.

Sutherland, Edwin H. (1934). *Principles of Criminology*. Philadelphia: J. B. Lippincott.

Teubner, Gunther. (1989). How the law thinks: Toward a constructivist epistemology of law. *Law and Society Review, 23*, 727–757.

Wilkins, Leslie T. (1973). Crime and criminal justice at the turn of the century. *Annals of the American Academy of Political and Social Science, 408*, 13–29.

Wilson, William Julius. (1987). *The Truly Disadvantaged: The Inner City, the Underclass, and Public Policy*. Chicago: University of Chicago Press.

Zimring, Franklin and Gordon Hawkins. (1991). *The Scale of Imprisonment*. Chicago: University of Chicago Press.

Conclusion

Remember in the first chapter the debates I had with my judicial friend from Sierra Leone? I have spent many hours attempting to demonstrate to him that whether a scholar is writing to strengthen the legal system or to express a scathing critique, both efforts are ideological and one-sided. The power of having a handbag of different lenses is that we have the tools to explore the foundations of claims and to make better theoretical sense of criminal justice.

This book channels our gaze at the criminal justice apparatus through eight orienting filters, all of which contain a certain set of meanings, concepts, and theoretical preferences. We are in essence recognizing a range of different views of reality. By not situating them in some sort of hierarchy of truth, the assumption is that our diversity of theoretical lenses renders our field of study dynamic, thought provoking, and—most importantly—productive. As we discussed throughout this book, a broad perspective leads to better research, which can ultimately translate to more enlightened practice.

The eight orientations discussed demonstrate clearly that theorizing CJ is a credible and useful endeavor—requiring at least as much academic rigor and complexity as theorizing crime. While assumptions about the why of crime can reveal aspects about the why of the criminal justice apparatus, that does not mean that the same theories used to study crime are suitable and adequate for understanding trends in social control, the behavior of law, the behavior of the state, the behavior of public organizations, or trends in crime control tactics and thinking. These distinct objects of study necessitate distinct theoretical systems.

The multi-metaphor approach helps us recognize and overcome the general tendency to oversimplify complex phenomena. For example, what explains exponential growth in police, courts, and corrections in the last thirty years? The rational/legal orientation provides one answer: growth is caused by a worsening crime problem forcing the system to react. This is a logical assumption, and most people take it for granted. But the seven other frames of reference also provide insight and understanding.

I could have applied forced reaction theory to my research documenting the growth of SWAT units and activities among U.S. police agencies. However, after using national, longitudinal-level data to test this theoretical proposition, we discovered the growth was not correlated with worsening crime or with an increase in crisis situations (Kraska & Cubellis 1997). It became clear after many years of study that much of the phenomenon could be explained by SWAT's cultural appeal (criminal justice as socially constructed reality). The paramilitary culture associated with these elite, special operations police units—futuristic/cyborg garb, advanced weaponry, high status of being the "Cop's cops," and aggressive marketing of paramilitary culture by for-profit vendors—was intoxicating for a large segment of paramilitary-minded police officers. This technocratic thinking and approach aligns with the rationalization of late-modern society.

Understanding criminal justice experiences, issues, and trends is a complex assignment. Multiple theoretical orientations provide the tools to map the terrain of this complexity. Because the format of this book segments perspectives into eight categories, a reader could mistakenly minimize the theoretical complexity of criminal justice. As we conclude our exploration, I want to stress again that these categories should not be thought of, or applied, as mutually exclusive. Although each perspective has distinct attributes, it also shares certain similarities, which can, in some cases, dovetail easily into another approach. It is vital to the learning process, in fact, that these eight orientations be mixed and matched when applied to specific research questions. Werner Einstadter and Stuart Henry (1995) offer this worthwhile advice:

> Consider theory [in our case, theoretical orientations] to be like a toolbox. Each of the different theories represent different tools. Just as the worker might decide that a job or a repair needs a saw to cut wood, glue or a hammer and nails to attach the wood to the existing structure, and a screwdriver and screws to secure it, so a criminologist might find that a type of crime or harm requires classical theory to analyze the offender's motives, strain theory to analyze the opportunity structure that shapes these motives, and Marxist theory to analyze why differences of opportunity exist. (p. 310)

David Garland, in telling the theoretical story of exponential CJ growth over the last thirty years, includes elements of structural functionalism (CJ as system), Foucault's work (CJ as late modernity), and radical theory (CJ as oppression). Jonathan Simon's (2001) explanation of the U.S. incarceration binge also incorporates a range of explanatory frameworks.

> We point to three different factors whose interrelationship has driven incarceration rates in ways quite different than might have been expected for each independently. First, we argue that changes in the political culture of the United States have made fear of crime a priority issue for politics [CJ as politics, socially constructed reality, and late modernity]. Second, the war on drugs, largely a product of this political priority of crime, produced an almost limitless supply of arrestable and imprisonable offenders [CJ as crime control vs. due process, socially constructed reality, and oppression]. Third, the growing integration of criminal justice agencies into a more transparent and interactive system has introduced a strong element of reflexivity into the system, which in turn produces strong internal pressures for growth [CJ as growth complex]. (p. 21)

Critical analysis and thinking are essential for the future construction of responsible practices. Creative practice stems from creative thought. As Simon (2003) explains in his work in progress, *Governing through Crime*, "There are times when the most important questions of all are not what should we do, but how should we think." What questions should we ask? What are the possible consequences—intended and otherwise—of a particular way of thinking and the actions it influences? What are the by-products of the approach or approaches selected?

Whether conscious or not, theory is implied in all practice. Conceiving of each orientation as a type of interpretive construct not only allows us to grasp a constellation of meanings, it also provides us with the tools for informed action. With thought and action being inextricably linked, filtering the criminal justice system and crime control efforts through multiple lenses allows for the possibility of seeing innovative solutions, effective policies, and just courses of action.

References

Einstadter, W., & Henry, S. (1995). *Criminological theory.* Fort Worth, TX: Harcourt, Brace.

Kraska, P. B., & Cubellis, L. (1997). Militarizing Mayberry and beyond: Making sense of American paramilitary policing. *Justice Quarterly, 14*(4), 607–629.

Simon, J. (2001). Fear and loathing in late modernity: Reflections on the cultural sources of mass imprisonment in the United States. *Punishment and Society, 3*(1): 21–33.

Simon, J. (2003). The land of the free and the home of the fearful. In *Governing through crime: Criminal law and the reshaping of American government* (chap. 1). Manuscript in preparation. Retrieved September 2, 2003, from http://personal.law.miami.edu/~jsimon/pdf/introdraft3.pdf

Index